The
Audubon Society
Guide to
Attracting Birds

The Audubon Societ

Second Edition

In Association with the CORNELL LABORATORY OF ORNITHOLOGY

Comstock Publishing Associates, a division of

CORNELL UNIVERSITY PRESS Ithaca and London

uide to Attracting Birds

Creating Natural Habitats for Properties Large and Small

STEPHEN W. KRESS

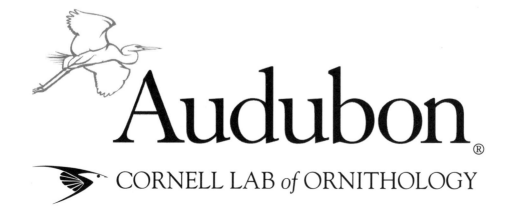

Audubon®

CORNELL LAB *of* ORNITHOLOGY

First published 2006
by Cornell University Press
First printing, Cornell Paperbacks, 2006

Library of Congress Cataloging-in-Publication Data

Kress, Stephen W.
   The Audubon Society guide to attracting birds : creating natural habitats for properties large and small / Stephen W. Kress ; foreword from first edition by Roger Tory Peterson. — 2nd ed.
      p.   cm.
   Includes bibliographical references and index.
   ISBN-13: 978-0-8014-8864-1 (pbk. : alk. paper)
   ISBN-10: 0-8014-8864-8 (pbk. : alk. paper)
   1. Bird attracting.   I. Title.
   QL676.5.K74   2006
   639.9'78—dc22

                                                                    2005027428

Audubon is a registered trademark of National Audubon Society, Inc.

The Audubon mission is to conserve and restore natural ecosystems, focusing on birds, other wildlife, and their habitats for the benefit of humanity and the earth's biological diversity.

Through its education, science, and public policy initiatives, Audubon engages people throughout the U.S. and Latin America in conservation. Audubon's Centers, and its sanctuaries and education programs, are developing the next generation of conservation leaders by providing opportunities for families, students, teachers, and others to learn about and enjoy the natural world. The science program is focused on connecting people with nature through projects like Audubon at Home and Great Backyard Bird Count. Audubon's volunteer Citizen Scientists participate in research and conservation action in a variety of ways, from monitoring bird populations and restoring critical wildlife habitat to implementing healthy habitat practices in their own backyards. Audubon's public policy programs are supported by a strong foundation of science, environmental education, and grassroots engagement. Working with a network of state offices, chapters, and volunteers, Audubon works to protect and restore our natural heritage.

To learn how you can support Audubon, call us at (800) 274-4201, visit our website at www.audubon.org, or write to Audubon, 700 Broadway, New York, New York 10003.

Printed in Canada

Cornell University Press strives to use environmentally responsible suppliers and materials to the fullest extent possible in the publishing of its books. Such materials include vegetable-based, low-VOC inks and acid-free papers that are recycled, totally chlorine-free, or partly composed of nonwood fibers. For further information, visit our website at www.cornellpress.cornell.edu.

Paperback printing
10   9   8   7   6   5   4   3   2   1

Contents

Foreword from the First Edition

No suburban garden is without birds or butterflies, but by imaginative planning you can easily double or triple their numbers. The environmentally oriented gardener can enjoy not only red, orange, yellow, and blue flowers but also red, orange, yellow, and blue birds such as cardinals, orioles, goldfinches, and jays.

During the past 20 or 30 years birdwatching has become much more sophisticated. So has attracting birds to the house and garden. The state of the art has gone far beyond the window feeder, the wren box, and the birdbath. There have been a number of primers designed for the needs of the white-breasted nuthatch type of bird watcher, but this new book by Stephen Kress goes much further; it opens new vistas. It not only offers more imaginative ideas for making the suburban backyard a Mecca for the local birds but also extends coverage to the more expansive acreages of farms, roadsides, and even wild areas.

A recent survey by the U.S. Fish and Wildlife Service arrived at an estimate of more than half a billion dollars spent yearly by Americans for birdseed. I suspect that the figure might be closer to a billion. Although a few critics have questioned whether it is really helpful to the birds to feed them except in periods of stress, I need only point out that a number of species have vastly extended their ranges during the past half century because of our largesse. Cardinals and tufted titmice, formerly regarded as southern, now reside permanently as far north as southern Canada and have established themselves throughout much of New England. Because feeders have enhanced their winter survival, mourning doves now winter north to the Maritime Provinces. Evening grosbeaks apparently can recognize a feeding table at a great distance when their nomadic flocks move southward from the boreal forests during those years when their natural food supply is insufficient to support them. Virtually confined to the northwest in Audubon's day, they now nest east to New England. If attractive birds such as these have extended their ranges and have become more numerous, how can we say they have not benefited?

We have been cautioned that we should not start feeding birds in the fall or at the onset of winter if we plan a midwinter holiday. It is reasoned that the birds might suffer if their source of food is cut off. This advice is perhaps valid in some parts of the country, but where I live, in Connecticut, everyone up and down our road feeds birds, so if I discontinue for a couple of weeks in January or even for a month, my white-throats, chickadees, and jays will simply go to the neighbors— to Mr. Schulze's feeding tray, or to the Kennedy's, who also feed birds.

I suspect that if I did not feed birds at all they would manage to survive; the reason I spend so much on hundreds of pounds of bird seed is that I enjoy watching the birds, and the more the merrier. At my studio, feeders are visible from both the north and south windows so I can watch the show while I work. At the main house, other feeders, facing south and east, have become the dining room for a large company of white-throated sparrows. By careful manipulation of the forsythia I have given them a secure fortress, which apparently is used as their social club, and by clumping the rhododendrons and other evergreen shrubs I have given them snug bedroom quarters.

On several occasions over the years a sharp-shinned hawk or a Cooper's hawk has attempted to dine on the diners, but the white-throats' impenetrable social club in the forsythia was their salvation. On the other hand, I have known a red-shouldered hawk living near the Washington Cathedral to come regularly to a feeding tray for suet, forcing the chickadees to wait their turn.

My friend, the late Herbert Mills, even operated a feeding station specifically for hawks. He kept a large supply of moribund mice in his refrigerator for just that purpose. He told me that at his feeder in southern New Jersey it was possible to see several evening grosbeaks feeding on sunflower seeds at one end of the feeding board while a red-tailed hawk devoured a mouse at the other.

During the course of my travels I have seen many innovative devices for attracting birds that are not described in this book. In Switzerland I watched a man weave a decoy stork's nest in the hopes that it might lure a pair of prospecting storks to the roof of his chalet. With the same thing in mind, another workman was nailing together a platform on the nave of a nearby church. A month later, on an island off the Baltic coast of Finland, I was shown boxes resembling little dog kennels that were being used as nesting boxes by scoters.

Although square wooden platforms on poles are widely used by ospreys, especially near my home in Connecticut, I was quite unprepared to see similar platforms accepted by merlins in the Canadian arctic. Well known are the small floating platforms and even rubber tires that are anchored offshore in ponds or lakes so that loons and geese may nest unmolested by raccoons and foxes.

The creation and management of spoil islands, sand and shell dredged and dumped from the ship channels, has had incredible success in some states such as North Carolina and Texas in building up populations of colonial birds. But unless high storm tides sweep things clean once in awhile, such islands need management. Sand and shell soon give way to grass, then shrubs. If there are to be terns and black skimmers rather than herons and other long-legged waders, plant succession must be arrested. Choices must be made—terns or herons?

Even the roofs of factories, office buildings, supermarkets, and shopping centers can offer secure nesting places for a few beleaguered species such as nighthawks, least terns, and even skimmers. There is a hazard, however, on roofs covered with pea gravel—least terns making a scrape and getting down to the tar base run the risk of hard-boiled eggs! At Manchester, New Hampshire, a management study is under way to see what can be done to help the nighthawks that are still nesting on some of the office buildings. Rooftop management is a wide-open field for enterprising local clubs. Unfortunately, our wood stork does not nest on buildings like its European relative.

The use of decoys was pioneered in Maine by the author of this book, first with puffins, then with common terns. Similar efforts have succeeded in inducing least terns and black skimmers to nest on selected sites along the Gulf coast and elsewhere.

There is no limit to the possibilities with decoys—including human. Let me explain. By erecting a scarecrow and putting the birdseed on its outstretched hand, many of the birds will not seem to know the difference when some days later you remove the scarecrow and substitute yourself in a sneaky sort of way.

Sometimes, quite unintentionally, birds may benefit from human activity in a larger way. In Toronto, when the subway system was being excavated, the earth was transported by dump truck to the edge of Lake Ontario where a long peninsula eventually formed. Initially about 70 pairs of ring-billed gulls took up residence on the sandspit. Today the number of ring-bills is close to 80,000 pairs, each of which raises an average of 2.3 chicks per nest. This means that by summer's end there are a third of a million birds. These multitudes of gulls give life and beauty not only to the Great Lakes but also to the beaches and bays along the entire Atlantic coast during the colder months.

Ring-bills can spot a McDonald's hamburger stand or any similar seaside eating place at the limit of gull vision. Near our home on the Connecticut River we have a very good restaurant called The Gull, the walls of which are adorned with paintings of gulls. I suggested to the management that they could have the real thing—live gulls hovering in front of the picture windows—if they would construct a long narrow box or ledge to hold waste scraps from the kitchen. It would give authenticity to the name of the restaurant. So far my idea has not been adopted.

There is no substitute for ingenuity and imagination. This manual will give you many ideas, but don't hesitate to try new ideas of your own. The birds will decide if they are valid.

Roger Tory Peterson

Preface

To some the term *bird attraction* brings to mind thoughts of feeding backyard land birds. In this book I interpret bird attraction in a much broader sense, based on the idea that the best way to attract birds is to enrich habitats by improving vegetation, natural foods, water supplies, and nest sites.

When I first considered writing a book about attracting birds, I hesitated because there were already many good books on the topic. There seemed, however, to be a need for a comprehensive book that presented ideas for improving wildlife habitat on large properties, such as farms and estates, as well as backyards. There also was a need to offer ideas for attracting large birds as well as small and to compile ingenious techniques for attracting birds as diverse as hawks, owls, quail, loons, and terns.

I could not have written this book without the help and enthusiastic support of many people, including Peter Prescott and Katherine Lenz, my editors at Cornell University Press. I especially thank my wife, Elissa, for her editing, suggestions, and encouragement. The manuscript also profited greatly from the helpful comments of many colleagues at Cornell University and elsewhere. For their generous assistance in the first edition, I thank Jane Bock, Daniel Decker, George Eickwort, Aelred D. Geis, Arthur Gingert, Gene Good, George Good, Daniel Gray, Peter Hyypio, John Kelly, Richard Malecki, Charles Smith, Sally Spofford, and Warren Stiles. In this second edition, I also thank David Bonter, Louise Chambers, John Confer, Michael DeMunn, Brian Harrington, Mitschka Hartley, James R. Hill III, Linda Kennedy, Daniel Klem Jr., Tess Present, Ron Rohrbaugh, Ken Rosenberg, Steven J. Saffier, Carl Schwartz, Peter D. Vickery, Roger Wells, and Jeff Wells.

It is my pleasure to acknowledge Anne Senechal Faust (AF), who prepared most of the illustrations in this second edition. I also thank Michael DeMunn (MD), William Dilger (WD), Camille Doucet (CD), Valerie Hayes (VH), Marion Murfey (MM), Orville Rice (OR), John Schmitt (JS), and Barry Van Dusen (BV), whose creative line drawings lend additional interest to these pages. Chapter opening illustrations are by Camille Doucet; other work may be identified by initials in the figure captions. Connie Krochmal and Terry Mingle assisted with research and compiled data, and I thank Beth Campbell for typing the manuscript. Finally, I thank the many generous people who shared their innovative ideas for attracting birds.

Stephen W. Kress
Ithaca, New York

Introduction

Improving the quality of land for wildlife is the single most constructive step that anyone can take to assist wild bird populations. Happily, it is well within almost everyone's capability to improve bird habitats by providing important food and cover plants. Such management is vitally important because of the alarming loss of natural landscapes in North America.

With nearly 80 percent of the wildlife habitat in the United States occurring on private lands[1] and an average of 2.1 million acres converted to residential use every year,[2] it is clear that what happens on private land will determine the fate of most North American birds.

The trend toward large farms with endless acres of single-crop plantings results in a similar monotony of bird life. As small family farms are lost, so are the grasslands, brushy fencerows, farm woodlots, and wetlands that accompany them.

Such varied habitats are vital to maintaining abundant and varied bird populations. In the same way, sprawling suburbia too often replaces natural habitats with sterile pavement and pesticide-soaked lawns, resulting in fewer kinds of birds. As the size of habitat parcels decreases, populations of forest and grassland birds usually decline, owing to local increases in predator populations.

Some species have clearly benefited by the changes humans have brought to the land. Even the names of the chimney swift, barn owl, and barn swallow show their long association with humans, but the benefits of this incidental relationship are more the exception than the rule. More often, land development tends to simplify plant and animal communities, resulting in fewer kinds of plants, birds, and other animals. Air and water pollution further deplete bird numbers by stressing vegetation and thus reducing the variety of natural foods and nesting

[1]U.S. Department of Agriculture, Natural Resources Conservation Service. 1996. *Framework for the Future of Wildlife.* 15 pages.

[2]Marlow Vesterby, and Kenneth S. Krupka. 2001. *Major Uses of Land in the United States, 1997.* Resource Economics Div., Economic Research Service, United States Department of Agriculture, Statistical Bulletin No. 973. 60 Pages.

places available to birds. Some contaminants, such as acid precipitation, weaken plant and wildlife communities far from the pollution source.

The loss of habitat and the trend toward monotonous landscapes have helped place 25 percent of North America's approximately 800 bird species onto the Audubon Watchlist, an early-warning ranking system for birds showing alarming population declines. The Watchlist includes many birds that migrate through backyards, such as the wood thrush, Canada warbler, and red-headed woodpecker.

The World Conservation Union's 1998 assessment revealed that at least one of every eight plant species in the world—and 29 percent of more than 16,000 plants in the United States—is under threat of extinction. According to Peter Raven, director of the Missouri Botanical Garden, a disappearing plant can take with it 10–30 dependent species of insects, higher animals, and even other plants. Clearly, protection and management of plant communities are essential to varied bird life.

In 1933, Charles Scribner's Sons published Aldo Leopold's *Game Management*. In the preface of this classic work, Leopold observed, "The central thesis of game management is this: game can be restored by the creative use of the same tools which have heretofore destroyed it—axe, plow, cow, fire, and gun." Although we now have chain saws and bulldozers in addition to axes and plows, the motives of those who guide these powerful tools are still what determines whether they will work to replenish or extinguish wildlife.

The opportunity to restore many wild bird populations rests on their remarkable ability to quickly replenish their numbers when they find good habitat. For example, in just four years with nothing slowing their increase, one pair of northern bobwhites could potentially increase to 500 birds. While these large increases are unlikely, understanding the reasons why such growth is restrained is the basis of good management.

Habitat management is key to any successful effort to increase wildlife numbers. The number of animals that can survive within a habitat is determined by limiting factors such as food, cover, water, and nesting sites. Other factors such as parasites, predators, display areas, and singing posts may also restrict populations. The challenge for those interested in increasing bird numbers is to first determine which factors are preventing a population from naturally growing.

When attempting to solve this puzzle, it is important to realize that limiting factors change from one season to the next. Food may curb numbers in the winter but not in the summer. Likewise, cover may be sufficient in the summer but not in the winter. Providing more nesting cover and food may be useless if there is an inadequate supply of open water or suitable nest sites. As soon as one limiting factor is identified and removed, another comes into play. If this one is removed, the population increases further until something else restricts growth. Eventually, such social factors as territoriality will affect bird numbers, but even territory size is not a fixed constraint, as most birds reduce the size of their territory where they find quality habitat.

When human-induced changes—such as the destruction of nesting vegetation or the introduction of nest competitors like house sparrows—create limiting factors, removal of these factors may quickly result in the return of the desired species. However, when *natural* limiting factors are removed, unforeseen and sometimes disastrous consequences may result. For example, limited supplies of natural foods once prevented Canada geese from staying more than a few weeks in the Horicon Marshes of Wisconsin before dispersing south to the Gulf Coast. When artificial feeding removed this limit, overcrowding resulted, setting the stage for disease that threatened the geese and other waterbirds.

This book rests on the idea that bird populations increase when successful action is taken to remove limiting factors. Because the results of management are often difficult to predict, careful planning and follow-up monitoring are essential. The chapters that follow are organized to help identify limits to growth and offer techniques and resources for improving habitat. Habitat improvement through vegetation manipulation is often slow, but for those with patience and an interest in gardening, the variety of birds that frequent your land will certainly increase.

Our presence on Earth has become so prevalent that there are few—if any— places left where human impacts are not affecting wildlife. The idea that nature should take its course and that there will somehow be a "new balance of nature" usually leads to less diversity, as more adaptive species such as European starlings, feral pigeons, and house sparrows thrive. This is especially true in cities and suburbs, but the same trend occurs elsewhere. On coastal islands herring and great black-backed gulls have replaced common and roseate terns; on former prairies cowbirds and red-winged blackbirds have replaced bobolinks and meadowlarks. Without concerted efforts to improve and protect land for birds, we will continue to lose native birds at both international and local levels, as generalist species dominate habitats ecologically simplified by human activities.

Many environmental problems seem beyond our grasp, but the tendency toward monotonous landscapes with few plant species is something that any property owner can do something about. This book shows how to increase the variety of birds that frequent your land by creating and managing plant communities that mimic the function of natural habitats.

Since the first edition was published in 1985, there have been many advances in our knowledge about bird management. For example, there is now broad consensus on the importance of native plantings and the problems associated with introduced plants. Hence, this edition recommends plants native to North America and includes information on removing invasives. There are also new methods for preventing damage by plant predators such as deer and rabbits.

Vast resources are now available through the Internet, and a number of enlightened state and federal agencies have excellent programs such as the Wildlife Habitat Incentive Program of the Natural Resources Conservation Service (U.S. Department of Agriculture) and the Partners for Wildlife Program (U.S. Fish and Wildlife Service) that provide funds for creating and enhancing wildlife habitat on private properties of all sizes. Also since the first edition, several national bird conservation plans have been published, including Partners in Flight (concerning land birds), the North American Waterfowl Plan, the North American Shorebird Plan, and the North American Waterbird Plan. Together, these plans comprise the National Bird Conservation Initiative, which identifies and prioritizes conservation concerns and offers management actions.

In response to the great need for educating private-land owners about healthy lawns and backyard conservation, Audubon has recently launched its Audubon at Home program, which focuses on reducing the use of lawn chemicals and fertilizers, while encouraging the creation of wildlife habitat using native vegetation. These and similar programs offer resources and support for landowners everywhere.

While the loss of bird habitats is alarming, there is encouraging new data about the popularity of birdwatching. The most recent survey of interest in birds has found that nearly one in five Americans is a bird watcher and they annually spend about $32 billion on equipment.[3] Many birders are gardeners and tens of thousands are participating in continent-wide citizen-science programs that further bird conservation. This bodes well for people improving the well-being of North American birds.

[3]United States Department of the Interior, Fish and Wildlife Service and United States Department of Commerce, U.S. Census Bureau. 2001 National Survey of Fishing, Hunting, and Wildlife-Associated Recreation. 116 pages, 4 Appendices.

My intent for this new edition of the *Audubon Society Guide to Attracting Birds* is to bring the best of these scattered resources into one volume. I hope to assist caring landowners and managers of properties ranging in size from urban balconies and suburban backyards to larger properties such as country estates, schoolyards, cemeteries, corporate parks, airports, golf courses, wildlife refuges, and parklands of all sizes. My hope is that managers of agricultural land, highways, greenways, and despoiled inner-city brownfields alike will find inspiration and techniques within these pages that will help them carry out the urgent and satisfying work of improving land for wild birds.

Birds brighten our lives with their song, color, and grace, but their well-being cannot be assumed. If we are to leave a heritage for future generations as rich as that which we know today, we must pursue a more proactive and responsible approach to bird conservation.

1 Backyard Habitats

Backyard bird gardeners and large landscape managers alike can increase the number and variety of birds by studying natural habitats and mimicking them at a manageable scale. For the small-property owner, this usually means increasing the variety of vegetation by replacing expansive, close-cropped lawns with creative landscaping that emphasizes a layering and clumping of native bird-attracting plants. If care is taken to select plants with high wildlife value, and then to plant them in appropriate places and not abandon them to deer, drought, and weeds, the result can be a property that is easy to maintain and alive with birds. Large-property owners, including farmers, have even more opportunities for improving habitat for wild birds—without losses in agricultural production. Regardless of property size, the same fundamental principle applies: manipulating habitat succession and the physical structure of vegetation can increase bird variety. The following projects will help to meet the needs of wild birds for food, water, cover, and nest sites by fulfilling their requirements with as much variety as possible.

Start with an Inventory and Develop a Plan

Before attempting to improve your land for birds, conduct an inventory to see which birds currently visit your property. Keep a list of species found on your property throughout the year; also conduct a dawn census of singing birds in late spring—these birds are ready to nest. In addition, list your most conspicuous trees, shrubs, and weeds. Map the distribution of your plant communities to create a record of what your property looks like before your management efforts begin. Be sure to include property lines, buildings, wetlands, changes in slope, and existing bird feeders.

With your inventory map complete, begin to plan on paper the changes that might improve your property for wildlife. Your plan will depend largely on the size of your property and available finances, as well as on which birds you hope to attract. The regional tables of recommended plants in Chapter 5 will prove useful in the early stages of your plan. From these you can decide which trees, shrubs, vines, and ground covers should be retained and encouraged and which should be replaced with better bird-attracting plants. The composition of plant communities and their arrangement on your property are the keys to successful bird attracting through the seasons.

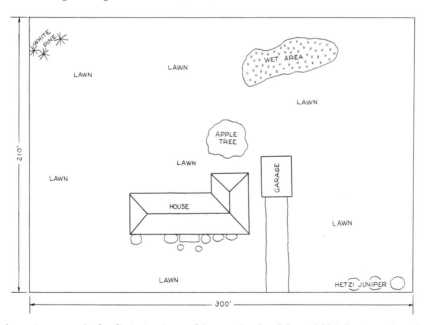

An inventory map is the first step toward improving land for wild birds. Anne Senechal Faust (AF)

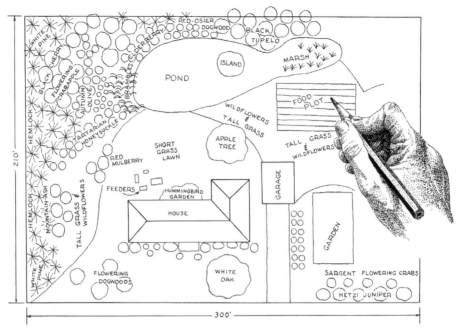

After completing the inventory map, create a management plan that illustrates the location of your specific management projects. This should include the composition and arrangement of plant habitats as well as locations of nest boxes, water features, and other improvements. (AF)

Optimizing Edge

Because of the abundant mix of food, cover, nest sites, perches, and other factors, bird variety is greatest where two or more plant communities come together. This is known as *edge effect*.

Rapidly growing shrubland (thicket) communities frequently thrive at woodland borders, and these usually have abundant fruit-producing shrubs and insect populations. Many shrubland plants, such as mesquite, juniper, hawthorn, raspberries, and roses, have well-armed stems that deter browsing mammals such as deer and rabbits. Such prickly thickets also provide excellent predator-safe nesting places.

In rural and suburban settings, shrubby edges and hedgerows, which often define property borders, will attract some of the species associated with shrublands. Such features are especially important because they provide shelter from the extremes of winter and summer weather, nesting places, protection from predators such as hawks, and abundant food in the form of insects and fruits.

When planting shrubby borders, mix several shrub species to vary the shape and density of your hedge, offering a greater selection of nest sites. Also select shrubs that fruit at different seasons to provide an ample food supply throughout the year.

Hedgerows are also useful for connecting separate woodlots and may increase the movement of forest birds between otherwise isolated forest islands. An inexpensive, although slow technique for developing a shrubby hedgerow is to till the soil where you want the hedge, then stretch a tight wire between two posts. Birds will soon perch on the wire and drop excrement, some of which will contain shrub seeds. A hedgerow of bird favorites like junipers, hawthorn, and roses will eventually develop.

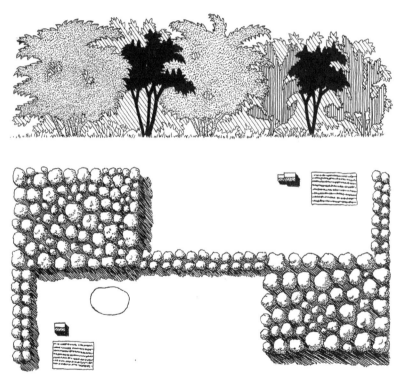

Shrubby hedgerows are one of the best ways to increase the variety of birds on your property. Upper diagram provides a vertical view of a hedgerow; lower diagram presents an aerial view. (AF)

NATURAL WAY TO PLANT A MIXED HEDGE

WIRE

PLOWED
SOIL

A wire stretched across a tilled plot of land allows a natural hedgerow to develop from seeds that drop in bird excrement. (AF)

Maximize Vegetation Levels

Even within the same habitat, different birds show strong preferences for specific elevations in which they feed and nest. This is most apparent in forests, where some species such as tanagers and grosbeaks sing and feed in the canopy level but nest in the subcanopy. Other birds, such as chipping sparrows, may feed on the ground, nest in shrubs, and sing from the highest trees. Such movements demonstrate the importance of a multileveled plan for wildlife plantings.

This principle is helpful in many different situations. Bird habitat in woodlots can be improved by planting shade-tolerant shrubs and vines within forest openings to improve food supplies and nesting places. Likewise, isolated trees in pastures and backyards will attract more birds if shrubs are planted at their bases, creating islands of vegetation with varied heights. The same principle applies when selecting plants for the borders of your backyard. Ideally, plant these in a stair-step arrangement, with the largest trees at the back of your property, stepping down to small trees, then large shrubs, small shrubs, and, finally, meadow plants. Limit close-cropped lawn to the immediate vicinity of your house.

Tall conifers are best located to the rear of your property or to the northern property border so that they provide maximum shelter from winter winds without excessively shading other plantings. Deciduous trees planted on the south side of buildings provide cooling summer shade; in winter, these leafless trees permit warming sunlight to reach buildings.

Compromise Some Lawn for Mixed Ground Cover

A small central patch of mown lawn is useful for viewing backyard birds. Birds that feed and nest in surrounding shrubs and trees will venture out onto the lawn—especially if lured there with feeders, baths, and dusting areas. But lawn itself, especially expansive rolling fields of it, is one of the most destitute bird habitats on earth. The simplest approach to reducing lawn is to just let it grow. This is best done by halting mowing near property borders while continuing to mow near the house. Soon the former lawn will turn to meadow and a surprising variety of wildflowers will emerge in the new habitat. Such meadows look more like a planned feature of the yard when the edges have an undulating margin.

To emphasize that your new lawn design is a plan and not a result of neglect, mow the borders, especially along a driveway, or mow a meandering path through the yard with a sign placed at the entrance that says "nature trail." Another approach is to erect a split-rail fence to define the border between lawn and meadow. Such fences are also excellent mounts for nest boxes.

Reduce lawn, but mow property borders. Lawn will soon change to meadow when mowing stops. One mowing per year in late summer is ample for preventing trees and shrubs from growing. Photograph by Stephen Kress (SK)

A split-rail fence creates an effective border between close-cropped lawn and meadow, while providing an excellent location for nest boxes. (SK)

For color, plant bird-attracting flowers and surround them with a border of flagstone or brick to neatly set this off as a managed rather than out-of-control area. Each autumn, rake leaves and place several inches of them underneath the shrubs. By spring the leaves will decompose into rich soil with an abundance of earthworms and insects for ground-feeding spring migrants.

Even robins that so capably pull earthworms from lawns may suffer if lawns are the only feeding habitat available. In West Newton, Massachusetts, a community with spacious lawns and many planted trees around the houses, researchers found that robins were not producing enough young to balance losses to the adult population. Although West Newton seemed to be ideal robin habitat, a closer examination found that the carefully groomed grounds around the homes had few brushy areas with little available leaf-litter. In April and May the robins fed successfully from the lawns, but in the drier months of June and July, when earthworms were not easily available in the lawns, the lack of moist leaf-litter among the carefully tended gardens and lawns left the robins with little alternative food for their young.

Achieve further variety in ground cover by planting borders and patches of low-growing perennial plants, such as bearberry, coralberry, and juniper, that can compete successfully with invading grasses and yet provide food and cover. These plants are more useful to birds than some better-known ground covers such as Boston ivy, pachysandra, cotoneasters, and periwinkle. Although these popular plants are effective alternatives to grasses, they provide little food or cover for birds and often escape into natural areas.

Close-cropped grass lawns make even less sense in dry or desert habitats. Ground-cover plants and shrubs that are especially adapted for arid climates (xerophytes) make both ecological and economic common sense.

The variety of birds will increase with more vegetation levels. While it may be difficult to establish shrubs under existing trees (middle), the arrangements shown in the top and bottom drawings are easier to create. (AF)

A small property with varied plant habitats provides many layers that offer useful structure for nesting, cover, and food. Diverse habitats will increase bird numbers and variety. (SK)

Properties with expansive lawns and few foundation plantings offer little in the way of food or cover for birds. (SK)

Leaf Mulch Beds

While some birds such as robins feed on earthworms and insects in grassy lawns, others such as towhees, fox sparrows, and white-throated sparrows prefer feeding among fallen leaves, where they can scratch and look for hidden insects. Rather than bagging raked leaves and setting them at the curb for pickup, consider creating leaf mulch beds under trees and shrubs where grass already has a difficult time growing. Let the leaves decompose under the shrubs and extend the mulch several feet out into the yard.

Rather than bagging leaves for curbside pickup, rake the leaves under shrubs to create leaf mulch beds for ground-feeding birds. (SK)

Changes in Slope

Ground-feeding birds such as sparrows, towhees, and wrens are attracted to abrupt changes in slope. In natural habitats birds frequently forage along stream banks, rock outcrops, and tree roots, as these habitats have a myriad of tiny nooks and crannies in which to dig and probe for hiding insects, worms, and other small animals. You can put this natural attraction to work in backyards by creating irregular elevation breaks.

On small properties, build a gently sloping soil mound with a steep rock face, or create rock gardens or stone walls. In northern habitats the steep face of an artificial slope should face south so that the first spring thaw will reveal foraging places previously hidden by snow. On larger properties the opportunities for creating varied slopes are even greater. Where space and means permit, use a bulldozer rather than a shovel and wheelbarrow for landscaping. Miniature cliffs landscaped with ground cover, rotting logs, and shrubs will vary the terrain, creating warm south-facing slopes to attract early-spring migrants, and cool, north-facing slopes where summer birds may forage. Changes in slope combined with rock-faced water pools are especially attractive.

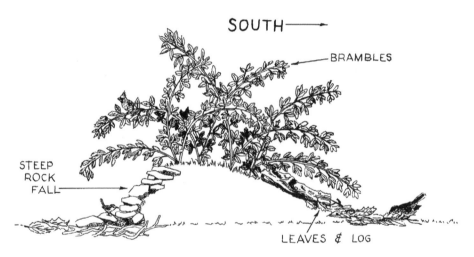

Even a small alteration in slope will help attract ground-feeding birds such as wrens and sparrows. (AF)

Dust Bathing

Many kinds of birds, including quail, pheasant, birds of prey, kinglets, and sparrows, enjoy taking a vigorous dust bath. Bathing movements in dust are remarkably like those in water, as birds fluff themselves up and flutter their wings in the dust. The function of dusting is little understood, but it may help to rid the bird's body of parasites such as feather lice.

A dusting area is another way to attract birds into an open viewing space. Even small backyards can accommodate a few square feet for a dusting area. Where space permits, a dusting area 3 feet on each side will accommodate several birds at a time. To create a dust bath, excavate soil about 6 inches deep and line the edges with bricks or rocks. To create a suitable dust mix, combine one-third each of sand, sifted ash, and soil.

Birds such as these bobwhites may dust to remove feather parasites. (AF)

Weed Food Patches

What is a weed? Ralph Waldo Emerson's answer was "a plant whose virtues have not yet been discovered." Studies of wild bird diets demonstrate the virtues of most backyard plants such as ragweed, lamb's-quarter, amaranth, bristle grass, and panic grass. These are among the most important wild bird foods. In contrast to perennials that produce relatively small amounts of seed each year, most annuals produce enormous amounts of seed (e.g., a single pigweed can produce more than 100,000 seeds). This strategy improves their odds for surviving from one generation to the next, while also providing a bountiful supply of seed for ground-feeding birds such as juncos, sparrows, and quail.

Weed seeds are so abundant and long-lived in soil that there is usually an ample supply available after tilling. An excellent way to favor growth of these plants is to establish a wild food patch. Depending on available space, this can be a 100- to 2000-square-foot patch of tilled soil or, if space permits, a rotating series of five strips that are plowed in different years in sequences such as 1-3-5-2-4 or 2-4-1-3-5. By repeating the sequence after the fifth year, the chance of shrub growth is eliminated and the rotation starts back to bare soil. Several long narrow patches are preferred over a single large patch because they offer more edge. After three years, perennial flowers such as goldenrod and asters usually replace the pioneering annual weeds.

A   PLANTED FOOD PATCH

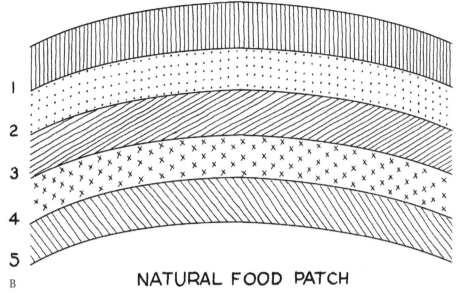

1
2
3
4
5

B

NATURAL FOOD PATCH

A five-strip tilled earth patch is an area where wildflowers and weeds are encouraged.
Such plants are important food sources for wild birds. These patches are similar to
giant bird feeders in that both provide concentrated supplies of food. (AF)

SOME COMMON UPLAND WEEDS

Bristle Grass (*Setaria* spp.)

Well named for their bristly seed heads, the bristle grasses are important
upland "weeds" for wild birds. Closely related to the cultivated millet found in
birdseed mixtures, bristle grasses are abundant and widespread throughout the
United States and southern Canada. The two most important members of this
genus are introduced annual grasses from Europe—yellow bristle grass (*Setaria
lutescens*) and green bristle grass (*S. viridis*). They commonly grow between rows
of cultivated crops and other disturbed soils.

At least 66 wild bird species feed on bristle grass seed, which comprises at
least 10 percent of the diet of 28 of these species. Bristle grass is an especially
important source of food for mourning doves, bobwhite quail, red-winged
blackbirds, indigo buntings, brown-headed cowbirds, dickcissels, horned larks,
Lapland longspurs, and pyrrhuloxias, as well as clay-colored, grasshopper, and
tree sparrows.

Backyard Habitats 19

Bristle grass (AF)

Crabgrass (*Digitaria* spp.)

Although there is a strong prejudice against crabgrass in lawns and gardens, these tenacious annual grasses are prolific seed producers and an important part of the diets of many seed-eating songbirds. Two European introductions from this genus, hairy crabgrass (*Digitaria sanguinalis*) and smooth crabgrass (*D. ischaemum*), are especially widespread and abundant in disturbed soils and lawns across North America. At least 21 species of birds eat crabgrass seed, but it is especially important for mourning doves, dark-eyed juncos, and Lapland longspurs, as well as the chipping, clay-colored, field, Lincoln's, savannah, and tree sparrows.

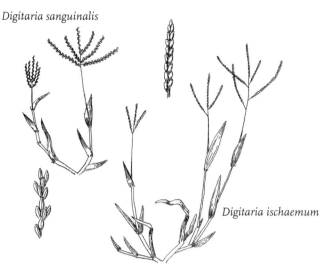

Digitaria sanguinalis

Digitaria ischaemum

Crabgrass (AF)

Panic Grass (*Panicum* spp.)

At least 160 species of panic grass grow in North America. Most are annual native grasses of dry uplands that grow best in cultivated or disturbed soils. Like the bristle grasses, the widespread and abundant panic grasses are very important foods for ground-feeding birds. Common witch-grass (*Panicum capillare*) and fall panic grass (*P. dichtomiflorum*) are two of the most common and ubiquitous species. Panic grasses are most common in the southeastern United States, but many kinds also occur in the north and west. At least 61 bird species eat panic grass seeds, most frequently bobwhite quail, wild turkeys, red-winged blackbirds, brown-headed cowbirds, blue grosbeaks, Smith's longspurs, pyrrhuloxias, and lark, clay-colored, Lincoln's, savannah, tree, song, swamp, and white-crowned sparrows.

Panic grass (AF)

Doveweed (*Croton* spp.)

Doveweeds (crotons) are important wild bird foods in the southern and prairie states. Their name comes from their popularity as food for mourning, ground, and white-winged doves. Prairie chickens, bobwhite quail, cardinals, pipits, pyrrhuloxias, and many other ground-feeding birds also favor doveweed seeds. Most doveweeds, such as wooly croton (*Croton capitatus*), are annual, but others, such as Gulf croton (*C. punctatus*), are perennial. Doveweeds are noted for their resistance to cattle grazing.

WOOLY CROTON

Doveweed (AF)

Knotweed (*Polygonum* spp.)

The knotweeds are a diverse group of mostly dry-habitat plants. Although they vary from low, creeping species, such as prostrate knotweed (*Polygonum aviculare*), to upright forms, such as erect knotweed (*P. erectum*) and black bindweed (*P. convolvulus*), a twining vine, all provide important seed supplies for wild birds. The large seeds of black bindweed are especially important to upland birds such as the greater prairie chicken and Hungarian partridge. At least 39 species of birds eat knotweed seeds. Ground-feeding birds, including rosy finches, horned larks, and McCown's longspurs, as well as fox, grasshopper, Harris', lark, savannah, song, and white-crowned sparrows, especially favor them.

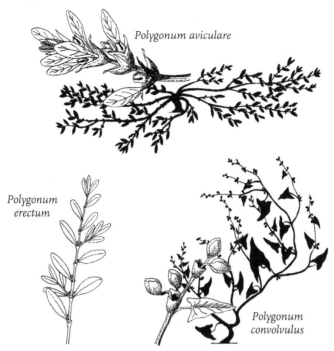

Polygonum aviculare

Polygonum erectum

Polygonum convolvulus

Knotweed (AF)

Lamb's-Quarter (*Chenopodium album*)

Lamb's-quarter is an introduced annual herb from Eurasia that grows commonly in disturbed garden and roadside soils throughout most of North America. An individual lamb's-quarter plant may produce 75,000 tiny seeds from June to October. At least 32 species of birds eat lamb's-quarter seeds. These include many ground-feeding birds, such as snow buntings, dark-eyed juncos, horned larks, McCown's longspurs, common red-polls, and white-crowned sparrows.

Lamb's-quarter (AF)

Pigweed (*Amaranthus* spp.)

Pigweeds are annual native plants of disturbed soils, such as vacant lots and waste areas. Some sources suggest that pigweeds are especially common in areas where pigs have rooted up the soil—a theory that may explain their unlikely name. Members of the amaranth genus are prolific seed producers—single plants are known to produce over 100,000 tiny seeds. As with ragweed, the best way to encourage a crop of pigweed is to thoroughly till the soil. Pigweeds, ragweeds, and other plants of disturbed soils can maintain themselves for only 2–3 years before perennials such as asters and goldenrods crowd them out. At least 47 species of birds eat pigweed seeds, which are especially important to mourning doves, snow buntings, and goldfinches, as well as chipping, clay-colored, Lincoln's, savannah, song, and white-crowned sparrows.

REDROOT PIGWEED

TUMBLE PIGWEED

Pigweed (AF)

Pokeweed (*Phytolacca americana*)

Pokeweed is a native, smooth-stemmed plant found in moist, disturbed soils. The poisonous taproot may produce plants that grow up to 12 feet tall. Each fall, pokeweed dies back to the ground; however, new stems may grow from the same root for 10 or more years. As many as 1000 juicy, dark purple berries ripen annually from August to October and are readily consumed by at least 52 kinds of birds. Mourning doves, catbirds, mocking-birds, thrushes, and cedar waxwings especially prefer pokeweed fruit. Some birds may become intoxicated after eating fermented pokeberry fruits.

Pokeweed (AF)

Ragweed (*Ambrosia* spp.)

Hay fever sufferers best know native ragweed for the allergic effect of its tiny pollen, but its reputation should also include its great importance as seed producers for wild birds. As such, ragweed has few rivals. No fewer than 60 bird species readily eat ragweed seeds. Common ragweed (*Ambrosia artemisiifolia*) is the most important ragweed in the east, as is western ragweed (*A. psilostachya*) in western states and provinces. These ragweeds have abundant, oil-rich seeds and frequently hold onto their tiny seeds well into the winter, long after most other seeds are covered by snow. Since ragweed seeds can live in the soil for years and wait for favorable growing conditions, the best way to get a good ragweed crop is to simply disturb the soil by tilling. Quail are especially fond of eating ragweed seeds, which are available from some quail restoration groups (see Chapter 4). Ragweed seeds are also

Ragweed (AF)

especially important for snow buntings, American goldfinches, dark-eyed juncos, horned larks, and common redpolls, as well as fox, Harris', song, white-crowned, and white-throated sparrows.

Sheep Sorrel (*Rumex acetosella*)

Sheep sorrel is a common plant in open, short-grass meadows. This diminutive member of the dock family is naturalized from Europe. It spreads by creeping perennial rootstock and occurs throughout most of North America in acidic, low-fertility soils. At least 29 species of birds eat sheep sorrel seeds, including many game birds and songbirds. Sheep sorrel seed also provides food for ruffed grouse, red-winged blackbirds, and hoary redpolls, as well as grasshopper, savannah, song, swamp, tree, and white-crowned sparrows.

Sheep sorrel (AF)

Sunflowers (*Helianthus* spp).

Most sunflowers grow in open, sunny habitats. More species thrive in the prairie and plains states than in any other region, but sunflowers occur throughout North America and some even grow in woodlands. Most, such as Jerusalem artichoke (*Helianthus tuberosus*), are perennials and grow each year from hardy rootstock. Common sunflower (*H. annuus*), however, is an annual with prolific seed production. Its cultivated varieties are among the most important wild bird foods. Some birds, such as chickadees, nuthatches, and titmice, prefer sunflowers over all other seeds and will feed exclusively on them if given the opportunity. At least 43 bird species eat sunflower seeds.

Sunflower (AF)

Cultivated Food Plots

Cultivated food plots can provide abundant, concentrated food supplies for wild birds. They are also useful for attracting birds to preferred areas. Several small rectangular food plots ranging from 100 to 2000 square feet and located near water or good cover are best. A useful goal is one half-acre food patch for every 20 acres of land. Larger plots are especially useful if deer are abundant, to ensure that some food is left for the birds. The simplest way to establish a food patch is to thoroughly till the soil and then broadcast a mixed bag of milo, millet, and sunflower seed onto the soil. Then rake the soil to lightly cover the seed. It is especially easy to grow a crop of milo in this manner. Fifteen pounds of mixed seed will cover a half-acre plot.

Garden Flowers for Songbirds

The seeds of many garden flowers are good additions to wild bird diets. When selecting flowers for your garden, keep birds in mind and choose some of their favorites. Most of the garden flowers recommended will grow in moist summer gardens throughout North America. The majority belong to the sunflower family, which explains their attractiveness to songbirds such as goldfinches and native sparrows. Most garden flowers require an open, sunlit area. For best results, place a slow-release fertilizer (most last for 3 months) on the soil for established plants, or mixed it into the soil for new plantings. Water, but don't soak; use mulch to retain soil moisture and minimize competing weeds. Be sure to let flower heads go to seed to provide fall and winter food. This also increases the chances for natural reseeding.

SOME BIRD-ATTRACTING FLOWERS FOR NORTH AMERICAN GARDENS

Aster (*Aster* spp.*)
Bachelor's button (*Centaurea hirta*)
⁺Basket flower (*Centaurea americana*)
Black-eyed Susan (*Rudbeckia* spp.)
Blessed thistle (*Carduus benedictus*)
Bluebells (*Campanula* spp.)
Calendula (*Calendula officinalis*)
California poppy (*Eschscholzia californica*)
China aster (*Callistephus chinesis*)
Chrysanthemum (*Chrysanthemum* spp.)
Coneflowers (*Echinacea* spp.)
⁺Coreopsis (*Coreopsis* spp.)
Cornflower (*Centaurea cyanus*)
Cosmos (*Cosmos* spp.)
⁺Dayflower (*Commelina* spp.)
Dusty miller (*Centaurea cineraria*)
Love-lies-bleeding (*Amaranthus caudatus*)
Marigold (*Tageses* spp.)
Phlox (*Phlox* spp.), especially Annual phlox (*P. drummondii*)
Portulaca (*Portulaca* spp.), especially moss rose (*P. grandiflora*)
Prince's feather (*Celosia cristata*)
Prince's plumes (*Celosia plumosa*)
Rock purslane (*Calandrinia* spp.)
⁺Royal sweet sultan (*Centaurea imperialis*)
Silene (*Silene* spp.)
Sunflower (*Helianthus annuus*)
Sweet scabious (*Scabiosa atropurpurea*)
Tarweed (*Madin elegans*)

*Abbreviation means that several species are available.
⁺Tolerates light shade.

Verbena (*Verbena hybrida*)
Zinnia (*Zinnia elegans*)

Goldfinches and other seed-eating birds feed on the mature seeds of zinnia, cosmos, coneflower, marigold, and other garden flowers. (AF)

Hummingbird Gardens

The ruby-throated hummingbird is usually the only hummingbird that visits eastern backyards, but sometimes 20 or more of these feisty midgets will frequent the same food patch, working it carefully for nectar and insects. Hummingbirds are much more common in the western and especially the southwestern states. At least 14 species occur occasionally in the western United States, and some are regulars throughout the year.

To attract hummingbirds to your property, plant bright-colored, tubular flowers. In general, orange and red flowers are the most frequently visited, but hummingbirds also occasionally visit yellow, pink, purple, and even blue flowers. Some trees and vines are also useful for attracting hummingbirds. Plant related flowers in large clumps to create a conspicuous display, and select a variety of species to provide continuous flowering from spring to fall.

An excellent planting design is based on the concept of layered vegetation. Grow a cascade of hummingbird-attracting plants on the side of your home by securing a trellis to a wall, then plant trumpet creeper vines or trumpet honeysuckle on the trellis. Layer shrubs such as bush fuschias and low hummingbird herbs such as salvias in front of the trellis.

Or devote a circular patch of yard to your hummingbird garden. In the center of the circle, plant trumpet vine or trumpet honeysuckle on an arbor and then encircle this with hummingbird shrubs, and an outer ring of hummingbird annuals or perennials from the following lists.

HUMMINGBIRD PLANTS FOR NORTH AMERICAN GARDENS
American columbine (*Aquilegia canadensis*); perennial
Bee balm (Oswego tea) (*Mondarda didyma*); native perennial
Bugleweed (*Ajuga repens*); creeping perennial
Butterfly milkweed (*Aesclepias tuberosa*); perennial; orange flowers also attract butterflies
Cardinal flower (*Lobelia cardinalis*); perennial; requires moist soil, partial shade
Columbine (*Aquilega canadensis*); perennial with orange-yellow flowers
Coralberry (*Symphoricarpos orbiculatus*); native shrub with attractive fruits
Dahlias (*Dahlia* spp.*); perennial
Evening primrose (*Oenothera* spp.); perennial wildflower
Four-o'clock (*Mirabilis jalapa*); perennial
Fuschias (*Fuschia* spp.); flowering shrub; hang in basket; also ornamental shrubs
Gladiolus (*Gladiolus* spp.); 'Flash' variety is 3–4 feet tall and bright red
Hibiscus (*Hibiscus* spp.); flowering shrub, especially variety 'Althaea'
Hollyhocks (*Althea* spp.); perennial
Honeysuckle, limber (*Lonicera divica*); shrubby vine
Honeysuckle, orange (*Lonicera ciliosa*); northwestern shrub
Honeysuckle, trumpet (*Lonicera sempervirens*); twining shrub
Horse chestnut (*Aesculus hippocastanum*); introduced flowering tree
Jewelweeds (*Impatiens* spp.); wildflower; a hummingbird favorite
Larkspur (*Delphinium* spp.); perennial
Madrone (*Arbutus menzilsii*); northwestern tree
Manzanitas (*Arctostaphylos* spp.); northwestern shrub

*Abbreviation means that several species are available.

Morning glory (*Ipomoea* spp.); annual vine

Nasturtiums (*Tropalolum majus*); annual

Paintbrushes (*Castillega* spp.); annual and perennial herbs

Petunias (*Petunia* spp.); annual

Phlox (*Phlox* spp.); perennial

Sage (*Salvia* spp.); especially pineapple sage (*S. elegans*) and autumn sage
(*S. greggii*); perennial in south and annual in north

Tiger lily (*Lilium tigrinum*); perennial

Trumpet vine (*Campsis radicans*); native vine

Zinnia (*Zinnia elegans*); annual

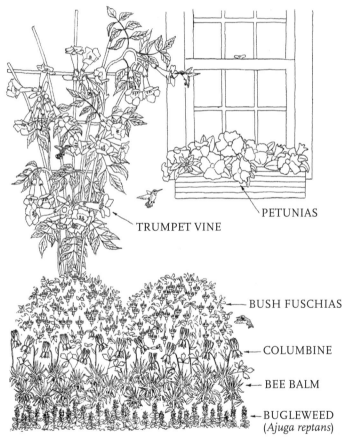

TRUMPET VINE

PETUNIAS

BUSH FUSCHIAS

COLUMBINE

BEE BALM

BUGLEWEED
(*Ajuga reptans*)

Multilevel hummingbird gardens based on the concept of layered vegetation are a colorful way to attract many hummingbirds to a small area. (AF)

Birds-of-paradise (*Poinciana gilliesii*); evergreen shrub; clustered yellow flowers
Citrus tree (*Citris* spp.); orange, grapefruit, and lemon trees
Coral bean (*Erythrina* spp.); southwestern tree
Fire pink (*Silene virginica*); bright red-flowered herb
Lemon bottlebrush (*Callistemon lanceolatus*); evergreen shrub, 6-inch red flowers
Mimosa tree (*Albizzia julibrissin*); introduced tree with pink-to-lilac flowers
Red buckeye (*Aesculus pavia*); small southeastern native tree with bright red
   flowers
Scarlet gilia (*Gilia aggregata*); southwestern herb
Scarlet runner bean (*Phaseolus coccineus*); cultivated legume vine
Wiegala (*Wiegala* spp.); deciduous shrub with white, pink, or red tubular flowers

*Check with local nurseries to determine tolerance for winter and summer temperature extremes.

Rooftop and Flower Box Gardens

Urban gardeners without backyards but with access to rooftops and balcony terraces can also attract birds by creating an oasis of green and colorful flowers. Even window boxes can help to attract hummingbirds. Consider making a rooftop garden by planting small trees and shrubs in large containers or wooden bins. Use a 1:1 mix of compost and soil-less potting mix. During summer, apply a 20-20-20 liquid fertilizer weekly and mix in a dry, organic, slow-release fertilizer. If possible, water the garden with rainwater. Such gardens are especially attractive during migration, when a variety of finches and sparrows will join resident birds such as jays and doves. Bright-colored flowers are the secret to lure hummingbirds. City birds such as pigeons, starlings, and house sparrows may dominate bird feeders, but gardens planted for birds will not encourage large numbers of these aggressive birds.

Conifer Plantations

A plantation of pine, hemlock, spruce, or other conifers in a corner of your yard or any odd area between agricultural fields adds pleasing variety to the landscape and benefits wild birds for several reasons. Some birds, such as crossbills, favor conifer seeds over all other foods. Conifers also provide excellent cover from both summer and winter temperature extremes and are favorite roosting and nesting places for owls. Look for regurgitated owl pellets and whitewashed tree trunks to locate roosting locations. Improve conifer stands for birds by leaving or creating snags, by pruning tree branches to create suitable nest supports, and by installing nest boxes for barred and screech owls (see Chapter 7).

Coniferous soils are usually too acidic for most understory and ground-cover plants adapted to deciduous forest soils. Consequently, conifer plantations often have sparse understory and few birds inhabit the forest floor and subcanopy levels. Where light levels permit, plant or encourage bird-attracting, acid-tolerant shrubs such as blueberry and huckleberry, and ground covers such as bunch-berry and bearberry.

Conifer plantations provide excellent winter cover for birds, excellent roosting places, and habitat for kinglets, nuthatches, and owls. (AF)

Brush Piles

Rather than disposing of fallen branches, reserve a corner of your backyard for a brush pile. The simplest approach is to heap branches on top of each other, but a foundation will greatly improve the value and life of the brush-pile for both birds and mammals. Several approaches are commonly used to build brush-pile foundations, but all rest on the need for animals to have a labyrinth of tunnels in which to hide from predators and obtain shelter from weather extremes. You can create such tunnels by laying four 6-foot-long logs (4–8 inches in diameter) directly on the ground and then laying another four logs of similar size perpendicularly on top of the first set. With branch stems pointing toward the ground, pile cut shrubs and pruned branches on top of the log foundation to form a peaked mound.

Another approach to building a foundation is to make three 1-foot-tall rock piles in a V formation, lay logs onto the rocks, and then pile branches on these. Or construct a brush pile over ceramic drainage tiles. Mound up large branches first and add small branches to the top of the pile.

Construct living shelters from conifers such as spruce or pine with well-formed lower branches. Construct a teepee-like shelter by slicing the underside of lower branches so that they fall to the ground, surrounding the tree trunk (if sufficient living bark is left intact, the branches may live in their new positions for several years). Such shelters provide excellent cover for game birds such as grouse and quail. In winter they also serve as useful places to install supplemental grain feeding stations.

BASES FOR BRUSH PILES

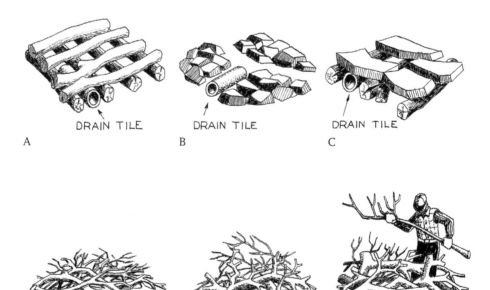

DRAIN TILE   DRAIN TILE   DRAIN TILE

A   B   C

A1   B1   C1

A brush-pile foundation should offer shelter to birds and other animals (A–C). On top of these foundations, pile branches (A1–C1). A living shelter is formed by slicing halfway through the underside of branches. (AF)

PLANTING TREES AND SHRUBS

Bird-attracting trees, shrubs, vines, and ground covers are available from local retail nurseries or mail-order nurseries, but native plants may be difficult to obtain. Many nurseries will special-order native plants, so start planning early to allow ample time before the planting season. This is especially appropriate in cases where development of natural areas is imminent.

The most important factors are careful selection of plants that are most likely to tolerate your climate and soil, testing of the soil before planting, careful preparation of the planting site, and continual care—especially during the months immediately following planting. It is sometimes suggested that if you have only $20 for planting a tree, it is best to spend $1 for the tree and put the rest into preparing the site and maintaining it afterward. This example may over-state the case, but it does emphasize the need for care in planting and continued maintenance.

Transplanting Wild Trees and Shrubs

Wild trees and shrubs from nearby woods and thickets have the advantages of being inexpensive, more resistant to insects and disease, and well adapted to your local climate and soil conditions. If done properly, moving wild trees and shrubs is not as simple as it might seem. First, you must get permission from a willing landowner; then search for a suitable specimen. Avoid overcollecting and removing rare plants that may be protected. It may take a long search to find a suitable tree or shrub for transplanting because many, if not most, wild plants have their roots and branches tangled with those of neighboring plants. Also, the main roots of wild plants may be few and widespread, making it difficult to transplant enough roots. To minimize these problems and give wild transplants the best chances for a long future, follow these five steps:

1. Make your selections for transplanting in early spring; plan to move the plants either the next winter or early the following spring. Select isolated shrubs and trees with no more than a 2-inch diameter at breast height (dbh). If a tree has a 2-inch dbh or a larger shrub is involved, prune the roots by using a sharp spade to make an 8-inch-deep incision circling the tree approximately 2 feet from the trunk. If the tree has a 1-inch dbh or the shrub is small, the encircling cut need be only 1 foot from the trunk. This root pruning should be done in early spring so that roots will branch during the following growing season, forming a less extensive but more compact and fibrous root system closer to the tree trunk or shrub crown. For larger plants, root pruning on one side in early spring and the other side later in the summer will reduce the chances of shocking the plant. Do not disturb the tree after root pruning. Remove the branches from neighboring trees that may shade the tree or shrub.

2. Late in the following winter or early next spring, dig up the root-pruned plant by making a new trench about 6 inches farther from the trunk than your initial incision. Dig up as much soil as possible with the roots and wrap the root mass in burlap to protect the roots from desiccation. This is especially important for evergreens.

3. As soon as possible after excavation, place the transplanted shrub at its new site. The depth of the prepared hole for the planting should approximate the height of the root system and be twice as wide as the root span. Before placing the tree in the hole, check for adequate drainage by filling it with water. If water remains in the hole 24 hours later, the soil is poorly drained and your transplant is likely to die unless it is a water-tolerant species. Sometimes digging it at least another foot deeper and then filling the bottom of the hole with gravel over a drain tile allows removal of excess water from the site.

    When setting the plant in the hole, take care to spread the roots in a natural way without bending or cramping them. Position the plant so the roots are at approximately the same depth as they were at the site from which they were removed. Incorporate leaf mold or peat moss at a ratio of 1 part to 3 parts soil into the backfill. You can also mix in bone meal or timed-release fertilizer to encourage root growth. Follow the directions for use of these products carefully.

Fill the hole three-fourths full with the soil mixture and water thoroughly to eliminate pockets of air. Then fill the remainder of the hole with loose, unpacked soil. With extra soil or strips of sod, build a shallow rim around the excavation to help retain water. Water once a week after planting if rainfall is not sufficient. You can conserve water by using a canvas soaker hose or water lance that applies water directly to the roots, and by spreading mulch over the planting hole.

4. After transplanting, remove approximately one-third of the branches by cutting them with sharp shears near the trunk or main branches. This pruning should be done so as to maintain the natural shape of the plant. On fruiting trees, trim vertical branches, favoring a more spreading contour. When vertical branches are eliminated, sunlight can better reach the lower limbs, favoring abundant fruit crop production.

The main purpose of such pruning is to reduce the leaves and stems, bringing these parts of the plant in balance with the reduced root system. Without sufficient pruning, the reduced root system might not be able to provide enough water for a full canopy of leaves during the transplant year and the plant may die of desiccation. Although pruning does reduce the size of your transplant, it is good insurance for a healthy start and rapid growth the next year.

5. The final step for protecting your transplant is to cover the base of the tree and planting hole with 3 or 4 inches of leaf or straw mulch. Mulches help prevent desiccation during the summer and reduce competition from weeds that would grow in the soil around your transplants. These weeds reduce the amount of water and soil nutrients available to the tree. Be sure to pull mulch away from the tree trunk during the winter to prevent mice from nesting near and gnawing the tender bark. Another useful precaution for newly transplanted trees is to wrap trunks with strips of heavy paper or burlap from 1 inch below the soil to the first branches. This will prevent bark damage from sunscald—a common problem for young and recently transplanted trees.

If the new tree is in an exposed site, you can protect it against wind damage by supporting it with guy wires attached to a post or three nearby stakes. Guy wiring also reduces wind vibration that could disturb recently planted roots. Surround the guy wires with sections of rubber hose to keep them from damaging the tree bark.

Competition from nearby tall grasses and other herbaceous plants is a common problem for many young trees and shrubs. When planted in a spring meadow or thicket, competing vegetation may not seem like a problem, but a month later, goldenrod and other tall annuals may tower over small woody seedlings, seriously depleting the supply of light and water. To reduce such competition, cut away nearby vegetation several times during the growing season. Scalping—using a shovel to remove sod from a 2-foot-diameter circle around the planting hole—is another technique for minimizing competition from grass and weeds. Cover the scalped area with 7 inches of mulch.

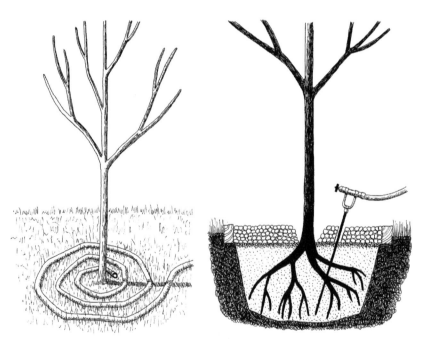

Two implements used for conserving water in arid habitats. The soaker hose (left) and water lance (right) both apply water to tree roots. (AF)

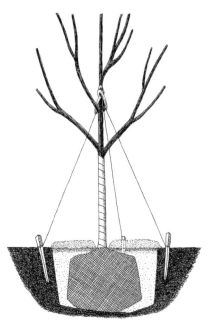

A staked wire support braces a newly transplanted tree in an exposed site against the threat of wind damage, which could cause improper settling and tilted posture. (AF)

Planting Bare-root Nursery Stock

Mail-order nurseries, state tree nurseries, and many local plant nurseries sell bare-root trees and shrubs that have usually been root-pruned and often stem-pruned before shipping. Such plants are easier to ship through the mail and are much less expensive than potted plants of the same size. Early spring is the best season to plant bare-root deciduous trees and shrubs. Summer is a stressful period for many plants because of heat and high evaporation rates, and in the fall there may not be enough time for bare-root plantings to develop adequate root systems before winter sets in.

The chances for a successful transplant are much higher if roots do not dry out. Although most nurseries pack bare-root stock in wet peat moss before shipping, it is very important to keep the roots moist until planting. Local nurseries are more likely to stock plants that are hardy to your climate. When plants arrive, check the roots carefully. If the roots appear dry, immediately soak them in water for several hours before planting. If it is too cold to plant outside when your order arrives, unpack the plants, sprinkle the tops and roots with water, and cover the roots with damp peat moss and a layer of burlap or canvas.

Keep new plants in a cool, frost-free place until you can plant them. If the weather is warm, but you are not yet ready to plant, temporarily protect them by placing them in a shallow trench in a cool, moist area. This technique is called *heeling in*. Spread the plants out along the trench, taking care to bury all roots completely. Water thoroughly and tamp the soil firmly to reduce air pockets near the roots. Keep the soil moist until you are ready to plant.

While planting, be certain to keep the roots moist. When placing a bare-root tree into a planting hole, spread the roots out to avoid kinking or twisting. This minimizes the risk of "girdling" roots (roots that wrap around each other) later in the life of the tree.

Continue by following steps 3 to 5 under Transplanting Wild Trees and Shrubs where appropriate.

Heeling in, or temporarily planting bare-root trees in a shallow trench, protects them until the final planting. (AF)

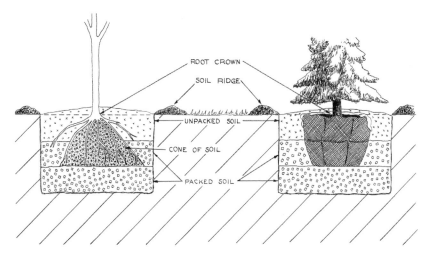

Soil profiles of bare-root tree (left) and balled and burlapped tree (right). (AF)

Planting Potted and Balled and Burlapped Trees and Shrubs

Local nurseries often have a good supply of trees and shrubs already potted, or with their root systems encased in soil and secured with burlap. Such nursery-grown plants are usually more expensive than collected or bare-root plants, but they have been transplanted and root-pruned several times before they reach the local nursery. These plants usually develop excellent root systems near the trunk, which gives them a very high chance of surviving the rigors of the transplant process. To plant balled and burlapped plants, loosen the burlap at the trunk but leave the burlap in place as you settle the plant into its hole. The burlap will soon rot away. If plastic burlap has been used to secure the ball, it should be removed completely. Likewise, any synthetic cord used to secure the root ball should also be removed to prevent girdling.

Remove potted plants from their containers and cut through any roots that have wrapped themselves around the root mass. Once encircling roots are removed, the soil around the roots should be loosened to spread out the roots. After placing the plants into their new holes, follow the same steps used to transplant wild trees and shrubs.

To determine the need for supplemental fertilizers and changes in soil acidity, contact your local Cooperative Extension Service office or nursery to arrange for a soil test. Test results can be a useful guide for establishing a fertilization program. Most local Cooperative Extension Service offices can provide fertilizer recommendations.

Protecting Plantings from Rabbits, Mice, and Deer

In winter, when tender twigs, seeds, and other favorite foods are already eaten or buried under snow, animals like mice, rabbits, and deer often turn to the tender bark, twigs, and buds of young trees and shrubs.

To reduce the chances of mouse damage, pull straw mulch away from the trunks of new plantings in late fall. Where mice and rabbits are common, wrap $\frac{1}{4}$-inch hardware cloth or plastic tree trunk protectors around tree trunks at least 2 feet higher than the average winter snow line. Some nurseries also sell a heavy plastic for wrapping around young trees and shrubs.

Deer management is most successful where there is a program of hunting (both bucks and does), combined with fencing and deterrents. Within city limits, hunting is usually inappropriate and public consensus is difficult to obtain. Yet some form of protection from deer remains necessary for new plantings. Protection is especially important for newly planted trees and shrubs that have just been purchased from nurseries, because their high nitrogen content is especially attractive to deer and rabbits.

To reduce browsing by deer, the best approach is to erect fencing around new plants. Although the cost is usually prohibitive, 8-foot-high fencing can protect entire yards and larger properties from deer browsing, but it is important to regularly walk along the fence to discover where trees have fallen on it, creating breaches where deer can enter the property. Likewise, it is important to install a gate over driveways and to keep it shut, especially after dusk hours. A cattle gate (steel bars spaced several inches apart and placed in the driveway) is an alternative as deer do not like to walk over the irregular surface. Protect individual plants with plastic deer mesh (available at garden shops) attached to posts and secured 6 feet from the ground. Select a deer mesh product with heavy-gauge material, ideally with a $2 \times 2\frac{1}{2}$ inch mesh.

For a more economic approach to discouraging deer browsing, hang strong-smelling soap from newly planted trees and shrubs or spread dried blood (available from garden shops) and hair clippings around favorite plants. Research that compared taste deterrents such as capsaicin (hot pepper) with odor-based products containing a rotten-egg smell found that the odor-based deterrents are most effective.[1] Deer Away/Big Game Repellent and Deer-Off Repellent Spray are two of the most effective commercial products and both contain the scent of rotten

[1]Paul D. Curtis, and Kristi L. Sullivan. 2001. *White-tailed Deer.* Wildlife Damage Management Fact Sheet Series. Ithaca, NY: Cornell Cooperative Extension.

eggs. Hinder is an odor-based deterrent containing ammonium soaps of higher fatty acids. It is among the few approved for use on edible crops. Paint Hinder full strength on the trunks of trees and shrubs to deter rabbits from gnawing them. Although producers of deterrents may suggest reapplying every 3 months, more frequent application (usually once a month) is important, especially following heavy rain. Deterrents are most effective when applied soon after damage is first noticed, as deer often keep returning to the same plants.

Because deer tend to avoid areas that smell of other mammals, the Deem family of Bernardsville, New Jersey, ties chunks of suet wrapped in cheesecloth to the tops of stakes and places them in front of and behind shrubs previously damaged by deer. These suet deer repellants also double as bird feeders.

Joe Sutowski, a nurseryman from Springfield, Vermont, recommends the following brew: Mix 1 cup of water with 6 cloves of garlic in a blender. Then add another cup of water, 2 tablespoons of alum, and 4 eggs. Blend to a smooth consistency and brush onto plants with broad sweeps. The mixture offers protection for about 6 months.

USEFUL SOURCES
On deer fencing:
   http://www.deerfence.com/
On deer repellents:
   http://www.woodstreamcorp.com/msds.asp and
   http://www.treehelp.com/index.asp

A

B

C

Devices for protecting plantings from browsing animals: 8-foot-tall deer fencing (A), individual enclosures (B), and trunk protectors to protect tender bark from sun scalding and damage from deer, rabbits, and mice (C). Photos by Stephen Kress (SK)

Forest Management

Prior to European settlement, about 50 percent of North America was covered in forest. About three-fourths of this was found in the eastern part of the continent, where expansive deciduous forests covered the Appalachians, Ohio Valley, and most of the southeastern coastal plain. At the same time, vast coniferous forests extended across Canada and down the mountains of the West Coast.

Forests in much of the eastern United States remained undisturbed until the late eighteenth century, but have since changed dramatically in area, age, size, shape, and structure as logging, agriculture, and settlements dominated the landscape. By the 1850s about 120 million acres of forest in the eastern United States was converted to farming and much of the remaining original forest was cut. Since the 1920s, about 20 percent of agricultural land has reverted to secondary-growth forest.

Although the amount of forest in eastern North America is increasing, the quality of secondary-growth forest is greatly compromised as a bird nesting habitat. Much of this secondary-growth forest is becoming increasingly fragmented and disturbed by highways, utility corridors, reservoirs, suburbia, and renewed logging. Invasive shrubs and vines such as kudzu, privet, Oriental bittersweet, and Japanese barberries especially impact eastern forests. Likewise, introduced diseases have decimated once-dominant native eastern forest tree species such as the American chestnut, American beech, and American elm. In addition, forests are plagued by epidemics from introduced insects such as the gypsy moth and wooly adelgid, which, respectively, plague oak- and hemlock-dominated forests.

Eastern forests are also stressed by acid precipitation and deer, which are altering the character and composition of forest communities by eliminating forest wildflowers, shrubs, and young trees. Even forest soils are changing as introduced earthworms consume much of the rich forest humus. These profound changes all effect nesting and migratory populations of forest birds.

Although there is much more ancient (previously uncut) forest in the western mountains and Pacific Northwest, much of the forest in this region is commercially harvested and is now dominated by second-growth forest. Likewise, the vast boreal forests of Canada are rapidly changing as intensive logging is replacing diverse natural forests with a more simplified, homogeneous forest similar to the industrial forests of Sweden and Norway.

North American forests are dynamic, changing habitats. Fortunately, research about forest bird management is helping foresters understand how to do a better job managing forest to benefit birds. Forest managers from private, commercial interests and agencies such as the U.S. Forest Service and U.S. Fish and Wildlife Service are now working together on behalf of migratory birds through Partners in Flight (PIF). PIF was established in 1990 to identify declining populations of migratory birds and address their conservation and management needs before species become endangered. Information about species of concern as identified by PIF is now widely known through the Audubon Watchlist program.

There is growing recognition that birds play a vital role in helping to keep forests healthy by controlling insect populations. Most of the forested land in eastern North America is held in private by small-property owners. Through proper management of privately owned forests and woodlots for wildlife, there is great potential to conduct sustainable forestry while also improving the habitat for both migratory and breeding birds. The following guidelines are especially relevant to the management of forests in eastern North America.

MANAGEMENT PROJECTS

Preserving Forest Interiors

Studies initiated by Chandler Robbins and associates of the U.S. Fish and Wildlife Service demonstrated that some forest birds such as the barred owl, red-shouldered hawk, red-eyed vireo, scarlet tanager, and ovenbird require large tracts of undisturbed, mature forest for nesting. Robbins found that in the heavily populated Baltimore-Washington, D.C. area these species required at least 200 acres of unbroken forest. Smaller areas apparently did not include enough habitat or protection from nest predators such as jays, crows, and grackles and nest parasites such as the brown-headed cowbird.

This and similar studies throughout forested North America point to the vulnerability of forest-interior birds to increasing fragmentation caused largely by spreading suburbs, housing developments, and associated roads. Depending on their management, even utility corridors for electricity, natural gas, and communications can interrupt the functional size of forests. Other concerns such as invasive plants, forest diseases, browsing by deer, logging, and acid precipitation also threaten forest birds and may contribute to a decline of some species.

While the populations of some forest birds such as the wood thrush and cerulean warbler are decreasing, many such as the ovenbird and red-eyed vireo are increasing and many others are stable. Data from the U.S. Fish and Wildlife Service's Breeding Bird Survey for 1980–2000 shows that 57 percent (43 of 75) of woodland species in northeastern United States are increasing in number.

These trends are largely linked to changes in the amounts of different kinds of forest. For example, upland forests are increasing in the Northeast as grasslands and shrubland mature into forest, but bottomland forests (frequented by cerulean warblers) are largely decreasing in the southeastern states as these forests are now mostly converted to agriculture and housing.

Although the general trends explain some population changes, there are many exceptions and there is growing insight into the complexities that influence bird populations. For example, researchers from the Cornell Laboratory of Ornithology discovered that populations of the wood thrush and most other forest thrushes are decreasing in the Northeast, coinciding with levels of acid precipitation. Acid rain leaches calcium from the soil, reducing snail and invertebrate populations that are an important part of thrush diets.

Wood thrush and other forest thrushes depend on abundant invertebrates, which they collect on the forest floor. John Schmitt (JS), © Cornell Laboratory of Ornithology

The wood thrush and cerulean warbler also require an adequate shrub layer for nesting, but this may be scarce where deer browse. Likewise, some species like the cerulean warbler and northern flicker usually nest near small gaps in an otherwise unbroken canopy. For many species, changes in bird populations are often complex and the reasons remain unclear, but ongoing research is identifying the requirements of individual species and these are helping managers improve forests for specific species. These population trends are detailed in the U.S. Fish and Wildlife Service's Web site.

The birds most sensitive to fragmented forest share several of the following characteristics: they migrate annually to tropical America, nest in forest interiors, are primarily insectivorous, build open nests on or near the ground in shrubs, have a low reproductive rate (usually one brood per year), and are relatively short-lived. A few examples of area-sensitive birds are the worm-eating warbler, ovenbird, and wood thrush.

Although unbroken forest might seem to be a uniform habitat, it is better described as a mosaic of slightly varied habitats or forest stands that differ in soil characteristics, climate, slope, and tree species. Often differences in forest are tied to past human disturbances that affect the depth and compaction of soil, such as logging, grazing, and fire. There may also be changes in the age and composition of adjoining woodlands resulting from earlier disruptions such as storm blowdowns, fire, and insect damage.

Forest birds usually require more than one habitat in their nesting cycle. By decreasing the size of forests, fragmentation can reduce the variety of habitats available within any given forest and the opportunities for birds to move between different habitats. Unfortunately, so little is known about the patterns of movement within forests that it is impossible to determine exact habitat requirements for most species.

Urban Forests and Greenways

Although large forests are necessary for maintaining productive nesting populations, it is also important to protect small urban forests such as greenway belts, forested stream banks, city parks, and cemeteries with mature landscapes. These can serve as corridors connecting larger forests, providing nesting habitat for forest birds. Urban woods are also important during migration, when flocks settle into small, forested oases for refueling.

Greenways are ribbons of natural habitat that run through urban areas. They protect open space and usually offer recreation opportunities such as bike trails. Greenways now occur in more than 500 North American cities. Researchers from North Carolina State University have documented the extent that both nesting and migratory bird populations use urban greenways, and have examined the nesting success of these city-dwelling birds. Studies show that even greenways that are 1000 feet wide are not able to support the full complement of breeding birds that nest in larger forests. However, such areas are critical "stopover" habitat for migrants. A key conclusion of this research is that 30-foot-wide bike paths with mowed shoulders will functionally break a 1000-foot-wide greenway into two 500-foot strips. If a greenway is less than 150 feet wide, then predators such as fox, skunk, and raccoon will find most nests. These researchers conclude that the minimum width for a greenway should be at least 150 feet.

Predators and Nest Parasites

The number of bird predators usually increases in fragmented forests. Fragmentation creates more edge and thus favors jays, grackles, squirrels, and chipmunks, which often prey on eggs and nestlings of other species. Rodent populations also tend to increase because there are few predatory hawks and owls in small fragmented forests. Such habitat may also pose a greater risk to humans as white-footed mice are hosts for the Lyme disease tick, which transmits the disease to humans.

Fragmented forests are also more vulnerable to nest parasitism from brown-headed cowbirds. Cowbirds lay their eggs in other birds' nests and let foster parents, generally warblers, vireos, or sparrows, raise their young. Cowbirds lay a clutch of six or more eggs, usually depositing each one in a different nest. After a few days, they lay a second clutch and may lay as many as three or four clutches in a season, totaling 11–20 eggs. A single female cowbird may deposit eggs in as many as 20 other birds' nests, often throwing out the host's eggs as she goes. At least 121 species have successfully reared brown-headed cowbird young. Many of these are forest-interior species, such as the worm-eating warbler and Kentucky warbler. These species build open-cup nests on the ground or in low trees and thus are vulnerable to cowbird parasitism, as well as predation. Encounters with cowbirds can eliminate chances for reproduction for an entire year, a major consequence since most small land birds live only a few years.

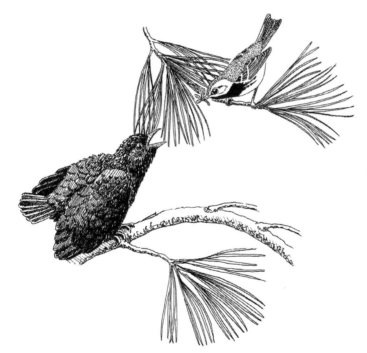

Brown-headed cowbirds lay their eggs in the nests of many species, including forest-interior species such as the black-throated green warbler. Foster parents then raise the young cowbirds. (AF)

The probability of finding forest-interior species in small patches of forest also depends on the proportion of forested land that surrounds the patch. For example, if 70 percent of the land surrounding a 50-acre woodland is mostly forested, then the woodland is much more likely to support forest-interior birds such as the scarlet tanager. In contrast, an isolated patch of woods the same size, but surrounded by agricultural land, is much less likely to support tanagers.

To benefit area-sensitive forest birds, it is important to minimize fragmentation and to preserve forest interiors. This can be accomplished by preserving large unbroken tracts of forest—the larger the better. Where some forest must be cut, the remainder will be better habitat for forest-interior birds if it is preserved in circular rather than linear shapes such as rectangles. Even oval-shaped forests have more edge than squares or circles.

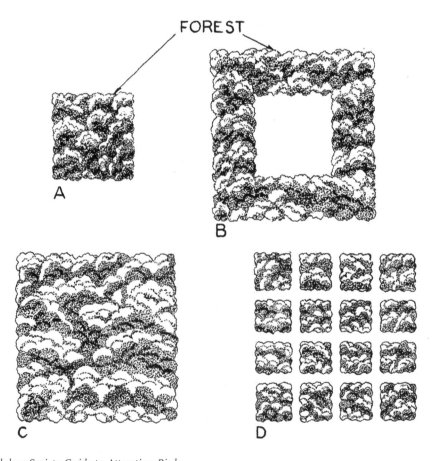

FOREST

A

B

C

D

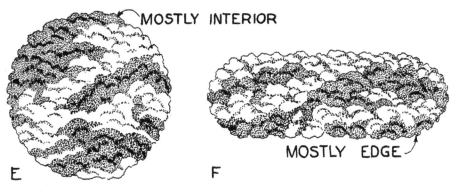

MOSTLY INTERIOR

MOSTLY EDGE

E   F

Patterns A, C, and E minimize fragmentation of the forest interior, allowing stable
nesting sites for forest-interior species and providing protection from predators.
Patterns B, D, and F have far more edge and open up the forest to a greater variety of
birds, which can lead to increased predation and brood parasitism by cowbirds. Block B
covers four times the area of A but has the same amount of forest and three times the
edge. Block D has four times the edge of C but covers the same area. Block F's oval
pattern has more edge than E's circular shape, but both have the same area. (AF)

Creating Woodland Openings

Where woodlands are significantly larger than 200 acres, it may be possible
to improve forests for interior-nesting birds without increasing the number of
edge-nesting birds by creating small woodland openings. Such gaps occur naturally every time a storm downs a large tree, insects or disease kills a group of
trees, or lightning starts a fire, but openings created by toppling trees with chain
saws can serve a similar purpose. Some species such as the northern flicker and
cerulean warbler greatly favor these gaps. Openings provide more varied nest
sites, increase the variety of trees and shrubs, and favor greater abundance and
diversity within insect populations. Such openings can also increase the fruiting
and regeneration potential of selected trees or favor important bird-attracting
trees that are intolerant of shade, such as oak, cherry, and serviceberry.

One useful technique for creating a forest opening and increasing food production is to select a large, healthy forest specimen of cherry, hackberry, oak, or
other fruiting tree. Measure the diameter of the tree in inches $4\frac{1}{2}$ feet above the
ground, multiply the diameter by 3. This gives the diameter of a circle (in feet)
that should have the selected tree in its center. Then remove all trees within the
circle except the central tree, making the borders irregular to give a more natural

appearance to the opening. For example, if the central tree has a 20-inch diameter at $4\frac{1}{2}$ feet, you would multiply 20 by 3, which would calculate to an opening 60 feet in diameter. After clearing the area, fruit production on the central tree will increase and shrubs will soon crowd into the sunlit opening. Preferred native bird-attracting shrubs could be planted in the clearing to further increase food production.

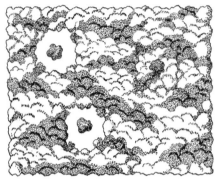

CREATING WOODLAND CLEARINGS

Clearing around a central tree within mature forest will enhance the food production of the selected tree and create a gap that is attractive to certain forest birds such as flickers. (AF)

Encouraging Forest Expansion

Tree planting is especially valuable where it is possible to connect nearby woodlands or where small (under 20 acres) fields are located near forest. In these circumstances, it is desirable to encourage the growth of forest or shrublands. This is best accomplished by planting islands of native bird-attracting trees and shrubs in the field. Birds will fly between adjacent forest and the planted islands, distributing seeds as they fly and naturally speeding the spread of trees and shrubs into the field.

This technique is also useful for changing urban brownfields such as landfills into urban forests. Studies in New Jersey have shown that species of trees, shrubs, and vines soon moved into landfills when birds were encouraged to fly out to isolated plantations. In this manner, first planting islands of vegetation and then letting birds plant the remainder of the landfill achieved reforestation.[1] This economical approach offers great promise for creating urban forests, especially where it is generally unlikely that expensive reforestation programs will be introduced.

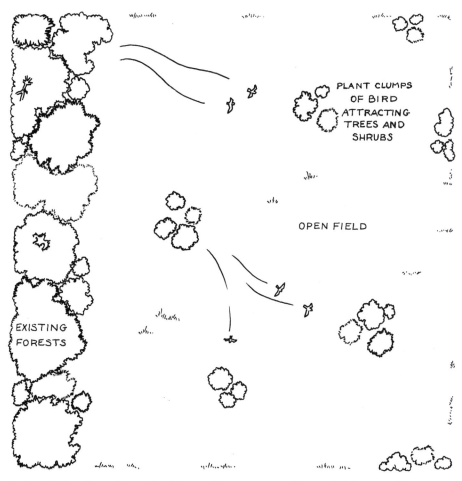

PLANT CLUMPS OF BIRD ATTRACTING TREES AND SHRUBS

OPEN FIELD

EXISTING FORESTS

Birds will distribute the seeds of forest plants, encouraging establishment of forest on adjacent fields. The technique is cost-effective and speeds the establishment of forest in areas such as urban landfills and reclaimed strip mines. Camille Doucet (CD)

[1]George R. Robinson, Steven N. Handel, and Victoria R. Schmalhofer. 1992. "Survival, Reproduction and Recruitment of Wood Plants after 14 Years on a Reforested Landfill." *Environmental Management* 16(2):265–271.

Corridors between Fragments

Corridors connecting fragmented forests offer a potential for benefiting forest-interior species, but there are risks because corridors may also serve as a conduit for transporting invasive plants and disease. Most studies looking for increases in the number of forest-interior species resulting from corridors have found that few species benefit. These studies suggest that forest-interior birds do best where they find large, unfragmented forests. Corridors are not a substitute or fix that makes small fragments acceptable.

Managing Snags for Cavity-Nesting Birds

Naturally developing mature forests can have a high proportion of dead or partially dead trees known as *snags*. Studies of upland forests show that 90 percent of the trees that reach an age of 20 years will die during the next 60 years. Depending on size, species of tree, and age since death, the snags will provide homes for cavity-nesting birds, ranging in size from the turkey vulture to the prothonotary warbler. Snags also provide places for nesting and roosting, as well as homes for many forest mammals such as mice, squirrels, and raccoons.

The abundance of suitable snags has changed dramatically since colonial days. Clearing of vast forests eliminated old-age timber stands with high proportions of large snags during the nineteenth century. Farmlands replaced forests throughout much of North America in the mid-1800s and early 1900s, a land use that no doubt greatly benefited open-country birds, including such cavity-nesters as tree swallows and bluebirds, which nested in the tops of rotting wooden fence posts. The regrowth of forest on old farmlands since about 1940 is providing vast forest lands once again, but most of this woodland is still too young to produce an abundant supply of old snags.

Removal of dead trees and snags is an unfortunate forestry practice. It is based on the assumption that dead trees may harbor tree diseases and that removal will make room for healthy trees or that they are an attraction for lightning and are thus a great fire hazard, especially in western forests. Fortunately, there is growing understanding that snags provide vital nest sites for woodpeckers and other cavity-nesting birds, most of which are insect-eaters.

Clear-cutting, the removal of an entire block of forest, prevents the occurrence of snags and thus contributes to a shortage of tree cavities. Although replanting usually follows such cutting, this practice leads to even-aged growth with few snags. Where clear-cutting is proceeding, it is important to leave widely dispersed snags. Also, live "reserve trees" should be selected for their potential as cavity trees and then girdled by removing a band of bark several inches wide or making two cuts through the bark that encircle the tree. Girdled trees will eventually die and become snags, and they will not create shade or compete with new tree crops. These "new" snags may persist for decades in the young, even-aged forest.

Another possibility is to leave small patches of live trees surrounding a few large snags as "lifeboat" or "legacy" patches within the center of a clear-cut. This island of live trees and snags may allow certain organisms (e.g., lichens used by birds for nest building) to persist in the new forest that grows back after clear-cutting. The patches will also provide homes for birds that prefer open country but require some large trees for nesting (e.g., certain hawks) and the birds that visit the island will disperse seed from the island out over the adjacent land.

When managing for snags in forests, it is important to remember that large snags are much more important than small snags. This is because large snags are necessary for large birds, but even small cavity-nesters will use large trees. The absence of old, dead, large-diameter trees is one of the most important differences between natural old-growth forests and forests managed for timber.

Although the shrublands and secondary forests that arise following clear-cutting have more species of insect-eating birds than mature forests do, these habitats can be further improved by leaving dead snags among the younger trees. In contrast, selective cutting is usually the best technique for managing forests for the greatest variety of birds, as such forests retain most of the interior-nesting species as well as many of the open-country species that continue to reside within patches of secondary growth. Even trees in small patch cuts or partial-cut patches can be removed without noticeable effect on the mix of birds that frequents forest. However, when selective cutting results in "high grading" (removal of all commercially valuable larger trees above a certain diameter), only undesirable trees will remain and this results in degraded forests for future timber harvest and for wildlife.

When managing for snags in forests, it is important to remember that large snags are much more important than small snags. © Michael DeMunn (MD)

Landowners interested in managing their forests for wildlife should consult a professional forester who has extensive interest in wildlife and who will mark the trees that should be cut and designate those that should remain. Proper timber management should maintain the full complement of tree ages, sizes, and species native to an area and the layers of shrub and understory trees that are essential for diverse bird communities. Healthy standing trees increase in value over time and provide seed crops to regenerate future forests, while providing birds with habitat for nesting, roosting, and feeding.

Woodpeckers are the principal developers of most nest cavities in trees because each nesting pair requires more than one cavity. If all conditions are ideal, a pair of woodpeckers uses only one cavity for nesting. However, predators and such nest competitors as starlings may cause a cavity to become unsuitable and the pair may have to look for another site. In addition to the nesting cavity, a pair of woodpeckers also requires two additional roosting cavities where they spend the night (woodpeckers do not usually sleep together), and some have the habit of regularly changing their sleeping place—a behavior that probably reduces vulnerability to nocturnal predators and results in even more tree cavities. After leaving their nest, young woodpeckers require additional roosting cavities. In total, a pair of woodpeckers requires *at least* four cavities during the year, one for nesting, two for adult roosts, and one or more for roosting fledglings.

Woodpeckers ranging in size from these pileated woodpeckers to sparrow-sized downy woodpeckers create cavities that provide nesting and roosting shelter for other forest birds. © Barry Van Dusen (BV)

Tree cavities may occur when limbs break off and heart rot fungus invades the tree interior. More frequently, however, woodpeckers create cavities as they excavate for insects in diseased heartwood (interior wood) and tunnel their nesting and roosting sites. Preserving or creating ideal snags for woodpeckers is the best way to create nesting cavities for other birds. Since most woodpeckers do not usually reuse their nesting cavities, such vacancies provide nest sites for cavity-nesters such as bluebirds, nuthatches, screech-owls, hooded mergansers, and prothonotary warblers that are not capable of excavating their own cavities. Chickadees and titmice serve the useful function of enlarging woodpecker-feeding holes into cavities large enough for their own use. Titmice, wrens, swallows, flickers, and others may enlarge such small cavities later until they become suitable for larger nesting birds. Mammals such as white-footed mice, flying squirrel, gray squirrel, and raccoon also help to enlarge tree cavities.

The numbers and variety of cavity-nesting birds are usually limited by the availability of suitable nesting and roosting sites in snags. When snags are removed from a forest, the number of cavity-nesting birds will decline. Since most cavity-nesting birds are insect-eaters, declines in such birds as woodpeckers, nuthatches, chickadees, and swallows can set the stage for outbreaks of destructive insects. Many foresters now recognize the value of cavity-nesting birds in suppressing population explosions of forest insects, and detailed studies describe the nesting requirements of these birds.

In general, larger snags are more useful for attracting cavity-nesting birds. Large snags, particularly those with a large diameter, have more surface for excavation and hence can support a greater number and variety of cavity-nesting birds. When birds nest in small-diameter trees, crowding may lead to fewer eggs and lower production of young.

Suitable trees for cavity excavation should have decayed heartwood at the appropriate height for a nest cavity. Trees that easily decay (e.g., basswood, maples, willow, American beech, and most pines) are especially preferred by woodpeckers because of the ease of channeling out the soft wood. The ideal tree for woodpecker excavation has rotten heartwood surrounded by a firm layer of living sapwood with intact bark. Rotten heartwood makes such trees easy to excavate, and the rough sapwood provides excellent defense from predators such as raccoons that cannot usually enlarge such nest openings.

While many birds will nest in completely dead trees, these nests are especially vulnerable to predators. Trees that have only sapwood rot without heartwood rot are the least suitable for cavity-nesters. In such hard-cored trees, such as decay-resistant oaks and cherry, small woodpeckers such as downy woodpeckers must dig shallow, thin-walled nest cavities, thus exposing eggs and nestlings to both predators and temperature extremes.

Creating Tree Cavities and Snags

The most direct way to create tree cavities is to drill 2-inch-diameter holes into the heartwood using a hand auger or battery-powered drill. This makes an excellent beginning for cavity excavators such as chickadees, especially if the heartwood is already rotten. Drill entrance holes about 3 inches below stout limbs on leaning trees so that openings point about 10 degrees below horizontal and the downward position of the opening provides some protection from rain. This position may also prove less conspicuous to predators.

You can also start cavities in trees by selecting a limb at least 3 inches in diameter and cutting it off about 6 inches from the trunk. As the cut limb rots, the tree will heal around the edges, but it will probably not close over the hole.

To create additional snags, select trees with at least a 12-inch dbh that are short-lived (e.g., poplars) or have minimal wildlife value (see plant-selection tables for your region to avoid girdling important wildlife-attracting trees). Proceed to girdle enough trees to bring the snags per acre up to the minimum for your forest type. Most state/provincial forestry or wildlife agencies can offer specific recommendations based on local research in specific forest types. For example, in 2002 the Maine Forest Service recommended leaving four living rough and rotten trees per acre including one with a dbh greater than 21 inches, four snags per acre including one with a dbh greater than 21 inches, and four downed logs per acre including one with a dbh greater than 21 inches.

To girdle a tree, use an axe to remove a 3- to 4-inch band of bark from around the entire circumference of the tree, cutting at least 1 inch below the bark. This interrupts the flow of food and water between the roots and leaves. The tree will die soon, but it will bring new life to the forest by increasing the population of cavity-nesting birds and mammals.

CUT LIMB
ABOUT 6"
FROM TRUNK

SAME SNAG
SEVERAL
YEARS LATER

3-4"

DRILLED HOLES SHOULD
POINT 10° BELOW THE
HORIZONTAL. TO SPEED
CAVITY FORMATION,
INOCULATE WITH ROTTING
WOOD.

(A) Girdle the tree by cutting a 3–4-inch-wide belt around the tree through the living tissue; (B) cut off a limb at least 3 inches in diameter, creating a stub 6 inches long; and (C) drill holes to encourage cavity-nesting species. (AF)

In the north central and northeastern hardwood forests, the U.S. Forest Service recommends for each 20-acre woodlot preserving 4 or 5 snags over 18 inches in dbh, 30–40 snags over 14 inches in dbh, and 50–60 snags over 6 inches in dbh. To optimize the number of tree cavities in your woodlot, provide woodpeckers with an abundant supply of quality snags. The following table describes the characteristics of preferred nesting trees for nine eastern woodpeckers.

Characteristics of Preferred Nesting Trees of Nine Eastern Woodpeckers

Species	When Using Territory	Territory Size (acres)	Minimum No. of Snags Used/Pair	Average dbh of Nest Trees (in.)	Average Height of Nest Trees (ft.)	Maximum No. of Pairs/100 Acres	Snags Needed/100 Acres to Maintain 100% of Cavity-Nesters
Downy woodpecker	All year	10	4	8	20	10	400
Hairy woodpecker	All year	20	4	12	30	5	200
Pileated woodpecker	All year	175	4	22	60	0.6	24
Common flicker	Breeding	40	2	15	30	2.5	150
Red-bellied woodpecker	All year	15	4	18	40	6.7	270
Red-headed woodpecker	Breeding	10	2	20	40	10	200
Black-backed three-toed woodpecker	All year	75	4	15	30	1.3	52
Northern three-toed woodpecker	All year	75	4	14	30	1.3	52
Yellow-bellied sapsucker	Breeding	10	1	12	30	10	100

Adapted from K. E. Evans and R. N. Conner. 1979. "Snag Management," in *Workshop Proceedings of Management of North Central and Northeastern Forests for Non-game Birds*. Forest Service Publication No. GTR NC-51. Washington, DC: U.S. Department of Agriculture.

Forest Management Guidelines

Studies of bird diversity in different forested habitats conducted by the New York Audubon Society and others suggest that a wide range of forest conditions is necessary to maintain the full complement of nongame wildlife species. Some species favor mature, unharvested forests while others prefer partially harvested or clear-cut forests. When counting individuals or species, selectively harvested forests usually have more songbirds than unharvested forests, because harvested forests provide habitat for many of the birds that favor mature conditions as well as those that prefer disturbed forests. This indicates that diverse timber-harvesting practices can result in habitat conditions that are favorable for many species, while also providing wood products through sustainable forestry.

The following list provides management actions for both small- and large-forest owners that are interested in sustainable forestry and habitat improvements for birds.[2]

1. Avoid fragmentation of existing contiguous forests. These areas have the potential of supporting the largest number of forest-interior species and they are more likely to meet the requirements of species that require large nesting areas. Protection of existing forest is easier than establishing new forest, and existing forest will have larger trees than newly created habitat. Maryland guidelines suggest that in eastern states, it is best to preserve blocks of at least 7500 acres of mature forest. In the Midwest, landscapes that remain at least 70 percent forested tend to minimize the adverse effects of fragmentation, especially hampering intrusion by the brown-headed cowbird.

2. Where possible, preserve existing old-growth stands with large, second-growth buffer strips around them and provide for the development of future old growth by leaving areas undisturbed or unharvested for 150 years or longer.

[2]J. R. Herkert, R. E. Szafoni, V. M. Kleen, and J. E. Schwegman. 1993. *Habitat Establishment: Enhancement and Management for Forest and Grassland Birds in Illinois.* Natural Heritage Technical Publication No. 1. Springfield, IL: Division of Natural Heritage, Illinois Department of Conservation. 20 pages; and K. V. Rosenberg, R. W. Rohrbaugh Jr., S. E. Barker, J. D. Lowe, R. S. Hames, and A. A. Dhondt. 1999. *A Land Manager's Guide to Improving Habitat for Scarlet Tanagers and Other Forest-Interior Birds.* Ithaca, NY: Cornell Laboratory of Ornithology. 24 pages.

3. Maintain well-developed shrub and herbaceous layers (e.g., wildflowers) to provide nesting places, food, and cover. Prevent cattle from grazing in forests; halt mowing, the removal of fallen trees, and snags; and prevent overbrowsing by deer.

4. Protect or plant vines such as wild grape and Virginia creeper as these provide cover, food, and nesting materials.

5. Manage forests to create blocks that are circular or square, as these have the least amounts of edge and are more likely to sustain forest-interior species than are narrower tracts. Forest-interior species are likely to occupy territories more than 110 yards from the forest edge.

6. Work to protect forests along streams and river bottoms as these are especially important to many of the most uncommon forest species.

7. Work with adjacent landowners to reforest gaps between existing forests. Use native trees to create larger forest blocks that will benefit area-sensitive species.

8. Establish conservation easements and other development restrictions to protect forested land in the long term. Consider creating a landowners' association among adjacent landowners.

9. Remember that uneven-aged forests with a well-developed but broken canopy usually provide the best habitat for forest birds.

10. Use single-tree or group-tree selection as the recommended harvesting technique. This mimics natural tree-fall dynamics and may benefit gap-dependent forest species such as hooded and mourning warblers. This method also creates a mosaic of different-size gaps from a single tree to $\frac{1}{4}$-acre patches and encourages trees that are important to wildlife such as cherry and oak. Avoid clear-cuts when managing for forest-interior species.

11. If single-tree selection is not possible, plan a rotation cutting that leaves the oldest sections adjacent to each other.

12. In timber harvest areas, preserve some large, undisturbed forested areas that can serve as refugia for forest birds. This approach also provides a source of forest seed and a core population of plant and bird life that can help to repopulate adjacent lands as forest matures. Ideally, these mature tracts should be in the center of the managed area. Avoid a checkerboard of small, different-aged plots.

13. Maintain broad forest connections, which prevent the isolation of smaller tracts and excessive edge.

14. Plant native trees in forest openings and also plant to connect existing stands.
15. Where mature and standing dead trees (snags) are less than one per acre, add nest boxes and/or girdle trees to enhance the number of snags.
16. Where forest management includes public use, encourage the public to use forest edges rather than the interior. Locate picnic and camping areas near the forest edge and existing road systems, rather than creating new roads into large forests.
17. Avoid creating mowed pathways along trails and walking paths through forests as these are attractive feeding areas for cowbirds and grackles.
18. Work to prevent utility corridors, impoundments, sewer lines, and other forest clearings within forested areas as these increase the amount of forest edge.
19. Eliminate cowbird-feeding opportunities by letting forest roadsides grow to at least 6–9 inches. Also avoid bare ground, pastures, feedlots, campgrounds, and bird-feeding stations near forests that are managed for forest-interior birds.
20. Maintain small woodlots of a few acres, parks, and forested city streets because they are very useful as migratory stopover habitat.
21. Avoid planting tree monocultures, especially of exotic species; these are less attractive to most forest birds. Monitor forested plots for nonnative, invasive plants and devise a removal plan if necessary.

USEFUL SOURCES

To participate in ongoing research about forest bird conservation, visit the Cornell Laboratory of Ornithology's Web site for the program Birds in Forested Landscape:
http://birds.cornell.edu/bfl/
For a national list of Forest Landowners Guides and State Forestry Offices:
http://www.na.fs.fed.us/pubs/misc/ir/index.htm
On migratory birds:
http://www.PartnersInFlight.org
http://www.audubon.org
On population trends:
http://www.mbr-pwrc.usgs.gov

3 Grassland Management

Grasslands support a unique mix of birds that are now largely dependent on human management. Throughout North America, agricultural lands such as hay fields, croplands, and pastures, and rangelands, along with commercial meadows such as airports, capped landfills, and reclaimed strip mines, have replaced natural meadows such as prairies and beaver meadows.

Grasslands dominated much of interior North America at the time of European exploration, with scattered grasslands extending to the Atlantic coast. The presence of eastern grasslands is a surprise to many, as there is a widely held misconception that European colonists encountered an expansive forest so dense that a squirrel could travel along the treetops from the Atlantic to the Mississippi. However, recent studies of ancient pollen and historic accounts from the first European explorers describe a very different scene.

When European colonists arrived in the eastern part of North America, they found considerable grassland and shrubland in addition to vast forests. In the more arid plains states and western mountains, a combination of low precipitation, grazing by bison, and fire favored the largest prairie grasslands in North America.

Many of these nonforested habitats were created when Native Americans burned the forest to create fields for agriculture and thickets for berry production. The practice also improved hunting for deer, rabbits, and other game. In addition to intentional burning, tornados and hurricanes interrupted continuous eastern forests, creating a mosaic of meadow, shrublands, and forests of varying age. Also, outbreaks of forest insects killed trees that provided fuel for natural fire sparked by lightning. Beavers were another major force affecting this mosaic. Beavers typically build dams that flood stream valleys. After cutting suitable trees, they move on to repeat the pattern elsewhere. Abandoned beaver dams fall into disrepair, and ponds progress from marshland to grassland. Plant succession eventually results in shrublands and forest, which entice beavers to return. Thus, birds that once depended on habitats created by bison, beavers, and Native Americans are now refugees in a very changed landscape.

At first the changes brought by European colonists favored grassland birds. In the 1800s nearly all of the original eastern deciduous forest was cut and most of it burned to create agricultural land and pasture for cattle. Grassland birds thrived during this period, but the regrowth of cleared land into young forest during the twentieth century has greatly reduced the amount of habitat for grassland specialists such as the bobolink, meadowlark, grasshopper sparrow, and upland sandpiper. The widespread use of chemical pesticides on breeding and wintering ranges, plantings of multiple crops of hay, and replacement of native grasslands with single-species cropland have also contributed to an alarming decline in the population of grassland birds. Today, native grasslands are largely replaced by modern agriculture and industrial meadows such as airports and landfills, but the quality of these habitats is greatly affected by adjacent housing, roads, and power lines that tend to degrade grasslands.

The Breeding Bird Survey of the U.S. Fish and Wildlife Service (U.S. Department of the Interior) was established in 1966 to document changes to North American bird populations. Since its inception, the survey has documented steady declines of grassland bird populations east of the Mississippi for 15 of the 19 species native to eastern United States. For example, the number of Henslow's sparrows has declined at the rate of 9 percent per year, grasshopper sparrows at 6 percent per year, and vesper sparrows and eastern meadowlarks at 3 percent per year. In contrast, populations of only 2 of 40 species of migratory eastern forest birds have declined at a rate more than 2 percent per year. Many grassland species west of the Mississippi are also decreasing in number, primarily due to habitat loss. Fortunately, most grassland birds readily colonize suitable habitat when it becomes available. This creates the opportunity to accomplish cost-effective management at sites that are already in some type of grassland production.

GRASSLAND MANAGEMENT PRACTICES[1]

Preservation:
1. Protect and conserve existing natural grasslands, including serpentine and emergent wetlands. Native grasslands with a high diversity of native plants are extremely rare. Actively preserve and manage such areas to provide quality habitat for native species, including grassland birds. Even small patches deserve protection for study and as a source of seed for restoration.
2. Within a regional context, protect a diversity of grassland habitats. These may range from wet sedge meadows to warm-season grasslands.
3. Save existing grasslands of 100 acres or more. Large tracts under private ownership offer excellent opportunities for helping grassland bird communities. Where grasslands this size are unavailable, focus efforts on grasslands at least 25 acres in size.

Management:
1. Try to keep grasslands adjacent or close to each other. Ideally, they should be less than $\frac{1}{2}$ mile apart, particularly if the areas are relatively small (25–100 acres). Consider planting or maintaining connecting grassy strips between separate patches to serve as corridors. Ideally, these corridors should be at least 600 feet wide.
2. Minimize the grassland edge-to-area ratio. Circular tracts are ideal, and square fields are better than rectangular ones. Most birds will not use linear grassland strips less than 600 feet wide or strips that are convoluted with irregular borders Birds that do nest in such areas will be vulnerable to predators.
3. Consider allowing grasslands that are adjacent to existing forest and less than 25 acres in size to revert to shrub habitat or forest. The rationale for

[1]Adapted from Maryland Partners in Flight. 1997. *Habitat Management Guidelines for the Benefit of Land Birds in Maryland*. Annapolis, MD: Maryland Partners in Flight.

this is that shrub-nesting birds will use smaller fields than grassland birds. Encourage this process by planting native trees and shrubs (such as hawthorns and dogwoods) in the grassland. This will speed the transition to a shrub habitat dominated by trees and shrubs with high value for shrub-nesting birds. Discourage nonnative plants from establishing.

4. Avoid fragmenting grasslands with roads, buildings, groves of trees, and row crops. Fragmentation especially reduces the chances of attracting area-sensitive species in great need of habitat, such as the upland sandpiper and Henslow's sparrow. Hedgerows dominated by woody vegetation taller than 10 feet or wider than 16 feet can also fragment grassland.

5. Avoid straight edges, especially where grassland meets the forest. Sharp edges are associated with higher predation and cowbird parasitism rates, as predators and cowbirds can perch along the edge and scan a longer distance for nests.

6. Avoid mowing native hay fields from April to August. This is the breeding season for most grassland birds. If mowing is necessary, consider the following:

   a. Avoid mowing from mid-May to mid-July—the core nesting period. Early-spring (March–April) mowing provides better winter habitat than late-summer or fall (August–October) mowing.

   b. If mowing is necessary during the breeding season, mow on a rotational basis and allow some blocks larger than 10 acres or strips wider than 300 feet to remain unmowed for at least a 6-week period. Stagger the location of mowed sections to maximize the amount of contiguous, unmowed area.

   c. Use an annual rotational mowing system that leaves some sections unmowed each year.

   d. Set the mower blade to 10 inches or higher.

7. Replace cool-season with warm-season grasses. Look for opportunities to establish these grasses at human-created sites such as capped landfills, reclaimed strip mines, and airports. This practice is especially recommended in eastern states. Low temperatures may prevent the use of warm-season grasses in western states. Check with local offices of the Natural Resources Conservation Service (U.S. Department of Agriculture) to determine the type of grassland appropriate for your area.

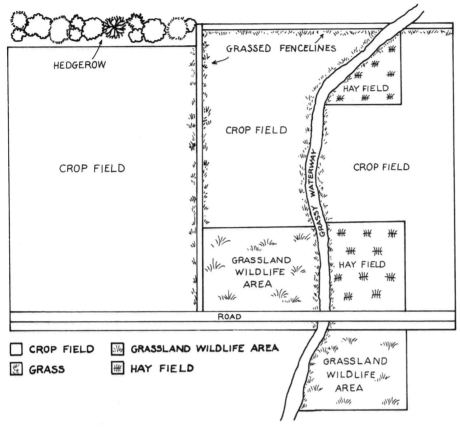

HEDGEROW

GRASSED FENCELINES

CROP FIELD

CROP FIELD

HAY FIELD

CROP FIELD

GRASSY WATERWAY

GRASSLAND WILDLIFE AREA

HAY FIELD

ROAD

□ CROP FIELD   GRASSLAND WILDLIFE AREA

GRASS   HAY FIELD

GRASSLAND WILDLIFE AREA

Recommended placement of grassland wildlife areas where a single, large unit cannot be established. Grassland wildlife plantings are connected to other grassed areas (e.g., hay field) by a grassed waterway. Likewise, grassed fencelines (wire fences with grass growing underneath) rather than brushy fencerows separate adjacent fields. Redrawn from *Habitat Establishment, Enhancement and Management for Forest and Grassland Birds in Illinois*. Division of Natural Heritage, Natural Heritage Technical Publication No.1. Springfield, IL. (CD)

MANAGING HAY FIELDS AND MEADOWS[2]

1. Limit mowing low-quality hay fields and meadows to once every 3 years. Schedule these mowings after August 1 to permit birds to nest. This mowing regime will keep fields in grass, prevent woody plants from invading the meadow, and reduce the risk of destroying second nesting broods.

2. For high-quality hay fields where farmers need to mow before August 1, avoid areas where birds are frequently seen. Leave borders or strips for nesting. These will provide food and cover for birds displaced by mowing. Likewise, situate low-quality hay fields near high-quality hay fields. Birds that fail to nest because of mowing will sometimes relocate to less-often-mowed fields.

3. Use mowing methods to reduce mortality. For example, raise mower blades to 6 inches; avoid night mowing as this kills both roosting and nesting birds; and use flushing bars on mowers to move birds ahead of the mower. Mow fields from the center out, making circular swaths. This provides better opportunities for birds to escape the mower.

4. Maintain patches of bare ground to attract killdeer and horned lark. These birds use such patches for nesting and feeding. Create bare patches by removing accumulated thatch, by intensively grazing goats or sheep (tethering them or creating electric-fenced enclosures), or by killing patches of vegetation under black plastic sheets or with glyphosate (Round-up). Rotate these methods throughout the field for best results.

5. Manage contiguous rather than isolated fields. Removing brushy fencerows creates one large field rather than equal-sized isolated fields. This is especially attractive to species requiring large fields, like the grasshopper sparrow and upland sandpiper. (Varying the frequency of mowing creates a mosaic of different-aged meadows, which leads to a greater diversity of grassland birds.) While brushy fencerows provide habitat for some shrubland birds, they compromise habitat for grassland specialists and can provide a source of seed for invasive shrubs such as multiflora rose and exotic honeysuckles.

[2]Andrea L. Jones and Peter V. Vickery. 1997. *Conserving Grassland Birds* (three parts). Lincoln, MA: Grassland Conservation Program, Center for Biological Conservation, Massachusetts Audubon Society.

6. If the meadow is grazed, rotate animals through several fields. Light grazing can lead to an ideal bird-nesting habitat by creating a mosaic of vegetation heights and density. In contrast, intensive grazing makes pasture unsuitable for most birds by removing the vegetation necessary for nesting, feeding, and shelter. To favor birds, keep at least 40 percent of the vegetative cover at a minimum height of 8–12 inches, and prevent grazing in some fields during the nesting season.

7. Reintroduce fire into the ecosystem. Burn fields in early spring after the snow melts and before the arrival of birds. Burning is an important tool for managing fields as it adds nutrients to the soil, discourages the growth of woody shrubs, and reduces the buildup of dead stems (thatch). Fields with too much thatch are not usually used for nesting. Generally, bird populations increase within a year or two following a burn. Prescribed burns should be conducted in accordance with the natural burn regime of the ecosystem with regards to the reburn interval.

Before burning, check with local fire authorities to obtain the necessary permits, and alert your neighbors. Consider temperature, humidity, and wind direction and speed. Obtain assistance and advice from your local fire department, office of Natural Resources Conservation Service, or Cooperative Extension Service.

NO-TILL FARMING

Where soil types permit, substitute "no-till" farming and avoid fall plowing. No-till equipment (such as seed drills) can plant crops such as corn without turning over the soil. This technique is much better for the soil and for wildlife.

Fall plowing of cornfields is intended to control infestations of corn borers, eliminate the need for cultivating wet spring soils, and promote decomposition and recycling of nutrients in corn stubble. However, fall plowing also dries out the soil and increases soil losses to wind and water erosion. The principal detriment to wildlife is that fall plowing turns under remnant stubble such as corn stalks that provide protective cover.

The Indiana Natural History Survey found 448 more birds per square mile in standing cornstalk fields than in fall-plowed fields. Twenty-nine kinds of birds feed on discarded corn, including the eastern bluebird, cardinal, American robin, northern bobwhite, mourning dove, tufted titmouse, and ring-necked pheasant.

By contrast, only 9 species inhabited fall-plowed fields. Fall plowing also affects wintering hawk populations, as the number of meadow mice declines, owing to lack of food and cover.

Corn stubble left standing over the winter provides vital cover and food for wildlife. (AF)

NATIVE GRASSLANDS

Little is known about the exact location of the former North American grasslands. Annual rainfall was once the principal factor limiting grassland communities. Tall-grass prairies (made up of primarily big bluestem and Indian grass) dominated roughly the eastern third of the grasslands region. Tall-grass prairies graded into medium-height and semiarid short-grass plains that extended to the base of the Rocky Mountains. Various wet meadow habitats occurred throughout North America that result from local hydrologic conditions.

Grassland managers seeking to restore quality bird habitat should select the grasses and the appropriate mix of wildflower species that are native to their area. In the eastern prairie region, where rainfall is more abundant, a mix of tall and medium habitats can be established to provide more varied wildlife cover. Short-grass mixtures are more appropriate in western prairie states.

Hay fields, pastures, and abandoned fields that are larger than 30 acres can provide useful habitat for grassland birds, especially if such areas are converted to warm-season grasses. These once dominated vast North American prairies in the Midwest and New England states prior to European settlement. Native prairies provide better habitat for grassland birds than do hay fields and pastures composed primarily of cool-season grasses introduced from Europe. The cool-season grasses (e.g., timothy, orchard grass, and Kentucky bluegrass) are favored by agriculture because they start growing earlier in the year than native warm-season grasses, permitting farmers to cut hay two to three times during a growing season.

In contrast, many native warm-season grasses such as big bluestem, little bluestem, and Indian grass grow in a bunching manner, leaving places for flowering plants to grow and runways between the bunches that provide nest sites and refuge from predators. Native grasslands also provide better perches for singing and a greater variety of seeds and insects, which are important foods for young birds. Unlike cool-season grasses that flatten to the ground in winter, warm-season grasses stand tall through the winter, providing vertical structure that offers excellent winter cover.

Our once-productive native grasslands can be restored by planting the proper mix of grasses, either as buffer strips or as large fields. Grasslands are further improved by seeding native wildflowers and legumes to provide additional wildlife food and nitrogen for the grasses. These greatly enhance both the appearance and the wildlife value of native grasslands.

Many warm-season grasses grow in "bunches," leaving passages for birds to walk and more secure nesting places. (©BV)

The following mixtures of perennial grass provide excellent cover and food for the short-eared owl, bobolink, meadowlark, and other grassland birds.

Recommended Mixes of Native Perennial Grasses

Tall mixtures (3–6 ft.) grow best in eastern prairie states. They provide important roosting, loafing, and cover for many . grassland birds

> Indian grass
> Big bluestem

Medium-height mixtures (2–3 ft.) provide important nesting places for the ring-necked pheasant, sharp-tailed grouse, and prairie chicken.

> Western wheatgrass
> Little bluestem
> Side oats grama

Short mixtures (1–2 ft.) grow in both eastern prairie states and western plains states where water limits the growth of taller grasses. Short grasses provide important cover and nest sites for such birds as meadow lark, quail, lark bunting, longspurs, and grassland sparrows

> Little bluestem
> Blue grama
> Buffalo grass

Wet mixtures (3–6 ft.) will tolerate occasional flooding or sites that have wet soils (but not frequent standing water). These grasses provide excellent cover in all seasons.

> Reed canary grass
> Indian grass
> Big bluestem
> Switch grass
> Western wheatgrass

WILDFLOWERS FOR MIDWEST/EASTERN WARM-SEASON GRASSLANDS

When establishing grasslands, mix perennial wildflower seed with the grass seed at the time of planting. Many varieties of native wildflower seed are available from suppliers of warm-season grasses, or they can sometimes be collected along roadsides or railroad tracks. Avoid mixing alfalfa, red, alsike, and white clovers into the warm-season grass mix, as they will compete with the warm-season grasses. Native prairie clovers are suitable. Contact your local office of the Natural Resources Conservation Service, Cooperative Extension Service, or state/provincial wildlife department to determine the best mix of grasses and wildlflowers for your location.

STEPS FOR CONVERTING AGRICULTURAL FIELDS AND MEADOWS TO WARM-SEASON GRASSLANDS

Site Preparation

The discussion that follows should be reviewed and adapted using advice from local agencies such as the Cooperative Extension Service, Natural Resources Conservation Service, and U.S. Fish and Wildlife Service. Specific recommendations are important in considering the best protocols for existing plant communities, soil types, climate, and size of the area intended for management. Timing of management practices is also critical and varies between regions. Several programs can provide technical support and grants for restoring grasslands on private lands (see Appendix C).

Weed management is the most significant problem to overcome when establishing warm-season grasses. Agricultural fields are the easiest sites to convert. Before starting restoration at such sites, research the herbicide history of the field, because if some chemicals (e.g., atrazine, Treflan, Avadex) have been used in the last 2–4 years, they will inhibit the germination and growth of prairie plants. Recently cultivated agricultural fields will not be free of weeds, but much of the preparation is already complete. Spot weeding with glyphosate (Round-up) is all that is necessary to remove occasional weeds. In early spring, use a light-duty cultivator or harrow to till the ground no more than 2 inches deep. Deeper tilling will only release more weed seed. To exhaust the supply of dormant weed seeds, till the field repeatedly about every 3 weeks until early June. Do not let the weeds grow more than 2 inches tall.

After weed control, pack the soil with a water-filled roller or agricultural packer to create a surface crust. This reduces air pockets that would dry out the roots of newly germinated seed, and ensures good contact between seed and soil for germination. If your footprint barely registers in the soil, then the site is sufficiently packed for planting. Plant with a seed drill or broadcast seed by hand. If seed is broadcast, then use the roller again to ensure good contact between seed and soil.

Old fields are more difficult to restore as they are usually full of perennial, nonnative weeds such as quack grass, smooth brome, and Canada thistle. It may take several years to control these species. If possible, burn the field in late fall or early spring to remove the accumulated litter and surface seed bank. If burning is not possible, then mow close to the ground with a rotary, sickle, or flail mower, and then rake off the surface litter.

Allow the vegetation to regrow to about 8 inches. Treat the field with glyphosate (e.g., Round-up) in late spring or early summer. Especially tough weeds such as Canada thistle and leafy spurge may require spot spraying. Additional treatments every 3–4 weeks may be necessary during the following growing season if weeds persist. Be certain to use licensed professionals that wear suitable safety equipment. Take care to follow directions carefully when applying herbicides.

Several weeks after the herbicide treatment, cultivate the field with a disk to turn under surviving weeds. To reduce erosion on steep sites or sites that receive water from a large drainage area, plant a summer annual such as sorghum, sudangrass, or millet, in mid-June, then till and plant oats in early fall.

Planting of summer annuals is not necessary where erosion is not a concern. Treat such sites with a second glyphosate treatment in mid-July. Wait 3 weeks and check for weeds. If few are present, do a final cultivation, pack the soil, and plant an early fall crop of buckwheat or oats (seed at 25–50 pounds per acre) to shade out and compete with weeds (use a seed drill on packed soil or broadcast seeds, then pack soil). Canada wild rye, native to the tall- and mixed-grass prairies, is widely used for this purpose as a short-lived perennial cover crop. It usually does not survive more than 8 years and gives slower-growing species a chance to establish. If perennial weeds are now under control, plant warm-season grasses the following spring. Spot control with glyphosate may still prove necessary.

If weeds are still abundant after the first year of treatment, treat the entire field again with glyphosate, cultivate, pack the soil (using a roller or bulldozer), and plant a cover crop of buckwheat, oats, or Canada wild rye. Continue spot control with glyphosate throughout the second growing season.

Conversion of cool-season grasslands can also be accomplished without herbicides, but there are additional environmental costs to consider because of the more intensive use of agricultural equipment. These include increased use of fuel, air pollution from tractors, erosion, and wear on equipment. This approach usually requires 2–3 years of repeated cultivation with cover crops of buckwheat or oats, followed by a year of allowing the cover crops to grow, before the field is suitably free of weeds.

- First year: Till the land to a depth of 6 inches using a tractor-pulled disk once a month, starting in early fall. Plant rye or oats by early September to compete with weeds. These crops will die off over the winter.
- Second year: Till just 1 inch deep once a month starting in early spring. Till more often if it is a wet year and less often if it is dry; tilling may

need to be deeper to kill deep-rooted plants such as Japanese knotweed. Shallow tillage turns under weeds without bringing up more weed seeds from deeper layers. The idea of repeated tillage is to exhaust the supply of dormant weed seeds and kill the roots of cool-season grasses. During late summer, plant a shade crop of buckwheat or oats to block light from competing weeds and protect the soil from erosion. Till the buckwheat under in early fall and plant a second buckwheat crop.

- Third year: If there are few weeds, plant warm-season grasses in the spring, seeding directly into the standing buckwheat, and mow the field high in early and late summer. Mowing above the low-growing warm-season grasses will keep weeds from seeding.

Seeding

The best time for seeding is midspring to early summer, when the soil has warmed to at least 50 degrees, there is adequate moisture for germination, and frost heaving is not a concern. It is best to use a seed drill calibrated for native grass seed (local conservation agencies may be able to provide this equipment or even conduct the seeding). If the seedbed is loose due to recent cultivation, compact it with a roller or the blade of a bulldozer before using the seed drill. The seedbed is firm enough when a footprint penetrates just $\frac{1}{4}$ to $\frac{1}{2}$ inch deep. If a seed drill is not available, use handheld equipment to broadcast seed onto a loose seedbed, then compact it with a roller or bulldozer to ensure good seed-to-soil contact.

Seed mixtures and seeding rates will vary from one location to another because of differences in soil type, soil moisture, and precipitation. Sellers of warm-season grass seed can provide advice on seed quantities, successful seeding mixes, and seeding rates for your area. In general, it is better to use low amounts of seed per acre to avoid growth that is too dense.

For a diversity of short and tall warm-season grasses, use a mix of switch grass, big and little bluestem, Indian grass, and side oats grama. The mix should also contain about 10 percent forbs. (Check with local agencies and seed sellers for wildflower species suitable for your area and to determine the proportion of grass seeds best suited for your soil type.) When combined, a mix of 3–5 pounds per acre of grass seed plus wildflower seed may be sufficient. Weeds must be monitored more aggressively in a low-density planting, but seed costs are lower, and the result is grassland with more structural diversity, which is highly attractive to grassland birds.

Postplanting Weed Control

Weed control is critical during the season after seeding, to allow the slower-growing warm-season grasses to become established. Mowing is a simple and effective method for controlling weeds in the new stand. Mow the meadow with a sickle bar mower, set at 4–5 inches, when weed growth reaches 6–10 inches (i.e., before weeds go to seed). The goal is to clip annual grasses and weeds while cutting, at most, just the leaf tips of the new warm-season grass seedlings. Leave cuttings in a thin layer on the ground. This mowing should result in no more than 6–8 inches of growth at the end of the season, a height sufficient to protect grass seedlings from winter frost heaving. Avoid weeding by hand as this tends to damage seedlings. However, problem weeds can be hand-cut at ground level, or treated individually with glyphosate using a wick-type applicator.

Second-Year Mowing

In the spring of the second year, mow the meadow several inches above the soil and remove the cuttings. This technique promotes early warming of the soil and germination of dormant seeds from the previous year's seeding. If weeds continue to be a problem in the second year, prevent them from setting seed via spot herbicide treatment or periodic mowing.

Ongoing Maintenance

Once established, a warm-season grassland should thrive with minimal maintenance. However, it will require either burning under the natural burn interval, or mowing and raking in late fall about every third year, to avoid invasion by woody plants.

PRESCRIBED BURNS

Fire is a natural way to control invading shrubs and trees and to maintain healthy grassland habitat. Grassland communities are adapted to fire and do best when they are occasionally burned. Yet, arranging a successful burn takes careful planning and some luck. Even professional grassland managers usually admit that successful burns are as much art as science.

Burn plans are developed for specific properties and should rely on advice from local professional fire ecologists whenever possible. Fire ecologists are often employed by agencies such as the U.S. Forest Service, U.S. Fish and Wildlife Service, Bureau of Public Lands, Natural Resources Conservation Service, state/

provincial conservation departments, universities through the Cooperative Extension Service, and nonprofit conservation groups such as The Nature Conservancy.

Some general considerations include the following:

- The goals of the prescribed burn
- Necessity of a burn permit from the local municipality
- Alternative plans for different wind directions
- What to do if the wind shifts direction during the fire
- How to respond to an escaped fire
- Time of day to burn
- Location of primary firebreaks
- Informing neighbors about the burn

As an example, the following procedures are used at the National Audubon Society's Appleton-Whittell Research Ranch (ARR) in southeastern Arizona:

- The burn plan was developed in cooperation with local/regional agencies associated with fire control (Bureau of Land Management, U.S. Forest Service, volunteer fire department) and divides the 8000-acre ranch into units of 700–1000 acres, using natural firebreaks such as dry washes and existing firebreaks (roads) as boundaries if possible. Blacklines are established to create temporary firebreaks by mowing and burning vegetation.
- This plan calls for burning about one unit per year so most parts of the ARR would burn approximately every 10 years, taking into account that some years are not suitable for burning (too dry, too windy, air quality too low). Timing of the burn is important, both from an ecological sense (usually it is considered best to burn when nature would burn) and to ensure the availability of adequate assistance.
- The burn plan is updated periodically to take into account changes such as wild fires. The burn plan describes in detail the sequence and patterns of ignition. Steps:
  1. During December–February, discuss with the burn boss the choice of burn unit and schedule date(s) for the burn, as well as alternative date(s).
  2. Two to 3 weeks prior to the burn date, contact local authorities for a burn permit to establish a blackline (boundary of burn area).
  3. Establish the blackline. For boundaries of burn units without natural firebreaks, use a tractor to mow one 6–8-foot-wide swath, skip a strip, then mow another swath.

4. The next step involves help from professionals. The inside (unmown) grass is torched and the fire is put out before it burns through the mown grass. This calls for a crew of about five people. One leads the way on a truck carrying a water tank and hoses, one torchs the standing grass, two follow closely behind the torch person to hose down the fire before it escapes, and one rides an all-terrain vehicle (ATV), with a sprayer about 50 feet behind the fire group to put out any embers that might have escaped notice. Boundaries created with natural firebreaks or roads may or may not need a blackline placed around the area to be burned.

5. On the day of the burn, have the burn permits in hand. Prescribed burns are usually scheduled late in the afternoon, so that rising humidity can help prevent fire from spreading. If conditions are within the prescription, the burn begins. Otherwise, wait for better conditions on an alternative date.

- The ARR equipment includes (in addition to a tractor and the ATV): radios, fireproof clothing, watertank on trailer, 15–25-gallon spray rigs for the ATV, flappers, shovels, and lots and lots of hoses! Professional fire crews will have additional equipment.

- If prescribed burning is rarely used in your area, develop an education program for neighbors, policy makers, and press. This will make the day of the burn much less stressful for everyone. It is also a great educational opportunity to explain the role and necessity for fire.

- IMPORTANT: If you live in a fire-adapted ecosystem, whether you are contemplating using prescribed fire or not, work to protect structures— homes, shops, barns, offices—and be prepared to protect and deal with people during and after a fire. If the public is likely to visit the area or a large staff is involved, then develop an evacuation plan, including a meeting point.

Bobolink

Habitat requirements

Grassland type: Upland meadow/pasture, wet meadow, old field (e.g., old hay fields, reclaimed grasslands, capped landfills).

Minimum grassland size: 5–10 acres.

Vegetation structure: Mixed-grass hay fields 8–12 inches high, and more than 8 years old, with relatively sparse ground cover, usually in lowlands with moist soil. Bobolinks prefer a mosaic of grasses, sedges, and scattered broad-leaved forbs with less than 25 percent shrub

Bobolink (©BV)

cover; they use shrubs, posts, and small trees as song perches.

Management suggestions

Mowing/haying: Mow hay fields every 1–3 years in August to prevent nest destruction; remove hay to prevent thatch buildup.

Grazing: Bobolinks tolerate light grazing (grass 8–12 inches high); they will not use heavily grazed pastures.

Prescribed burning: Burn patches every 2–5 years, but not the entire area in one year. Bobolinks will nest in a field during the growing season following a burn; they avoid recently burned areas that remove all litter.

Restoration: Plant late-maturing hay species (i.e., warm-season native grasses) rather than legumes; restore habitat on eroded, marginal farmland; use no-till method for reseeding. Bobolinks will renest if their nest is destroyed before June 20; they have high site fidelity when breeding is successful, and have the greatest nesting success far from forest edges.

Meadowlark

Habitat requirements

Grassland type: Upland
    meadow/pasture, old field, (e.g., hay
    fields, croplands, reclaimed grass-
    lands, capped landfills, airports,
    shrubby overgrown fields). Western
    meadowlarks require shorter, more
    sparse vegetation than eastern
    meadowlarks and drier, more open
    situations.

Minimum grassland size: 15–20 acres.

Vegetation structure: Sparse to dense
    grass-dominated cover 10–20 inches
    high, preferably in low-lying areas
    with damp soils, and a thick layer of
    dead grass; meadowlarks use scat-
    tered shrubs, and tall forbs 15 inches high for song perches; they prefer
    mixed-grass fields to alfalfa.

Meadowlark, Orville Rice (OR), © Cornell
Laboratory of Ornithology

Management suggestions

Mowing/haying: Mow every 1–3 years in August to avoid nest destruction.

Grazing: Leave fields ungrazed for 2 years or allow light grazing to more than
    5 inches high, leaving scattered forbs; rotate grazing to maintain a variety of
    grass height and density during the breeding season.

Prescribed burning: Meadowlarks nest 2–4 years following a burn as shrubs
    regrow; they avoid areas with a thick litter layer.

Restoration: Restrict surface tilling during the breeding season; plant warm-
    season native grasses in moist areas. Meadowlarks will renest if their nests
    are destroyed early in the season—they are sensitive to human disturbance
    while breeding.

Grasshopper Sparrow

Habitat requirements

Grassland type: Upland meadow/pasture, old field, sand-plain grassland (e.g., cultivated grasslands, coastal heathlands, blueberry barrens, reclaimed grasslands, capped landfills).

Grasshopper sparrow (©BV)

Minimum grassland size: 30 acres, preferably 50–100 acres

Vegetation structure: Short bunch grasses (4–12 inches high) with minimal litter and grass cover, patches of bare ground, scattered tall forbs (8–25 inches high), and short shrubs (1–8 inches high) for song perches. The grasshopper sparrow favors well-drained upland sites and is absent from fields with more than 35 percent shrubs.

Management suggestions (one or more of the following, if necessary, to produce the above conditions)

Mowing/haying: Mow fields annually outside breeding season (May 1–August 5).

Grazing: Allow light to moderate grazing to maintain short and sparsely bunched vegetation.

Prescribed burning: Burn every 5–7 years (as appropriate for region) but leave sufficient unburned breeding habitat each year. This sparrow nests in burned and unburned areas, increasing for 4–5 years following a burn until the litter cover increases.

Restoration: Plant native warm-season bunch grasses rather than sod-forming grasses on well-drained or sandy soils with a mixture of scattered forbs and shrubs.

Savannah Sparrow

Habitat requirements

Grassland type: Upland
meadow/pasture, old field, sandplain
grassland, salt meadow (e.g., cultivated fields, hay fields, pastures, suc-
cessional fields, blueberry barrens,
coastal grassland, airports).

Minimum grassland size: 20–40 acres.

Vegetation structure: Dense ground
vegetation with mixture of short and
tall grasses (1–24 inches high) in
moist habitat with a thick layer of
dead grass and scattered saplings,

Savannah sparrow (©BV)

shrubs, and forbs (1–10 inches high); use fields of all ages from alfalfa to
grass.

*Management suggestions (one or more of the following, if necessary, to produce the
above conditions)*

Mowing/haying: Mow yearly after mid-August to maintain short grasses.

Grazing: Allow light grazing with approximately 40 percent vegetation cover
(grass height to 10 inches).

Prescribed burning: Populations increase 2–4 years following a burn every 5th
year and then decrease because of greater litter cover, short grasses, and not
enough short shrub.

Restoration: Plant fields with mixture
of tall and short grasses and forbs.

Vesper Sparrow

Habitat requirements

Grassland type: Upland
meadow/pasture, old field, sand-
plain grassland (e.g., crop fields,
weedy edges of potato fields, pastures, pine barrens, blueberry
barrens, gravel pits, forest clearings).

Minimum grassland size: 30 acres.

Vegetation structure: Open sparse,

Vesper sparrow (©BV)

short grass (1–8 inches high) on dry upland sites with low grass and forb density with scattered shrubs or small trees (height less than 12 inches) for singing perches

Management suggestions (one or more of the following, if necessary, to produce the above conditions)

Mowing/haying: Mow frequently to provide foraging areas; leave nesting areas unmowed during breeding season (April 15–August 30).

Grazing: Allow moderate grazing to maintain 20–40 percent of vegetation at 10 inches tall.

Prescribed burning: Burn early spring or late fall; for grasslands larger than 60 acres, burn 20–30 percent yearly; for smaller grasslands, do not burn more than 50–60 percent of the area in a given year. The vesper sparrow responds positively to short sparse vegetation created by burning.

Restoration: Plant native warm-season grasses in well-drained fields with lighter soils (sand and gravel), avoid heavy clays; provide undisturbed sparse vegetation and song perches along borders of crop fields. In crop fields, nests will be confined to field edges; foraging will occur in nearby brush and woods.

Upland Sandpiper

Habitat requirements

Grassland type: Upland meadow/pasture, old field, sandplain grassland (e.g., pastures, old hay fields, dry meadows, airfields, blueberry barrens, extensive mixed agricultural areas).

Minimum grassland size: 150 acres, preferably 200–300 acres.

Vegetation structure: Provide mixture of short grass (feeding) and tall (24 inches) grass (breeding) interspersed with patches of bare ground and some tall singing perches; avoid fields with uniform grass and legumes and dense litter layer.

Management suggestions

Mowing/haying: Mow nesting areas after mid-July, every 1–3 years (provide 6–8-inch-high grass in nesting area for spring arrival).

Upland sandpiper (©BV)

Grazing: Allow moderate grazing (to grass height of 8–12 inches) with some scattering of forbs; restrict cattle May 1–July 15 in nesting areas.

Prescribed burning: Burn only a portion of large areas in a year to provide unburned habitat in spring; burn every 5–10 years after September 1 or before May 1. The upland sandpiper nests in recently burned fields (prefers second year after burn) with short new growth and no litter.

Restoration: Plant native warm-season bunch grasses in large fields or combine existing fallow fields to provide mosaic of habitat types for feeding and breeding areas.

SUGGESTED NATIVE GRASSES FOR WARM-SEASON GRASSLANDS

Little Bluestem

(*Schizachyrium scoparius*)

This warm-season grass forms 1½–4-foot-tall bunches in dry or moist soils. It is drought tolerant and flowers in July–October. It grows in sandy fields and disturbed areas in full sun, often invading old fields in the Northeast. Little bluestem grows best in light, textured soil with average fertility. It does not grow well

Little bluestem, Valerie Hayes (VH)

in rich soils. Plant the seed in late summer to early fall or early spring. Agricultural uses are soil stabilization, range reseeding, landscaping, and forage. It does not grow well with close mowing or grazing.

Big Bluestem (*Andropogon gerardii*)

One of the tallest native grasses, big bluestem typically reaches 3–8 feet or higher and has a bunch-forming habit. It is very drought tolerant and adaptable. Big bluestem grows in sunny, open places along roadsides and shores and in both moist and dry fields. It grows in poor to well-drained soils that are coarse sand to clay. Plant big bluestem in spring or summer when the soil is warm. It has multiple agricultural uses for pasture, forage, and hay.

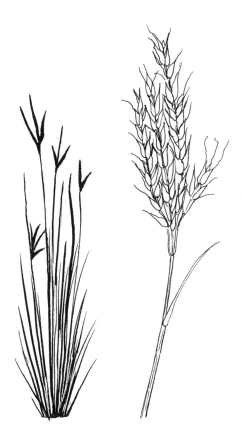

Big bluestem (VH)

Switch Grass (*Panicum virgatum*)

Slow-growing and drought tolerant, this 2–7-foot-tall bunch grass is an excellent choice for sunny areas with dry soils, but it can become a monoculture, crowding out other species. Switch grass flowers in July–September and serves as a valuable winter food and cover for birds. It grows on many types of soil but thrives on fertile and moist sandy soil, tolerating moderate salinity. Plant the seed in early spring or late summer or early fall. It blooms the first year if planted early, but takes 1–2 years to become well established. Agricultural uses include pasture, forage, and erosion control.

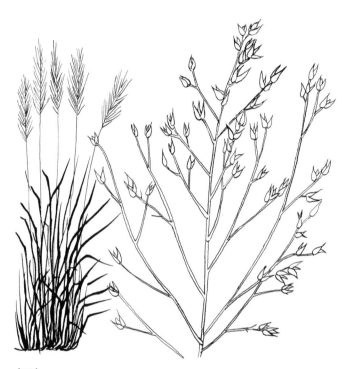

Switch grass (VH)

Indian Grass (*Sorghastrum nutans*)

This drought-tolerant grass is an excellent choice for dry, sunny fields with dry to moist soil and poor to average fertility. It is often planted with big bluestem as it grows to a similar height of 2–9 feet. Like other bunch grasses, it provides excellent structure for nesting and abundant hiding places for fledging birds. Indian grass flowers from July to September, creating an abundant seed source in fall and winter. It is a good choice for pasture and range, serving as a nutritious food for livestock.

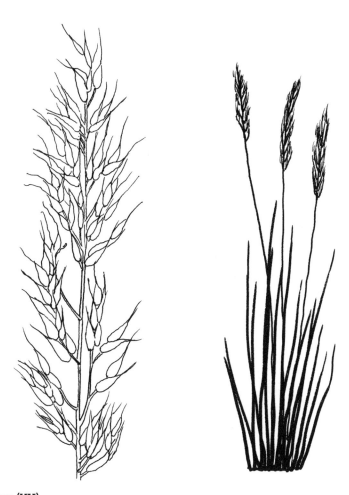

Indian grass (VH)

Side oats Grama (Tall Grama Grass) (*Bouteloua curtipedula*)

    This bunch grass grows to a relatively low height, 1–3 feet. It is drought tolerant and a good choice for sunny areas in dry woods and prairies. It prefers dry to moist soils and grows best in well-drained rocky or shallow areas. It matures quickly and can bloom the first year if the seed is planted in early spring. Its agricultural uses include pasture, range, and erosion control.

Side oats grama (VH)

Buffalo Grass (*Buchloe dactyloides*)
This perennial, warm-season grass has great potential as a drought-tolerant turf for lawns and other areas where a mowed look is desirable. It does not grow in bunches, but spreads by sending out surface runners. Its natural habit of growing just 6–12 inches requires minimal or no mowing. It is a soft, blue-green color during the growing season and turns golden brown when dormant. Buffalo grass is native to the prairies of the Great

Buffalo grass (VH)

Plains, where it is hardy between zones 3 and 7. It provides seeds for sparrows, finches, and other ground-feeding birds, and many species use its fine leaves for building nests. Buffalo grass is a good companion to plant with side oats grama, which provide a bunched habitat for nesting.

USEFUL SOURCES

For warm-season grass and wildflower seed:

　　Ernst Conservation Seed: http://www.ernstseed.com/

　　Prairie Nursery: http://www.prairienursery.com

　　Prairie Moon Nursery: http://www.prairiemoonnursery.com

On prescribed fire:

　　http://www.Firewise.org

For information on species recommendations:

　　Conserving Grassland Birds: Managing Large Grasslands Including Conservation Lands, Airports, and Landfills over 75 Acres for Grassland Birds.

　　Conserving Grassland Birds: Managing Small Grasslands, including Conservation Lands, Corporate Headquarters, Recreation Fields and Small Landfills for Grassland Birds.

　　Conserving Grassland Birds: Managing Agricultural Lands, including Hayfields, Crop Fields, and Pastures for Grassland Birds.

　　Andrea L. Jones and Peter D. Vickery, Undated. Grassland Conservation Program, Center for Biological Conservation. Lincoln, MA: Massachusetts Audubon Society, in collaboration with Silvio O. Conte National Fish and Wildlife Refuge and the USFWS North American Waterfowl Management Program. Three parts: each 17 pages.

4 Shrubland Management

Shrublands (also called scrub) are early succession habitats dominated by shrubs and young trees. Even within the same region, shrublands result from many different circumstances, such as tornado blowdowns, succession of beaver ponds, and clear-cuts. Usually, each type of shrubland supports a distinctive group of birds, and each species has specific habitat requirements. Yellow-breasted chats, for example, often nest only in thickets with shrubs, small trees, and tangles less than 6 feet high. Where chats do nest in areas with an overstory of trees, a dense thicket of shrubs is found below. Like most grassland birds, shrubland species such as chats are dependent on large areas of uninterrupted habitat, rarely nesting in a shrubland smaller than 5 acres. Because thickets are generally temporary communities, chats usually nest in one location for about 5 years before the shrubland changes to young forest. This pattern is not unique to chats. It is replayed with many other species that depend on shrubland habitat.

The rate that shrublands change to forest depends largely on the availability of tree seeds. Small patches of shrubland surrounded by forest change much more rapidly than larger shrublands, which may persist for 40 years.

Shrubland birds such as the gray catbird, thrashers, towhees, buntings, chestnut-sided warbler, and field sparrow are threatened by widespread loss of habitat as forest replaces shrubland communities. In addition, vast shrubland habitats are disappearing because of development. Like grassland species, most shrubland birds have been steadily declining in numbers (especially in eastern North America) since at least the 1960s. The Breeding Bird Survey, sponsored by the U.S. Fish and Wildlife Service, has documented this trend. Since the beginning of the survey in 1966, populations of the yellow-billed cuckoo, golden-winged warbler, prairie warbler, painted bunting, and field sparrow have declined by more than 1 percent each year.

Eastern towhee populations are declining faster than that of any other shrubland bird, with an annual decrease of 5.5–10.2 percent from 1966 to 1989. Such declines are pushing some species, such as golden-winged warblers, near extinction. From 1992 to 2003, the numbers of golden-winged warblers have decreased as much as 13 percent per year in some parts of their range. Of the 16 nesting shrubland species east of the Mississippi, only the blue grosbeak has shown an increase in population and this is due to range expansion. Prior to European colonization, these species occupied shrublands that grew up near beaver dams, habitat burned by native Americans, and thickets that appeared in storm-damaged forests. Today, new natural shrublands rarely form because the young woods that covers much of the countryside is not as vulnerable to storm damage.

Shrubland birds are also in trouble in areas dominated by agriculture. Here, they are refugees in a landscape where vast fields of single-species crops have replaced the small family farms that were often separated by shrubby fencerows. Similarly, the close-cropped lawns that dominate suburbia offer little benefit for shrubland birds. Yet, even in these intensely managed landscapes, there are opportunities to create suitable shrubland habitat.

MANAGEMENT PRACTICES

Clear-cuts

Although vast clear-cuts on steep terrain result in erosion and sedimentation of streams, small clear-cut patches on level terrain can lead to quality shrubland habitat, especially where managers permit natural vegetation to regrow.

Unlike grassland and forest birds, most shrubland species do not require vast areas of uniform habitat. For example, shrubland birds usually quickly occupy clear-cut forests in Maine, and there is no significant difference in preference for cuts ranging in size from 5 to 277 acres. Surveys of clear-cuts in Connecticut show similar results—cuts ranging from 1½ to 52 acres are equally attractive to shrubland birds. In these clear-cuts, the prairie warbler, chestnut-sided warbler, and blue-winged warbler were equally frequent regardless of the size of the area. Only the eastern towhee was more abundant in the larger cuts. In the Green Mountains National Forest in Vermont, chestnut-sided and mourning warblers nested in cuts as small as 1 acre.

Utility Corridors

The land occupied by utility corridors (e.g., electric, gas, and communication lines) offers a great opportunity to create and manage habitat for shrubland birds. Presently, most utility companies in the northeastern United States use selective spraying with herbicides to manage tree height under power lines. This technique has largely replaced the practice of broadcast spraying and the use of heavy equipment such as brush hogs and industrial mowers. The practice of selective herbicide application and cutting of individual trees requires relatively low maintenance.

These practices provide an excellent habitat for shrubland birds and allow for long-term management of the area, which is necessary for these species. The initial steps in this approach are expensive and labor-intensive, but long-term projects in Connecticut and Maryland point to its value and the possibility of maintaining stable shrublands. In Connecticut, the field sparrow, white-eyed vireo, and blue-winged, chestnut-sided, and prairie warblers have nested under managed power lines for 40 years. Similar management methods in Maryland and Pennsylvania demonstrate that birds nesting in these corridors are highly productive. Creating shrub-dominated wildlife corridors is especially important under utility lines that pass through forests, because the process of clearing the forest serves to fragment otherwise large forests and to favor nest predators such as crows, jays, grackles, and cowbirds. The following techniques were developed for creating bird-friendly shrublands under utility corridors, but the same techniques will work to establish a shrub-dominated habitat elsewhere.[1]

1. When utility corridors are first cleared, all trees in the corridor are cut and treated with herbicide, leaving behind shrubby species that will serve as a seed source for a shrub community. If the trees are cut but not treated with herbicide, the result is multiple stems (coppice growth) that

[1]Adapted from Maryland Partners in Flight. 1997. *Habitat Management Guidelines for the Benefit of Land Birds in Maryland.* Annapolis, MD: Maryland Partners in Flight.

soon lead to more trees than shrubs. To get to a state where herbicides can be used selectively, nearly 100 percent of the trees must be removed initially. A mix of herbaceous and shrubby habitat will favor early-succession birds such as indigo buntings and blue-winged and golden-winged warblers. Leaving mostly shrubs and a few trees will favor later-succession birds such as catbirds and towhees.

2. Along the edges of the corridor, cut the tops from tall trees that would reach the power line and girdle them to create dead snags for woodpeckers and other cavity-nesting birds. Pile the canopy branches and other cut vegetation into brush piles to provide shelter and feeding places for sparrows, juncos, wrens, and other birds.

3. There is little need for further management for 3–4 years, but at that time, spray emerging trees with an herbicide that works to girdle them without cutting. A recommended mixture is 10 percent Weedone 170, 20 percent Garlon 4, 1 percent Becker-Underwood red indicator dye, and 69 percent fine-grade mineral oil. Five gallons of the mixture usually treats at least 1 acre. Do not use this mixture in wetlands.

   Typically, a team of workers equipped with backpack pumps spread themselves out 10–15 feet apart, walking the length of the corridor. They identify tall-growing species and spray these at about knee height. The red dye helps to indicate treated trees. Spraying can happen during the growing or dormant season, but it is easier to identify trees during the growing season. After the trees are removed, shrubs and vines can spread out and grow in a denser form that eventually slows the advance of more trees.

4. Make the wildlife corridors as wide as possible. The only limitation should be allowing for safe distances to the wires; in practice this usually sets a limit of 300 feet for width because of the cost of clearing.

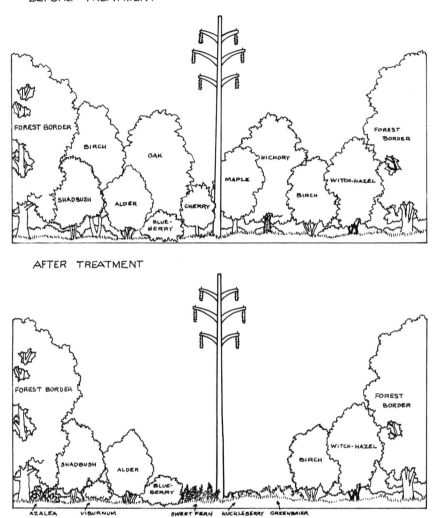

BEFORE TREATMENT

FOREST BORDER
BIRCH
OAK
SHADBUSH
ALDER
CHERRY
BLUE-BERRY
MAPLE
HICKORY
BIRCH
WITCH-HAZEL
FOREST BORDER

AFTER TREATMENT

FOREST BORDER
SHADBUSH
ALDER
BLUE-BERRY
BIRCH
WITCH-HAZEL
FOREST BORDER
AZALEA   VIBURNUM   SWEET FERN   HUCKLEBERRY   GREENBRIER

CREATION OF A STABLE SHRUBLAND UNDER POWER TRANSMISSION LINES.

Utility corridors provide opportunity for the creation of shrubland habitat by selectively cutting and killing trees. (CD)

Suburban Shrublands

Neighborhoods committed to reducing lawn area and replacing it with shrubby property borders can help to create functional shrubland. Since some shrubland birds such as the chestnut-sided warbler and common yellowthroat will nest in relatively small areas of an acre or more, the opportunity exists for city blocks to become suburban shrubby "islands." This takes commitment from the majority of block neighbors, but the benefits of turning relatively bird-hostile habitat into productive city shrubland is a promising possibility. The native shrubs listed in Chapter 5 can help to enhance existing shrubs and hedges to create such habitat.

NEIGHBORHOOD SHRUBLAND PLAN

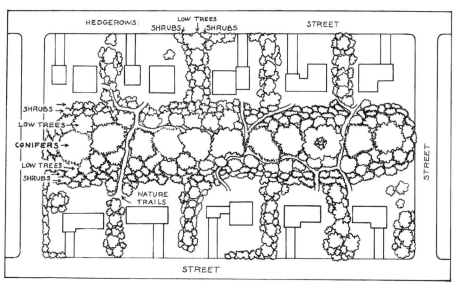

Working together, neighbors could declare their city block a "bird sanctuary" by reducing the amount of lawn and replacing it with adjoining plantings that provide habitat for a wide variety of shrubland birds. (CD)

WINDBREAKS

In the windy prairie states and provinces, windbreaks (also called *shelterbelts*) are well recognized as an important technique for protecting crops, soils, buildings, and livestock from the impact of wind. The use of windbreaks, along with other soil conservation techniques, has greatly reduced losses to wind erosion since the dust bowls of the 1930s. Plantings serving as wind protection can double as a useful wildlife habitat, especially for shrubland birds such as towhees, catbirds, and brown thrashers.

Although a 2- or 3-row windbreak will provide adequate shelter for crops and buildings, wildlife windbreaks should contain at least 6 rows. Where possible, they should consist of up to 11 rows. Wide shelterbelts, with trees and shrubs of varying heights, can offer excellent cover and food for both birds and mammals on landscapes that otherwise could not support wildlife.

A 6-row windbreak is approximately 60 feet wide and would cover almost $1\frac{1}{2}$ acres if it were 1000 feet long. An 11-row windbreak would be approximately 200 feet wide and would cover just over $4\frac{1}{2}$ acres if it were 1000 feet long. Such large amounts of agricultural land committed to wildlife windbreaks obviously require taking land from crop production, but the value of shelterbelts is so great that they usually more than pay for themselves. For example, a study in Nebraska found that agricultural lands adjacent to windbreaks produced an average of 55 bushels per acre, while unprotected cropland produced only 10 bushels per acre. The difference results from less water loss in the protected field and therefore greater water availability for crops. Windbreaks can also be moneymakers if valuable hardwoods such as black walnut or a row of Christmas trees are planted.

The ideal wildlife shelterbelt should contain a central row of tall conifers edged by deciduous trees, with both tall and small shrubs at the edges. The conifers provide seed crops and shelter from the extremes of both summer and winter weather, the deciduous trees provide food and nesting cavities, and the shrubs provide additional nest sites, fruit, and places to feed on insects. Creating a row of herbaceous cover on the outside edges of the windbreak provides additional feeding and nesting habitat for pheasant, quail, and ground-feeding birds such as sparrows.

To establish a wildlife windbreak, plant large trees 10 feet apart, small trees 8 feet apart, and shrubs 6 feet apart. Keep the following considerations in mind as you select and plant the trees and shrubs:

1. Plant the tallest trees in the center and the lowest shrubs on the outside.
2. Within each row, vary the kinds of trees and shrubs.
3. Select trees and shrubs that fruit at different times of the year.
4. Plant the conifers in a weaving row to give a more natural appearance and to avoid an open parklike appearance under the conifers.
5. Mix fast-growing and slow-growing trees and shrubs to provide cover in both the near and distant future.
6. Plant a 10–15-foot-wide buffer strip of perennial cover (grass, alfalfa, and clover) on the outside edge.
7. Sacrifice some width to increase the length of windbreaks if space is a limiting factor, as the length is more important than the width.
8. Erect fencing to exclude cattle and other livestock until windbreak plantings become well established.

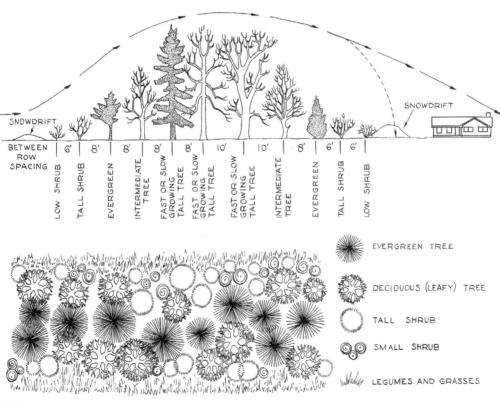

(AF)

SHRUBBY FENCEROWS

Shrubby fencerows provide adequate cover for wildlife and offer great benefit to cropland by increasing the number of insectivorous birds and predacious insects. These help reduce agricultural pests. A comparative study in Ohio found 32 times as many songbirds in brushy fencerows as in open cropland, and 60 times as many aphid-eating ladybird beetles as in sod fencelines. To provide useful cover, brushy fencerows should be at least 10 feet wide and 150 feet long.

Some Bird-Attracting Windbreak Plantings for Northern States and Provinces (South Dakota and Points North)

Trees	Height (ft.)	Shrubs	Height (ft.)
Colorado blue spruce	80–100	Chokecherry	6–20
White spruce	80–100	Saskatoon serviceberry	6–12
Austrian pine	70–90	Scarlet elder	2–12
Bur oak	70–80	Red-osier dogwood	4–8
Scotch pine	60–75	Silverberry	3–8
Green ash	30–50	Silver buffaloberry	3–7
Common hackberry	30–50	Snowberry	3–6
Black willow	30–40	Common juniper	1–4
Downy hawthorn	15–25		

Some Bird-Attracting Windbreak Plantings for Central Prairie and Plains States (Nebraska South to Northern Texas)

Trees	Height (ft.)	Shrubs	Height (ft.)
Ponderosa pine	150–180	American cranberry viburnum	6–15
Black walnut	70–90	Skunkbush sumac	6–12
Bur oak	70–80	Red-osier dogwood	4–8
Eastern redcedar	40–50	Silver buffaloberry	3–7
Common hackberry	30–50	Coralberry	2–5
Flowering crabapples	15–30	Common juniper	1–4
Hawthorns	15–25	Prairie rose	1–2
Osage orange	10–50		
Chokecherry	6–20		

DEVELOPING SHRUBLAND HABITAT IN UNUSED AREAS

Creative landscaping can turn unused areas in the backyard or back forty into productive wildlife habitat. In urban backyards options may be limited to secluded corners, but rural properties and farmland have many possibilities for wildlife improvement, such as gullies, quarries, rock piles, corners of farm fields, pond margins, and abandoned roads. These areas can be productive stopover habitat for migrants and breeding places, but they may also be dangerous traps for birds if cats are permitted to roam through them (see Chapter 8 regarding house cats).

The first step in improving such areas is to select and establish wildlife-attracting vegetation and to plant this in clumped formation. Clumps of the same tree or shrub (five or more) are useful for several reasons. Plants of the same species are likely to fruit at the same time, thus making larger food supplies available and more conspicuous. Also, some shrubs such as mulberry and hollies have both male and female plants, necessitating a close supply of pollen to ensure successful pollination. In addition, planting at least five of each species provides some insurance that if one or two die, there will still be a few survivors. As space permits, plant in clumps several different shrubs or trees selected to provide food at different seasons. Ideally, planting should provide food and cover throughout the year, which means including both evergreen and deciduous selections.

A circular, clumped planting is a good choice where space permits as it provides more interior habitat, which is safer from nest predators such as grackles and jays. Such plantings might surround a rock outcrop, eroded gully, or sinkhole. Position tall trees and shrubs in the middle of the circle and surround them with a border of low shrubs. In areas where cowbirds are significant nest parasites, avoid leaving a lone snag protruding from such plantings as this is very attractive to cowbirds. In prairie states, the areas between pivotal irrigators also provide opportunities for wildlife plantings.

Clumped plantings can also help to speed up conversion of small meadows to shrubland. To favor the growth of shrub habitat, scatter plantings of hawthorn, chokecherry, brambles, redcedar, and other sun-tolerant shrubs in open fields. Soon birds will fly out to the plantings to feed and roost and in the process they will bring seed from adjacent habitats. This cost-effective approach is helping to rapidly transform strip mines, landfills, and other wasteland into valuable wildlife habitat at many "brownfield" sites near urban areas.

Field border strips, adapted from the odd-area principle, are created by planting useful strips of warm-season perennial grasses and legumes in such areas as woodland borders, borders of drainage ditches, and margins between crop fields, as well as areas adjacent to cropland and along pipelines and power lines through woodlands. Using this technique, the farmer establishes a 15–30-foot-wide strip of grass and legume. Perennial grasses and legumes provide excellent cover and food in these otherwise unproductive areas. Rather than just strips of eroded soil or spindly crops, these odd areas can support towhees, chats, the blue grosbeak, song sparrow, and quail, to name only a few.

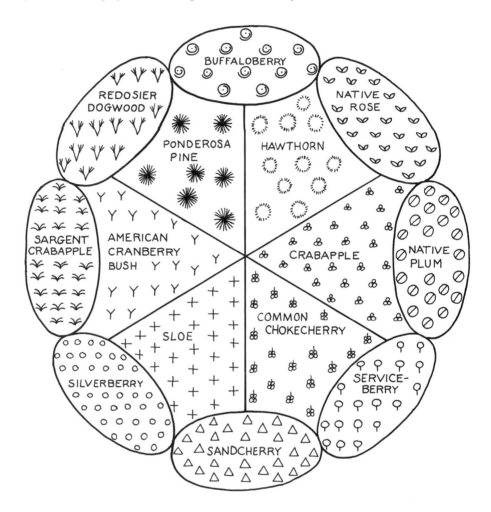

WILDLIFE PLANTING FOR AN OPEN AREA

Circular planting for an open area. (CD)

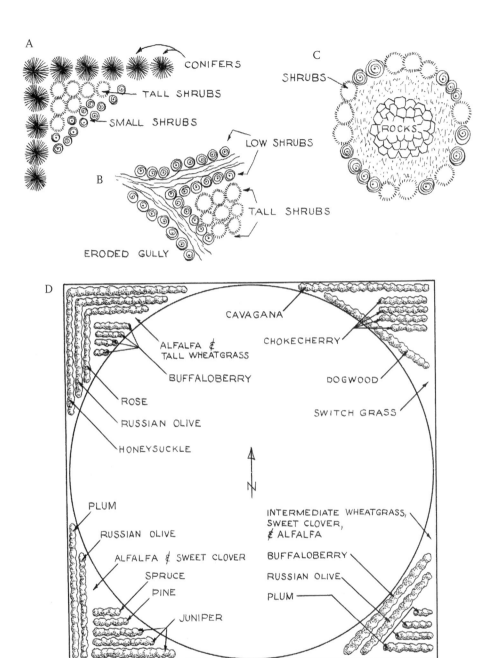

A

CONIFERS
TALL SHRUBS
SMALL SHRUBS

B

LOW SHRUBS
TALL SHRUBS
ERODED GULLY

C

SHRUBS
ROCKS

D

CAVAGANA
ALFALFA & TALL WHEATGRASS
BUFFALOBERRY
ROSE
RUSSIAN OLIVE
HONEYSUCKLE
CHOKECHERRY
DOGWOOD
SWITCH GRASS
N
PLUM
RUSSIAN OLIVE
ALFALFA & SWEET CLOVER
SPRUCE
PINE
JUNIPER
INTERMEDIATE WHEATGRASS, SWEET CLOVER, & ALFALFA
BUFFALOBERRY
RUSSIAN OLIVE
PLUM

Odd areas, such as corners of fields (A), gullies (B), rock piles (C), and corners around pivot irrigators (D), can provide useful food and cover. (AF)

FIELD BORDER STRIP

The edges of an agricultural field can be a productive wildlife area when planted to grass and legumes. (AF)

REVIVING NEGLECTED APPLE TREES

Throughout the Northeast and Pacific Coast regions, neglected apples trees are reminders of abandoned farmsteads and orchards. Long after they are abandoned, such apple trees continue to provide useful wildlife food crops, but shading from larger trees and competition from crowding invasive shrubs greatly reduces the value of these useful bird-attracting trees. The fruit, seeds, and buds of apple trees are eaten by at least 28 bird species and by almost as many kinds of mammals. Also, many cavity-nesting birds such as screech-owls, bluebirds, nuthatches, and chickadees find shelter in the hollowed wood for roosting and nesting.

Crabapples, hawthorns, and other fruit and nut trees are also important sources for bird food. Abandoned orchards or other lands dominated by these trees can become managed shrublands that provide excellent habitat for both shrubland-nesting birds and migrants. Because these fruit-producing trees are usually low-growing, they can also become excellent birding hotspots because birds that forage there are much more visible than those that feed in high forest canopy.

Overgrown trees will usually benefit from the following techniques for improving fruit production and tree health.[2]

1. Remove all other shrubs and trees from the trunk out to the drip line of the apple tree. If large overtopping trees shade the apple tree, remove these on at least three sides, especially toward the south.

2. Carefully examine the apple tree. Look for dead branches, diseased wood in the trunk, and the presence of more than one stem. If there is more than one stem, select the largest and most vigorous and remove the smaller, competing stems by cutting them off as near the ground as possible. If the largest stem is badly diseased or broken, remove it and select the next largest, most vigorous stem for improvement.

3. Remove all the dead branches from the apple tree. Cut the branches off with a pruning saw or pruning shears as close to the living branches as possible.

4. Remove approximately one-third of the remaining live growth to open up thick clusters of branches. Clip off 1–2 feet from the ends of vigorous side branches and vertical sucker shoots. Do not remove the short spur branches that grow on the sides of larger branches because they bear fruit. If the tree is a young sapling with few side branches, the top may be cut off to encourage branching.

5. Fertilize the tree by spreading a 10-10-10 fertilizer uniformly over the area covered by the tree. Apply 1 pound per inch of trunk diameter up to a maximum of 10 pounds per tree.

[2]Adapted from *Care of Wild Apple Trees.* New Hampshire Cooperative Extension Service. Folder 70. Also see William Lord. 2001. *Care of the Mature Backyard Apple Tree.* Durham: University of New Hampshire Cooperative Extension.

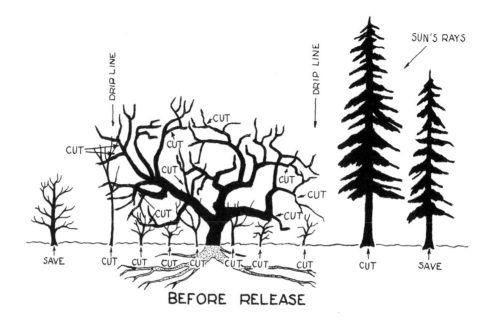

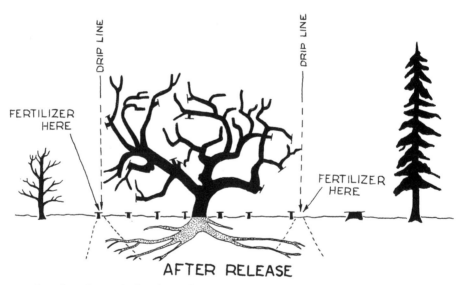

A neglected apple tree before (above) and after (below) release from competition with nearby vegetation. (AF)

Bobwhite chicks stay close to their parents. (CD)

Like other grassland and shrubland birds, many populations of North American quail are in trouble. Two species, northern bobwhite and scaled quail, are showing significant population declines across their ranges. Of the other four North American species, two (California and Gambel's quail) seem to be doing well at this time, and the other two (Montezuma and mountain quail) are unknown. Of all the quail, the northern bobwhite's status is especially alarming. According to the U.S. Fish and Wildlife Service's annual Breeding Bird Survey, bobwhite populations have declined by 70–90 percent since 1966, with an annual decrease of 4–6 percent in the center of its range.

As quail are found in at least 44 states and their effective management assists many other grassland and shrubland species, the popular appeal of these charismatic birds could serve as the focus for habitat restoration with broad benefit for many other native birds.

Northern bobwhite originally frequented prairie grasslands, where it found abundant high-quality habitat under tall bunch grasses like bluestem and Indian grass. The nineteenth-century transition of eastern forest into a patchwork of small farms edged by stone walls and brushy fencerows was also ideal for quail, especially where they found spilled grain and standing stubble for winter cover. In contrast, today's agriculture is usually not quail friendly.

Throughout much of the quail's range, sprawling, corporate-owned farms and intensely grazed pastures are replacing small, family-owned farms and the shrubby fencerows that benefited quail and other shrubland birds. Large farms are harvested by massive equipment, and fields may be tilled in the fall to facilitate early-spring planting. Like grassland birds, quail that attempt to nest in hay fields may lose their nests and young when fields are mowed in the spring. Likewise, the loss of native prairies and the succession of shrublands to forest in eastern states have greatly reduced the amount of quality habitat.

In addition to broad-scale changes in habitat, local factors also affect quail. Where coyote and other large predators are removed, small predators such as fox, skunk, and feral cats further reduce quail populations. Once populations are low, severe winters and new threats such as introduced fire ants (which prey on hatching quail eggs) and escaped pathogens from diseased poultry can further drive down populations.

Once quail disappear from part of their range, they are slow to repopulate, as they are not migratory and most young stay near their hatching place. Given these changes, it is not surprising that quail are becoming rare and that the bobwhite's emphatic call has dropped from the background chorus across much of North America.

Although quail populations are threatened for many reasons, several encouraging circumstances favor recovery. There is perhaps more known about the ecology and population dynamics of northern bobwhite than any other North American bird. The bobwhite is also prolific (laying 12–16 eggs each year) and much that is known about captive rearing could help restoration programs.

The greatest challenge for bobwhite management is the restoration and ongoing management of quality habitat. The management of private land on a large scale will bring the greatest gains, but even small-scale improvements on family farms and rural backyards can collectively help to revive quail populations. Quail have a very dedicated following among hunters and birders, who would like to see quail populations increase. The following discusses some techniques that will help to bring the quail back to your property.

Improving Land for Bobwhites[3]

The preferred habitat for bobwhites is a mixture of grassland, cropland, brushy areas, and woodland interspersed to provide abundant areas of "edge"—margins

[3]Adapted from publications by Roger Wells, National Habitat Coordinator, Quail Unlimited, Inc., 868 Road 290, Americus, KS 66835. Tel.: 316-443-5834. Web site: http://www.qu.org/down/oads/quail_in.doc.

where two or more cover types come together. Grasslands are utilized mainly for nesting cover and brooding; cropland, for feeding and dusting; and brushy areas, thickets, and woodlands, for escape cover, loafing, and winter protection. The greater the interspersion of type combinations, the greater the amount of edge and the more bobwhite quail.

Controlled burns

Burning improves habitat by removing accumulated dead vegetation (litter), stimulating new growth, and controlling excessive shrubs. In this way, burning slows succession, favoring early-succession habitats. Burning prairie and other grassland benefits quail for four reasons: (1) The litter is removed from the ground level, which aids in bird movement; (2) burned areas attract a greater density and diversity of insects that are critical to quail chicks; (3) seed production is greater on burned prairies; and (4) the ability of birds to feed on those seeds is improved because there is less accumulated litter. When learning to use fire as a management tool, first check with the local fire department to obtain the necessary permits. Some fire departments will be willing to assist. In areas where there are nearby homes, it is a good-neighbor policy to inform adjacent property owners. You may also find assistance at the local office of the Cooperative Extension Service, Natural Resources Conservation Service, or U.S. Fish and Wildlife Service (see Appendix C).

- Burning conditions: After establishing 6–12-inch-wide firebreaks by mowing or disking in the fall, wait for the ideal conditions for a burn. The best season is early spring before new grass begins to immerge. Burn when there is a 5–15-mph wind. Preferably burn in calm weather 1–3 days after a rain when the humidity is above 40 percent. Remember that wind tends to increase in speed throughout the day and generally decreases toward evening.
- Creating varied habitat: For the best wildlife response, burn in small units. For areas 40–60 acres or larger, burn only one-third annually. Burn smaller habitats every third year. This provides varied habitat for nesting and brooding.
- "Hot" and "cool" burns: If control of excessive woody plants is the goal of the burn, then a "hot" fire is best. Hot fires travel with the wind and generate considerable heat as they consume the litter. Wildlife managers usually prefer "cool" fires. These are generally set to back into the wind or where the line of fire is parallel with the wind. Cool fires are easier to

control and do a good job of leaving some woody cover intact. Cool late-afternoon and nighttime burns are very good. The purpose is not generally to completely sweep the entire area black with a fire but rather to enhance the "crazy quilt" pattern. Night fires set when the wind is decreasing and humidity is rising tend to go out in some spots and burn through heavier cover, creating a patchwork design.

Disking and mowing

Quail populations may be low in an area simply because vegetation is too thick for them to easily walk between their sources of food, covers, and water. Disking (turning over the soil by a tractor-pulled disk) or mowing pathways provides travel lanes for quail. Of the two approaches, annual disking is preferred as it exposes bare soil that quail use for dusting and a place where chicks can easily hunt for insects. Soil disturbed by disking also encourages a growth of annual "weeds" such as ragweed (*Ambrosia* spp.) and bristlegrass (*Setaria* spp.) that provide a good winter source of seeds.

- Depth and width: Disk strips about 3–4 inches deep, enough to kill existing vegetation. The strips can vary in width, but 10–15 feet is the minimum. Strips up to 30 feet wide are also suitable as long as they are left to grow annual weeds and grasses.
- Grassy strips: Mow where disking is impractical because of the probability of erosion or because the soil is too shallow and rocky. Mowed strips should also be at least 10–15 feet wide.

Food plots

Food plots are usually $\frac{1}{4}$–2 acres. The larger plots are necessary where deer are also feeding. Plant only one-half to one-third of the plot annually and allow the remaining portion to grow into summer annuals in the idle years. Be sure to allow space in the plot for the quail to easily walk among the plants. Take soil samples from any food plot to determine the fertility and recommended fertilizer rates. Follow the recommended rates for producing a milo or corn crop.

A thick mat of annual grasses such as crabgrass or foxtail will hinder the quail's ability to forage for seed. Cultivate rows at least once to get the grain-seed plants off to a good start ahead of weeds and grasses. Use the following seeding rates for the various food plot crops:

Crop	Pounds per acre
Milo (with planter)	4–5
—— (broadcast)	6–8
Soybeans (with planter)	30–40
—— (broadcast)	50–80
Corn (with planter)	12–15
—— (broadcast)	15–20
Sunflowers (with planter)	3–4
—— (broadcast)	4–8
Proso millet	20–30

Legume seeding

Legumes are important to hen quail in spring as they come into breeding condition. Green legumes also attract a diverse array of insects beneficial to quail chicks. In late winter, broadcast alfalfa or clover seed by hand onto bare soil or use a seed drill. Plant legumes in portions of food plots or in disked travel lanes.

Half-cutting and shrub planting

Quail use shrubs for roosting and travel lanes. Where there are few shrubs, consider providing shrubby cover by providing "half-cuts" or planting shrubs. The half-cutting technique involves cutting a tree one-half to two-thirds of the way through, leaving a hinge of attached bark. When the tree falls, it remains alive, creating a living brush pile. The technique is especially successful when trees already support wild grape or greenbrier, as these proceed to cover the entire brush pile. Where possible, half-cut several nearby trees so they fall onto each other, making a brush pile 20–50 feet in diameter. This is particularly useful for creating roosting places and shelter for sparrows, juncos, wrens, towhees, and many other birds.

In places where there is no woody cover, consider establishing windbreaks, hedges, or small shrub thickets by selecting native plants for your area from the recommended tables in Chapter 5. Low-growing, evergreen or dense shrubs provide the best cover. Depending on your location, plant junipers, blackberries, American plum, fragrant sumac, shrubby dogwood, blackberry, currants, granjeno (spiny hackberry), or coyote bush (chaparral). Protect new plants from fire and grazing for at least several years and remove weeds that compete for moisture.

Reintroducing Quail

In addition to the habitat improvement suggestions described in the previous section, it is possible to restore quail within their existing range where populations have disappeared. Quail restoration without habitat improvement is certain to fail.

Where quail are missing from the landscape, consider releasing captive hatched birds to restore a wild population. Quail biology lends itself to restocking, as young birds are not fed by their parents and have many inherent behaviors such as flocking, covey formation, winter roosting, and predator avoidance. There is concern that captive released quail that interbreed with native quail could impair the genetics of the relic native population or could introduce disease. However, this concern does not apply in areas where the native population is already absent and where disease can be avoided by obtaining birds from reliable breeders and by using appropriate hygiene while rearing birds in captivity. Here are some tips for quail restoration by rearing and releasing quail chicks.

1. First assess the feasibility of the project by evaluating the habitat. This should consist of a patchwork of meadows edged by thicket, shrubby fencerows, or windbreaks. The habitat can be further improved by the habitat techniques described earlier. Also check with your state/provincial wildlife department to obtain a permit.

2. Consider predator populations. Predators are ubiquitous, but some habitats have exceptionally large populations of free-ranging house cats and these areas will likely prove unsuitable for quail.

3. Build or dedicate a shed for the purpose of rearing quail chicks. The shed should be approximately 10 × 12 feet with an attached 4 × 10 foot entry and storage space for feed and supplies. The building should be completely tight, to prevent weasels, raccoons, and other predators from entering.

4. Cover the floor of the quail house with several inches of clean wood shavings (not sawdust) and place an 8-foot-diameter, 18-inch-tall corrugated cardboard circle (available from poultry supply houses) in the center of the shed. Take care to bury the bottom of the cardboard into the shavings to prevent chicks from escaping.

5. Obtain about 200 one-day-old quail chicks from a reputable breeder and place them within the cardboard circle. Smaller numbers may be better during the first year while techniques are being developed, but eventually larger numbers are necessary for restoration success.

6. Provide red heat lamps or a commercial brooder for the chicks, keeping them at 95 degrees Fahrenheit for the first week. Then slowly decrease the heat by 5 degrees each week over the next 5 weeks. Provide quail/turkey starter food in shallow trays for the first 2 weeks and then transfer the food to large hopper feeders for the next 4 weeks. Provide water in special quail-chick water jugs with shallow dishes, to prevent the tiny chicks from drowning. Later, replace these with larger jugs that need to be filled every few days.

7. Tend the new chicks as infrequently as possible. Provide food and water at night using a flashlight covered with a red filter or a camouflage mask or wearing a "big bird" costume by day. This approach is recommended to prevent the chicks from imprinting on humans. Otherwise, they will be as tame as little chickens and will be especially vulnerable to predators.

8. After the first 12 days, heap wood shavings into the corners of the shed (to reduce the risk of the chicks smothering each other if too many crowd into a corner) and remove the cardboard circle. Continue to provide food and water, making minimal visits to the birds.

9. When the birds are about 6 weeks old, release them by following one of these two options:

   a. A hard release involves letting the birds free when they are 5–6 weeks old (do not release if the outside temperature is likely to fall below freezing). Birds released at this age are likely to act like wild birds, as their natural instincts will dominate their behavior. Quail released in this manner are also more likely to avoid predators than those reared in the flight pen described below, but they are also more likely to disperse far from the release site.

   b. Soft release is an alternative for locations where there are relatively few predators (especially feral cats, fox, and hawks). This approach is more likely to keep birds in the vicinity, but they will be tamer. Young quail are fed continuously in the quail house and released through a small door into an attached aviary that is approximately 15 feet wide and 30 feet long. Cover the walls and roof of the aviary with chicken wire and install several strands of electric fence on the aviary walls to discourage raccoons and other predators. To discourage predators from digging into the pen, bury 2-inch-square welded wire in a 1-foot-deep trench, bending it away from the aviary. The pen should also have a human-sized access door for maintenance.

A releasing cone is the key feature for the soft-release technique. Construct the cone from hardware cloth, so that it measures 24 inches long with a large opening approximately 6 inches tall and 9 inches wide. The small end of the cone is 3 inches tall and just 2½ inches wide. To position the cone, cut a hole in the rear wall of the aviary and place the cone inside the pen, wiring the large end to the hole in the pen. The cone permits quail to leave one at a time and prevents large predators such as raccoons from gaining access to the pen and the quail house. Quail learn to go out the small opening, and the large opening makes it easy for them to return. If the majority of the birds stay in the pen, open the access door to let out at least one-third of the birds.

Quail reared in this way will leave the pen and often venture to bird feeders, gardens, and other areas near the pen during the day, but they usually return to roost and feed in the flight pen with the remaining birds. Quail reared in this manner will be quite tame and especially vulnerable to predators, but some may reach breeding age (5 months) and produce a next generation that will act more like wild birds.

10. In either approach, continue to provide food in brushy habitat near the release site.

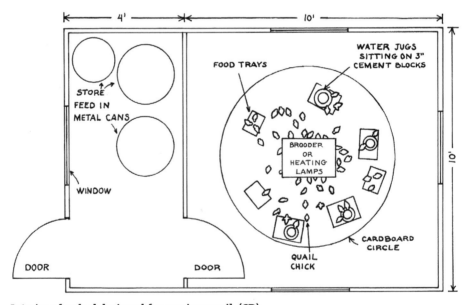

Interior of a shed designed for rearing quail. (CD)

An alternative technique to establish quail is to place day-old chicks in a self-contained unit called "The Surrogator," which provides heat, water, and food without exposing the chicks to humans. Five-week-old birds, imprinted at the site, are then released into suitable habitat.

USEFUL SOURCES
"The Surrogator" is available from Quail Restoration Technologies, 18953
    W. 301 Street South, Bristow, OK 74010:
    http://www.quailrestoration.com
Quail chicks, brooders, and water jugs are available from Murray McMurray
    Hatchery, Webster City, IA 50595-0458:
    http://www.mcmurrayhatchery.com
Automated feeders are available from Sweeney Enterprises, 321 Waring
    Welfare Road, Boerne, TX 78006:
    http://www.SweeneyFeeders.com
Suggested reading: David Howell, ed. Bobwhite Basics (brochure from the
    Southeast Quail Study Group). Available from: Quail Unlimited, 868 Road
    290, Americus, KS 66835:
    http://www.quailunlimited.org

5   Selecting Plants

Most of our knowledge of wild bird food habits comes from painstaking studies of stomach contents conducted by the U.S. Fish and Wildlife Service and its predecessor, the U.S. Biological Survey. Not surprisingly, there is much more known about the food habits of the ring-necked pheasant, bobwhite, and ruffed grouse than other species, since the research of both federal and state wildlife agencies has historically focused on game species.

Relatively little is known about the food habits of nongame birds, and this is especially true for insect-eating birds such as warblers and flycatchers. There is even debate about whether purple martins really favor a diet of mosquitoes (as sometimes claimed by makers of martin housing). Certainly, there is much to learn about wild bird food preferences, and anyone with a pair of binoculars and a keen eye can make useful observations.

The tables that appear later in this chapter list plants that are well known or show promise as important food and cover for wild birds. They are included to assist with inventories of existing vegetation (for protection and enhancement) and to provide lists of bird-attracting plants that could be planted to improve habitat quality for wild birds. For the purpose of this chapter, North America is divided into five major plant/animal regions: Northeast, Southeast, prairies and plains, mountains and deserts, and Pacific Coast. These regions are subdivided into three categories: recommended plants (those that show the greatest value for attracting birds); a repeat list of recommended plants described in detail from other regions; and other good choices (recommended plants with somewhat less promising value).

The plant descriptions and tables in this chapter refer to the following plant characteristics:

Plant names

Common and Latin names follow *Hortus Third*, compiled by Liberty Hyde Bailey and Ethel Zoe Bailey, revised and expanded by the staff of the Liberty Hyde Bailey Hortorium (New York: Macmillan, 1976), or *Checklist of North American Plants for Wildlife Biologists*, by Thomas G. Scott and Clinton H. Wasser (Washington, D.C.: The Wildlife Society, 1980).

Native vs. Alien

Nearly all of the recommended plants listed are native to North America. There are many good reasons for favoring natives when selecting plantings, the most important of which is that they have demonstrated their ability to survive in our climate and they are likely useful to native birds for food and nesting places. Native species are more likely to fruit when birds experience the greatest need for food and they provide the best nutrition, packaged in an easily digested form just the right size for swallowing. They are also more likely to survive weather and water extremes.

The eastern deciduous forest alone has 300 species of trees, shrubs, vines, and ground covers that rely on birds to distribute their seeds. Birds are ideal for this as they can carry seeds miles from the parent tree, often dropping them in ideal habitat. Further, the process of digestion increases germination by removing the fleshy seed coat. In contrast, seeds that fall under the parent tree are likely doomed for lack of light and water.

The colorful berries of many bird-attractive plants such as hollies, flowering dogwood, hawthorns, and crabapples are further testimony to this intimate relationship. Those plants with white, blue, or black fruits usually advertise that fruits are ripe (and seeds are mature) by a brilliant foliage display. Blueberries, shrubby dogwoods, and Virginia creeper are but a few of the plants that use "foliage flags" to attract birds.

The coevolution of native plants and birds is impressive when one considers that native plants ripen their fruit at the peak of migration, offer fruits that are just the right size for swallowing, and provide nutrients that are especially important to birds such as lipids (fats), which are necessary for migration, and sugars, which fuel rapid metabolism for flight. Native shrubs also offer better nesting sites. For example, robins that nest in hawthorns usually produce more young than those that nest in invasive buckthorn and honeysuckle, as hawthorns provide safer nest sites within their tangles of long thorns.

The primary reason to avoid introduced plants (those not native to North America) is that they may escape cultivation and create a monoculture, competing with a healthier, more diverse flora that provides food and cover for birds throughout the seasons.

Oriental bittersweet, Japanese honeysuckle, kudzu, multiflora rose, and Norway maple are vivid examples of introduced species that have spread out of control in eastern North America. Pasture grasses and even runaway garden flowers like purple loosestrife and dame's rocket demonstrate that the problems with invasive, alien plants are not limited to trees and shrubs. In the lists that follow, the few recommended alien plants, such as crabapples and Chinese junipers, have been cultivated successfully in North America for at least several decades without invasive problems and have well-demonstrated value for attracting birds.

Height

The heights given for recommended plants are either ranges of mature specimens or maximum height. Mature height can vary greatly depending on such factors as available water, fertility, and exposure to wind. Plants growing in the northern plains, mountains, and deserts are especially influenced by these factors.

Evergreen or deciduous

Trees and shrubs are grouped within Other Good Choices by their evergreen or deciduous character. This information for ground covers and vines appears in a separate column in the Other Good Choices tables.

Zone

Within each region, plant-hardiness zones suggest the northern distribution or limit to plant growth. The zone system used here follows the 1990 plant-hardiness zones established by the U.S. National Arboretum, Agricultural Service, U.S. Department of Agriculture, and the American Horticultural Society. The zones are based on more than 50 years of weather data used to chart average annual low temperatures. To identify appropriate bird plantings for your property, find your plant-hardiness zone by looking at the map of zones. Then look for recommended plants that are hardy within your home region.

These zones are only estimates, and microclimate differences can account for as much as one or even two zone differences, even though the microclimates may be only a few miles or even feet apart. For example, it has been estimated that the north- and south-facing sides of the same home receive sunlight that may be the equivalent in microclimate of areas at least 300 miles apart. The south side of a home receives considerably more light than the north side and this is the best place to locate plants with more southern distributions. Likewise, low valleys and gorges serve as frost pockets and should be planted with vegetation suited to a more northern climate. Plant zones follow *Hortus Third* and the American Horticultural Society's *A-Z Encyclopedia of Garden Plants*, edited by Christopher Brickell and Judith D. Zuk (New York: DK Publications, 1997).

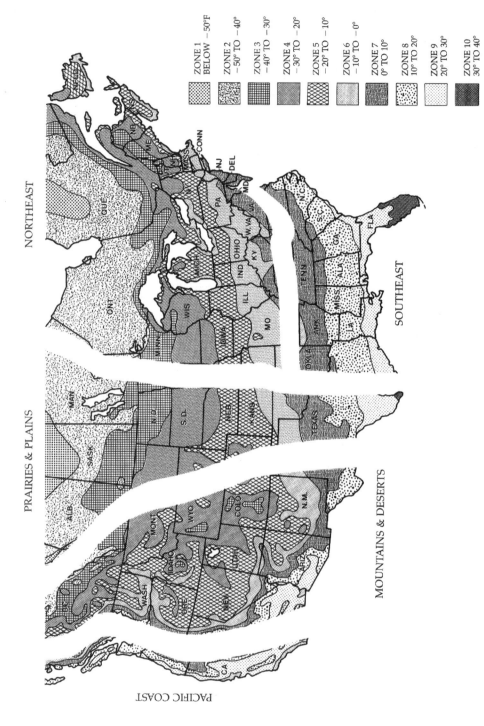

Vegetation regions and U.S. Department of Agriculture plant-hardiness zones. Zones indicate approximate range of average annual minimum temperatures. (AF)

ZONE 1 BELOW −50°F
ZONE 2 −50° TO −40°
ZONE 3 −40° TO −30°
ZONE 4 −30° TO −20°
ZONE 5 −20° TO −10°
ZONE 6 −10° TO −0°
ZONE 7 0° TO 10°
ZONE 8 10° TO 20°
ZONE 9 20° TO 30°
ZONE 10 30° TO 40°

NORTHEAST

PRAIRIES & PLAINS

SOUTHEAST

MOUNTAINS & DESERTS

PACIFIC COAST

Soil

Consider your soil type and available soil moisture when selecting plants. This is especially important for dry climates. Just as grass lawns are inappropriate and a waste of precious water in arid areas, many shrubs and trees with high moisture requirements make poor choices where water is scarce. The lists in the tables contain excellent choices for native bird plantings in arid regions.

Light

Light requirements vary greatly from one plant to the next. Consider your intended planting site before making selections.

Fruit period and type

Because seasons vary dramatically in length and timing from north to south, the fruiting periods are listed by season rather than month. When selecting plantings, choose a mix of fruiting periods so that some fruit is available from summer through winter. *Fruit* is a general term for describing the casings that surround plant seeds. The following text and tables refer to fruit by specific type such as *achene, pome, drupe, capsule, samara,* and *cones.* The fruit types are illustrated and described here.

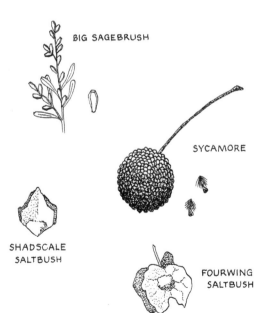

BIG SAGEBRUSH

SYCAMORE

SHADSCALE
SALTBUSH

FOURWING
SALTBUSH

Achene, a nonsplitting fruit that contains one seed closely surrounded by a membranous case (e.g., saltbush, sycamore, sagebrush). (AF)

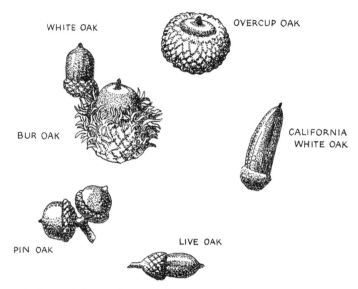

WHITE OAK

OVERCUP OAK

BUR OAK

CALIFORNIA
WHITE OAK

PIN OAK

LIVE OAK

Acorn, the nut of an oak tree. A hard woody cup usually partially or wholly surrounds it. (AF)

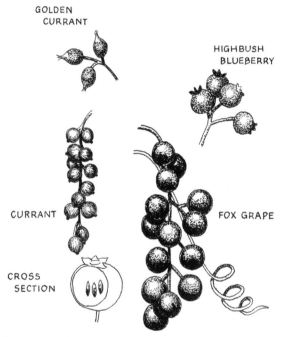

GOLDEN
CURRANT

HIGHBUSH
BLUEBERRY

CURRANT

FOX GRAPE

CROSS
SECTION

Berry, a pulpy fruit with immersed seeds (e.g., grape, blueberry, currant). (AF)

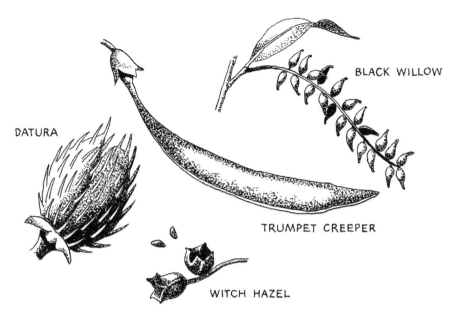

Capsule, a dry, usually many-seeded fruit with one or more cavities in which the fruit splits open when mature (e.g., witch-hazel, black willow, trumpet creeper). (AF)

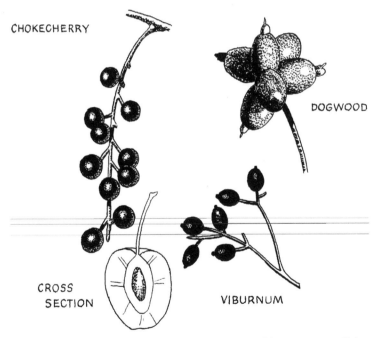

Drupe, one-seeded fruit with a fleshy outer wall and a hard bony inner wall (e.g., cherry, sumac, viburnum, hackberry). (AF)

Drupelet, a tiny drupe that often occurs in clusters called *aggregate fruits* (e.g., raspberry). (AF)

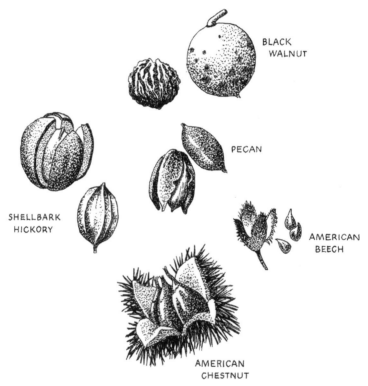

Nut, a hard, usually one-seeded fruit that does not split open (e.g., hickory, walnut, pecan, beech, chestnut). (AF)

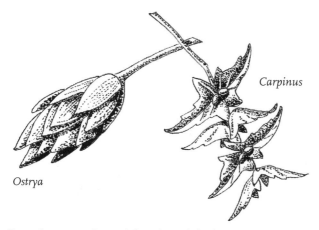

Carpinus

Ostrya

Nutlet, a small nut (e.g., musclewood, hornbeam). (AF)

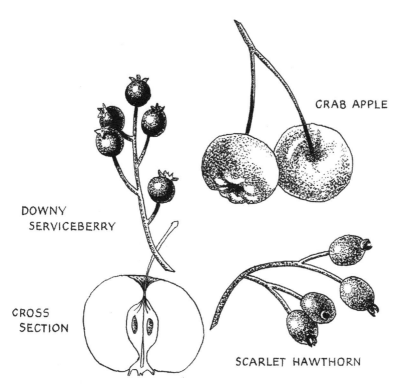

CRAB APPLE

DOWNY
SERVICEBERRY

CROSS
SECTION

SCARLET HAWTHORN

Pome, a fleshy fruit with a central core containing several seeds (e.g., apple, pear, rose, crabapple). (AF)

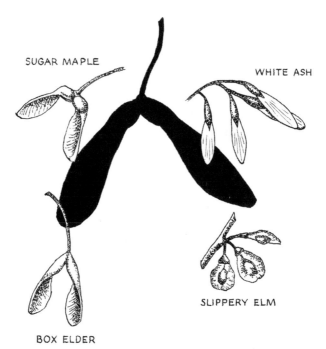

SUGAR MAPLE

WHITE ASH

SLIPPERY ELM

BOX ELDER

Samara, a nonsplitting winged fruit (e.g., maple, ash, elm). (AF)

RECOMMENDED PLANTINGS FOR THE NORTHEAST

Eastern Redcedar (*Juniperus virginiana*)

Eastern redcedar (actually a juniper) is an excellent choice for providing food, cover, and nest sites for songbirds. This hardy native tree thrives as far north as zone 2 and occurs naturally as far south as Georgia and west to Minnesota and Texas. Only female plants produce the blue, berry-like cones, so it is best to plant several trees to improve the chances of good fruit crops. The fruit ripens in September and stays on the tree through the winter. Eastern redcedar usually grows to about 50 feet tall with a spread of 15–25 feet, but some trees are much taller. Plant redcedar in open, sunlit sites. It prefers limestone-derived soils, but it will grow in a variety of sites and frequently thrives in poor, overgrazed, and eroded soils. The dense, prickly branches provide excellent nest sites for the northern mockingbird, brown thrasher, gray catbird, chipping sparrow, and many others. As their name suggests, cedar waxwings frequent this useful tree. They not only consume fruit but also nest and roost in its dense cover. At least 54 species are known to eat redcedar fruit.

EASTERN REDCEDAR *Juniperus virginiana* **(AF)**

Eastern White Pine (*Pinus strobus*)

Eastern white pine's importance as a lumber tree is legendary, but its significance to wildlife is often overlooked. Its large cones produce an abundant crop of highly nutritious seed that is readily consumed by at least 38 bird species. Some birds, such as the red crossbill, favor white pine over all other sources of food. Birds that cannot actively shred cones will pick the seed from the ground. Cones usually appear when the trees are about 10 years old. White pine will often grow 100 feet tall with a spread of 20–25 feet, which ranks it as the largest conifer in the Northeast.

EASTERN WHITE PINE *Pinus strobus* **(AF)**

Its usefulness to birds does not stop with its seed crops, as its billowy foliage and branch structure provide abundant nest sites. Mourning doves favor white pine for nesting, and many cavity-nesters, such as chickadees, nuthatches, and woodpeckers, excavate cavities in its soft wood. White pine is hardy north to zone 4 and occurs naturally from Newfoundland to Minnesota and southward in the Appalachians to Georgia.

Black Cherry (*Prunus serotina*)

Few trees attract as many birds as our native black cherry. This rapidly maturing deciduous tree grows to about 50 feet tall with a spread of 30 feet and may live from 150 to 700 years. In early spring it has many drooping flower spikes. Abundant small, dark purple fruit become available in early summer. Most black cherries have heavy fruit crops every 3 or 4 years. Black cherry grows wild in open fields and thickets throughout most of eastern North America, from Quebec and North Dakota, and south to Texas and Florida. It is hardy as far north as

BLACK CHERRY *Prunus serotina* (AF)

zone 2 and grows in a variety of soils, ranging from rich and moist to light and sandy. Avoid planting cherries in places where fruit will fall on driveways, sidewalks, and patios. Although this cherry offers few suitable nest sites and sparse cover, at least 47 species readily consume the fruit, including the ruffed grouse, Northern flicker, red-headed woodpecker, northern mockingbird, rose-breasted grosbeak, and white-throated sparrow.

Flowering Crabapples (*Malus* spp.)

Flowering crabapples are highly decorative, small deciduous trees. One species, sweet flowering crabapple (*Malus coronaria*), is native from southern Ontario to Tennessee, but most of the 80 or more cultivated varieties (cultivars) available in northeastern North America are hybrids from crossing several alien species. Crabapples are usually hardy only as far north as zone 4, but that still leaves many varieties that are useful for planting even in northern

Maine and southern Canada. Crabapples vary in height from 8 to 50 feet. Some, like sargent crabapple (*M. sargentii*), are twice as broad as they are tall. They all require open, sunlit sites, but tolerate a variety of soils. For attracting the greatest variety of birds, it is best to select trees that have small fruits, because these are most readily plucked and swallowed. You should also try to choose crabapples that hold their fruits into winter when food supplies from other trees become scarce. Some of the types best known for these

FLOWERING CRABAPPLES *Malus* spp. (AF)

characteristics are Arnold, Bob White, Donald Wyman, Japanese, Dorothea, Hillieri, Jackie, Mary, Potter, sargent, Siberian, snowbank, Toringo, drifter, and tea.

Flowering Dogwood (*Cornus florida*)

Flowering dogwood is one of the most important and widely distributed wildlife trees in the eastern United States. Showy white flower clusters and brilliant red fruits enhance this dogwood's graceful form. Flowering dogwood is hardy in zone 5 and occurs as a common understory tree in eastern deciduous forests from Maine to Kansas and south to Florida and Texas. Fruits

FLOWERING DOGWOOD *Cornus florida* (AF)

are first available in August and most are usually consumed by November. Flowering dogwood's fall foliage varies from russet to deep red. Since these attractive native trees usually grow only to 10–30 feet with a spread of 25 feet, they are an excellent choice for small properties. They are also one of the best selections for enhancing deciduous woodlands, border, and larger residential properties. Where the fungus dogwood anthracnosis occurs, the trees should be planted in full sun. Mulching and pruning diseased wood can also provide some measure of control. Flowering dogwood grows in a wide variety of sites, including thoroughly drained uplands and moist stream banks. Among the 36 species that eat the nutritious fruit are 6 species of thrush, northern flicker, pileated woodpecker, summer tanager, evening grosbeak, and pine grosbeak.

Hawthorns (*Crataegus* spp.)

These small, round-topped deciduous trees make up a widespread group of similar species. With the exception of a few distinctive types, hawthorn identification baffles even the most astute botanists. Hawthorns grow best in open, sunlit habitats. In the spring hawthorns are covered with white and pink flowers, followed by an abundant crop of small orange or red pome fruits. As a group, hawthorns are easily recognized by single large, unbranched spines that grow from leaf axils. They

HAWTHORNS *Crataegus* spp. (AF)

are an excellent choice for yards and property borders, but you must take care not to let them become shaded by competing vegetation. Hawthorn fruits are readily consumed by at least 18 bird species, especially cedar waxwings. Their dense, forked branches provide choice nesting places for robins, cardinals, blue jays, and others. Cockspur hawthorn (*Crataegus crus-galli*) and Washington hawthorn (*C. phaenopyrum*) are two native species that are especially useful for attracting birds and these are often available at nurseries. Both bear prolifically, and are hardy as far north as zone 5.

White Oak (*Quercus alba*)

This magnificent tree may grow 100 feet tall with a massive trunk 4 feet in diameter. White oaks that grow in open areas may develop massive canopy spreads of up to 165 feet across, but such trees will not grow as tall as forest oaks. Where there is ample sun and water, white oaks will grow relatively fast, and under optimal conditions they may live for 500 years or more. This is certainly not a tree for a small urban yard, but where space permits, few trees are as grand as this fine native giant. White oak produces an annual acorn crop and these are very important food for mammals and birds. Wild turkeys, mallards, and wood ducks swallow whole acorns, but smaller birds such as flickers, red-headed woodpeckers, and blue jays must peck open the acorns. At least 28 species consume acorns. Several, including the turkey, ruffed grouse, and northern bobwhite, also consume tender leaf buds. White oak is hardy north through zone 6 and occurs from southern Maine to southeastern Minnesota and south to eastern Texas and Florida.

WHITE OAK *Quercus alba* **(AF)**

Downy Serviceberry (*Amelanchier arborea*)

Serviceberries, named for their habit of flowering about the time of Easter, are the small trees and shrubs that give the first color to the spring woods. They are also known as *juneberry* because their fruit often appears in June, and they are also called *shadbush* or *shadblow* because shad (fish) often spawn during this season. Their white flowers decorate spring woodlands from March to June, usually weeks before the canopy closes. By June, small purple fruits begin to appear. Downy service-

DOWNY SERVICEBERRY *Amelanchier arborea* **(AF)**

berry is one of the most common and widely distributed members of this important native group. It is hardy as far north as zone 3, and ranges from Quebec south to Florida and west to eastern Minnesota and eastern Texas. This forest understory tree grows 20–40 feet tall with a spread of 30 feet and can develop a trunk 16 inches in diameter. Serviceberry is an excellent choice for shady yards or as an additional planting in northeastern woodlands. Commercial stock is available from nurseries, but where it is abundant, transplanting root cuttings that are approximately 3–6 inches long can easily propagate it. Downy serviceberry is an important food for at least 19 species of woodland birds, including the ruffed grouse, hairy woodpecker, wood thrush, red-eyed vireo, scarlet tanager, and rose-breasted grosbeak. Closely related members of this genus, such as shadblow serviceberry (*Amelanchier canadensis*) and smooth serviceberry (*A. laevis*), are equally useful for attracting woodland birds. Nurseries often sell shrub forms of these species.

Highbush Blueberry (*Vaccinium corymbosum*)

This dense deciduous shrub provides food and useful nest sites for many birds. Highbush blueberry grows 6–15 feet tall and 5 feet wide, and is native along the Atlantic coast from eastern Maine to northern Florida. It is found west through northern Ohio, southern Wisconsin, and southern Ontario, and may be cultivated as far north as zone 4. Temperatures below –20 degrees Fahrenheit (–29 degrees Celsius) can kill small plants. High-

HIGHBUSH BLUEBERRY *Vaccinium corymbosum* **(AF)**

bush blueberry prefers soils that are slightly acidic, sunlit, and well drained. It is ideal for planting in clumps in meadows or for creating hedges. Since it is shade intolerant, it should not be planted near larger trees. Most plants bear fruit when 8–10 years old, although under ideal conditions some plants fruit when only 3 years old. Its dense growth form provides excellent cover, and it is a favorite nest site for the gray catbird. Blueberries are a preferred food for the American robin, eastern bluebird, orchard oriole, and at least 34 other species.

Brambles (*Rubus* spp.)

Brambles is the collective name for blackberries, raspberries, dewberries, and thimbleberries, which comprise this complex of hundreds of closely related plants. Brambles vary greatly in height and tendency to form spiny dense tangles, but all produce fruit that is readily consumed by birds. At least 49 bird species eat bramble fruit. They are highly preferred by the wild turkey, ruffed grouse, northern bobwhite, blue jay, gray catbird, veery, cedar waxwing, orioles, yellow-breasted chat, and many others. Brambles also provide dense

BRAMBLES *Rubus* spp. (AF)

cover and excellent nest sites safe from predators. Brambles are available at most nurseries or they can be transplanted easily from the field. For maximum fruiting and branching, they should be pruned and fertilized. Most bramble species native to the Northeast are hardy as far north as zone 4. Bramble patches planted at the edges of woodlands or corners of small properties are one of the best ways to increase the numbers and variety of thicket-nesting birds on your property.

Red-Osier Dogwood (*Cornus stolonifera*)

Red-osier dogwood reaches a maximum height of only 4–8 feet with a spread of 10 feet or more. This deciduous shrub provides dense cover during the summer and produces a large crop of small white drupes that are about $\frac{1}{4}$ inch in diameter. The fruits are first available in July, but most are consumed by birds or have fallen from the shrubs by October. Red-osier has bright red stems in

RED-OSIER DOGWOOD *Cornus stolonifera* (AF)

winter and spreads by creeping stolons that grow through the soil and rise nearby to produce new shrubs. Red-osier occurs as far north as the tree line in Canada. Warm temperatures seem to limit its southern distribution, as it is not found south of Washington, D.C. It is hardy in zone 2 and occurs west to California and Alaska. Red-osier fruits are readily eaten by at least 18 bird species, including the wild turkey, ruffed grouse, American robin, gray catbird, and purple finch. It grows in a great variety of soils, but is especially useful in most sites or as a streamside planting to reduce soil erosion.

American Elder (*Sambucus canadensis*)

American elder is an excellent choice for providing late-summer food and nesting cover in moist areas. This 3- to 10-foot-tall deciduous shrub with a spread of 12 feet produces abundant annual crops of tiny dark purple fruits that are readily consumed by at least 33 species of birds. American elder forms dense thickets along sunny pond and stream edges and other moist habitats. These provide excellent nesting habitat and shelter during extreme weather. It

AMERICAN ELDER *Sambucus canadensis* (AF)

has large white flower clusters from late June to August, and its fruit ripens from late July to September.

American elder is hardy north to zone 4 and grows naturally from Nova Scotia west to Manitoba and south to Georgia and Louisiana. It is best propagated from rooted cuttings or seeds. Young plants will grow only a few inches their first year, but individual canes may grow as much as 15 feet in subsequent years. Annual pruning will greatly improve fruit production. For this purpose, leave five or six 1-year canes and one or two older canes for each shrub. If space permits, leave some plants unpruned to provide dense nesting cover. For shady areas, scarlet elder (*Sambucus pubens*) is a good choice. Mixtures of both elders offer varied colors and a greater seasonal availability of fruit. The scarlet elder fruits from June through August, a full month earlier than American elder.

Winterberry (*Ilex verticillata*)

This deciduous shrub is named for its bright red fruits, which persist on the bare branches into the winter months. It is an excellent choice for providing a shrubby border; its abundant clusters of scarlet fruit make it attractive to humans and birds throughout the winter. Birds eat most of the fruit by spring. Winterberry grows about 15 feet tall and spreads a similar amount. It can tolerate some shade but does best in partial to full sun. It grows in a variety of soils, including wet areas. Like other hollies, there are male and female plants. Dwarf

WINTERBERRY *Ilex verticillata*, Marion Murfey (MM)

males are available to provide ample pollen. Winterberry is hardy to zone 5 and occurs from Maine to northern Florida. For more acidic soils, consider planting inkberry (*Ilex glabra*). This broadleaf evergreen shrub grows 6–8 feet tall and 8–10 feet wide. Plant this species between zones 4 and 9. The fruits of both hollies are eaten by the cedar waxwing, American robin, northern mockingbird, brown thrasher, and gray catbird.

Wild Grapes (*Vitis* spp.)

There are at least 20 different species and varieties of wild grapes in the Northeast. These climbing deciduous vines provide very attractive fruit and nest sites. At least 52 bird species eat wild grapes. Grape tangles are common nest sites for the eastern kingbird, northern mockingbird, gray catbird, and brown thrasher. The loose, peeling bark is a favorite nest-building material for at least 16 species, including the veery, cedar waxwing, northern cardinal, and 8 species of warbler. The best nest sites are where grapevines

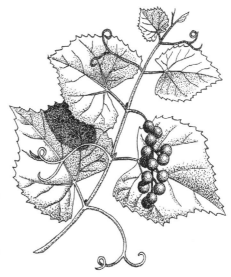

FOX GRAPE *Vitis labrusca* (AF)

smother large shrubs, creating dense thickets. Most grapes, such as fox grape (*Vitis labrusca*), grow best in open sunny areas where they find moist soils, but others, such as summer grape (*V. aestivalis*), grow in upland woods. Riverbank grape (*V. riparia*) is one of the hardiest and most widespread wild grapes growing along streams north through zone 3 to Quebec, south to Tennessee, and west to Manitoba and New Mexico.

American Mountain-Ash (*Sorbus americana*)

American mountain-ash is a moderate-sized deciduous tree or large shrub that reaches a maximum of 40 feet with a spread of 22 feet. It has blue-green foliage that turns a brilliant orange-red in the fall. Its large, showy white spring flowers and cluster of red fruit make this an attractive choice for both small urban yards and larger properties. It is hardy through zone 2, occurring in northern Quebec and south into the Appalachians of Georgia. It grows best in sunlit, moist soil, but also does well in thin mountain soils and light shade. American mountain-ash prefers slightly acidic soils, ranging from a pH of 4.7 to 6.0. Warm temperatures limit its southern distribution.

AMERICAN MOUNTAIN-ASH *Sorbus americana* (AF)

Fruits are usually available in August or September and continue through the winter, but they are such a common source of food for cedar waxwings, eastern bluebirds, gray catbirds, and at least 13 other species that they seldom last past early fall. Occasionally, the fruit ferments on the trees, intoxicating birds. Waxwings are noted for their vulnerability. For this reason, plant the tree away from roads. European mountain-ash (*Sorbus aucuparia*) is more available in the nursery trade and is a suitable substitute.

Red Mulberry (*Morus rubra*)

Few trees are as attractive to songbirds as red mulberry. At least 44 bird species consume the red fruits of this native deciduous tree. The fruits ripen from June to August and are usually consumed as soon as they become available. The inconspicuous green male and female flowers usually grow on different trees. Although pollen is spread by the wind, a nearby male tree may be necessary for a good fruit crop. Red mulberry grows 25–40 feet tall with a spread of 50 feet and thrives in a variety of habitats including open forest and thickets. Red mulberry is hardy as far north as zone 6, occurring from Massachusetts to southern Florida and west to southern Michigan and central Texas. It grows naturally in rich floodplain soils with a pH range from 6.0 to 7.5. Red mulberry is an excellent choice for a central backyard bird tree, but take care not to locate it near sidewalks or other areas where the accumulation of fallen fruit will be a problem.

RED MULBERRY *Morus rubra* (AF)

Avoid substituting white mulberry, also known as *Russian mulberry*. This invasive tree was introduced from Asia and is hybridizing with native red mulberry.

Inkberry (*Ilex glabra*)

There are relatively few native evergreen shrubs that survive in the Northeast, so bird gardeners should pay special attention to this native shrub (sometimes called *gallberry*). It prefers somewhat acidic and sandy soils; it tolerates shade and grows best in full sun. Inkberry can grow 6–10 feet tall and 10 feet wide and is densely covered in leathery, dark green leaves. The variety "Compacta" has a denser growth habit and a somewhat smaller form with a

INKBERRY *Ilex glabra* (VH)

height and spread of 4–6 feet. Like other members of the holly family, inkberry has both male and female plants, making it necessary to plant the shrub in clusters for best fruiting potential. It typically bears black (rarely white) fruit in the fall and holds these through the winter. These dense shrubs provide nesting habitat for mockingbirds and robins and the fruit are eaten by at least 9 species. Turkeys, mockingbirds, and robins especially like the fruit. The bluebirds, hermit thrush, rufous-sided towhee, and flickers also eat the fruit. Inkberry is hardy in zones 4–9.

Staghorn Sumac (*Rhus typhina*)

Staghorn sumac shrubs form brilliant scarlet clumps on the fall landscape, and their winter-persistent fruits are consumed by at least 21 bird species. This native deciduous shrub spreads from the original central plant at a rate of about 3 feet a year, eventually creating a large circular clone that may be 12 feet tall and 20 feet wide. Sumac clones begin to lose their vigor after about 15 years, but cutting stems back to the soil can rejuvenate them. The open nature of the stems and general absence of suitable forked branches create few good nest sites, but some ground-nesting birds find shelter under the sumac's shade. Staghorn sumac is hardy as far north as zone 4 and occurs on eroded and disturbed soils from Nova Scotia and the Gaspe Peninsula of Quebec south to North Carolina and west to Iowa. The closely related and equally

STAGHORN SUMAC *Rhus typhina* (AF)

important smooth sumac (*Rhus glabra*) occurs from southwestern Quebec to southern British Columbia and all contiguous 48 states.

Virginia Creeper (*Parthenocissus quinquefolia*)

This native deciduous vine produces small blue berries that are a favorite food for at least 35 bird species. In addition to thrushes and woodpeckers, several species of vireos and warblers also eat the fruits. Virginia creeper will climb the tallest trees, and although it sometimes smothers small shrubs, you should try encouraging it or at least tolerating it because of its great importance to birds. Virginia creeper is easy to identify even at great distances because it is the only vine that turns a brilliant, crimson color. It is hardy north through zone 4 and has a wide distribution from Quebec to Florida and west to Mexico. Virginia creeper readily climbs trellises and stone walls. It enhances woodlands or even isolated trees with brilliant fall color and bird-friendly fruit, which is available from August through the winter.

VIRGINIA CREEPER *Parthenocissus quinquefolia* **(AF)**

WOODBINE, P. 205

Other Good Choices for the Northeast

Name	Zone	Native (N) or Alien (A)	Height/spread (ft.)	Light	Preferred Soil	Fruit Period	Fruit Type	Remarks
Evergreen Trees								
ARBORVITAE, EASTERN (*Thuja occidentalis*)	4–7	N	20–40/10–15	Sun/half sun	Moist	Early fall/fall	Cone	Forms dense hedges; used as nest site by grackles, robin, and house finch; seeds are a preferred food for pine siskin
FIR, BALSAM (*Abies balsamea*)	4–6	N	40–60/15	Sun/shade	Moist	Late spring/early summer	Cone	A favorite nesting tree for robin and mourning dove; sensitive to smoke; not good for large cities; seeds eaten by at least 13 species, including evening grosbeak, purple finch, and pine grosbeak
HEMLOCK, EASTERN (*Tsuga canadensis*)	3–8	N	50–80/30	Variety	Moist loam	Early fall/fall	Cone	Very shade tolerant; preferred nest site for robin, blue jay, wood thrush; also important food tree for chickadees; forms hedges when trimmed; intolerant of air pollution

Species	Zones	Native	Height/Spread	Light	Soil	Fruiting season	Fruit	Remarks
HOLLY, AMERICAN (*Ilex opaca*)	6–9	N	40–50/20–40	Shade/part shade	Dry	Early fall, persistent until spring	Red drupes	Male and female flowers on separate plants; highly ornamental, makes excellent hedges or specimen tree. Difficult to transplant, plant in protected areas in north. At least 13 species use it for food, cover, and nesting
PINE, PITCH (*Pinus rigida*)	5–7	N	40–60/50	Sun	Dry/moist	Late fall/summer	Cone	Best pine for poor, sandy, or even gravelly locations
PINE, RED (*Pinus resinosa*)	2–7	N	To 80/20–25	Sun/half sun	Dry/drained	Late summer/fall	Cone	Heavy seed crops occur every 3–7 years; very hardy, will grow in even poor soil; at least 48 bird species eat the seeds of this and other pines
SPRUCE, COLORADO BLUE (*Picea pungens*)	3–8	N	80–100/15	Sun/half sun	Drained	Early fall/winter	Cone	Important nesting and winter cover; at least 19 species eat seeds from these and other spruce; preferred food for crossbills, evening grosbeak, and red-breasted nuthatch
SPRUCE, RED (*Picea rubens*)	2–5	N	60–70/30–40	Sun/shade	Moist/drained	Early fall/fall	Cone	
SPRUCE, WHITE (*Picea glauca*)	2–6	N	80–100/10–20	Sun/half sun	Drained	Late summer/late fall	Cone	

Other Good Choices for the Northeast—cont.

Name	Zone	Native (N) or Alien (A)	Height/spread (ft.)	Light	Preferred Soil	Fruit Period	Fruit Type	Remarks
Large Deciduous Trees								
ASH, BLACK (Fraxinus nigra)	2–8	N	40–70/25	Sun	Moist/drained	Early summer/early fall	Samara	Moderate value to wildlife; cardinal and pine grosbeak are attracted to seeds
ASH, GREEN (Fraxinus pennsylvanica)	2–9	N	30–50/70	Sun/half sun	Moist/dry/drained	Early fall	Samara	Tolerant of city conditions; a good landscaping species; seeds are a preferred food of wood duck, bobwhite, evening grosbeak, purple finch, and pine grosbeak
ASH, WHITE (Fraxinus americana)	4–9	N	70–100/50	Sun/half sun	Dry/rich/moist	Early–late fall	Samara	Winged seed is preferred food for evening grosbeak, purple finch, and others; hardy, disease resistant, and attractive for lawns
ASPEN, BIGTOOTH (Populus grandidentata)	4–9	N	30–70/40	Sun/half sun	Dry/moist/drained	Late spring/early summer	Capsule	Buds and catkins are a preferred food of ruffed grouse, and buds are readily

144

Species	Zones		Height/Spread	Sun	Soil	Flowering	Fruit	Notes
ASPEN, QUAKING (*Populus tremuloides*)	1–8	N	40–60/30	Sun/half sun	Dry/moist	Late spring/early summer	Capsule	eaten by evening grosbeak and purple finch; catkins eaten by at least 8 bird species; especially important for ruffed grouse
BEECH, AMERICAN (*Fagus grandifolia*)	4–8	N	40–70/25	Sun/shade	Moist/drained	Early–late fall	Nut	Nut crop provides excellent food for many birds and mammals; excludes grass beneath it, but forms imposing appearance with spreading crown; at least 25 bird species eat its fruit
BIRCH, GRAY (*Betula populifolia*)	5–6	N	20–30/10	Sun	Waste lands/moist/dry	Fall	Samara	Good seed crops every 1–2 years; seeds eaten by at least 12 species, including wood duck, ruffed grouse, goldfinch, juncos, pine siskin, and chickadees
BIRCH, PAPER (*Betula papyrifera*)	2–7	N	50–80/30	Sun/half sun	Moist/drained	Late summer/early fall	Samara	
BIRCH, SWEET (*Betula lenta*)	4–7	N	50–60/40	Sun/shade	Moist/fertile/	Late summer/	Samara	Good seed crops every 1–2 years; seeds eaten by at least

145

Other Good Choices for the Northeast—cont.

Name	Zone	Native (N) or Alien (A)	Height/spread (ft.)	Light	Preferred Soil	Fruit Period	Fruit Type	Remarks
BIRCH, YELLOW (*Betula alleghaniensis*)	4–7	N	60–70/30	Sun/half sun	Cool/moist/drained	Late summer/fall	Samara	12 species, including wood duck, ruffed grouse, goldfinch, juncos, pine siskin, and chickadees
BUTTERNUT (*Juglans cinerea*)	4–7	N	40–60/70	Sun	Moist/dry/drained	Early–late fall	Nut	Nuts are favorite of Carolina wren, chickadees, nuthatches, and red-bellied woodpecker; fast growing
COTTONWOOD, EASTERN (*Populus deltoides*)	2–9	N	80–100/70	Sun/half sun	Moist	Spring/early summer	Capsule	Soft wood excavated for nest sites by woodpeckers; prefers floodplains and riverbanks
GUM (TUPELO), BLACK (*Nyssa sylvatica*)	5–9	N	40–60/75	Sun/half sun	Moist/dry	Early fall	Purple drupe	Especially favored by thrush and woodpeckers, with at least 37 species eating the fruit; excellent for ponds and bottomlands

Species	Zone	Native	Height/Spread	Light	Moisture	Season	Fruit	Notes
HACKBERRY, COMMON (*Celtis occidentalis*)	5–9	N	30–50/50	Sun/shade	Dry	Early fall/late winter	Red or purple drupe	Especially useful to birds because fruits often persist into winter. At least 25 species eat the fruit; often used as windbreak or street planting
HICKORY, MOCKERNUT (*Carya tomentosa*)	5–8	N	40–50/39	Sun/shade	Drained	Fall	Nut	At least 18 bird species eat hickory nuts—frequently cleaning up after squirrels, which break open the nuts; among the birds eating hickory nuts are cardinal, white-breasted nuthatch, rufous-sided towhee, red-bellied woodpecker, bobwhite, ring-necked pheasant, and wild turkey
HICKORY, PIGNUT (*Carya glabra*)	5–8	N	50–70/70	Sun/shade	Drained	Fall	Nut	
HICKORY, SHAGBARK (*Carya ovata*)	5–8	N	70–80/50	Sun/half sun	Dry/light drained	Early fall	Nut	
LARCH, EASTERN (*Larix laricina*)	1	N	40–80	Sun	Moist	Late summer/early fall	Cone	Frequent nest tree and an important seed tree for crossbills and purple finch

147

Other Good Choices for the Northeast—*cont.*

Name	Zone	Native (N) or Alien (A)	Height/spread (ft.)	Light	Preferred Soil	Fruit Period	Fruit Type	Remarks
MAPLE, BOX ELDER (*Acer negundo*)	2	N	50–75	Sun/shade	Moist/tolerates poor soil	Late summer/fall	Brown samara	Preferred winter food of evening grosbeak and purple finch; very hardy, fast growing, but short-lived; used in shelterbelt plantings
MAPLE, RED (*Acer rubrum*)	4–9	N	50–70/30	Sun/half sun	Moist	Early summer/summer	Red samara	Spectacular red fall color; very hardy and may live 150 years
MAPLE, SILVER (*Acer saccharinum*)	4–9	N	60–80/50	Sun/half sun	Moist/dry	Early summer	Green or red samara	Grows fast, but relatively short-lived; buds favored by evening grosbeak; city tolerant
MAPLE, SUGAR (*Acer saccharum*)	4–8	N	69–100/40	Sun/shade	Fertile/moist/drained	Early summer/fall	Samara	Intolerant of city conditions; source of maple syrup; orange-yellow fall foliage; good nest tree for robins and vireos

OAK, BLACK (*Quercus velutina*)	5–8	N	80–150/80	Sun/half sun	Rich/moist/drained	Early–late fall	Acorn	Popular shade tree that may live for 200 years; acorn crops about every third year; preferred food for turkey, bobwhite, blue jay, and rufous-sided towhee
OAK, BUR (*Quercus macrocarpa*)	4–9	N	80–150/30	Sun	Dry/drained	Fall	Acorn	Tolerates city conditions; poor soils; a favorite food of the wood duck
OAK, NORTHERN RED (*Quercus rubra*)	4–9	N	60–80/70	Sun/half sun	Moist/rich/drained	Early–late fall	Acorn	Tolerates city conditions; acorns eaten by many birds; preferred by turkey, grouse, grackles; excellent shade tree; 3–5 years between acorn crops
OAK, PIN (*Quercus palustris*)	5–8	N	60–75/40	Sun/half sun	Moist	Early–late fall	Acorn	Useful ornamental in yards, along streets for unusually broad crown; at least 29 bird species eat the acorns of this and other oaks
OAK, SCARLET (*Quercus coccinea*)	5–9	N	70–80/50	Sun/half sun	Dry/sandy	Fall	Acorn	Preferred food for grackles, blue jay, turkey; ornamental use for red fall color. Biennial acorn crop
PERSIMMON, COMMON (*Diospyros virginiana*)	5–9	N	30–50/35	Sun	Dry/moist/drained	Early–late fall	Orange-yellow berry	Fruit preferred by mockingbird, gray catbird, and cedar waxwing; disease resistant

Other Good Choices for the Northeast—*cont.*

Name	Zone	Native (N) or Alien (A)	Height/spread (ft.)	Light	Preferred Soil	Fruit Period	Fruit Type	Remarks
POPLAR, BALSAM (*Populus balsamifera*)	2–9	N	60–80/25	Sun	Dry/ drained	Early summer	Capsule	A hardy northern tree; buds are a favorite food for ruffed grouse
SASSAFRAS, COMMON (*Sassafras albidum*)	5–8	N	10–50/50	Sun	Dry/ moist	Late summer/ fall	Blue drupe	At least 22 bird species eat this fruit; it is preferred by pileated woodpecker, eastern kingbird, gray catbird, eastern bluebird, and red-eyed vireo; colorful orange leaves in fall
SWEETGUM, AMERICAN (*Liquidambar styraciflua*)	6–9	N	50–120/40	Sun/ half sun	Dry/ moist/ drained	Fall	Com- pound capsule	Seeds favored by finches, sparrows, turkey, mourning dove, and bobwhite; heavy seed crop every 3 years; highly disease resistant
TULIP TREE, NORTH AMERICAN (*Liriodenfron tulipifera*)	6–9	N	60–150/50	Sun	Moist/ drained	Fall	Samara	A beautiful ornamental; flower nectar is used by ruby-throated hummingbird; hardy; a good street tree

Species	Zone	N/A	Size (ht/spread)	Sun	Soil	Season	Fruit	Notes
WALNUT, BLACK (*Juglans nigra*)	5–9	N	70–120/70	Sun/half sun	Rich bottom-land/drained	Early–late fall	Nut	Edible nuts and very valuable wood. Excellent specimen tree. Nuts preferred by many birds and mammals; roots release toxins that may kill some plants; should be isolated
WILLOW, BLACK (*Salix nigra*)	5–9	N	To 50/25–35	Sun	Moist/wet	Spring/summer	Capsule	Useful to birds as a nest site; good naturalizer for low, wet ground; problems include invasive roots; keep distant from dwellings; buds are preferred food of ruffed grouse and pine siskin

Small Deciduous Trees

Species	Zone	N/A	Size (ht/spread)	Sun	Soil	Season	Fruit	Notes
APPLE, COMMON (*Malus pumila*)	4–7	A	20–30/40	Sun	Clay loam/variety	Fall	Green-red pome	Used for nest site by eastern bluebird, red-eyed vireo, great crested flycatcher, and American robin; fruits eaten by many birds; fragrant spring blossoms
CHERRY, PIN (*Prunus pensylvanica*)	2–8	N	10–30/30	Sun	Dry	Summer/early fall	Red drupe	Grows best in disturbed or waste places. Eastern bluebird attracted to fruits, which are edible; best planted in clumps away from walks and patios; very valuable wildlife food

Other Good Choices for the Northeast—*cont.*

Name	Zone	Native (N) or Alien (A)	Height/spread (ft.)	Light	Preferred Soil	Fruit Period	Fruit Type	Remarks
CHOKECHERRY, COMMON (*Prunus virginiana*)	2–8	N	6–20/25	Sun	Rich/drained	Summer/fall	Red/black drupe	A pioneer species in old fields, along streams, and pastures. Good boundary planting along fences, and so on; at least 43 bird species eat its fruit; wilted leaves of all cherries are poisonous to livestock
DOGWOOD, ALTERNATE-LEAF (*Cornus alternifolia*)	4–8	N	20–30/20	Sun/shade	Moist/rich/dry drained	Summer/early fall	Blue-black drupe	An attractive small tree or shrub; make excellent hedge, or plant in forest; at least 34 bird species eat the fruit, and it is a preferred food for downy woodpecker, brown thrasher, wood thrush, eastern bluebird, and cedar waxwing
HAWTHORN, COCKSPUR (*Crataegus crus-galli*)	5–7	N	20–30/30	Sun	Well drained	Late summer/late winter	Red pome	White flowers in May; fruits persist through winter

152

Name	Zone	Origin	Height/Spread	Light	Soil	Fruit Season	Fruit	Notes
HOP HORNBEAM, AMERICAN (Ostrya virginiana)	5–9	N	20–45/40	Sun/half sun	Dry/drained	Late summer/fall	Brown nutlet	Fruits highly preferred by ruffed grouse; useful understory tree with its tolerance to shade; known for strong wood
HORNBEAM, AMERICAN (Musclewood) (Carpinus caroliniana)	2–9	N	20–40/50	Sun/shade	Dry/moist	Late summer/fall	Brown nutlet	Seed preferred by ruffed grouse; attractive trunk
MOUNTAIN-ASH, EUROPEAN (Sorbus aucuparia)	2–7	A	30–45/22	Sun	Dry/moist/drained	Fall/late fall	Yellow-scarlet pome	Similar to American mountain-ash; many cultivated varieties, a readily available and useful tree
MOUNTAIN-ASH, NORTHERN (Sorbus decora)	2–8	N	To 15/15	Sun	Dry/moist/drained	Early fall/winter	Orange pome	Sometimes grows as a shrub. Most northern distribution of our native species

Evergreen Shrubs

Name	Zone	Origin	Height/Spread	Light	Soil	Fruit Season	Fruit	Notes
HUCKLEBERRY, BOX (Gaylussacia brachycera)	6, 7	N	To 2/5	Sun	Dry/acid/drained	Summer/late summer	Black berry	51 bird species are known to eat the fruit of huckleberries; these low shrubs are frequent nest sites; berries eaten by ruffed grouse, flicker, blue jay, and red-headed woodpecker
JUNIPER, CHINESE (Juniperus chinensis)	5–9	A	2–12/20	Sun/half sun	Dry/moist/drained	Persistent	Blue-green berry	At least 19 cultivated varieties are known; fruits appear only on female plants

Other Good Choices for the Northeast—cont.

Name	Zone	Native (N) or Alien (A)	Height/spread (ft.)	Light	Preferred Soil	Fruit Period	Fruit Type	Remarks
Cultivars of Chinese juniper:								
Hetzii juniper	5–9	A	10–12/12	Sun/half sun	Dry/moist/drained	Persistent	Blue-green berry	Rapid growth, spreads to 12–15 ft., with blue-green foliage
Pfitzerana juniper	5–9	A	To 6/10–15	Sun	Dry/moist/drained	Persistent	Blue-green berry	Vase-shaped form with spreading branches; the most prolific fruiter
Sargentii juniper	5–9	A	To 2/6–9	Sun	Dry/moist/drained	Persistent	Blue-green berry	Spreads to over 6 ft. wide
JUNIPER, COMMON (*Juniperus communis*)	2–6	N	1–4/3–20	Sun	Sterile	Early–late fall	Blue-black berry	Only female plant has berries; cultivated variety *depressa* (Canadian) juniper is vase-shaped, 3–4 feet tall; seven cultivated varieties; excellent cover for sandy, barren land
YEW, CANADA (*Taxus canadensis*)	2–8	N	To 3/8–10	Shade	Moist/drained/rich humus	Summer/early fall	Red drupe-like	Most useful as cover and nest site; sparse fruiting with only 7 bird species known to eat the fruit

Tall Deciduous Shrubs

ALDER, HAZEL (*Alnus serrulata*)	5–8	N	6–12/10–20	Sun	Moist/ swampy	Late summer/ fall	Cone	Useful naturalizer for ponds, stream borders; reproduces quickly in full sun; seeds important food
ALDER, SPECKLED (*Alnus rugosa*)	5–9	N	15–25/13	Sun	Moist/ swampy	Late summer/ fall	Cone	for goldfinches, pine siskin, and redpolls; fruit persists into winter
BAYBERRY, NORTHERN (*Myrica pensylvanica*)	2–6	N	3–8/5–12	Sun/ half sun	Dry/ sandy	Early summer/ summer	Gray waxy berries	Hardy plant that grows well in swamp soils or sand dunes; berries attract at least 26 bird species; red-winged blackbird commonly uses it for nesting; aromatic; much fruit; coastal
BUTTONBUSH, COMMON (*Cephalanthus occidentalis*)	5–10	N	3–12/8	Sun/ shade	Wet	Early fall/ early winter	Brown nutlike capsule	May form dense stands providing nesting sites for wetland birds; 7 types of waterfowl eat these seeds; ruby-throated hummingbird readily feeds at its flowers; often grows in standing water
CHOKEBERRY, BLACK (*Aronia melanocarpa*)	5–9	N	To 10/10	Sun/ half sun	Moist/ dry	Late summer/ late fall	Black berry	Fruits eaten by at least 12 bird species, and preferred by cedar waxwing and brown thrasher; berries persist into the winter; also notable for brilliant fall foliage

Other Good Choices for the Northeast—cont.

Name	Zone	Native (N) or Alien (A)	Height/spread (ft.)	Light	Preferred Soil	Fruit Period	Fruit Type	Remarks
CHOKEBERRY, RED (*Aronia arbutifolia*)	5–9	N	2–8/5	Sun/half sun	Wet/dry	Late summer/late fall	Red berry	
CRABAPPLE, SARGENT (*Malus sargentii*)	5–8	A	5–8/8–15	Sun	Well-drained	Late summer/early winter	Red pome	May grow twice as wide as tall; pruned, it forms a hedge; profuse white blooms in May
CRABAPPLE, TORINGO (*Malus sieboldii*)	5–9	A	3–10/10	Sun	Well-drained	Fall/late winter	Red-yellow pome	White flowers; sometimes grows as small tree; winter-persistent fruits
ELDER, SCARLET (*Sambucus pubens*)	5–8	N	2–12/13	Sun	Dry/rocky/drained	Early summer/early fall	Red berry	At least 23 bird species eat these colorful fruits; it is a preferred food of red-bellied woodpecker, American robin, veery, and rose-breasted grosbeak; highly decorative with abundant red berries. European *S. racemosa* is similar

Common name (scientific name)	Zones	Native	Height/spread	Light	Soil/moisture	Bloom/fruit time	Fruit	Comments
HAWTHORN, ONE-FLOWER (*Crataegus uniflora*)	7–9	N	3–8	Sun/half sun	Dry/sandy	Fall	Yellow/red pome	At least 36 bird species eat hawthorn fruit; this shrubby species provides good nest sites for birds, such as willow flycatcher
HAZEL, AMERICAN (*Corylus americana*)	5–9	N	To 10/7–12	Sun	Dry/moist	Summer/fall	Brown nut	Nuts preferred by ruffed grouse, ring-necked pheasant, blue jay, and hairy woodpecker; nuts survive into winter; also good cover
ROSE, PASTURE (*Rosa carolina*)	5–9	N	5–7/4–6	Sun	Dry	Summer/early fall Persistent over winter	Scarlet hip	Dense thickets provide excellent nest sites; rose hips are eaten by at least 20 bird species, and are preferred by mockingbird, Swainson's thrush, and cedar waxwing
ROSE, SWAMP (*Rosa palustris*)	5–8	N	To 8/3	Sun	Damp	Late summer/early fall	Scarlet hip	
SERVICEBERRY, ALLEGHENY (*Amelanchier laevis*)	4–9	N	20–25/25	Sun/half sun	Moist to wet	June–August	Purple-black pome	At least 36 bird species are known to eat serviceberries; these two shrub forms offer abundant summer foods
SERVICEBERRY, SHADBLOW (*Amelanchier canadensis*)	5–7	N	20–25/10	Sun/half sun	Swamps	Early-late/summer	Purple pome	

Other Good Choices for the Northeast—cont.

Name	Zone	Native (N) or Alien (A)	Height/spread (ft.)	Light	Preferred Soil	Fruit Period	Fruit Type	Remarks
SUMAC, SHINING (WINGED) (*Rhus copallina*)	5–9	N	4–10/10	Sun	Dry/ rocky	Fall	Red drupe	31 bird species are known to eat the fruits of sumac, especially catbird, wood thrush, eastern bluebird, and starling. Sumac fruits remain on branches into late winter and thus serve as "emergency" food
SUMAC, SMOOTH (*Rhus glabra*)	2–8	N	10–15/8	Sun	Variety/ tolerates poor soils	Late summer/ fall	Red drupe	
VIBURNUM, AMERICAN HIGHBUSH CRANBERRY (*Viburnum trilobum*)	2–7	N	6–15/12	Sun	Moist/ dry/ drained	Fall/ spring	Red drupe	A very hardy shrub useful for borders and hedges. The fruit survives the winter and thus offers a late-winter emergency food. It is preferred by only ruffed grouse, brown thrasher, and cedar waxwing, but an additional 29 bird species occasionally eat the fruit.

Plant	Zone		Size	Light	Soil	Fruiting	Fruit	Notes
VIBURNUM, ARROWWOOD (*Viburnum dentatum*)	2–8	N	To 15/10	Sun/half sun	Moist	Late summer/late fall	Blue drupe	Excellent cover and nesting sites; forms dense thickets; tolerates city pollution; useful planting for pond and stream edges
VIBURNUM, BLACKHAW (*Viburnum prunifolium*)	3–9	N	8–15/8–12	Sun/shade	Dry/moist/drained	Fall/spring	Blue-black drupe	Reddish fall color and attractive white spring flowers; at least 8 bird species eat these winter-persistent fruits
VIBURNUM, HOBBLE BUSH (*Viburnum alnifolium*)	4–7	N	To 10/12	Shade	Moist	Summer/fall	Purple drupe	Useful understory planting in woodland; fruits eaten by at least 6 bird species
VIBURNUM, MAPLELEAF (*Viburnum acerifolium*)	4–8	N	3–6/4	Sun/shade	Dry/drained	Summer/winter	Purple drupe	Highly tolerant of different soil and light conditions; at least 10 bird species are known to eat this fruit
VIBURNUM, NANNYBERRY (*Viburnum lentago*)	2–8	N	8–25/10	Sun/shade	Dry/moist/drained	Late summer/fall	Blue-black drupe	Forms dense clumps and can be pruned to form hedges; very hardy plant with wide range; at least 11 bird species eat these winter-persistent blue-black drupes
VIBURNUM, WITHEROD (*Viburnum cassinoides*)	2–8	N	6–12/5–6	Sun/shade	Moist	Early fall/winter	Blue-black drupe	Salt tolerant; good coastal planting; ornamental flowers and fruits; at least 9 types of bird eat this fruit

Other Good Choices for the Northeast—cont.

Name	Zone	Native (N) or Alien (A)	Height/spread (ft.)	Light	Preferred Soil	Fruit Period	Fruit Type	Remarks
WILLOW, PUSSY (*Salix discolor*)	2–8	N	10–20/12–15	Sun	Low/ moist	Spring/ late spring	Capsule	Buds eaten by ruffed grouse; favorite nest site for American goldfinch
WINTERBERRY, COMMON (*Ilex verticillata*)	4–8	N	5–15/15	Sun/ half sun	Wet/ rich/ slightly acidic	Late summer/ fall	Red berry	Attractive fruits in fall, survive in winter; many birds attracted by berries, including mockingbird, catbird, brown thrasher, and hermit thrush
Small Deciduous Shrubs								
BLACKBERRY, ALLEGHENY (*Rubus alleghениensis*)	3–9	N	3–8/4–8	Sun	Drained	Summer/ early fall	Black dru- pelets	Like other members of the raspberry genus, this is a very important late-summer bird food; at least 40 bird species eat raspberry/blackberry fruit in the Northeast
BLUEBERRY, LOWBUSH (*Vaccinium angustifolium*)	3–8	N	To 2/2	Sun	Acid/ drained	Early summer/ fall	Blue berry	Blueberries are very important wildlife food; no fewer than 37 bird species are known to eat blueberries, and they are preferred food for 24 of these

Name	Zones		Height/Spread	Light	Soil	Fruiting season	Fruit	Notes
BUCKTHORN, ALDERLEAF (*Rhamnus alnifolia*)	5–9	N	2–3/4	Shade	Damp	Late summer/fall	Black drupe	Dark fruits and leaves; highly ornamental; dense foliage makes this plant good in border plantings, 15 bird species eat the berries, including mockingbird, pileated woodpecker, and brown thrasher
CORALBERRY (*Symphoricarpos orbiculatus*)	2–6	N	2–5/6	Sun/shade	Dry/drained/moist	Early fall/early winter	Purple/red berry	Hummingbirds attracted to flowers; this hardy shrub forms dense thickets and is useful in erosion control; at least 14 bird species eat the colorful berries
CURRANT, AMERICAN BLACK (*Ribes americanum*)	5–8	N	To 5/3–4	Sun/half sun	Dry/moist/drained	Early summer/early fall	Black berry	Attractive spreading shrub, but an alternate host for white-pine blister-rust disease; choice food for many birds, but plant away from white pine
DANGLEBERRY (*Gaylussacia frondosa*)	5–9	N	3–6/3–4	Sun	Acid/drained	Early summer/early fall	Dark blue berry	Attractive when used in borders and clumps. Berries eaten by ruffed grouse, mourning dove, mockingbird, and scarlet tanager, among others

Other Good Choices for the Northeast—cont.

Name	Zone	Native (N) or Alien (A)	Height/spread (ft.)	Light	Preferred Soil	Fruit Period	Fruit Type	Remarks
DEWBERRY, NORTHERN (*Rubus flagellaris*)	4–9	N	1–2/6–10	Full sun	Dry/ drained	Summer	Black dru- pelets	As with other members of the raspberry family, this shrub provides both important summer food and nest sites. At least 49 northern bird species eat raspberry fruit and 12 species nest in its shelter
HONEYSUCKLE, AMERICAN FLY (*Lonicera canadensis*)	4–8	N	3–5	Shade	Moist	Early– late summer	Red berry	Provides food and shelter for at least 20 bird species, including catbird, robins, and goldfinches
HONEYSUCKLE, SWAMP FLY (*Lonicera oblongifolia*)	4–6	N	2–5/2–4	Sun/ half sun	Moist	Summer/ early fall	Red berry	
HUCKLEBERRY, BLACK (*Gaylussacia baccata*)	2–7	N	To 3/3	Sun/ half sun	Dry/ rocky/ sandy	Summer/ early fall	Black berry	Attractive ornamental with edible sweet fruits; forms low shrub with crown to 4 ft.; at least 24 bird species eat huckleberry fruit

Name	Zones		Height/Spread	Sun	Soil	Bloom	Fruit	Notes
HUCKLEBERRY, DWARF (*Gaylussacia dumosa*)	5–9	N	1–2	Sun	Wet	Early summer/fall	Black berry	Useful ground cover in wet meadows and boggy areas
MEADOWSWEET, NARROWLEAF (*Spirea alba*)	4–7	N	1–4/3	Sun	Neutral damp	Summer/fall	Inconspicuous follicle	Important to wildlife as cover or nest site; forms thickets
RASPBERRY, BLACK (*Rubus occidentalis*)	4–7	N	3–6/4–8	Sun	Rocky/rich	Summer	Black drupelets	At least 40 bird species eat raspberry fruits in the Northeast; these thicket-forming shrubs grow in a wide variety of soils, but require full sun; at least 12 bird species nest in the protection of their prickly arching stems
RASPBERRY, RED (*Rubus idaeus*)	3–9	A	3–6/3–5	Sun	Drained/poor	Summer	Red drupelets	
ROSE, MEADOW (*Rosa blanda*)	2–7	N	1–4/4–6	Sun/half sun	Dry/moist/rocky	Summer/early fall	Scarlet hip	Persistent fruits and dense thicket growth provide important food and cover for wildlife; natural hedges; frequent nest site for many birds; valuable as food for at least 20 bird species

163

Other Good Choices for the Northeast—*cont.*

Name	Zone	Native (N) or Alien (A)	Height/spread (ft.)	Light	Preferred Soil	Fruit Period	Fruit Type	Remarks
ROSE, VIRGINIA (*Rosa virginiana*)	4–9	N	To 6/5	Sun	Dry/ moist/ drained/ sandy	Summer	Scarlet hip	
SERVICEBERRY, BARTRAM (*Amelanchier bartramiana*)	3–8	N	2–4/3–4	Sun/ half sun	Rich/ peaty/ variety	Early summer/ early fall	Purple black pome	Flower and fruits later than other serviceberries; berries are a preferred fruit for cedar waxwing, eastern bluebird, and many others; at least 40 Northeast bird species eat serviceberry fruit
SERVICEBERRY, RUNNING (*Amelanchier stolonifera*)	5–8	N	1–3/5	Sun	Dry/ moist/ drained	Summer	Black pome	Low, dense shrub that grows in sand and gravel; as with other serviceberries, this an important summer food for many songbirds
SNOWBERRY, COMMON (*Symphoricarpos albus*)	4–7	N	3–4/6	Sun/ shade	Dry/ drained/ moist/ limestone/ clay	Late summer/ late spring	White berry	Late fall and winter fruiting makes this a valuable wildlife plant. It tolerates city conditions and does well planted as a lawn border or

Plant				Light	Soil	Season	Fruit	Notes
								in the forest understory; at least 8 bird species eat the berries
SPICEBUSH, COMMON (*Lindera benzoin*)	5–9	N	2–8/10	Sun/shade	Fertile/moist/drained	Summer/fall	Red drupe	A forest understory tree; fruits eaten by at least 15 bird species; preferred food of wood thrush and veery
ST. JOHN'S-WORT, SHRUBBY (*Hypericum spathulatum*)	5–8	N	1–4/1–4	Half sun/shade	Rocky/sandy	Late summer/winter	Reddish brown achene	Wide crown makes it highly ornamental; especially attractive blooms; good as mixed border species; fruits eaten by 5 bird species, including ring-necked pheasant, bobwhite, and junco

Ground Covers (less than 12 in. tall)*

Plant				Light	Soil	Season	Fruit	Notes
BEARBERRY (*Arctostaphylos uva-ursi*)	2–6	N	E	Sun/half sun	Drained/acid	Summer/fall	Red berry	Fruit persistent to spring; can grow in very poor soil; forms large mats; 34 bird species are known to eat its fruit
BILBERRY, BOG (*Vaccinium uliginosum*)	1–6	N	E	Sun	Dry/drained	Late summer/fall	Blue berry	Alpine and bog habitats in northeastern United States; good for rock gardens and other shallow soils; at least 87 bird species are known to eat its blue berry fruits

Other Good Choices for the Northeast—cont.

Name	Zone	Native (N) or Alien (A)	Height/spread (ft.)	Light	Preferred Soil	Fruit Period	Fruit Type	Remarks
BUNCHBERRY (*Cornus canadensis*)	2–7	N	D	Shade	Cool/moist/acid	Late summer	Red drupe	Large white bracts look like flowers; preferred food for Philadelphia vireo, warbling vireo, and veery
COWBERRY (*Vaccinium vitis-idaea*)	1–6	N	E	Sun	Dry/drained	Fall	Red berry	An arctic ground-cover mat; occurs south to northern Maine and Minnesota; larger berries at lower elevations
CROWBERRY, BLACK (*Empetrum nigrum*)	4–6	N	E	Sun to half sun	Cool/moist/acid	Summer/late summer	Black berry	Grows best over rock and gravel; at least 40 bird species are known to eat these berries, including many ducks and shorebirds
JUNIPER, CREEPING (*Juniperus horizontalis*)	3–9	N	E	Sun	Drained	Late summer/winter	Blue-green berry	Grows best over gravel or shallow soil
Cultivars of creeping juniper: Bar Harbor juniper	3–9	N	E	Sun	Shallow	Late summer/winter	Blue-green berry	6–12 in. tall and forms a mat 7 ft. wide

Name	Zones			Light	Soil	Season	Fruit	Notes
Andorra juniper or plumose	3–9	N	E	Sun	Shallow	Late summer/winter	Blue-green berry	18 in. tall and forms a mat 7 ft. wide
Blue rug juniper	3–9	N	E	Sun	Shallow	Late summer/winter	Blue-green berry	3–6 in. tall and forms a dense mat 10 ft. wide
JUNIPER, SARGENT (*Juniperus chinensis var. sargentii*)	5–9	A	E	Sun	Drained	Late summer/winter	Blue-green berry	Forms large mats 12 in. tall and up to 10 ft. across; most useful as cover; plant male and female bush for a berry crop
PARTRIDGEBERRY (*Mitchella repens*)	3–9	N	E	Shade	Moist/acid	Summer/late summer	Red berry	Creeping mat; berries eaten by grouse and at least 8 other bird species
STRAWBERRY, CULTIVATED (*Fragaria chiloensis*)	5–10	N	E	Sun/half sun	Drained	Spring/summer	Red berry	Cultivated strawberries provide cover and food for at least 29 bird species
STRAWBERRY, WILD (*Fragaria virginiana*)	4–8	N	E	Sun/half sun	Drained	Spring/summer	Red berry	Wild strawberry of east; small fruits than above
WINTERGREEN (*Gautheria procumbens*)	4–8	N	E	Half sun/shade	Cool/moist	Late summer/early fall	Red berry	Slow-growing, trailing plant for shady areas; at least 10 bird species eat these red berries

Other Good Choices for the Northeast—cont.

Name	Zone	Native (N) or Alien (A)	Height/spread (ft.)	Light	Preferred Soil	Fruit Period	Fruit Type	Remarks
Vines*								
AMPELOPSIS, HEARTLEAF (*Ampelopsis cordata*)	5–9	N	D	Shade	Moist/ drained/ fertile woods	Late summer/ late fall	Blue berry	May be cultivated on trellis; good cover for walls and fences; at least 10 bird species eat its fruit, including flicker, wood thrush, and brown thrasher
BITTERSWEET, AMERICAN (*Celastrus scandens*)	2–8	N	D	Sun	Dry/ drained	Late summer/ early winter	Red and yellow pod	Climbs to 60 ft.; attractive yellow fall color; excellent ornamental; plant male and female plants nearby; at least 15 bird species eat its fruit
GRAPE, NEW ENGLAND (*Vitis novae-angliae*)	5–7	N	D	Sun	Fertile/ drained	Early fall	Black berry	Grapes attract many birds, especially cardinal and catbird; easily cultivated on

168

Species	Zone			Light	Moisture	Fruit season	Fruit	Notes
GRAPE, FOX (*Vitis labrusca*)	5–8	N	D	Sun/shade/variety	Dry/moist/drained	Late summer/fall	Black-amber berry	arbors; at least 52 bird species eat grapes; they are preferred food for 24 species; many insect-eating birds, such as vireos, warblers, flycatchers, and cuckoos, are known to nest among grapevines or use grape bark in their nests
GRAPE, FROST (*Vitis vulpina*)	6–8	N	D	Sun	Rich soils/bottom land/drained	Fall	Black berry	
GRAPE, RIVERBANK (*Vitis riparia*)	3–7	N	D	Sun	Moist	Late summer/early fall	Blue-black berry	
GRAPE, SUMMER (*Vitis aestivalis*)	4–8	N	D	Sun	Dry	Fall	Black berry	
GREENBRIER, CAT (*Smilax glauca*)	6–9	N	D	Sun/variety	Swampy to drier woodland edges	Fall	Blue-black berry	Forms impenetrable tangle that offers excellent cover, food, and nest sites for at least 19 bird species; berries are preferred food for mockingbird, catbird, and Swainson's thrush
GREENBRIER, COMMON (*Smilax rotundifolia*)	5–8	N	D	Sun	Moist/drained	Early fall	Blue-black berry	Similar to above, but has strong thorns; fruits survive through winter; at least 20 bird species eat this fruit

Other Good Choices for the Northeast—*cont.*

Name	Zone	Native (N) or Alien (A)	Height/spread (ft.)	Light	Preferred Soil	Fruit Period	Fruit Type	Remarks
HONEYSUCKLE, TRUMPET (*Lonicera sempervirens*)	4–9	N	Semi to E	Sun	Drained	Late summer/ fall	Red berry	Hardiest of all the honeysuckle vines; excellent for hummingbirds
MOONSEED, COMMON (*Menispermum canadense*)	6–8	N	D	Sun/ shade/ variety	Moist/ drained	Late summer/ fall	Black drupe	Ivy-like foliage climbs to 12 ft.; useful ground cover; dies back in winter; 5 bird species known to eat this fruit
TRUMPET CREEPER, COMMON (*Campsis radicans*)	5–9	N	D	Sun	Dry/ moist/ drained	Late summer/ fall	Capsule	Forms shrubby vine to 30 ft.; decorative orange flowers attract hummingbirds

*D, deciduous; E, evergreen.

Loblolly Pine (*Pinus taeda*)

This fast-growing pine grows to 100 feet tall with a variable spread and thrives on a variety of sunlit soils from poorly drained coastal plains to well-drained hill country. Sometimes it grows in pure stands, but frequently mixes with shortleaf pine (*Pinus echinata*). Loblolly and other southern pines produce abundant seed crops that provide an important food source for the Carolina chickadee, brown-headed nuthatch, rufous-sided towhee, and many other birds. Loblolly pine occurs

LOBLOLLY PINE *Pinus taeda* (AF)

as far north as North Carolina and is found west to eastern Texas and south through most of Florida. On deep, sandy soils, consider planting long-leaved pine (*P. palustris*). It has graceful needles up to 15 inches long and is the longest-living pine native to this region.

American Holly (*Ilex opaca*)

The evergreen foliage of American holly makes it a useful cover tree for birds throughout the year. Large specimens grow to 50 feet and may spread up to 20 feet. The brilliant red fruits are produced only on female trees, so when selecting plants it's best to choose specimens with fruit if possible. It is important to plant at least one male tree nearby. For maximum benefit to birds, trees should be planted in clumps or in a hedge, although this tree is also an excellent choice as a foundation planting, especially at the corners of large buildings. American

AMERICAN HOLLY *Ilex opaca* (AF)

holly thrives in partial shade and a variety of soils ranging from rich and moist to sandy. It is hardy only as far north as zone 6, naturally occurring from Massachusetts to Florida and west to southern Illinois and Indiana. At least 12 species of birds eat American holly fruit. The northern mockingbird, eastern bluebird, and cedar waxwing especially prefer it. American holly grows slowly, but it can live for over 200 years.

Red Buckeye (*Aesculus pavia*)

This native deciduous shrub or small tree of the southeastern United States makes an excellent specimen for the yard or for use as part of a border planting in front of larger trees. It grows about 15 feet tall with a spread of 10 feet. In early summer, it provides nectar and insect food for ruby-throated hummingbirds within its clusters of red flowers. The variety "Atrosanguinea" has especially dark, red flowers.

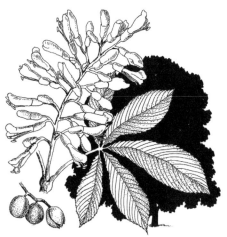

RED BUCKEYE *Aesculus pavia* (CD)

Sugar Hackberry (*Celtis laevigata*)

The small, orange-to-black fruits of sugar hackberry are among the favorite foods of the cedar waxwing, yellow-bellied sapsucker, northern mocking-bird, and at least 23 other species. This deciduous native tree usually grows in moist woodlands, but it will also grow in drier areas and thus makes an excellent choice for a backyard bird-attracting tree. In forest habitats, sugar hackberry grows to 100 feet tall and 40 feet wide, self-pruning its lower branches to create a straight trunk. In sunny habitats, it retains lower branches and is not as tall. The fruits ripen in late summer and stay on the

SUGAR HACKBERRY *Celtis laevigata* (AF)

trees through the winter. Sugar hackberry produces the most fruit when it is 30–70 years old. It is hardy as far north as zone 7, and occurs from Virginia and southern Indiana south to eastern Texas and central Florida.

Shagbark Hickory (*Carya ovata*)

This distinctive hickory usually has abundant nut crops every other year. It grows in well-drained soils and prefers an open, sunny habitat, but it will also grow in partial shade, frequently occurring on dry hillsides in mixed forests of hickory and oak. It grows slowly to a height of 80 feet and a spread of 50 feet, and usually does not produce large fruit crops until it is about 40 years old. Shagbark hickories are certainly long-term investments for wildlife, as they may live to be 300 years old. Hickory

SHAGBARK HICKORY *Carya ovata* (AF)

fruits are eaten by the wild turkey, mallard, wood duck, and many smaller birds that pick at nut scraps after they have been cracked open and discarded by squirrels. A few of the smaller birds that eat hickory nuts are the Carolina chickadee, white-breasted nuthatch, pine warbler, and Eastern towhee. Shagbark hickory has an extensive distribution throughout southeastern Canada and the United States. It is hardy north to zone 5, and occurs from southern Quebec and Nebraska south to northeastern Texas and north central Florida. It does not occur along the Atlantic or Gulf coastal plains.

Live Oak (*Quercus virginiana*)

A beautiful symbol of the Deep South, the live oak is also a very important tree for wildlife. As with all oaks, the meaty nuts are important to both birds and mammals. In the Southeast, acorns are preferred foods for the wild turkey, wood duck, northern bobwhite, common grackle, scrub jay, brown

LIVE OAK *Quercus virginiana* (AF)

thrasher, and many others. Live oak grows in a wide variety of soils, but does best in coastal sandy soils. It occurs commonly in coastal locations from Virginia south through Florida and west to eastern Texas. Its tolerance to salinity makes it an excellent selection in coastal habitats. Live oak has dark green, evergreen leaves and usually grows to about 50 feet with a spread of 60–100 feet. Acorns ripen in September and are usually available until December.

Common Persimmon (*Diospyros virginiana*)

The fruit of common persimmon is a favorite of the American robin, northern bobwhite, eastern bluebird, eastern phoebe, cedar waxwing, and at least six other species of eastern bird. The fleshy 1½-inch-diameter yellow fruits ripen from September to November. This 30–50-foot-tall tree with a spread of 35 feet usually grows in moist soils or in old fields and roadsides, and first fruits when it is about 6 feet tall. Common persimmon is hardy as far north as zone 5, occurring from southern Connecticut south to Florida and west to Texas and Kansas. It usually grows in sunny habitats and does best in light soils.

COMMON PERSIMMON *Diospyros virginiana* (AF)

Black Tupelo (*Nyssa sylvatica*)

Black tupelo (black gum) generally grows in moist woodlands, but it is also an excellent tree for backyards or for landscaping pond banks. It usually grows to about 60 feet in height with a spread of 30 feet. The branches are heavy with small, dark blue fruit by late August or October. The wood thrush, common flicker, rose-breasted grosbeak, cedar waxwing, starling, and

BLACK TUPELO *Nyssa sylvatica* (AF)

many others consume these. In the fall, just as its fruit is ripening, the foliage turns to blazing scarlet and vermilion. Black tupelo is hardy as far north as zone 5 and occurs from Maine to Missouri and south to Texas and Florida.

Cabbage Palmetto (*Sabal palmetto*)

Cabbage palmetto grows in sandy soils along the Atlantic coast from North Carolina to Florida, where it is the state tree. This branchless tree grows up to 80 feet tall and 15–22 feet wide and produces large clusters of small black drupelike fruits. The fruit is frequently eaten by many kinds of birds, including the northern bobwhite, northern cardinal, eastern phoebe, and red-bellied woodpecker. Since cabbage palmetto grows in disturbed soils, it readily colonizes roadsides and old fields. Such new habitats are permitting

CABBAGE PALMETTO *Sabal palmetto* **(AF)**

this useful native tree to become increasingly common. Its tolerance of various soil and water conditions, plus its value as a bird-attracting plant, make it an excellent choice for landscaping.

Yaupon Holly (*Ilex vomitoria*)

Depending on growing conditions, the Yaupon holly can grow 15–25 feet tall with a spread of 10–15 feet. Yaupon fruits best in open sunlight, but it also grows well in partial shade. It prefers moist, sandy soils with good drainage. This native, evergreen shrub makes an excellent wildlife hedge, providing abundant nest sites and fruit. The plentiful red drupe fruits are about $\frac{1}{2}$ inch in diameter, they ripen in October, and stay on the branch through the winter.

YAUPON HOLLY *Ilex vomitoria* **(AF)**

As with most hollies, fruits usually appear only on female plants, but occasionally both male and female flowers grow on the same shrub. The gray catbird, northern mockingbird, brown thrasher, northern bobwhite, and many songbirds readily eat Yaupon fruits. It is hardy as far north as zone 7 and occurs from West Virginia south to the Gulf coast and northern Florida.

American Beautyberry (*Callicarpa americana*)

This native deciduous shrub of southern forests is an excellent choice for light-shade habitats. Small bluish flowers appear in leaf axils from March to June, and these form large clusters of lustrous pink-purple fruit by August. The fruit stays on the plants until midwinter, and since the berries contain about 80 percent water, they are an excellent moisture source for birds during dry fall and winter seasons. At least 12 bird species consume the fruit, a favorite winter food for the northern bobwhite. American beautyberry pro-

AMERICAN BEAUTYBERRY *Callicarpa americana* (AF)

duces the most fruit when it grows in sunny, well-drained soils, but it also thrives in partial-shade habitats such as open pine forests. This 3–6-foot-tall shrub spreading to 5 feet is hardy as far north as zone 7, occurring north to Maryland and Tennessee and south to eastern Texas and central Florida.

Spicebush (*Lindera benzoin*)

This deciduous shrub is named for its aromatic leaves and twigs. It is native under forest canopies from Massachusetts to northern Florida. It is hardy to zone 5. Spicebush grows to about 8 feet tall and can spread to 10 feet. In the shade, it has sparse foliage and shows off its graceful form. In partial to full sun it takes on a more

SPICEBUSH *Lindera benzoin* (VH)

compact form; it prefers moist, fertile soils. Its aromatic characteristics apparently give it protection from deer browsing. Spicebush fruit is high in lipid content, which makes it a favorite of thrushes (especially the wood thrush and veery). These and at least 13 other species consume most of the large, fleshy fruit as soon as they ripen.

Christmas Berry (*Lycium carolinianum*)

This evergreen shrub or small tree can grow 10 feet tall and 6 feet wide. It occurs along coastal areas, where it grows on sandy mounds and ridges in salt marshes. It is hardy within zones 8–10. It has solitary white or bluish flowers in summer and these mature to bright red, juicy berries by late fall and winter. It grows well in a variety of soils but thrives in low-organic-matter soils, mixed with sand in poor drainage areas. Christmas berry is a favorite food of the American robin, white-crowned pigeon, and northern mockingbird.

CHRISTMAS BERRY *Lycium carolinianum* (VH)

Common Greenbrier (*Smilax rotundifolia*)

This stout woody vine climbs to 30 feet, creating dense tangles that are very attractive to birds. It has inconspicuous green flowers from April to August and small, blue-black berries that ripen by September. These are among the favorite fruits of the wild turkey, ruffed grouse, northern mockingbird, Swainson's thrush, and at least 16 other bird species. In addition to the importance of the fruit, several species such as the gray catbird and northern cardinal choose greenbrier as a favorite

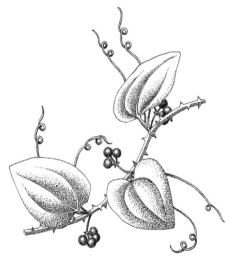

COMMON GREENBRIER *Smilax rotundifolia* (AF)

nesting place. New clumps can be established by transplanting rootstock. These usually produce vigorous new canes 2 years later. Common greenbrier is hardy north to zone 5, and occurs from Nova Scotia to Florida and west to Texas and Michigan. It grows best in low, moist areas but will also thrive in drier woods and forest edge. Some no doubt regard this thorny vine as a weed, but its fruit and dense cover make it a valuable planting for creating hedgerows at property borders or corners.

Trumpet Creeper (*Campsis radicans*)

Trumpet creeper is a native vine of the southeastern forests, where it can climb 30 feet or more to the forest canopy. It can develop a massive stem 5–6 inches in diameter and requires a very sturdy support. Plant it in full sun and give it ample space to grow. Trumpet creeper is a favorite of ruby-throated hummingbirds, which can completely disappear within the deep, tubular orange flowers as they search for nectar and insects. The flowers appear in clusters of 4–12 at the tips of branches. *Campsis flava flava* ("Yellow Trumpet") has yellow flowers. Trumpet creepers are hardy within zones 5–9.

TRUMPET CREEPER *Campsis radicans* (CD)

Trumpet Honeysuckle (*Lonicera sempervirens*)

This semievergreen native vine has oval leaves and clusters of coral-colored, trumpet-shaped, tubular flowers. The 2-inch-long flowers are favorites of ruby-throated humming-birds, which readily visit the flowers for nectar and insects. Some of the flowers produce bright red fruits that are eaten by songbirds. It occurs in forest edge, thickets, and other sunny locations

TRUMPET HONEYSUCKLE *Lonicera sempervirens* (CD)

throughout the eastern states as far west as Texas. Trumpet honeysuckle can grow to 20 feet and spread to 12 feet. It is an excellent choice for a trellis or fence or it can serve as a ground cover. This twining vine prefers full to partial sunny locations and grows best in moist or well-drained soils.

Additional Recommended Plantings for the Southeast*

Evergreen Trees
HEMLOCK, EASTERN (*Tsuga canadensis*)
REDCEDAR, EASTERN (*Juniperus virginiana*)

Large Deciduous Trees
HACKBERRY, COMMON (*Celtis occidentalis*)
MAPLE, RED (*Acer rubrum*)
MAPLE, SUGAR (*Acer saccharum*)
MULBERRY, RED (*Morus rubra*)
OAK, BLACK (*Quercus velutina*)
OAK, NORTHERN RED (*Quercus rubra*)
OAK, PIN (*Quercus palustris*)
OAK, SCARLET (*Quercus coccinea*)

Small Deciduous Trees
CRABAPPLES, FLOWERING (*Malus* spp.)
DOGWOOD, ALTERNATE-LEAF (*Cornus alternifolia*)
DOGWOOD, FLOWERING (*Cornus florida*)
HOP HORNBEAM, AMERICAN (*Ostrya virginia*)
MOUNTAIN-ASH, AMERICAN (*Sorbus americana*)
MOUNTAIN-ASH, EUROPEAN (*Sorbus aucuparia*)
SASSAFRAS (*Sassafras albidum*)

Evergreen Shrubs
HOLLY, INKBERRY (*Ilex glabra*)
HUCKLEBERRY, BOX (*Galussacia brachycera*)
JUNIPER, COMMON (*Juniperus communis*)
YEW, CANADA (*Taxus canadensis*)

Deciduous Shrubs
ALDER, SPECKLED (*Alnus rugosa*)
BAYBERRY (*Myrica pensylvanica*)

BLACKBERRIES (*Rubus* spp.)
BLUEBERRY, HIGHBUSH (*Vaccinium corymbosum*)
BUTTONBUSH (*Cephalanthus occidentalis*)
DOGWOOD, RED-OSIER (*Cornus stolonifera*)
DOGWOOD, SILKY (*Cornus amomum*)
ELDER, AMERICAN (*Sambucus canadensis*)
HUCKLEBERRY, DWARF (*Gaylussacia dumosa*)
ROSE, PASTURE (*Rosa carolina*)
ROSE, SWAMP (*Rosa palustris*)
SUMAC, SMOOTH (*Rhus glabra*)
SUMAC, STAGHORN (*Rhus typhina*)
VIBURNUM, HOBBLEBUSH (*Viburnum alnifolium*)
VIBURNUM, MAPLELEAF (*Viburnum acerifolium*)
VIBURNUM, SOUTHERN ARROWWOOD (*Viburnum dentatum*)
WINTERBERRY (*Ilex verticillata*)

Ground Covers
BEARBERRY (*Arctostaphylos uva-ursi*)
BUNCHBERRY (*Cornus canadensis*)
CROWBERRY, BLACK (*Empetrum nigrum*)
DANGLEBERRY, BLACK (*Gaylussacia frondosa*)
JUNIPER, CREEPING (*Juniperus horizontalis*)
JUNIPER, SARGENT (*Juniperus chinensis sargentii*)
PARTRIDGEBERRY (*Mitchella repens*)
STRAWBERRIES (*Fragaria* spp.)
WINTERGREEN (*Gautheria procumbens*)

Vines
AMPELOPSIS, HEARTLEAF (*Ampelopsis cordata*)
CREEPER, VIRGINIA (*Parthenocissus quinquefolia*)
GRAPE, FOX (*Vitis lambrusca*)
GRAPE, FROST (*Vitis vulpina*)
GRAPE, SUMMER (*Vitis aestivalis*)
GREENBRIER, CAT (*Smilax glauca*)

---

*See detailed descriptions under Recommended Plantings for the Northeast.

Other Good Choices for the Southeast

Name	Zone	Native (N) or Alien (A)	Height/spread (ft.)	Light	Preferred Soil	Fruit Period	Fruit Type	Remarks
Evergreen Trees								
MAGNOLIA, SOUTHERN (*Magnolia grandiflora*)	7b–9	N	To 50/50	Sun	Moist/drained	Summer/fall	Rose drupe	At least 19 bird species eat this fruit, including catbird, fish crow, northern flicker, eastern kingbird, mockingbird, and wood thrush
MAGNOLIA, SWEETBAY (*Magnolia virginiana*)	5b–9	N	To 35/20	Sun	Moist/drained	Fall	Red drupe	Choice food of eastern kingbird, mockingbird, robin, wood thrush, and red-eyed vireo
PIGEON PLUM (*Coccoloba diversifolia*)	10, 11	N	To 60/20–30	Sun	Sandy/organics	Summer	Red drupe	Excellent for streets and yards; fruit is a favorite of pileated woodpecker, fish crow, and white-crowned pigeon
PINE, LONGLEAF (*Pinus palustris*)	7–10	N	To 125/40	Sun	Sandy	Fall	Cone	Grows very well near the sea; often a nest site; choice food for northern cardinal, brown-headed nuthatch, and tufted titmouse

181

Other Good Choices for the Southeast—*cont.*

Name	Zone	Native (N) or Alien (A)	Height/spread (ft.)	Light	Preferred Soil	Fruit Period	Fruit Type	Remarks
PINE, SAND (*Pinus clausa*)	9, 10	N	To 60/20	Sun	Sandy/infertile	Persistent	Cone	Nest site of scrub jay; occurs in coastal Florida
PINE, SHORTLEAF (*Pinus echinata*)	6–9	N	To 100/35	Sun	Sandy/loam	Fall	Cone	Frequent nest site; many species eat the seeds
PINE, SLASH (*Pinus elliottii*)	8, 9	N	To 100/35–50	Sun	Sandy/loam	Fall	Cone	One of the most rapid-growing, early-maturing eastern trees
PINE, VIRGINIA (*Pinus virginiana*)	5–9	N	To 40/50	Sun	Dry/drained	Fall	Cone	Often a nest site; the seed is a choice food for bobwhite, northern cardinal, Carolina chickadee, brown-headed nuthatch, and song sparrow
REDBAY (*Persea borbonia*)	8–11	N	To 70/20	Sun	Moist	Late summer/fall	Blue or purple drupe	Choice food of eastern bluebird, robin, and bobwhite; grows in swamps and along streams

Tall Deciduous Trees

Name	Zones	Native	Height/Spread	Light	Soil	Season	Fruit	Notes
HAWTHORN, BLUEBERRY (*Crataegus brachyacantha*)	8, 9	N	To 40	Sun/half sun	Sandy loam	Summer/fall	Bright blue-black pome	Frequent nest site; thorny shrubs provide safe cover; at least 36 bird species eat the fruit of hawthorns
HICKORY, WATER (*Carya aquatica*)	7–9	N	To 100/39	Sun	Moist	Fall	Nut	Fair food for wood duck and mallard
OAK, BLACKJACK (*Quercus marilandica*)	6–9	N	To 30/50	Sun/half sun	Dry/sandy/sterile	Fall / 1 year*	Acorn	Frequent nest sites for hawks and many other kinds of bird; choice food for bobwhite, wood duck, common grackle, brown thrasher, blue jay, red-headed woodpecker, and wild turkey
OAK, CHESTNUT (*Quercus prinus*)	6–8	N	60–80/60–70	Sun/half sun	Dry/sandy/gravelly	Fall / 2–3 years*	Acorn	
OAK, LAUREL (*Quercus laurifolia*)	8, 9	N	60–70/70	Varied	Moist	Fall / 1 year*	Acorn	
OAK, POST (*Quercus stellata*)	5–9	N	40–50/40–50	Sun/half sun	Dry/sterile	Fall / 2–3 years*	Acorn	
OAK, SPANISH RED (*Quercus falcata*)	7–9	N	To 80/40	Sun/half sun	Dry/sandy/clay	Fall / 2–3 years*	Acorn	

Other Good Choices for the Southeast—*cont.*

Name	Zone	Native (N) or Alien (A)	Height/spread (ft.)	Light	Preferred Soil	Fruit Period	Fruit Type	Remarks
OAK, SWAMP CHESTNUT (*Quercus michauxii*)	6–9	N	60–80/ 80–100	Sun/ half sun	Moist	Fall 3–5 years[*]	Acorn	
OAK, WATER (*Quercus nigra*)	6–9	N	60–70/40	Sun/ half sun	Moist	Fall 1–2 years	Acorn	Frequent nest sites for hawks and many other kinds of bird; choice food for bobwhite, wood duck, common grackle, brown thrasher, blue jay, red-headed woodpecker, and wild turkey
OAK, WILLOW (*Quercus phellos*)	6–9	N	60–80/50	Sun/ half sun	Drained	Fall 1 year[*]	Acorn	
PECAN (*Carya illinoensis*)	6–9	N	To 150/70	Sun	Dry/ moist/ drained	Early fall	Nut	A favorite of wood duck and eaten by at least 9 other bird species. Largest of all hickories
Small Deciduous Trees								
BLACKHAW, RUSTY (*Viburnum rufidulum*)	5–8	N	16–18/15	Sun	Sandy/ loam	Summer/ fall	Blue-black drupe	Choice food of eastern bluebird and cedar waxwing; semievergreen

Name (Scientific name)	Zone	N	Size	Light	Moisture	Season	Fruit	Notes
BUCKTHORN, CAROLINA (*Rhamnus caroliniana*)	6–9	N	25–35/10–15	Sun/shade	Moist/drained	Fall	Red/black drupe	Berries eaten by many songbirds, especially catbird
DAHOON (*Ilex cassine*)	7b–9	N	To 40/8–15	Sun/shade	Moist/drained	Fall/winter	Red/yellow berry	Provides many birds with a good food source through the winter
FARKLEBERRY (*Vaccinium arboreum*)	6–10	N	To 30/6–13	Sun/shade	Dry/drained	Early fall	Black berry	Fruits eaten by many kinds of bird, especially favored by mockingbird
FRINGE TREE, WHITE (*Chionanthus virginicus*)	5–9	N	20–25/10	Sun/half sun	Moist/drained	Fall	Dark blue drupe	Fruit eaten by many kinds of bird; often eaten by pileated woodpeckers; tolerates city conditions
HAWTHORN, PARSLEY (*Crataegus marshallii*)	3–9	N	15–25/15–20	Sun	Swampy	Late summer/winter	Bright red pome	The thorny thickets make good cover, providing brood-rearing areas for ruffed grouse
OAK, BLUEJACK (*Quercus incana*)	8–10	N	To 20	Sun/half sun	Dry/sandy	Fall	Acorn	Very productive acorn producer; choice food of northern bobwhite and Eastern towhee
OAK, CHAPMAN (*Quercus chapmanii*)	8–10	N	To 25	Sun	Well drained	Matures in first season	Red drupe	Covers wide areas with shrubby growth, giving much cover and food to many birds. Annual acorn crop

Other Good Choices for the Southeast—*cont.*

Name	Zone	Native (N) or Alien (A)	Height/spread (ft.)	Light	Preferred Soil	Fruit Period	Fruit Type	Remarks
PLUM, AMERICAN (*Prunus americana*)	6–8	N	20–30/10–15	Sun/shade	Dry/moist/drained	Summer/fall	Red drupe	Occasional nest site; fruit eaten by many kinds of bird, including bobwhite, robin, ring-necked pheasant, and red-headed woodpecker
POSSUM, HAW (*Ilex decidua*)	6–9	N	10–20/6–20	Sun/half sun	Dry/moist/drained	Fall/winter	Red berry	Good winter food for eastern bluebird, robin, cedar waxwing, purple finch, red-bellied woodpecker, and many others
VIBURNUM, POSSUM HAW (*Viburnum nudum*)	7–9	N	20/6	Sun	Swampy/sandy/acid	Fall	Pink to blue drupe	Good protection for birds in wet areas; food for bobwhite
WAX, MYRTLE (*Myrica cerifera*)	7–9	N	To 40/15	Sun	Moist/sun	Fall/winter	Blue-gray nutlet	A good winter food source for many songbirds

Evergreen Shrubs

Name	Zone	Native (N) or Alien (A)	Height/spread (ft.)	Light	Preferred Soil	Fruit Period	Fruit Type	Remarks
BLUEBERRY, GROUND (*Vaccinium myrsinites*)	7–10	N	To 3/2–3	Sun	Drained/sandy	May	Purple/black berry	Among the most important summer and early-fall foods for grouse

CHERRY LAUREL, CAROLINA (*Prunus caroliniana*)	7–10	N	To 18/15–25	Varied	Varied	Persistent	Black berry	Choice food of bluebird, mockingbird, robin, and cedar waxwing
COCOPLUM (*Chrysobalanus icaco*)	10–11	N	To 15/15	Sun	Poorly drained/neutral	All seasons	Yellow drupe	Fruits are high sugar and fat content and are likely eaten by many species
GALLBERRY, LARGE (*Ilex coriacea*)	7–9	N	To 8/20	Varied	Sandy/acid	Fall	Black berry	Male and female plants needed for fruit set; berries needed for fruit set; berries cedar waxwing, robin, and eastern bluebird; occasional nest site for mockingbird, nest site for mockingbird, brown thrasher, and Eastern towhee
HOLLY, MYRTLE-LEAFED (*Ilex myrtifolia*)	7–11	N	To 23/8–12	Varied	Sandy/acid	Fall/winter	Red/orange berry	
JUNIPER, JAPANESE GARDEN (*Juniperus chinensis* var. *procumbens*)	4–8	A	To 1/10	Sun/half sun	Drained	Late spring/summer	Blue berry	Provides good ground shelter; plant male and female for fruit Shore juniper is very salt tolerant
JUNIPER, SHORE (*Juniperus conferta*)	5–9	A	To 1/indefinite	Sun/half sun	Moist/drained	Late spring/summer	Blue berry	
OAK, DWARF LIVE (*Quercus minima*)	7–11	N	To 3	Varied	Sandy/clay	August/November	Acorn	Acorns are favored turkey food

Other Good Choices for the Southeast—*cont.*

Name	Zone	Native (N) or Alien (A)	Height/spread (ft.)	Light	Preferred Soil	Fruit Period	Fruit Type	Remarks
PALMETTO, DWARF (*Sabal minor*)	8, 9	N	To 8/10	Sun	Varied	Year-round	Black drupe	Good for songbird food; good nest site for ground-nesting birds, such as the warbler
SEAGRAPE (*Coccoloba uvifera*)	10–11	N	To 25/25–40	Sun	Sandy/neutral	Fall	Purple clusters of berries	Excellent planting along roadsides and large properties where there is room for it to spread; the fruit are eaten by northern mockingbird, fish crow, pileated woodpecker, and white-crowned pigeon

Deciduous Shrubs

Name	Zone	Native (N) or Alien (A)	Height/spread (ft.)	Light	Preferred Soil	Fruit Period	Fruit Type	Remarks
DEERBERRY, COMMON (*Vaccinium stamineum*)	5–9	N	6/10–15	Sun/shade	Dry/drained	Late summer	Green to purple berry	Important food of ruffed grouse, bobwhite, and other ground-feeding birds
DEVIL'S WALKING STICK (*Aralia spinosa*)	5–8	N	35–50/16	Part shade	Dry/moist	Fall	Black berry	Thorny shrubs that offer excellent cover and food eaten by many sparrows and thrushes

188

OAK, RUNNING (*Quercus pumila*)	7–9	N	6/50	Sun/shade	Dry/drained	Summer/fall	Acorn	Acorns eaten by wild turkeys and ruffed grouse
Vines[+]								
GRAPE, WINTER SWEET (*Vitis cinerea*)	5–10	N	D	Sun/shade	Moist/drained	Fall	Black/purple berry	Grapevines overtopping other plants provide nest sites for such birds as northern cardinal, catbird, and brown thrasher; these also use grape bark in their nests
GREENBRIER, LAUREL (*Smilax laurifolia*)	7–9	N	E	Sun/half sun	Moist	Late summer/persistent	Black berry	Provides excellent cover, food, and nest sites for many birds, including flicker, pileated woodpecker, ruffed grouse, and red-bellied woodpecker
SNAILSEED, CAROLINA (*Cocculus carolinus*)	7–9	N	D to semi-E	Sun	Moist/dry/drained	Late summer/persistent	Red drupe	Pea-size fruit; often persists through winter; only female plant bears fruit; eaten by brown thrasher, mockingbird, and eastern phoebe
SUPPLEJACK, ALABAMA (*Berchemia scandens*)	6–9	N	D	Sun	Moist/rich	Summer/fall	Blue/black drupe	Climbs to 15–20 ft.; at least 14 bird species eat its fruit

*Intervals between acorn crops.

[+]D, deciduous; E, evergreen.

Ponderosa Pine (*Pinus ponderosa*)
The Ponderosa pine is a huge tree that is native to the west—it may grow to a towering 150 feet with a spread of 20–25 feet and develop a trunk diameter of 5–8 feet. It usually grows in large single-species stands, but it can be effectively planted in shelterbelts to provide cover through the year for birds and serve as an effective windbreak. Ponderosa pine is drought and fire resistant but is not very resistant to insects. This impressive tree tolerates

PONDEROSA PINE *Pinus ponderosa* **(AF)**

many types of soils and grows at elevations ranging from 2000 to 10,000 feet. It first produces seed when it is about 20 years old and doesn't reach maximum production until it is 150 years old. Good seed crops occur every 2–5 years. The tiny, abundant seeds (12,000 to a pound) are important food for the blue grouse, band-tailed pigeon, Lewis' woodpecker, and many others. Ponderosa pine and its many varieties grow on dry, rocky hillsides from South Dakota and western Nebraska south to western Texas and west along the Pacific coast from California to British Columbia.

Common Chokecherry (*Prunus virginiana*)
This common shrub or small tree of fencerows and thickets produces abundant fruits that range in color from red to black. The fruits are tart tasting and readily consumed by at least 43 bird species—they are especially favored by the eastern bluebird. Common chokecherry grows 6–20 feet tall with a spread of 25 feet and sometimes forms extensive thickets. It has also been used with some success for

COMMON CHOKECHERRY *Prunus virginiana* **(AF)**

erosion control, since it thrives in full-sun locations with a great variety of soils, including sand. Chokecherry is hardy north through zone 2 and has a widespread distribution from Newfoundland to British Columbia and south to Georgia and California.

Common Hackberry (*Celtis occidentalis*)

Common hackberry grows on rocky hillsides, open pastures, and moist stream banks, from the mid-Atlantic states west to Manitoba, North Dakota, Nebraska, and Kansas. Since it is a drought-resistant native tree, it makes an excellent choice for a shelterbelt planting. It is adaptable to a great variety of sites but appears to thrive best on sunlit, alkaline soils. Common hackberry grows to 30–50 feet with a spread of 50 feet and produces an annual crop of ¼-inch red or purple

COMMON HACKBERRY *Celtis occidentalis* (AF)

drupe fruits, which may survive through the winter if they are not quickly consumed by birds. At least 24 bird species eat common hackberry fruit—the wild turkey, northern flicker, northern mockingbird, Swainson's thrush, and cardinal especially favor it.

Bur Oak (*Quercus macrocarpa*)

The bur oak is a hardy native western tree, capable of withstanding the wind and droughts that eliminate most trees from this region. Large bur oaks may grow 150 feet tall and 30 feet wide and live for 350–400 years. Its flowers appear from April to May and the distinctive large acorns ripen from August to September. This grand oak usually produces good nut crops every 2–3 years. The wood duck, jays, greater

BUR OAK *Quercus macrocarpa* (AF)

prairie chicken, northern bobwhite, and wild turkey eat the acorns. Bur oak grows well on well-drained land in eastern Texas, Oklahoma, Arkansas, and Louisiana east to Georgia and north to Nova Scotia. It grows along rivers west to the Dakotas and Manitoba. Bur oak can withstand temperatures in the coldest regions of the northeastern and north central United States.

Cockspur Hawthorn (*Crataegus crus-galli*)

This native round-topped tree is an ideal choice for moderate-sized backyards as it only grows to 25 feet with a spread of 30 feet. Hawthorns are an excellent native tree choice for several reasons. This species is named for its long, curved thorns that help to protect the fruit. The spines also deter predators from approaching bird nests.

COCKSPUR HAWTHORN *Crataegus crus-galli* (CD)

Saskatoon Serviceberry (*Amelanchier alnifolia*)

Saskatoon serviceberry varies in growth form, depending on soil and water availability. In rich, moist soils it forms dense thickets or grows 6–12 feet tall as a small tree with a spread of 12 feet. In hard, dry soils it often grows prostrate or takes on a stunted appearance. Saskatoon serviceberry has fragrant white flowers in May, and sweet and juicy purple-black pome fruits each July and August. This hardy serviceberry grows in open woods, thickets, stream banks, and

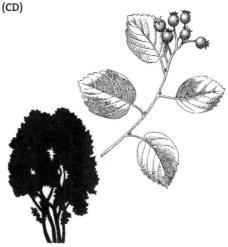

SASKATOON SERVICEBERRY *Amelanchier alnifolia* (AF)

canyons from South Dakota and Colorado to western Canada and north to Alaska. It also occurs through California to New Mexico. Its fruit is eaten by many kinds of birds, including the blue grouse, mountain quail, black-billed magpie, American crow, American robin, and Swainson's thrush.

Buffalo Currant (*Ribes odoratum*)

Buffalo (clove) currant is a spine-forming shrub that grows to a maximum height of about 6 feet with an equal spread. It is a popular cultivated plant whose berries are sometimes used in jams and jellies. Buffalo currant has fragrant, bright yellow flowers from April to May and blackish purple smooth berries that ripen from June to September. Many types of songbirds eat the fruits as soon as they ripen. Buffalo currant grows along woodland borders, cliffs, rocky hillsides, and other open habitats. It prefers well-drained soil and is a

BUFFALO CURRANT *Ribes odoratum* **(AF)**

common plant on open, sandy habitats from Minnesota and South Dakota south to Louisiana and east Texas. Buffalo currant adapts well to cultivation and is an excellent bird-attracting addition to property borders, fencerows, and other open habitats.

Silver Buffaloberry (*Shepherdia argentea*)

This is an excellent native deciduous shrub for the northern Great Plains and mountain slopes. It can withstand extreme cold and windy locations and thrives in most soils (including alkali). It is hardy within zones 3–7. Once established, it will tolerate drought. Silver buffaloberry usually grows 5–6 feet tall and can spread to 12 feet. Birds will find both cover and nest sites within its spine-tipped branches. Silver buffaloberry has male and female flowers on different plants, so it is important to plant several to provide

SILVER BUFFALOBERRY *Shepherdia argentea* **(CD)**

pollination and a good crop of the bright red or orange berries. These are eaten by a wide variety of birds including the sharp-tailed grouse and robins.

Gray Dogwood (*Cornus racemosa*)
This shrubby, deciduous dogwood grows on a wide variety of sites, from swampy lowlands to higher, well-drained areas. It is a principal component of shrublands throughout the eastern United States, especially in the Southeast and lower prairie states where it forms thickets along waterways and in old fields. It grows well in full sun or partial shade. It is a good choice for pond shores or as a planting to enhance a forest border. It has round, white drupe fruit that appear on bright red stems arising off of gray branches. The

GRAY DOGWOOD *Cornus racemosa* (VH)

fruit ripen about the same time as the leaves turn a striking burgundy color, in August–October, and they persist on the shrubs into early winter. It can grow 10–15 feet tall, with a similar spread. At least 16 species feed on the fruits. It is a preferred food for woodpeckers, catbirds, robins, bluebirds, and other thrushes. Gray dogwood is hardy within zones 5–7.

Several other shrubby dogwoods are also excellent choices for this region. Rough-leaved dogwood (*Cornus drummondii*) is very drought tolerant and spreads by underground stems to form thickets. Red-osier dogwood (*C. stolonifera*) has dramatic red or yellow stems; silky dogwood (*C. amomum*) is similar with metallic, blue fruits.

Possumhaw (*Ilex decidua*)
As its Latin name suggests, this holly loses its large, dark green leaves in the fall, displaying dense clusters of scarlet fruit. The $\frac{1}{4}$–$\frac{1}{3}$-inch-diameter fruits ripen in September while the leaves are still green. This large shrub may grow 20–30 feet tall, but more typically reaches 10–15 feet with a spread of 5–10 feet. Possumhaw grows in a variety of soils, including dry, alkaline, and wet soils. It produces its heaviest crops of fruit when it grows in full sun. Use possumhaw as part of a hedge or along property borders—it is too large for a

POSSUMHAW *Ilex decidua* **(CD)**

house foundation planting. Possumhaw is hardy to zone 5. This plant is an excellent winter food source for the red-bellied woodpecker, purple finch, eastern bluebird, cedar waxwing, and many other songbirds.

Snowberry (*Symphoricarpos albus*)

Snowberry is a thicket-forming deciduous shrub that grows on rocky hillsides, gravel banks, and other sites that are too difficult for most other shrubs. In good soil, common snowberry grows up to 6 feet tall with a spread of 6 feet, but plants in poor sites are usually much smaller. It lives in both sunny and shady habitats—plants in the sun produce more of the white berries associated with its name. The berries mature in August and September and usually stay on the shrub through the winter, making snowberry an important source of winter food for many birds, including the ruffed grouse, ring-necked pheasant, American robin, cedar waxwing, and pine grosbeak. The snowberry is an attractive native

SNOWBERRY *Symphoricarpos albus* **(AF)**

shrub and an excellent bird-attracting plant for waste areas, hedges, and property borders. It is hardy as far north as zone 4, and occurs from Nova Scotia south to Pennsylvania and west to Colorado.

Skunkbush Sumac (*Rhus aromatica* var. *flabelliformis*)

This drought-resistant, deep-rooted shrub makes an excellent shelterbelt planting for the plains and prairies. Skunkbush sumac is a hardy, deciduous shrub that grows about 12 feet tall and earns its name from the offensive smell that results from crushing its leaves. It can be propagated from root cuttings. Its red fruit ripens in August and September and is eaten by at least 25 bird species, including the ruffed grouse, evening grosbeak, American robin, northern bobwhite, and greater prairie chicken. It grows best in open, sunny habitats on limestone soils, but can live in a great variety of sites. Skunkbush sumac occurs from the Dakotas south into northern Mexico and west to California.

SKUNKBUSH SUMAC *Rhus aromatica* var. *flabelliformis* (AF)

Rusty Black Haw Viburnum (*Viburnum rufidulum*)

This native viburnum with a spread of 15 feet typically grows at the edge of woods, prairie edges, stream sides, and thickets on the southern plains. It grows well in full sun or partial shade and thrives in dry to moist, well-drained soils. It has many small white flowers in late spring that form showy, flat clusters up to 6 inches across. These develop into fleshy, dark purple fruits by September and October, when the leaves turn an attractive burgundy color. Rusty black haw is a favorite food of many songbirds, especially the cedar waxwing, northern flicker, America robin, and purple finch. Wild turkey and ruffed grouse also eat the fruit. It is hardy to zone 5.

In the northern plains states, nannyberry (*Viburnum lentago*) can be a substitute. Like rusty black haw, nannyberry can grow 20 feet tall but is hardier and can survive throughout the north plains in zone 2. It has a spread of 10 feet.

RUSTY BLACK HAW VIBURNUM *Viburnum rufidulum* (CD)

Additional Recommended Plantings for the Prairies and Plains*

Evergreen Trees
ARBORVITAE, EASTERN (*Thuga occidentalis*)
REDCEDAR, EASTERN (*Juniperus virginiana*)
SPRUCE, COLORADO BLUE (*Picea pungens*)

Large Deciduous Trees
ASH, GREEN (*Fraxinus pennsylvanica*)
ASPEN, QUAKING (*Populus tremuloides*)
BIRCH, PAPER (*Betula papyrifera*)
CHERRY, BLACK (*Prunus serotina*)
CHERRY, PIN (*Prunus pensylvanica*)
COTTONWOOD, EASTERN (*Populus deltoides*)
HACKBERRY, SUGAR (*Celtis laevigata*)
MAPLE, BOX ELDER (*Acer negundo*)
OAK, POST (*Quercus stellata*)
PECAN (*Carya illinoensis*)
WALNUT, BLACK (*Juglans nigra*)
WILLOW, BLACK (*Salix nigra*)

Small Deciduous Trees
APPLE, COMMON (*Malus pumila*)
CRABAPPLE, FLOWERING (*Malus* spp.)
HAWTHORN, WASHINGTON (*Crataegus* spp.)

MOUNTAIN-ASH, AMERICAN (*Sorbus americana*)
MOUNTAIN-ASH, EUROPEAN (*Sorbus aucuparia*)
MOUNTAIN-ASH, NORTHERN (*Sorbus decora*)

Deciduous Shrubs
BUTTONBUSH (*Cephalanthus occidentalis*)
CORALBERRY (*Symphoricarpos orbiculatus*)
CURRANT, AMERICAN BLACK (*Ribes americanum*)
DOGWOOD, RED-OSIER (*Cornus stolonifera*)
ELDER, AMERICAN (*Sambucus canadensis*)
ELDER, SCARLET (*Sambucus pubens*)
RASPBERRY, BLACK (*Rubus occidentalis*)
RASPBERRY, RED (*Rubus ideaeus*)
VIBURNUM, AMERICAN CRANBERRY (*Viburnum trilobum*)

Ground Cover
BEARBERRY (*Arctostaphylos uva-ursi*)
BUNCHBERRY (*Cornus canadensis*)
JUNIPER, CREEPING (*Juniperus horizontalis*)
STRAWBERRY (*Fragaria* spp.)

Vines
AMPELOPSIS, HEARTLEAF (*Ampelopsis cordata*)
BITTERSWEET, AMERICAN (*Celastrus scandens*)
CREEPER, VIRGINIA (*Parthenocissus quinquefolia*)
GRAPE, FOX (*Vitis labrusca*)
GRAPE, RIVERBANK (*Vitis riparia*)
GREENBRIER, COMMON (*Smilax rotundifolia*)
HONEYSUCKLE, TRUMPET (*Lonicera sempervirens*)
MOONSEED, COMMON (*Menispermum canadense*)
TRUMPET CREEPER, COMMON (*Campsis radicans*)

---

*See detailed descriptions under Recommended Plantings for the Northeast and Recommended Plantings for the Southeast.

Other Good Choices for the Prairies and Plains

Name	Zone	Native (N) or Alien (A)	Height/spread (ft.)	Light	Preferred Soil	Fruit Period	Fruit Type	Remarks
Deciduous Trees								
BIRCH, ALASKAN PAPER (*Betula papyrifera* var. *humilis*)	1–5	N	To 30	Sun	Dry/moist	Late summer/early fall	Samara	This Alaskan variety is hardier and shorter than eastern forms; seeds and buds are a favorite food of ruffed grouse, pine siskin, and American goldfinch
COTTONWOOD, PLAINS (*Populus sargentii*)	2–7	N	60–90/40	Sun	Moist	Spring/summer	Capsule	Frequent along streams in western plains; buds eaten by grouse
ELM, SLIPPERY (*Ulmus rubra*)	4–9	N	To 60/49	Sun	Dry/moist/rich/drained	Spring	Samara	Buds are eaten by birds; fruit is a favorite food of purple finch and American goldfinch
HACKBERRY, NETLEAF (*Celtis reticulata*)	6–9	N	To 21/25	Sun	Dry/rocky/sandy	Late summer	Red-brown drupe	Berries rich in calcium; food for Bullock's oriole, robin, roadrunner, and northern flicker

199

Other Good Choices for the Prairies and Plains—*cont.*

Name	Zone	Native (N) or Alien (A)	Height/spread (ft.)	Light	Preferred Soil	Fruit Period	Fruit Type	Remarks
HAWTHORN, DOWNY (*Crataegus mollis*)	4–7	N	15–25/25	Sun	Dry	August/ October/ November	Red pome	These hardy hawthorns can survive the harsh conditions of the northern plains. As a group, hawthorns are known to attract at least 36 kinds of fruit-eating birds
HAWTHORN, FIREBERRY (*Crataegus chrysocarpa*)	3–9	N	To 13	Sun	Dry/ moist/ rocky	Early fall	Red pome	
HAWTHORN, FLESHY (*Crataegus succulenta*)	3–9	N	To 20	Sun	Dry/ moist/ rocky	Early fall	Red pome	
HAWTHORN, GLOSSY (*Crataegus nitida*)	4–9	N	20–30	Sun	Dry	Fall/ winter	Red pome	Glossy, dark green leaves turn brilliant red in fall; disease resistant, fruits persist through winter

Name								Notes
MULBERRY, TEXAS (*Morus microphylla*)	7–10	N	10–20/30	Sun	Moist/drained	Spring	Black compound drupe	A thicket-forming tree that does best in limestone soils; plant male and female trees nearby to produce fruit. A favorite of Gambel's and harlequin quail and many kinds of songbird; provides excellent cover. At least 23 bird species are known to eat buds and tender twigs; these include ruffed, blue, spruce, and sharp-tailed grouse.
WILLOW, PEACH-LEAVED (*Salix amygdaloides*)	5–7	N	40–60/49	Sun	Moist	Spring	Capsule	Willows should not be planted near underground plumbing as roots may clog pipes
WILLOW, SANDBAR (*Salix interior*)	2–10	N	To 30	Sun	Moist/alluvial	Spring	Capsule	

Evergreen Shrubs

Name								Notes
JUNIPER, ASHE (*Juniperus ashei*)	7–9	N	6–20/15–25	Sun	Dry/sandy/gravel	Fall/year-round	Blue berry	Copious seed production; important food for robin; central to southwest Texas. Forms dense thickets between 600 and 2000 ft.

Other Good Choices for the Prairies and Plains—*cont*.

Name	Zone	Native (N) or Alien (A)	Height/spread (ft.)	Light	Preferred Soil	Fruit Period	Fruit Type	Remarks
JUNIPER, ONE-SEED (*Juniperus monosperma*)	5–10	N	20–30	Sun	Dry/rocky	Fall/year-round	Blue berry	Rapid growing for junipers; excellent nesting cover; as with all junipers only the female bears fruit; important food for Gambel's quail and several kinds of songbird
JUNIPER, ROCKY MOUNTAIN (*Juniperus scopulorum*)	4–7	N	30–40/12	Sun	Alkaline/dry/sandy	Fall/year-round	Blue berry	Drought resistant; similar in appearance to eastern redcedar; not recommended for eastern part of this region
PINE, AUSTRIAN (*Pinus nigra*)	4–8	A	70–90/25	Sun to part shade	Varied/sandy/poor	Fall/winter	Cone	Excellent cover and abundant seed production; use only where protected from direct wind; northern plains
SPRUCE, BLACK HILLS (*Picea glauca* var. *densata*)	3–6	N	To 70	Sun to half shade	Moist	Fall	Cone	More resistant to winter desiccation than Colorado blue spruce; northern plains

Deciduous Shrubs

BLACKBERRY, HIGHBUSH (*Rubus ostryfolius*)	6–9	N	3–8/6–12	Sun/half sun	Dry/moist/drained	Summer	Black berry	At least 63 bird species are known to eat the fruit of blackberries and raspberries; also excellent cover
CHERRY, BESSEY (*Prunus besseyi*)	3–6	N	To 2/3–6	Sun	Dry	Summer/early fall	Black drupe	A prostrate shrub; fruit eaten by ring-necked pheasant and other birds; dense form provides excellent nesting cover
CHERRY, DWARF SAND (*Prunus pumila*)	4–9	N	3–5/7	Sun	Dry/moist/drained	Summer	Black drupe	A prostrate shrub that thrives in sandy soil; provides good nesting cover and food
CURRANT, WAX (*Ribes cereum*)	5–8	N	2–4	Sun	Dry	Summer	Red berry	Wild currants and gooseberries provide excellent cover and food for many song and game birds. At least 33 bird species eat *Ribes* berries. This species of currant thrives in dry, rocky soils and prairies
DOGWOOD, ROUGH-LEAVED (*Cornus drummondii*)	4–9	N	4–8/10–15	Sun/part shade	Dry/drought tolerant	Fall	White drupe	Spreads 20 ft. to form thickets; attracts more than 40 species to fruit including quail, turkey, cardinal, bluebird, brown thrasher, thrushes and vireos, flickers, kingbirds, and cedar waxwing

Other Good Choices for the Prairies and Plains—*cont.*

Name	Zone	Native (N) or Alien (A)	Height/spread (ft.)	Light	Preferred Soil	Fruit Period	Fruit Type	Remarks
GOOSEBERRY, MISSOURI (*Ribes missouriense*)	5–9	N	5–6/3–6	Sun/shade	Dry/moist/drained	Summer/early fall	Purple-black berry	Prickly stems; large, abundant fruit; excellent cover
JUNEBERRY, ROUNDLEAF (*Amelanchier sanguinea*)	5–8	N	8–12/3–6	Sun/shade	Well drained	Summer	Purple-black pome	Serviceberries (*Amelanchier*) are eaten by at least 36 bird species; this hardy shrub has great potential for wildlife plantings
OAK, SHIN (*Quercus mohriana*)	7–10	N	To 20	Sun	Dry	Fall	Annual acorn	Sometimes grows to a small tree
PLUM, SANDHILL (*Prunus angustifolia*)	6–10	N	To 20	Sun/varied	Dry/drained/sandy/light	July/August	Red/yellow drupe	Forms dense thickets; fruit eaten by several types of bird
ROSE, PRAIRIE WILD (*Rosa arkansana*)	5–9	N	1–2/4–8	Sun to light shade	Drained	Summer	Purple pome	At least 38 bird species eat wild roses. This native prairie rose offers good shelter and food for prairie chicken, sharp-tailed grouse, and ring-necked pheasant

SILVERBERRY (*Eleagnus commutata*)	2–6	N	3–8/6	Sun/shade	Varied	Summer/fall	Silvery drupe	Very silver foliage; livestock won't eat leaves; forms thickets; eaten by ring-necked pheasant and prairie chicken. A very hardy shrub of the northern plains

Vines

GRAPE, BUSH (*Vitis acerifolia*)	6–10	N		Sun	Dry/drained/sand	Summer	Purple-black berry	Forms dense thickets; good nest sites for many kinds of bird, especially cardinals and catbirds; Missouri south
GRAPE, MUSTANG (*Vitis mustangensis*)	5–8	N		Sun/shade	Moist/drained	Summer	Purple-black berry	Very vigorous grape that can survive great drought and heat. Fruit often persists into winter
WOODBINE (*Parthenocissus vitacea*)	4–8	N		Sun/shade	Moist/drained	Summer/fall	Blue berry	Fruits eaten by many bird species; will cling to brick or stone; rapid growing, drought resistant

Colorado Blue Spruce (*Picea pungens*)

The stately Colorado blue spruce may grow up to 150 feet tall with a spread of 15 feet and develop a trunk diameter 3 feet wide. It is native along hillside streams and canyons at altitudes from 6500 to 11,000 feet in New Mexico, Arizona, Colorado, Utah, Idaho, and Wyoming. Many horticultural varieties are planted in diverse habitats throughout the northern states and most of southern Canada. Spruce needles are important food for the blue

COLORADO BLUE SPRUCE *Picea pungens* (AF)

and spruce grouse, and the seeds are eaten by many types of northern land birds including crossbills, chickadees, pine grosbeak, red-breasted nuthatch, pine siskin, and cedar waxwing. Good seed crops usually occur every 2–3 years. Colorado blue spruce creates excellent nesting sites and protected roosting cover during extremes of summer and winter.

Quaking Aspen (*Populus tremuloides*)

Quaking aspen is one of the most widely distributed trees in North America. It occurs from sea level to 10,000 feet, from New England to California and south to the mountains of Mexico. Within this wide range, it thrives best in the Rockies and coastal ranges, where vast aspen forests grow. Most quaking aspen reach a height of 20–40 feet, but occasionally a tree can grow to 100 feet with a spread of 30 feet. It is a fast-growing, hardy tree that

QUAKING ASPEN *Populus tremuloides* (AF)

thrives on sunlit, poor rocky soils that often result from logging and burning.

It also grows near pond edges, stream banks, and other moist habitats as far north as zone 1. Leaf buds are this aspen's principal attraction for birds. Winter buds are one of the most important foods for the ruffed grouse and a surprising variety of other birds, including the northern shrike, northern oriole, rose-breasted grosbeak, and pine grosbeak. Several cavity-nesting birds, including the yellow-bellied sapsucker, downy woodpecker, and black-capped chickadee, frequently excavate in this aspen's soft wood.

Cascara Buckthorn (*Rhamnus purshiana*)

CASCARA BUCKTHORN *Rhamnus purshiana* **(AF)**

Cascara buckthorn is a small deciduous shrub or tree, 20–40 feet tall. It is best known for the medicinal qualities of its bark, which are processed into a commercial laxative. Its black, juicy berries are about ½ inch in diameter and ripen in late summer. The evening grosbeak, purple finch, pileated woodpecker, ruffed grouse, band-tailed pigeon, Steller's jay, American robin, western tanager, and many others readily consume cascara buckthorn fruits. This important wildlife tree often grows in fencerows with hawthorn, crabapple, and serviceberry, but it is also moderately shade tolerant, and occurs in coniferous forests as an understory tree. Cascara buckthorn grows on rich bottomland and dry hillsides from British Columbia to California and east to the Rocky Mountains of Idaho and Montana.

Golden Currant (*Ribes aureum*)

Golden currant is a native spineless shrub that usually grows about 3–8 feet tall with a spread of 6 feet. It is commonly cultivated for its juicy fruit, and it makes an excellent wildlife planting for food and cover. Golden currant is named for its bright yellow flowers, which appear from March to June. Quarter-inch fruits that vary in color from red or yellow to black follow the flowers. The shrub grows naturally in shady ravines and stream edges, where grouse and quail frequently eat its fruit. At least 33 bird species are known to

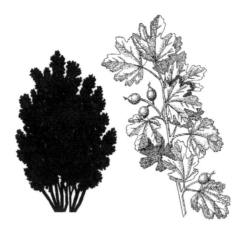

GOLDEN CURRANT *Ribes aureum* (AF)

eat *Ribes* fruit. Golden currant has a wide distribution in the western mountains. It occurs at altitudes from 3500 to 8000 feet in New Mexico and Arizona, and west in the mountains to California and north to Washington and neighboring Canada.

Desert Willow (*Chilopsis linearis*)
This drought-resistant shrub or small tree resembles willows because of its leaves, but its spectacular pink and rose flowers clearly distinguish it. These blossoms are very attractive to hummingbirds. Desert willow, which can have a spread of 6–25 feet, grows rapidly at first, then slows down as it reaches its maximum height of 25 feet. Or it can grow as a 6-foot-tall spreading shrub. The trumpet-shaped flowers appear in late spring through summer,

DESERT WILLOW *Chilopsis linearis* (CD)

depending on elevation. The flowers develop into catalpa-like pods. It thrives in direct sun in dry, open areas. It is hardy in zones 8 and 9.

Desert Olive (*Forestiera neomexicana*)

This evergreen shrub is a fairly fast-growing, drought-resistant choice for creating shrubby fencerows and screens in dry, well-drained soil under full sun. It typically grows 6–10 feet tall and spreads as wide. Male and female flowers occur on separate plants, so plants should be grouped in clusters to obtain crops of the blue-black fruit. The fruit occur in early summer through fall. Scaled quail and desert songbirds readily eat the fruits. It is hardy within zones 7–9.

DESERT OLIVE *Forestiera neomexicana* (CD)

Sugar Bush (*Rhus ovata*)

This evergreen shrub varies in height from 2½ to 10 feet. It is an excellent choice for dry, rocky habitats. It has white or pink flowers from late spring to early summer and is named for its sweet-tasting, red hairy fruits, which ripen in the fall. It grows best in full sun or part shade and prefers well-drained soils. It is hard to establish sugar bush in hot weather, so it should be planted in early spring or fall. At least 15 bird species feed on the red fruits, including the golden-crowned sparrow, yellow-rumped warbler, juncos, northern flicker, and roadrunner. It is hardy within zones 9 and 10.

SUGAR BUSH *Rhus ovata* (CD)

Douglas Hawthorn (*Crataegus douglasii*)

Douglas hawthorn is widely distributed through the northwestern states and adjacent Canada. It grows in a variety of sunny habitats, including stream edges, abandoned fields, and open rangeland. This hawthorn often takes the form of a 5–10-foot-tall, many-branched shrub or a small tree that may grow 15–30 feet tall with a spread of 6–9 feet. Its glossy green leaves and abundant white blossoms make it an attractive plant in the wild or in cultivated areas. Its flowers appear from May to July and its ½-inch black, juicy fruit ripens from July to September. Although this hardy native is not commercially available, it is a common shrub or tree from the Pacific coast across the plains to Michigan. With property owners' permission, speci-

DOUGLAS HAWTHORN *Crataegus douglasii* **(AF)**

mens can be located for transplanting, but be careful to transplant small hawthorns to avoid damage to the deep taproot. This adaptable tree is a good food source for many types of fruit-eating birds, including Townsend's solitaire, American robin, ruffed grouse, cedar waxwing, pine grosbeak, and hermit thrush.

Green Mountain-Ash (*Sorbus scopulina*)

Green mountain-ash is a native shrub that occurs in rocky soils at altitudes from 6000 to 10,000 feet in western mountains from New Mexico north to Alberta and British Columbia. This stout shrub grows from 3 to 15 feet tall and 5 feet wide. It has abundant white flowers in June, and orange pome fruits that mature from July to December. Although green mountain-ash is rarely cultivated, its tolerance of dry mountain soils shows promise for this shrub as a wildlife planting. Moun-

GREEN MOUNTAIN-ASH *Sorbus scopulina* **(AF)**

tain-ash fruit is eaten by many kinds of western woodpeckers, thrush, and grouse.

Blueberry Elder (*Sambucus caerulea*)

Blueberry elder is a spreading shrub that sometimes grows as a 30–40-foot-tall tree with a spread of 15 feet. As with other members of the elderberry group, blueberry elder is one of the best choices for attracting a great variety of songbirds. Blueberry elder has yellowish white flowers from April to August and produces abundant, sweet, and juicy fruits from August to September and sometimes as late as December. It grows best in low, moist

BLUEBERRY ELDER *Sambucus caerulea* (AF)

areas at elevations from 2000 to 8000 feet, from western Texas and New Mexico west to southern California and north in the coastal ranges to British Columbia. Quail, flickers, and woodpeckers consume the abundant fruits. The western kingbird, black phoebe, black-headed grosbeak, Swainson's thrush, phainopepla, band-tailed pigeon, and many others readily eat the fruit. This important wildlife planting is an excellent choice for landscaping pond and stream edges and other moist habitats.

Mesquite (*Prosopis juliflora*)

Mesquite is a common tree or shrub of the southwestern United States. It grows best on moist stream banks and canyons, but it also spreads to upland sites and sometimes creates serious problems for cattlemen, as it shades out grasses on overgrazed range. Mesquite grows up to 30 feet tall with a spread of 20 feet, though it is a much lower shrub in most of its range, and it is so rugged that it can live in areas

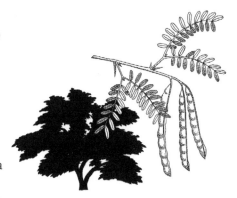

MESQUITE *Prosopis juliflora* (AF)

occupied by few other shrubs or trees. Mesquite owes its tenacity to its long taproot system, which may reach as much as 60 feet down to groundwater. Its principal value to birds is its thorny branches and foliage, which provide excellent cover and nest sites. Mesquite seeds are especially important to Gambel's quail, scaled quail, white-winged dove, and ravens. Because of its value as a cover plant, mesquite should be protected for wildlife cover in rocky soils, streamside habitats, and other property "corners" where few other woody plants will grow.

Prickly Pear Cactus (*Opuntia* spp.)
Members of this highly diverse cactus group are especially adapted to the arid habitats of the western United States, especially the Southwest. In overgrazed lands, *Opuntia* spp. may be the dominant vegetation, and its well-armed prickly shelter gives abundant cover to many small animals. The principal benefit of this species group to birds is its abundant crop of juicy fruits and seeds. The white-winged dove, Gambel's quail, scaled quail, curve-billed thrasher, golden-fronted

PRICKLY PEAR CACTUS *Opuntia* spp. **(AF)**

woodpecker, cactus wren, and many others often eat them. Some botanists have described more than 100 *Opuntia* species in the United States. These vary greatly in size from low, creeping forms that are only a few inches tall to some, such as the sonora jumping cholla (*O. fulgida*), that may grow up to 12 feet tall.

Grouseberry (*Vaccinium scoparium*)
A low deciduous shrub, grouseberry is usually only 4–12 inches tall, but under ideal conditions it can grow up to 6 feet. It produces a crop of sweet, red or wine-colored fruits that mature by July through September. As with most members of the huckleberry-blueberry group, the fruit is a favorite bird food. The grouseberry's fruits are eaten by many bird species, including the ring-necked pheasant, pine grosbeak, hermit thrush, and Swainson's thrush. Grouseberry grows at altitudes from 6000 to 11,500 feet in shaded pine forests. It is usually found in moist, well-drained soils, and is naturally distributed from northern New Mexico west to the mountains of California and north to British Columbia and Alberta.

GROUSEBERRY *Vaccinium scoparium* **(AF)**

Western Thimbleberry (*Rubus parviflorus*)

As with most members of the bramble group, western thimbleberry is an important wild bird food. This is an especially prolific, spineless, fruiting species. It is adaptable to a variety of light conditions, occurring in woodlands, borders, and open habitats in the mountains of New Mexico north to British Columbia and Alaska. Fragrant white flowers appear during June and July and are followed by red fruits, which ripen during August and September. The fruits are consumed by

WESTERN THIMBLEBERRY *Rubus parviflorus* **(AF)**

many types of land birds, including the western kingbird, cedar waxwing, common flicker, gray catbird, northern bobwhite, Swainson's thrush, red-headed woodpecker, and pine grosbeak. This attractive shrub is often available through commercial suppliers.

Canyon Grape (*Vitis arizonica*)

Canyon grape is a vigorous climbing vine well adapted for dry habitats. It endures drought and cold but cannot withstand excess moisture. Canyon grape occasionally develops a stem diameter of 1 foot—plants with 6-inch diameters are common. It sometimes overtops small shrubs and trees, creating an ideal nesting habitat for many kinds of songbirds. Its sweet, black fruit ripens from July to August. Canyon grapes are highly prized for jellies and preserves, and are readily consumed by several species of quail and songbirds, including the common flicker, northern mockingbird, western bluebird, and western kingbird. This hardy grape occurs in ravines and gulches between altitudes of 2000 and 7500 feet in most of New Mexico, Arizona, and Colorado.

CANYON GRAPE *Vitis arizonica* **(AF)**

Additional Recommended Plantings for the Mountains and Deserts

Evergreen Trees
Juniper, One-Seed (*Juniperus monosperma*)
Juniper, Rocky Mountain (*Juniperus scopulorum*)
Pine, Austrian (*Pinus nigra*)
Pine, Ponderosa (*Pinus ponderosa*)
Spruce, White (*Picea glauca*)

Deciduous Trees
Cherry, Black (*Prunus serotina*)
Chokecherry, Common (*Prunus virginiana*)
Maple, Box Elder (*Acer negundo*)
Poplar, Balsam (*Populus balsamifera*)

Evergreen Shrubs
JUNIPER, CHINESE (*Juniper chinensis*)
JUNIPER, COMMON (*Juniper communis*)
JUNIPER, CREEPING (*Juniper horizontalis*)
LILAC, WILD (*Ceanothus* spp.)

Deciduous Shrubs
BUCKTHORN, ALDERLEAF (*Rhamnus alnifolia*)
BUFFALOBERRY, SILVER (*Shepherdia argentea*)
CURRANT, WAX (*Ribes cereum*)
DOGWOOD, RED-OSIER (*Cornus stolonifera*)
ELDER, SCARLET (*Sambucus pubens*)
RASPBERRIES (*Rubus* spp.)
ROSE, WOODS (*Rosa woodsii*)
SERVICEBERRY, SASKATOON (*Amelanchier alnifolia*)
SILVERBERRY (*Eleagnus commutata*)
SNOWBERRY, COMMON (*Symphoricarpos albus*)
SUMAC, SKUNKBUSH (*Rhus aromatica*)
SUMAC, SMOOTH (*Rhus glabra*)

Vines
CREEPER, VIRGINIA (*Parthenocissus quinquefolia*)
HONEYSUCKLE, TRUMPET (*Lonicera sempervirens*)
WOODBINE (*Parthenocissus vitacea*)

Other Good Choices for the Mountains and Deserts

Name	Zone	Native (N) or Alien (A)	Height/spread (ft.)	Light	Preferred Soil	Fruit Period	Fruit Type	Remarks
Evergreen Trees								
ASH, VELVET (*Fraxinus velutina*)	6–8	N	20–30/30	Sun	Moist/drained	Fall	Samara	A variable, semievergreen tree; very alkali and drought resistant; ash seeds are eaten by at least 9 bird species, including evening and pine grosbeaks
FIR, DOUGLAS (*Pseudotsuga menziesii*)	4–7	N	75–100/20–30	Sun	Dry/moist/drained	Fall	Cone	Thrives best on northern exposures; needles are important winter food of blue grouse, but there are few other records of bird use
FIR, GRAND (*Abies grandis*)	5, 6	N	To 120/15–25	Sun/part shade	Moist/drained	Fall	Cone	At least 10 species of birds feed on the needles and seeds of these large evergreens; as with Douglas fir, they are most useful as food for grouse, but when planted in yards,

Species	Zone	N	Size	Light	Soil	Season	Fruit	Notes
FIR, SUBALPINE (*Abies lasiocarpa*)	3–6	N	60–100/10–12	Sun/shade	Cool/moist/deep	Fall	Cone	they provide important nest sites and cover
FIR, WHITE (*Abies concolor*)	4–7	N	80–100/15–22	Sun/shade	Dry/moist/drained	Fall	Cone	
HEMLOCK, MOUNTAIN (*Tsuga mertensiana*)	6–8	N	75–100/20	Sun/shade	Cool/deep/moist/drained	Fall	Cone	Excellent choice for hedges or shady habitat. Preferred foods of chickadees and pine siskin; abundant seed crops every 2–3 years
HEMLOCK, WESTERN (*Tsuga heterophylla*)	7, 8	N	125–175/20–30	Sun/shade	Dry/moist/drained	Fall	Cone	
JUNIPER, ALLIGATOR (*Juniperus deppeana*)	7, 8	N	30–50/12	Sun	Dry/rocky/sterile	Fall	Blue-green berry	These drought-resistant junipers provide excellent cover and food; at least 26 bird species are known to eat juniper berries; plant male and female to provide a fruit crop: pinyon jay and
JUNIPER, UTAH (*Juniperus osteosperma*)	5–9	N	To 20	Sun	Dry/rocky/sandy	Fall	Blue-green berry	Townsend's solitaire eat these berries

Other Good Choices for the Mountains and Deserts—cont.

Name	Zone	Native (N) or Alien (A)	Height/spread (ft.)	Light	Preferred Soil	Fruit Period	Fruit Type	Remarks
JUNIPER, WESTERN (Juniperus occidentalis)	6–8	N	15–30/3–10	Sun	Dry/rocky	Fall	Blue-green berry	
OAK, CANYON LIVE (Quercus chrysolepis)	7–9	N	60–80/30	Sun	Dry/drained	Fall	Biennial acorn	Varies in form from large tree to small shrub, depending on available water; grows in sand or loam soils, sometimes
OAK, GAMBEL (Quercus gambellii)	4–7	N	15–30/10–12	Sun	Dry/drained	Late summer	Annual acorn	creating dense ground covers; acorns eaten by acorn woodpecker, and scaled and Montezuma quail
PINE, LIMBER (Pinus flexilis)	6–7	N	25–50/20–28	Sun	Dry/drained	Fall	Cone	Adaptable to many soil types and shows tolerance to wind; named for the flexible nature of young branches
PINE, LODGEPOLE (Pinus contorta var. latifolia)	4–8	N 50	70–80/	Sun	Dry/moist/drained/sandy	Late summer/fall	Cone	Intolerant of pollution; tall trees often fall in strong winds

PINE, PINYON (*Pinus edulis*)	5–8	N	10–40/20–25	Sun	Dry/drained	Fall	Cone	Slow growing and drought resistant; seeds eaten by at least 9 bird species, including Montezuma quail and wild turkey
PINE, SUGAR (*Pinus lambertiana*)	6–8	N	175–200/30	Sun	Moist/drained	Fall	Cone	Tallest pine, with enormous cones (26 in.); seeds are especially important to quail and grouse, but also eaten by many kinds of songbirds
PINE, WESTERN WHITE (*Pinus monticola*)	6–8	N	90–150/20–25	Sun	Rich/moist/drained	Fall/winter	Cone	At least 54 bird species eat pine seeds, and western white pine is one of the most important seed providers in this region; shade tolerant when young; requires full sun when mature
PINE, WHITEBARK (*Pinus albicaulis*)	4–7	N	10–40/47	Sun	Dry/drained	Late summer/fall	Cone	Very resistant to wind; sometimes taking a prostrate or shrub form when under stress from strong, persistent wind
SPRUCE, ENGELMANN (*Picea engelmannii*)	3–8	N	60–120/15	Sun/shade	Rich/moist/drained	Fall	Cone	Important food for blue and spruce grouse, which eat the needles; seeds usually produced every third year

Other Good Choices for the Mountains and Deserts—cont.

Name	Zone	Native (N) or Alien (A)	Height/spread (ft.)	Light	Preferred Soil	Fruit Period	Fruit Type	Remarks
YEW, PACIFIC (Taxus brevifolia)	6–10	N	20–50/8–18	Sun/shade	Moist/deep	Fall	Red berry	Most shade-tolerant forest tree in the Northwest; berries eaten by ruffed grouse
Deciduous Trees								
ALDER, ARIZONA (Alnus oblongifolia)	7–9	N	20–30	Sun	Moist/drained	Fall	Nutlet in cone	Useful plantings along streams, ponds, and other moist-soil habitats; alders provide excellent cover and nest sites for songbirds; seeds are important food for goldfinch, siskins, and redpolls
ALDER, SITKA (Alnus sinuata)	1–8	N	5–30/12	Sun	Moist	Fall	Nutlet in cone	
ALDER, THINLEAF (Alnus tenuifolia)	6–8	N	6–25/25	Sun	Moist/drained	Fall	Nutlet in cone	
ALDER, WHITE (Alnus rhombifolia)	5–8	N	40–100/70	Shade	Moist	Fall/spring	Nutlet in cone	

Species	Zone	N	Size	Light	Moisture	Season	Fruit	Notes
BIRCH, WATER (*Betula occidentalis*)	4–8	N	20–25/6–9	Sun	Moist/ mineral	Fall	Samara	Catkins and buds are important food for grouse; birch seeds are favorite foods for redpoll and pine siskin
CHERRY, BITTER (*Prunus emarginata*)	7, 8	N	35–40	Sun	Dry/ moist/ drained	Spring/fall	Drupe	Large tree to shrub; forms dense thickets; eaten by at least 9 bird species, including Townsend's solitaire, bluebird, and band-tailed pigeon
COTTONWOOD, BLACK (*Populus trichocarpa*)	5–9	N	To 100/30	Sun	Moist/ sandy/ gravelly	Spring	Capsule	Ten bird species are known to eat cottonwood buds; especially important to ruffed grouse, greater prairie chicken, and sharp-tailed grouse; also eaten by evening grosbeak and purple finch; fairly salt tolerant, especially Fremont cottonwood
COTTONWOOD, FREMONT (*Populus fremontii*)	7–9	N	To 100/50	Sun	Dry/ drained	Spring	Capsule	
COTTONWOOD, NARROWLEAF (*Populus angustifolia*)	3–10	N	50–70/15–35	Sun	Moist/ drained	Spring	Capsule	
DOGWOOD, PACIFIC (*Cornus nuttallii*)	7–9	N	10–40/25	Sun/ shade	Drained	Late summer/ fall	White drupe	Fruit readily eaten by grouse, quail, flicker, bluebird, purple finch, and Swainson's thrush

221

Other Good Choices for the Mountains and Deserts—*cont.*

Name	Zone	Native (N) or Alien (A)	Height/spread (ft.)	Light	Preferred Soil	Fruit Period	Fruit Type	Remarks
HAWTHORNS (*Crataegus* spp.)	3–9	N	20–35/20–30	Sun/half sun	Drained/rich	Fall	Black pome	At least 36 bird species eat these fruits; occurs along banks of mountain streams or rich bottomlands; often forms thickets; sometimes grows as a shrub North: *C. erythropoda*, *C. columbiana*, and *C. succulenta* Central: *C. chrysocarpa*, *C. rivularis*, and *C. succulenta* South: *C. tracyi* and *C. wootoniana*
MAPLE, BIGTOOTH (*Acer grandidentatum*)	6–8	N	30–40/30	Sun	Drained	Fall	Samara	Large trees to shrubs; tolerates poor soils; buds eaten by evening and pine grosbeaks
MAPLE, ROCKY MOUNTAIN (*Acer glabrum*)	5–8	N	20–30/6–15	Sun	Dry/drained	Late fall	Samara	

MESQUITE, SCREWBEAN (*Prosopis pubescens*)	7–10	N	15–30/25	Sun	Dry/moist	Summer/fall	Legume	Grows in river bottoms and canyons; varies from large tree to small shrub, depending on conditions; spiny, forms thickets; grows in wide variety of soils including gravel; eaten by bobwhite, roadrunner, and Gambel's quail
OAK, ARIZONA WHITE (*Quercus arizonica*)	6–10	N	To 40	Sun	Dry/drained	Fall	Annual acorn	Sometimes grows as a shrub; resists heavy grazing and is drought tolerant; oaks are very important wildlife food; at least 63 bird species are known to eat acorns
OAK, GAMBEL (*Quercus gambelii*)	4–7	N	25–35/10–12	Sun	Dry/drained	Fall	Annual acorn	
SYCAMORE, ARIZONA (*Platanus wrightii*)	7–9	N	60–80/20	Sun	Moist/drained	Fall	Achene	A favorite food of goldfinches; also eaten by band-tailed pigeon
WILLOW, COYOTE (*Salix exigua*)	4–6	N	To 15/15	Sun	Moist/drained	Early summer	Capsule	Stabilizes stream banks; provides excellent cover and nest sites for many kinds of songbirds; buds eaten by grouse
WILLOW, PACIFIC (*Salix lasiandra*)	1–9	N	To 30	Sun	Moist/drained	Early summer	Capsule	

223

Other Good Choices for the Mountains and Deserts—cont.

Name	Zone	Native (N) or Alien (A)	Height/spread (ft.)	Light	Preferred Soil	Fruit Period	Fruit Type	Remarks
Evergreen Shrubs								
ACACIA, CATCLAW (*Acacia greggii*)	6–10	N	To 30/6–13	Sun	Dry	Summer/ spring	Legume	A preferred food of quail and doves; thorny, excellent cover; sometimes grows as a small tree
ELDER, MEXICAN (*Sambucus mexicana*)	7–10	N	To 30/25–35	Sun	Moist	Year-round	Black berry	This semievergreen shrub of the Southwest can grow to a small tree with up to an 18-in.-diameter trunk; occurs in low, moist habitats, such as ditches, stream borders, and moist grasslands; at least 12 bird species eat the fruit
HACKBERRY, SPINY (*Celtis pallida*)	7–10	N	10–20/8–10	Sun	Dry	Summer/ fall	Yellow drupe	A valuable bird food and cover; plant in the southern part of this region; fruits are eaten by cactus wren, cardinal, pyrrhuloxia, scaled quail, and green jay

224

Species								Remarks
HONEYSUCKLE, MEXICAN (*Justicia spicigera*)	8–11	N	2–3/1–2	Sun/part shade	Dry/drained	Spring/summer	Yellow/orange flowers attract hummingbirds	Excellent hummingbird shrub. Similar forms use shrimplant (*J. brandegeana*), Brazilian plume flower (*J. carnea*), and chuprosa (*J. californica*)
MANZANITA, GREEN-LEAF (*Arctostaphylos patula*)	7–9	N	1–10/6	Sun	Dry/drained	Year-round	Brown berry	Creeping mat or shrub of Southwest mountains; occurs in dry, gravelly soils, often in association with ponderosa pine; fruit eaten by grouse and quail
MANZANITA, POINT-LEAF (*Arctostaphylos pungens*)	7–10	N	1–10/3–7	Sun	Dry/drained	Summer/spring	Brown dark red berry	
OAK, PALMER (*Quercus palmeri*)	6–9	N	To 25	Sun	Dry/drained/sandy	Summer	Biennial acorn	Large, dense shrub, sometimes grows as a tree; grasslands and canyons of the Southwest
OREGON-GRAPE (*Mahonia nervosa*)	5–8	N	To 2/3	Sun/shade	Dry/drained	Fall	Berry	Dense foliage offers excellent cover; several cultured varieties available; berries eaten by ruffed and blue grouse

225

Other Good Choices for the Mountains and Deserts—*cont.*

Name	Zone	Native (N) or Alien (A)	Height/spread (ft.)	Light	Preferred Soil	Fruit Period	Fruit Type	Remarks
SALTBUSH, BIG (*Atriplex lentiformis*)	8–10	N	6–10	Sun	Dry	Fall/ winter	Achene	Growing in dense patches, it provides excellent cover for quail and other desert wildlife; when pruned it forms excellent hedges for arid climate cities of the Southwest and California. Deciduous in dry areas
SALTBUSH, DESERT HOLLY (*Atriplex hymenelytra*)	6–9	N	2–5	Sun	Dry	Early fall	Achene	Decorative and good cover for arid habitats; native to Southwest; 29 bird species are known to eat saltbush fruit
Deciduous Shrubs								
ACACIA, MESCAT (*Acacia constricta*)	7–11	N	6–18/6–20	Sun	Dry/ sandy	Summer	4-in. black pods/ legumes	A common, spiny shrub of harsh soils in the extreme southern part of this region; seeds eaten by scaled quail and white-winged dove

	Zones	Native	Height/Spread	Light	Moisture	Fruiting	Fruit	Notes
BLUEBERRY, WESTERN BOG (*Vaccinium occidentale*)	5–9	N	To 4	Sun	Moist/drained	Late summer	Blue berry	Blueberries and huckleberries are very important wildlife foods, with at least 87 bird species known to eat the fruits
CEANOTHUS, FENDLER (*Ceanothus fendleri*)	5–9	N	To 3/3	Sun/shade	Dry/drained	Late summer/early fall	Red/brown capsule	Useful for quail food and cover, and as a nest site for many kinds of songbirds
CHERRY, BITTER (*Prunus emarginata*)	7, 8	N	3–12	Sun/shade	Dry/moist/drained	Spring/early fall	Black drupe	Large shrub to small tree; forms dense thickets providing good nest cover and food for at least 6 bird species
CONDALIA, KNIFE-LEAF (*Condalia spathulata*)	7–10	N	To 10/10–20	Sun	Dry	Early summer	Black drupe	Very thorny, rounded shrubs of deserts and dry foothills in the southwest; ideal nest sites for songbirds; important food for scaled quail
CONDALIA, LOTEBUSH (*Condalia lycioides*)	7–9	N	To 10	Sun	Dry/drained	Early summer	Purple drupe	
CONDALIA, LOTEWOOD (*Condalia obtusifolia*)	7–10	N	To 10	Sun	Dry	Early summer	Black drupe	
CURRANT, STICKY (*Ribes viscosissimum*)	4–9	N	1–4/6	Sun/shade	Drained	Late summer/early fall	Black berry	Thornless shrub with roots up to 4 ft. deep; at least 33 bird species eat fruits of the currants and gooseberries

Other Good Choices for the Mountains and Deserts—*cont.*

Name	Native (N) or Alien (A)	Zone	Height/spread (ft.)	Light	Preferred Soil	Fruit Period	Fruit Type	Remarks
CURRANT, WAX (*Ribes cereum*)	N	5–8	2–4	Sun	Dry	Summer	Red berry	At least 33 bird species eat currants and gooseberry; wax currant is a very important bird food and cover plant throughout this region; it grows in green, sunny fields, or forest openings; an important food for grouse
DOGWOOD, BROWN (*Cornus glabrata*)	N	8–10	To 10/3–7	Sun	Moist	Late summer/fall	Drupe	Large shrub or small tree that, along with other western dogwoods, provides important food for grouse, quail, woodpeckers, and bluebirds; brown dogwood forms dense thickets along mountain streams
DOGWOOD, MINER'S (*Cornus sessilis*)	N	5–10	To 10/3–9	Sun	Moist	Late summer/early fall	Drupe	

Name	Zone	N	Height	Light	Moisture	Season	Fruit	Notes
ELDER, BLACK-BEAD (*Sambucus melanocarpa*)	6–9	N	3–12/13	Sun/shade	Moist	Late summer	Blue berry	At least 111 bird species are known to eat elderberry fruits; bunchberry elder is a small shrub that occurs on the eastern slopes of the Rocky Mountains; the larger black-bead elder grows along mountain streams and canyons in the conifer belt from New Mexico to southern Alaska
ELDER, BUNCHBERRY (*Sambucus microbotrys*)	3–9	N	To 5	Sun/shade	Moist/drained	Late summer	Red berry	
HACKBERRY, WESTERN (*Celtis douglasii*)	3–9	N	To 20/20–25	Sun/shade	Dry/moist/drained	Summer/winter	Brown drupe	Grows in dry, gravelly soils; fruits eaten by band-tailed pigeon, evening grosbeak, roadrunner, and many others; hackberry fruits are eaten by at least 20 bird species
HONEYSUCKLE, BEARBERRY (*Lonicera involucrata*)	4–8	N	To 10/10	Sun/shade	Moist/drained/calcereous	Late summer	Brown berry	Grows in lime soils in woods and meadows to 10,500 ft.; fruit eaten by at least 6 bird species, including cedar waxwing, pine grosbeak, and Swainson's thrush; flowers are visited by blue-throated and magnificent hummingbirds

Other Good Choices for the Mountains and Deserts—*cont.*

Name	Zone	Native (N) or Alien (A)	Height/spread (ft.)	Light	Preferred Soil	Fruit Period	Fruit Type	Remarks
HONEYSUCKLE, HAIRY WHITE (*Lonicera albiflora*)	6–9	N	To 9	Sun	Moist/drained	Fall	Blue berry	A thicket-forming shrub or climbing vine of the Southwest; occurs in thickets and banks of streams; eaten by bobwhite, catbird, robin, and hermit thrush
HONEYSUCKLE, UTAH (*Lonicera utahensis*)	6–8	N	To 5	Shade	Dry/drained	Summer/early fall	Yellow/red berry	An erect, clump-forming shrub; fruit eaten by hermit thrush, Townsend's solitaire, robin, and ring-necked pheasant
MOUNTAIN-ASH, ALPINE (*Sorbus occidentalis*)	6–9	N	To 30	Sun	Moist/dry/drained	Late summer/winter	Red pome	At least 11 bird species readily eat mountain-ash fruit, including evening grosbeak, pine grosbeak, robin, blue grouse, and Clark's nutcracker;
MOUNTAIN-ASH, GREEN (*Sorbus scopulina*)	6, 7	N	To 15/5	Sun/shade	Moist/drained	Summer/winter	Red pome	

Species				Light	Moisture	Season	Fruit	Comments
MOUNTAIN-ASH, SITKA (*Sorbus sitchensis*)	5–9	N	To 15/6–8	Sun	Moist/dry/drained	Late summer/early winter	Red pome	frequently forms dense thickets
OLIVE, DESERT (*Forestiera pubescens*)	7–10	N	6–10/15	Sun	Dry/moist/drained	Early summer/early fall	Black drupe	Widely distributed spreading shrub of dry river bottoms in the Southwest; principal food of scaled quail in Texas; also eaten by robins
RASPBERRY, BOULDER (*Rubus deliciosus*)	4–8	N	To 6/8	Sun	Dry/moist/drained	Summer/early fall	Dark purple drupelet	Plants of dry, rocky soils; offers excellent cover and nest sites for mockingbirds; at least 146 bird species are known to eat the fruits of these exceptionally important plants
RASPBERRY, WHITEBARK (*Rubus leucodermis*)	3–9	N	To 5/6–12	Sun	Dry/moist/drained	Summer/early fall	Dark purple drupelet	
ROSE, WOODS (*Rosa woodsii*)	3–8	N	To 3/5	Sun/half sun	Moist/drained	All year	Red hip	Widespread thicket-forming rose throughout the Rocky Mountains from 3–500 to 10,000 ft.; largest flowers of any wild western rose; fruits eaten by hermit thrush, Swainson's thrush, ruffed grouse, and other game birds

Other Good Choices for the Mountains and Deserts—*cont.*

Name	Zone	Native (N) or Alien (A)	Height/spread (ft.)	Light	Preferred Soil	Fruit Period	Fruit Type	Remarks
SAGEBRUSH, BIG (*Artemisia tridentata*)	4–9	N	2–10/8	Sun	Dry/drained	Fall	Achene	Occurs widely in the West, growing in dry and stony soils in deserts and up to timberline; principal food and cover for sage grouse; an indicator of alkaline-tree soils
SERVICEBERRY, LONGFLOWER (*Symphoricarpos longiflorus*)	7, 8	N	3–4	Sun	Dry	Summer	White berry-like drupe	Occurs in rocky foothills and canyons from 4000 to 8000 ft.; the fruit of this and other snowberries is eaten by at least 26 bird species; special importance to grouse and other game birds
SERVICEBERRY, UTAH (*Amelanchier utahensis*)	4–9	N	4–25	Sun	Dry/drained	Summer	Blue/black pome	Small to large shrub of rocky soil and dry hillsides; as with other serviceberries, this is an important food for songbirds
SNOWBERRY, MOUNTAIN (*Symphoricarpos oreophilus*)	6–8	N	To 4/1–3	Sun	Dry/moist/drained	Late summer	White berry-like drupe	Occurs in rocky soils of southwestern mountains from 5000 to 9000 ft.; has ornamental value

Name	Zones		Height	Light	Soil	Season	Fruit	Notes
SNOWBERRY, ROUNDLEAF (*Symphoricarpos rotundifolius*)	8, 9	N	To 3	Sun	Dry/drained	Late summer/early fall	White berry-like drupe	Highly ornamental, slender plant; long cultivated; occurs in mountain canyons from 4000 to 10,000 ft.
WOLFBERRY, ANDERSON (*Lycium andersonii*)	6–10	N	1–9/3–7	Sun	Dry/sandy	Spring	Red berry	Tolerant of alkaline soils; excellent cover; important food for verdin, gila woodpecker, and many other types of desert bird; flower nectar used by black-chinned hummingbird

Ground Covers (less than 1 ft. tall)

Name	Zones		Height	Light	Soil	Season	Fruit	Notes
BLUEBERRY, DWARF (*Vaccinium caespitosum*)	4–7	N		Sun	Dry/drained	Summer/early fall	Blue berry	Creeping timberline shrubs that produce highly attractive berries; among the birds eating these fruits are cedar waxwings; ruffed grouse, flicker, hermit thrush, and pine grosbeak
WHORTELBERRY, GROUSE (*Vaccinium scoparium*)	3–8	N		Sun/shade	Dry/moist	Summer	Blue berry	
WINTERGREEN (*Gaultheria humifusa*)	6, 7	N		Sun/shade	Drained	Late summer	Berry	Small evergreen shrubs; form mats grow on sandy or other soils; at least 7 bird species are known to eat the fruits of wintergreens

233

Other Good Choices for the Mountains and Deserts—cont.

Name	Zone	Native (N) or Alien (A)	Height/spread (ft.)	Light	Preferred Soil	Fruit Period	Fruit Type	Remarks
WINTERGREEN, BUSH (*Gaultheria ovatifolia*)	6–8	N		Sun	Drained	Late summer	Berry	
Vines*								
GRAPE, CANYON (*Vitis arizonica*)	7–9	N	D	Sun	Moist/drained	Summer/persists to fall	Blue-black berry	Grows best in moist, sandy soils; eaten by many types of bird, including Gambel's and scaled quail
HONEYSUCKLE, CHAPARRAL (*Lonicera interrupta*)	7–10	N	E	Sun	Dry	Summer/winter	Berry	Attractive fruits for Townsend's solitaire, thrashers, towhees, Swainson's thrush, and wrentit; chaparral honeysuckle is an evergreen and sometimes grows as a shrub
HONEYSUCKLE, ORANGE (*Lonicera ciliosa*)	6–9	N	D	Sun/shade	Dry/drained	Summer/early fall	Red berry	

*D, deciduous; E, evergreen.

Shore Pine (*Pinus contorta*)

Shore pine is a native of the coastal region from northern California to Alaska. It usually grows to only 15–35 feet with a spread of 25 feet, and takes on a twisted and contorted form as its Latin name suggests. Away from the coast it becomes shrubby, and in more protected areas it takes on a straight-trunk form. At even higher and more protected altitudes, shore pine eventually grades into an important lumber

SHORE PINE *Pinus contorta* (AF)

tree, the lodgepole pine. Shore pine tolerates the rigors of the Pacific Coast zone so well that it may live to over 200 years. It is an excellent shelter planting for windy coastal areas and is one of the best choices for sandy or rocky soils. This is a popular residential tree because of its pleasing pyramidal shape and its dense foliage, which serves as a good visual screen, offering excellent shelter for birds. It is hardy to zone 5. Shore pine's cones are about 2 inches long and mature during August and September, providing tiny seeds that are eaten by many bird species.

Pacific Madrone (*Arbutus menziesii*)

Usually Pacific madrone takes the form of a 15-foot-tall evergreen bush or small tree, but in ideal conditions it may grow to an 80-foot-tall tree with a spread of 50 feet. It is native from British Columbia to California in the coastal ranges and is hardy in zone 9. Madrone is notable for its distinctive reddish brown bark that peels in thin flakes. During spring it has bell-shaped, pale pink or white flowers that arise in clusters at the ends of branches. Red or orange fruits are

PACIFIC MADRONE *Arbutus menziesii* (VH)

extremely attractive to birds in late October and November. Madrone grows best in rich, well-drained soils. It takes on a spreading form when planted in the open, and grows tallest when planted in groves. The fruit is a favorite food of the band-tailed pigeon, wild turkey, California and mountain quail, thrushes, finches, and other songbirds.

California Live Oak (*Quercus agrifolia*)

This large native oak once dominated vast coastal regions from Santa Barbara to the Mexican border. Unfortunately, human population growth has eliminated almost all of the great coastal oak groves, leaving only a few remnant reminders of their former grand stature. California live oak may develop a trunk diameter of 12 feet and a remarkable spread of 130 feet, though even a tree this large will only grow about 75 feet tall. This adaptable evergreen oak can live in many habitats,

CALIFORNIA LIVE OAK *Quercus agrifolia* (AF)

from windblown coastal sites to steep mountainsides, canyon walls, and open plains. Within these varied habitats, it prefers dry, well-drained soils, and can thrive in sand, loam, gravel, and other soil types. In very dry sites, it may grow no higher than a small shrub. California live oak produces an acorn crop each year, and California quail, jays, woodpeckers, chestnut-backed chickadee, plain titmouse, and many others eat this fruit. This California native is adaptable to normal garden conditions and is hardy in zone 9. Young trees may be started from rooted nursery stock or acorns. Regular watering is not necessary, but it encourages rapid growth in young live oaks.

Pacific Dogwood (*Cornus nuttallii*)

Closely related to the spectacular flowering dogwood of the east, the Pacific dogwood has even larger flowers and leaves than its eastern relative. It inhabits the Pacific coastal mountains at elevations between 4000 and 6000 feet from Vancouver Island, British Columbia, to the mountains of San Diego County and is hardy to zone 8. This attractive tree grows to 60 feet tall with a spread of 25 feet, but usually it is much smaller. Pacific dogwood is a popular cultivated tree. It has inconspicuous clusters of yellow-green flowers surrounded by 4–6 white bracts. This showy flower cluster measures up to 6 inches across. The fruit clusters ripen from October to November, and consist of 30–40 bright red berry-like drupes. The tree's fall color is as spectacular as its spring show, as the leaves turn a brilliant burgundy red. The fruits are one of the favorite foods of the band-

PACIFIC DOGWOOD *Cornus nuttallii* (AF)

tailed pigeon and are also eaten by the flicker, hermit thrush, cedar waxwing, warbling vireo, purple finch, American robin, and pileated woodpecker.

Holly-Leaved Buckthorn

(*Rhamnus crocea*)

Buckthorn holly is a native evergreen shrub that usually grows only 2–3 feet tall and 3–10 feet wide. Rarely, it grows as a tree, which can reach a height up to 25 feet. It produces red fruits in August and September that make an attractive contrast with the lustrous holly-like leaves. Holly-leaved buckthorn grows best on sunny, dry hillsides in Arizona and southern California, where it is hardy to zone 9. It is an excellent bird-attracting choice for

HOLLY-LEAVED BUCKTHORN *Rhamnus crocea* (AF)

this dry climate, as it provides excellent nesting places in its dense foliage. Its berries are eaten by many kinds of birds, including the phainopepla, northern mockingbird, California thrasher, and Swainson's thrush. Plants transplanted from the country to moderately well-watered residential settings acquire a glossy foliage, the brown of lower leaf surfaces usually disappears, and the plants develop a less dense growth form, sometimes reaching a height of 5 feet. Since the male and female flowers are on different plants, it is necessary to plant several for a good fruit crop.

Holly-Leaved Cherry (*Prunus ilicifolia*)

Holly-leaved cherry, sometimes known by the Indian name *Islay*, is an evergreen shrub or small tree, 6–28 feet tall and a spread of 20 feet, with glossy green leaves. In its native habitat from San Francisco Bay south through the coast ranges of California to Baja California, holly-leaved cherry grows in many soil types, including sand, loam, and clay. It inhabits the dry chaparral,

HOLLY-LEAVED CHERRY *Prunus ilicifolia* **(AF)**

where it tolerates alkali soils and demonstrates its resistance to drought and fire. Yet when transplanted to more moderate climate, holly-leaved cherry makes a fine residential planting or pruned hedge. It is hardy within zone 9. Holly-leaved cherry has small white flowers from March to May and sweet, dark red or purple fruits that often remain available into December. The fruit is eaten by many kinds of birds, including the hairy woodpecker, scrub jay, phainopepla, and Swainson's thrush. Its dense foliage also provides excellent protection for bird nests.

Four-Wing Saltbush (*Atriplex canescens*)

This erect, evergreen shrub, 6 feet tall and 8 feet wide, will tolerate even the most arid western habitats. Four-wing saltbush is widely distributed in southern California to western Texas and Oklahoma and north to eastern Washington and Alberta. It is hardy within zone 7. It thrives in a great variety of sunny, arid conditions, including grassy uplands, sandy deserts, and salt and alkali flatlands. Its principal value to birds is its ability to reduce soil erosion and provide shade and nesting cover in these harsh environments. It produces an annual crop of $\frac{1}{4}$–$\frac{3}{4}$-inch-long winged seeds during August and September. Gambel's quail, horned lark, and other ground-feeding birds eat the seeds. Four-wing saltbush is an excellent planting for conservation lands.

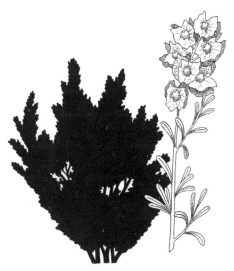

FOUR-WING SALTBUSH *Atriplex canescens* **(AF)**

Toyon (*Heteromeles arbutifolia*)

This native evergreen shrub is also known as *California holly* because of its holly-like leaves and clusters of red or orange berries in late winter. Usually, toyon grows to about 5–10 feet, but under ideal conditions it may reach 25 feet in height with an equal spread. It is native to the Sierra Nevada foothills and southern California to Baja. Its natural habitat is the edge of oak woodlands and mixed pine-oak woods. It is

TOYON *Heteromeles arbutifolia* **(VH)**

not easily transplanted from the wild, so nursery-grown plants are best. It should be planted in deep, rich soil and watered infrequently but deeply in the first winter after transplanting. The fruits are readily eaten in winter by many songbirds including the northern mockingbird, western bluebird, hermit thrush, and many woodpeckers. Toyon is hardy within zones 8–10.

Red-Flowering Currant (*Ribes sanguineum*)

This deciduous shrub is native to the coast ranges from California to British Columbia. It is named for its clusters of 10–30 drooping red flowers, which hang from March to June. These develop into blue-black berries. Red-flowered currant grows 4–12 foot tall with a spread of 6 feet. It should be planted in either sun or shade; it is fairly drought resistant but thrives with moderate water. It is hardy within zones 6–8. Hummingbirds often visit the flowers and quail, flickers, and thrushes readily eat the fruit.

RED-FLOWERING CURRANT *Ribes sanguineum* (VH)

From central to southern California, fuchsia-flowering gooseberry (*Ribes speciosum*) can be a substitute. This evergreen shrub grows 3–6 feet tall and 6 feet wide. In addition to attracting hummingbirds and songbirds, it provides excellent nesting cover among its spiny stems. It tolerates heat and drought and makes an excellent choice for creating hedges in coastal areas. It is hardy within zones 7–9.

Tall Red Huckleberry (*Vaccinium parvifolium*)

Tall red huckleberry is a deciduous shrub that grows 4–12 feet tall and 6 feet wide. It occurs mainly in the redwood region from California's Santa Cruz Mountains, north in the humid coastal zone to Alaska. It is hardy to zone 5. Tall red huckleberry has a spreading, cascading shape. It should be planted in acid soils under partial shade. The greenish or whitish flowers are often tinted with pink and appear in leaf axils in May and June. The clear,

TALL RED HUCKLEBERRY *Vaccinium parvifolium* (AF)

bright red fruits are about ¼ inch in diameter and ripen from June to September. The fruit is eaten by many kinds of song and game birds, including several species of grouse, the American robin, black-capped chickadee, wrentit, Swainson's thrush, and northern flicker.

Desert Honeysuckle (*Anisacanthus thurberi*)

This extraordinary hummingbird-attracting shrub is native to dry habitats in Arizona, New Mexico, Texas, and northern Mexico. Also known as *flame flower*, its 1½-inch tubular flowers are yellow-orange or red and occur on spikes at the ends of branches. It resembles true honeysuckle, but it is not even closely related. It is 4½ feet tall and 3 feet wide. This is an excellent backyard plant for arid areas. It should be planted in full sun and cut back to the ground each year in the winter. Desert honeysuckle is hardy in zones 8–10.

DESERT HONEYSUCKLE *Anisacanthus thurberi* (CD)

Several other plants within this genus also offer promise as backyard hummingbird plants.

Pacific Waxmyrtle (*Myrica californica*)

Pacific waxmyrtle is a large, native evergreen shrub or small tree that grows 10–35 feet tall with a spread of 3–7 feet. Dark green glossy foliage and dense form make it a popular choice for cultivation in residential areas as a specimen tree or pruned hedge. Pacific waxmyrtle occurs along the Pacific coast from Los Angeles to Washington, and is found most commonly near beaches and in salt marshes. It develops purplish, waxy, nutlike fruits in July that persist over the winter until the following June. Like those of its close relative, eastern bayberry, these fruits are important food for many types of birds, including the northern flicker, tree swallow, chestnut-backed chickadee, towhees, wrentit, and yellow-rumped warbler. It is hardy to zone 8.

PACIFIC WAXMYRTLE *Myrica californica* (AF)

Salal (*Gautheria shallon*)

This low-growing, spreading shrub is an excellent ground cover for coastal gardens in the Pacific Northwest. It produces pink flowers in the spring that mature into purple, $\frac{1}{2}$-inch-diameter fruits from midsummer to fall. It can be planted in both sun and shade and prefers acid soils. It grows about 4 feet tall and spreads rapidly to about 5 feet by sending out wandering surface roots that grow into branches. It makes an excellent cover for steep banks. It is hardy within zones 6–8. The fruits are a favorite of wrentits and pheasants. It provides excellent nesting cover.

SALAL *Gautheria shallon* (CD)

Mexican Bush Sage (*Salvia leucantha*)

This bushy, evergreen shrub is extremely attractive to hummingbirds. It can be planted at property borders where it has plenty of room to spread. It usually grows 3–4 feet tall and 3 feet wide and is notable for its arching shape, with each branch tipped by a long display of purple, pink, or white flowers that have long periods of bloom. It is native to central and eastern Mexico, where it lives in tropical and subtropical coniferous forests. It grows well in sun or light shade and in loamy, gravelly, and sandy soils; it tolerates drought with only occasional watering. If old stems are cut to the ground, new ones will bloom continuously through summer and fall. Mexican bush sage is hardy from zones 8 to 10 or can be used as an annual farther north. It is a favorite of Anna's hummingbird, but it is also attractive to all other western hummingbirds.

MEXICAN BUSH SAGE *Salvia leucantha* **(CD)**

Autumn sage (*Salvia greggii*) is also highly attractive to hummingbirds. It is a dwarf, evergreen shrub with red-lipped flowers. It is hardy from zones 7 to 9.

Wild Lilac (*Ceanothus* spp.)

This group of about 55 native species includes a wide variety of mostly evergreen shrubs, from creepers to small trees. Wild lilacs are named for their spectacular bloom of blue flowers, which range from powder blue to deep cobalt. The variety of forms provides great flexibility for gardeners, but these are relatively short-lived shrubs, usually lasting just 5–10 years. They typically live in areas with minimal water such as dry hillsides, so they require little water in gardens and can readily succumb with too much

WILD LILAC *Ceanothus griseus horizontalis* **(CD)**

watering. They should be planted where they will receive full or partial sun. Wild lilacs include the Point Reyes creeper (*Ceanothus gloriossus*), which grows to just 4–20 inches with a spread of 5 feet, or mahala mats (*C. prostratus*), an even more low-growing form that creates mats 8 feet in diameter. In contrast, blue blossom (*C. thrysiflorus*) is one of the hardiest evergreen species, growing

6–21 feet tall with a spread of 8–30 feet. Wild lilacs provide both cover and food for birds. Many songbirds including towhees, white-crowned sparrow, and western bluebird eat the small fruit capsules.

Additional Recommended Plantings for the Pacific Coast

Evergreen Trees
ARBORVITAE, EASTERN (*Thuja occidentalis*)
FIR, DOUGLAS (*Pseudotsuga menziesii*)
FIR, SUBALPINE (*Abies lasiocarpa*)
FIR, WHITE (*Abies concolor*)
HEMLOCK, MOUNTAIN (*Tsuga mertensiana*)
HEMLOCK, WESTERN (*Tsuga heterophylla*)
JUNIPER, ROCKY MOUNTAIN (*Juniperus scopulorum*)
JUNIPER, WESTERN (*Juniperus occidentalis*)
PINE, LODGEPOLE (*Pinus contorta* var. *latifolia*)
PINE, PONDEROSA (*Pinus ponderosa*)
PINE, WESTERN WHITE (*Pinus monticola*)
YEW, PACIFIC (*Taxus brevifolia*)

Deciduous Trees
ALDER, SITKA (*Alnus sinuata*)
ALDER, THINLEAF (*Alnus tenuifolia*)
ALDER, WHITE (*Alder rhombifolia*)
ASPEN, QUAKING (*Populus tremuloides*)
BIRCH, PAPER (*Betula papyrifera*)
BUTTONBUSH, COMMON (*Cephalanthus occidentalis*)
CHERRY, BITTER (*Prunus emarginata*)
COTTONWOOD, BLACK (*Populus trichocarpa*)
DOGWOOD, WESTERN (*Cornus occidentalis*)
HAWTHORN, COCKSPUR (*Crataegus crus-galli*)
HAWTHORN, DOUGLAS (*Crataegus douglasii*)
HAWTHORN, DOWNY (*Crataegus mollis*)
HAWTHORN, WASHINGTON (*Crataegus phaenopyrum*)
MAPLE, ROCKY MOUNTAIN (*Acer glabrum*)
MOUNTAIN-ASH, AMERICA (*Sorbus americana*)
MOUNTAIN-ASH, EUROPEAN (*Sorbus aucuparia*)
MULBERRY, RED (*Morus rubra*)
POPLAR, BALSAM (*Populus balsamifera*)

Evergreen Shrubs
ACACIA, CATCLAW (*Acacia greggii*)
CACTUS, PRICKLY PEAR (*Opuntia* spp.)
CURRANT, GOLDEN (*Ribes aureum*)
JUNIPER, CHINESE (*Juniperus chinensis*)
JUNIPER, COMMON (*Juniperus communis*)
SALTBUSH, DESERT HOLLY (*Atriplex hymenelytra*)
SNOWBERRY, COMMON (*Symphoricarpos albus*)
SNOWBERRY, MOUNTAIN (*Symphoricarpos oreophilus*)
SNOWBERRY, ROUNDLEAF (*Symphoricarpos rotundifolius*)
SUMAC, SKUNKBUSH (*Rhus aromatica*)
THIMBLEBERRY, WESTERN (*Rubus parviflorus*)
WOLFBERRY, ANDERSON (*Lycium andersonii*)

Deciduous Shrubs
BUCKTHORN, CASCARA (*Rhamnus purshiana*)
BUFFALOBERRY, SILVER (*Shepherdia argentea*)
DOGWOOD, BROWN (*Cornus glabrata*)
DOGWOOD, MINER'S (*Cornus sessilis*)
DOGWOOD, RED-OSIER (*Cornus stolonifera*)
ELDER, BLACK-BEAD (*Sambucus melanocarpa*)
ELDER, BLUEBERRY (*Sambucus caerulea*)
MOUNTAIN-ASH, ALPINE (*Sorbus occidentalis*)
MOUNTAIN-ASH, GREEN (*Sorbus scopulina*)
RASPBERRY, WHITEBARK (*Rubus leucodermis*)
ROSE, NOOTKA (*Rosa nutkana*)
SAGEBRUSH, BIG (*Artemisia tridentata*)
SALTBUSH, BIG (*Atiplex lentiformis*)
SERVICEBERRY, SASKATOON (*Amelanchier alnifolia*)

Ground Cover
BEARBERRY (*Arctostaphylos uva-ursi*)
BILBERRY, BOG (*Vaccinium uliginosum*)
BUNCHBERRY (*Cornus canadensis*)
JUNIPER, CREEPING (*Juniperus horizontalis*)
STRAWBERRY (*Fragaria* spp.)
WINTERGREEN (*Gaultheria humifusa*)

Vines
HONEYSUCKLE, ORANGE (*Lonicera ciliosa*)
HONEYSUCKLE, CHAPARRAL (*Lonicera interrupta*)

Other Good Choices for the Pacific Coast

Name	Zone	Native (N) or Alien (A)	Height/spread (ft.)	Light	Preferred Soil	Fruit Period	Fruit Type	Remarks
Evergreen Trees								
CHERRY, CATALINA (*Prunus lyonii*)	8–10	N	15–35	Sun	Dry/drained	Late summer/early fall	Purple-black drupe	Native to several southern California islands; fruit is readily eaten by many kinds of songbirds; often cultivated as an ornamental tree
FIR, NOBLE (*Abies procera*) (formerly nobilis)	5, 6	N	60–225/20–28	Sun	Drained	Fall	Cone	Long-lived and rapid growth; seeds are food for chickadees, jays, nuthatches, and many other species; native to Cascade Mountains of Oregon and Washington
FIR, SHASTA RED (*Abies magnifica*)	6–8	N	60–200/15–20	Sun	Drained	Early fall	Cone	Abundant seed crop every 2–3 years; choice food for blue grouse, pine grosbeak, and many other species; native to Oregon Cascades; good ornamental value

JUNIPER, CALIFORNIA (*Juniperus californicus*)	8, 9	N	10–30	Sun	Dry	All year	Blue-green berry	Berries eaten by at least 10 bird species, including mockingbird, Townsend's solitaire, varied thrush, and cedar waxwing; excellent cover for dry soils
LAUREL, CALIFORNIA (*Umbellularia californica*)	7–9	N	20–75/40	Sun/shade	Moist/drained	Fall	Drupe	Depending on growth conditions, a shrub, tree, or creeping ground cover; eaten by Steller's jay and Townsend's solitaire
OAK, BLUE (*Quercus douglasii*)	7–9	N	20–60/40	Sun	Dry/drained	All year	Annual acorn	Acorns are eaten by wild turkey, band-tailed pigeon, quail, jays, and many other species; both oaks occur in scattered groves along lower, dry mountain slopes
OAK, ENGELMANN (*Quercus engelmannii*)	7–10	N	20–50	Sun	Dry/drained	All year	Annual acorn	
PINE, DIGGER (*Pinus sabiniana*)	8, 9	N	40–80/15–20	Sun	Dry/moist/drained	All year	Cone	Native to dry foothills of northern and central California
PINE, JEFFERY (*Pinus jeffreyi*)	6–8	N	60–200/20–25	Sun	Drained	Fall	Cone	Occurs naturally high in the mountains; cones sometimes grow to 15 in. long

247

Other Good Choices for the Pacific Coast—*cont.*

Name	Zone	Native (N) or Alien (A)	Height/spread (ft.)	Light	Preferred Soil	Fruit Period	Fruit Type	Remarks
PINE, MONTEREY (*Pinus radiata*)	7–9	N	40–100/25–40	Sun	Drained	On exposure to heat	Cone	Cones occur every 3–5 years; commonly planted in gardens and yards in coastal zone near San Francisco
PINE, TORREY (*Pinus torreyana*)	7–9	N	20–40/25–40	Sun	Drained	All year	Cone	Native to coastal southern California; dense foliage and often twisted trunks give this tree interesting ornamental value for coastal land birds
Deciduous Trees								
CRABAPPLE, OREGON (*Malus diversifolia*)	3–9	N	10–30/12–20	Sun	Moist/drained	Fall	Purple pome	Native on the Pacific coast from Alaska to northern California; sometimes occurs as a shrub; a favorite food of robin and ruffed grouse; many cultivated varieties are also available; some other flowering crabapple species and varieties hardy to Alaska include Japanese hopa, radiant, pink cascade, sparkler, and dolgo

MADRONE (*Arbutus menziesii*)	7–9	N	20–100/50	Sun	Dry/ moist/ drained	Summer/ winter	Orange/ red berry	Native in the foothills and lower mountain slopes of coastal ranges from British Columbia to southern California; fruit persists through early winter; at least 5 bird species eat its fruit, including band-tailed pigeon and wild turkey
MAPLE, CALIFORNIA BOX ELDER (*Acer negundo* var. *californicum*)	3–10	N	20–40/16–39	Sun/ shade	Dry/ moist	Summer/ fall	Samara	Native to streams and valleys of coast ranges; extensively cultivated for street and park plantings; its seeds are eaten by at least 4 bird species, including evening grosbeak and ring-necked pheasant
OAK, OREGON WHITE (*Quercus garryana*)	7–9	N	35–60/30	Sun	Dry/ drained	All year	Annual acorn	Acorns are important food for turkey, band-tailed pigeon, Lewis' woodpecker, and ring-necked pheasant; Oregon white oak often occurs as a shrub
OAK, VALLEY WHITE (*Quercus lobata*)	7–9	N	40–125/50	Sun/ shade	Dry/ drained	Fall	Annual acorn	

Other Good Choices for the Pacific Coast—cont.

Name	Zone	Native (N) or Alien (A)	Height/spread (ft.)	Light	Preferred Soil	Fruit Period	Fruit Type	Remarks
SYCAMORE, WESTERN (*Platanus racemosa*)	8–10	N	40–90/ 70	Sun	Drained/ moist	Fall/ winter	Achene	Grows along streams and adjacent floodplains in central and southern California; seeds are a favorite goldfinch food
WILLOW, SCOULER (*Salix scouleriana*)	2–8	N	4–30	Sun	Dry/ moist/ drained	Summer	Capsule	Very common tree of mountain and stream banks from southern Alaska to southern California; excellent for stabilizing stream banks; 23 bird species, especially grouse and quail, are known to eat the tender buds and twigs of willows

Evergreen Shrubs

Name	Zone	Native (N) or Alien (A)	Height/spread (ft.)	Light	Preferred Soil	Fruit Period	Fruit Type	Remarks
BUCKTHORN, CALIFORNIA (COFFEE BERRY) (*Rhamnus californica*)	7–9	N	To 8/10	Sun	Dry	Early fall	Drupe	Eaten by at least 7 bird species, including band-tailed pigeon

Name	Zone	N	Height	Light	Soil	Bloom	Fruit	Notes
BLADDERBUSH (*Isomeris arborea*)	7–10	N	To 7/3–6	Sun	Loamy	Summer/fall	Capsule	Usually grows in alkaline soils; semievergreen; good cover year-round; spreads to 6 ft.
COYOTE BRUSH (DWARF CHAPPARAL BROOM) (*Baccharis pilularis*)	9, 10	N	To 6/5	Sun	Dry/wet	Summer/fall	Achene	Excellent cover plant for difficult growing conditions; provides dense cover and low hedges about 2–3 ft. tall. Ideal shelter for quail and other ground birds. Occurs from California coast to high desert.
CHRISTMAS BERRY (TOYON) (*Heteromeles arbutifolia*)	8–10	N	10–20/25	Sun/shade	Dry/drained	Late fall/winter	Red pome	Occurs on lower mountain slopes from central to southern California; extensively cultivated for attractive dark green leaves and red fruit; fruits are eaten by at least 7 bird species, including band-tailed pigeon and California quail
GRAPE, OREGON (*Mahonia nervosa*)	7, 8	N	To 2/3	Sun/shade	Dry/drained	Late summer	Berry	Forms dense, low thickets; resistant to black stem rust; excellent cover

Other Good Choices for the Pacific Coast—*cont.*

Name	Zone	Native (N) or Alien (A)	Height/spread (ft.)	Light	Preferred Soil	Fruit Period	Fruit Type	Remarks
HUCKLEBERRY, EVERGREEN (*Vaccinium ovatum*)	7–9	N	To 10/10	Sun/shade	Moist/drained	Late summer	Black berry	Important food for blue grouse and many types of songbirds; at least 87 bird species are known to eat blueberry and huckleberry fruits
MANZANITA (*Arctostaphylos manzanita* and *A. diversifolia*)	7–10	N	12–15/10	Sun	Dry/drained	Year-round	Red berry	Occurs along California coast and in coastal mountains of southern California; fruit eaten by at least 8 bird species, including California jay, band-tailed pigeon, fox sparrow, wrentit, and mockingbird
SALTBUSH, BREWER (*Atriplex brewerii*)	9, 10	N	1–5	Sun	Dry	Early fall	Achene	Excellent cover for dry habitats; salt tolerant; makes good windbreaks and hedges (with pruning); semievergreen
SALTBUSH, DESERT (*Atriplex polycarpa*)	5–10	N	To 6/3–7	Sun	Dry	Fall	Achene	Male and female plants; semievergreen; spreads 6 ft.

Species	Zone	Native	Height	Light	Soil	Fruiting season	Fruit	Comments
SUMAC, LAUREL (*Rhus laurina*)	9, 10	N	10–20	Sun	Dry/drained	Early fall/persistent over winter	Red drupe	Thick evergreen leaves produce dense shade and endure salt, extreme heat, and drought; at least 6 bird species are known to eat fruit, including quail and wrentit; occurs in coastal southern California
SUMAC, LEMONADE (*Rhus integrifolia*)	9, 10	N	To 30	Sun	Dry/drained	Late summer	Red drupe	
SUMAC, SUGAR (*Rhus ovata*)	9, 10	N	To 10	Sun	Dry/drained	Late summer/persistent over winter	Red drupe	

Deciduous Shrubs

Species	Zone	Native	Height	Light	Soil	Fruiting season	Fruit	Comments
BLACKBERRY, CALIFORNIA (*Rubus macropetalus*)	8, 9	N	To 6/6–12	Sun	Dry/moist/drained	Late summer	Black drupelets	Climbing or shrublike; fruits readily consumed by at least 12 bird species
CHOKECHERRY, WESTERN (*Prunus virginiana* var. *demissa*)	2–9	N	10–20/6–7	Sun/shade	Dry/moist/drained	Summer/early fall	Red/purple drupe	Forms dense thickets and provides prolific fruit that are consumed by at least 6 bird species, including ring-necked pheasant and sharp-tailed grouse

Other Good Choices for the Pacific Coast—*cont.*

Name	Zone	Native (N) or Alien (A)	Height/spread (ft.)	Light	Preferred Soil	Fruit Period	Fruit Type	Remarks
ELDER, PACIFIC RED (*Sambucus callicarpa*)	8, 9	N	To 20	Sun/half sun	Dry/moist/drained	Late summer/early winter	Red berry	Thrives in rich, moist soil; prolific fruits are readily eaten by at least 8 bird species, including California quail, robin, and Swainson's thrush
OSOBERRY (*Osmaronia cerasiformis*)	4–10	N	To 12/12	Shade	Well drained	Late summer	Purple-black drupe	Fruits readily eaten by many kinds of bird
ROSE, BALDHIP (*Rosa gymnocarpa*)	6–9	N	To 3/3–10	Sun	Dry/drained	Fall	Red hip	Pink flowers; excellent cover; food for at least the following: ruffed and blue grouse
ROSE, CALIFORNIA (*Rosa californica*)	4–9	N	To 10/4–6	Sun	Dry/drained	Fall	Red hip	Swainson's thrush, Townsend's solitaire, ring-necked pheasant, and bluebird
SALMONBERRY (*Rubus spectabilis*)	4–9	N	To 6/6–12	Sun	Dry	Summer	Yellow/red drupelet	Readily eaten by robin, blackbird, cedar waxwing, pine and black-headed grosbeak, and band-tailed pigeon

Name	Zones	Native	Height	Light	Soil	Season	Fruit	Description
SERVICEBERRY, WESTERN (*Amelanchier florida*)	2–7	N	3–20	Sun	Dry/moist/drained	Late summer	Blue pome	An important food for at least 10 western bird species, including flicker, cedar waxwing, western tanager, evening grosbeak, and black-headed grosbeak

Ground Cover

Name	Zones	Native	Height	Light	Soil	Season	Fruit	Description
GROUND, ROSE (*Rosa spithamea*)	6–9	N	10 in.	Sun	Dry/drained	All year	Red hip	Low bush provides good cover and fruit for ground-feeding birds
MANZANITA, PINE-MAT (*Arctostaphylos nevadensis*)	7, 8	N	6 in.	Sun	Dry/drained	Summer/early fall	Red berry	Creeping evergreen mat; white flower and persistent fruit; provides excellent food into winter for grouse, jays, and band-tailed pigeon
STRAWBERRY, CALIFORNIA (*Fragaria californicus*)	7–10	N	6 in.	Sun	Dry/moist/drained	Spring/summer early	Red berry	At least 7 bird species eat strawberry fruit, including California quail, mockingbird, brown towhee, robin, and black-headed grosbeak
STRAWBERRY, WOOD (*Fragaria bracteata*)	5–9	N	6 in.	Sun/half sun	Dry/moist/drained	Spring	Red berry	A perennial herb; occurs in prairies and open, dry woods; at least 9 bird species are known to eat this fruit, including cedar waxwing, ruffed grouse, song sparrow, pine grosbeak, robin, and black-headed grosbeak

Other Good Choices for the Pacific Coast—*cont.*

Name	Zone	Native (N) or Alien (A)	Height/spread (ft.)	Light	Preferred Soil	Fruit Period	Fruit Type	Remarks
Vines								
GRAPE, CALIFORNIA (*Vitis californica*)	7–9	N		Sun	Moist/ drained	Summer/ fall	Purple berry	Tall climbing vine with fragrant flowers; fruits are favorites of many kinds of bird, including flicker, grouse, quail, mockingbird, wrentit, western bluebird, and cedar waxwing
GREENBRIER, CALIFORNIA (*Smilax californica*)	7–9	N		Sun/ shade	Moist/ drained	Summer/ fall	Berry	Smooth or prickly vine that often spreads by rootstocks; fruits eaten by mockingbird, thrasher, robin, and Swainson's thrush
HONEYSUCKLE, PINK (*Lonicera hispidula*)	7–9	N		Sun	Dry/ drained	Summer/ persists through winter	Red berry	Evergreen vine that sometimes grows as a 12-ft. shrub; white or purple flowers; fruits eaten by at least Townsend's solitaire, robin, towhee, and wrentit

USEFUL SOURCES

For a complete list of invasive plants in the United States including Hawaii:
   http://www.nps.gov/plants/alien/list/c.htm
For an Internet version of the zone map with more detail:
   http://www.usna.usda.gov/Hardzone/ushzmap.html
For descriptions and photographs of most North American plants:
   http://plants.usda.gov/links.html

6 Pools, Ponds, and Wetlands

In dry habitats of the southwestern states, water may be more attractive to birds than food. Even in the moist Pacific Northwest and northeastern states, water may be locally scarce during the summer, and for most of the northern winter it becomes mostly inaccessible, locked in ice and snow.

Birds can get much of their water needs from their food, and many consume drops of water or flakes of snow from vegetation and other surfaces, but all species require at least some water for drinking. Also, birds ranging in size from eagles to hummingbirds bathe in water during all seasons. Most waterfowl, wading birds, and shorebirds are, of course, totally dependent on very specific aquatic habitats. Providing clean water at the proper level in the correct habitat at the right time of year is one of the most useful management tools for attracting birds and improving wildlife habitat.

WATER PROJECTS

Birdbaths

A predator-safe birdbath that offers open water throughout the year will help to attract birds that seldom visit feeders, such as warblers and vireos. Birdbaths are usually sold with raised pedestals or stands, but many species seem to prefer baths at ground level, the usual place where rain puddles appear in nature. The principal advantage of a raised birdbath is protection from predators such as house cats, which might easily pounce on birds that are vulnerable while water-soaked and busy splashing. Raised birdbaths are also more conspicuous and easier to maintain where there are deep winter snow accumulations.

A wide variety of birdbaths are available from commercial suppliers, but it is easy to provide water from homemade baths and pools. Garbage can lids are an ideal shape for a birdbath. They can be used on the ground, supported with bricks, or secured on top of a ceramic drain tile with a weight tied to the handle. Plastic lids are not as useful because the surfaces are very slick, thus making it difficult for birds to work their way into the bath and gain secure footing.

Slope and water depth are the most important factors when selecting a bird-bath. Make sure that your birdbath has a very gentle incline into the water and that the water in the bath is not more than 2 or 3 inches deep. Birds will not bathe in many manufactured baths because the sides are too steep.

The location of the birdbath often determines which types of bird it will attract. Bold species, such as robins and jays, will visit birdbaths in open areas or near shrubs, but warblers, wood thrush, and other secretive birds are more likely to visit baths that are tucked into shady, protected spots. The only problem with such sites is vulnerability to lurking house cats. If house cats prowl your property, keep your birdbaths in the open, at least 15 feet from shrubs and on a pedestal at least 3 feet off the ground.

Water supplies should be dependable. When water is available consistently, birds will visit the bath as part of their daily routines. Unpredictable water sources are rarely visited. Also, the water in birdbaths should be changed every few days and the surface scrubbed clean of algae that may thrive in the bird-fertilized water. Avoid using detergents or disinfectants for cleaning bird baths, except for an occasional rinse with a 10 percent bleach solution followed by a thorough scrubbing. Regular maintenance is especially important to keep the baths from breeding mosquitoes. In many areas mosquitoes carry the West Nile virus, a deadly plague for native birds with serious human health consequences.

You can make your birdbath more attractive by creating motion on the water's surface. Dripping water is especially alluring to warblers. Burbling, gurgling, or dripping water appeals to birds, but fast-moving, powerful sprays may startle and disperse them.

The simplest way to create dripping is to install a specially designed water adapter. The several models available consist of a narrow-diameter hose that leads to a hook-shaped, copper tube which drips water into the birdbath. Some devices create a miniature fountain spray that is also attractive, especially for hummingbirds.

Another method to achieve a similar effect is to hang a bucket with a hole punched in its bottom over the bath. Experiment with the size of the hole, starting with a small nail hole, enlarging it until a regular pattern of water drips from the bucket (about 20–30 drops per minute). Keep the bucket covered to reduce evaporation and the chance of detritus clogging the drip hole.

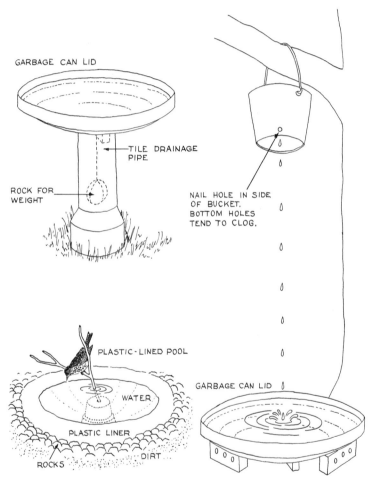

Examples of birdbaths made from everyday materials, such as garbage can lids, metal buckets, and drainage pipes. Water dripping from a bucket into a bath creates surface motion attractive to small birds. (AF)

WATER DRIP

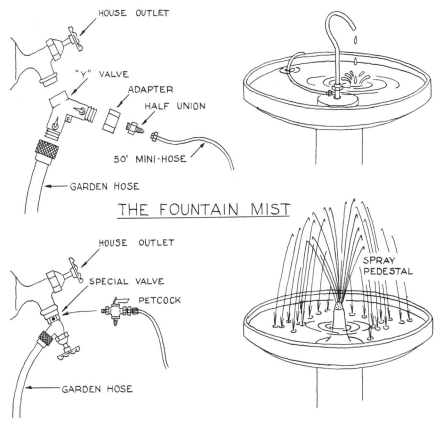

HOUSE OUTLET

"Y" VALVE

ADAPTER

HALF UNION

50' MINI-HOSE

GARDEN HOSE

THE FOUNTAIN MIST

HOUSE OUTLET

SPECIAL VALVE

PETCOCK

SPRAY PEDESTAL

GARDEN HOSE

Commercial dripping and misting devices create movement on the surface of birdbaths and make them more appealing to birds. (AF)

Birds will use open water in birdbaths throughout the winter, but it is best to provide this in plastic or granite structures, as ceramic and concrete baths will eventually freeze and crack. Keep the birdbath water ice-free by using a water heater. The simplest and least expensive design consists of a light fixture mounted in the base of a flowerpot. A shallow ceramic or plastic dish with thin walls rests on top of the flowerpot. A heavy-gauge outdoor power cord, which leads to an outdoor power receptacle, fits through the drain hole in the bottom of the pot. For added safety, check with an electrician to be sure that the receptacle has a ground fault interrupter. The size of the light bulb will depend on the severity of your winters. A 40-watt light bulb is usually adequate.

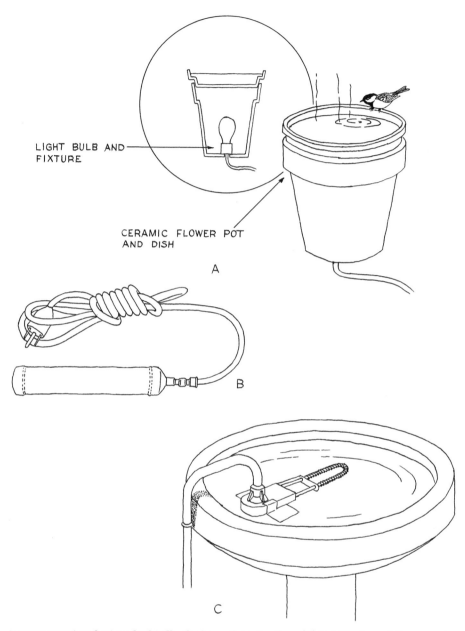

LIGHT BULB AND
FIXTURE

CERAMIC FLOWER POT
AND DISH

A

B

C

Water-warming devices for birdbaths keep them ice-free: (A) light bulb and flower pot,
(B) thermostatic heater designed for use in poultry houses, and (C) Nelson heater
designed especially for birdbaths. (AF)

Commercial water heaters, specifically designed for birdbaths, are also available at most garden stores and bird feed shops. The first, a thermostat-controlled heater designed for use in poultry houses, warms water to about 50 degrees Fahrenheit (9 degrees Celsius) and then turns off. Hold this heater in place with a brick or other heavy weight. The second, the Nelson heater, is specially designed for birdbaths, with a flat base and curved stem that mounts over the side of the bath. Its thermostat keeps water at 40–50 degrees Fahrenheit (5–9 degrees Celsius). Heaters increase evaporation, so it is important to keep replacing water in the bath to keep the heaters covered.

Backyard Pools

Where space permits, an in-ground pool designed expressly for birds will attract many species and add an interesting touch to your bird-feeding area, especially if it is creatively landscaped with ferns or other low rock-garden plants. Such pools are especially useful in arid or hot climates. The following steps are for a pool designed to merge a classic water lily habitat with a shallow area for birds to bathe and drink.

1. Choose a location where you can readily view the pool. Place the pool far enough from bird feeders so that it is not always filling with seed hulls and discarded grain, and distant from trees that will drop leaves into the pool. Also pick a site within reach of an electric outlet with a ground fault for the pump. The location should be near a water spicket as it will be necessary to frequently add water to the pool.
2. Use a garden hose or long length of rope to outline the site of the future pool. Move the rope on the ground until you find a pleasing shape.

(SK)

3. Then use a shovel to excavate the hole to a depth of about 3½ feet in the center, with a lip about 1 foot deep and 1 foot wide around the perimeter. The lip provides a shelf for placing potted aquatic plants. A minimum depth of 3 feet in the center is necessary for fish to overwinter in northern climates, and small fish are important to control mosquitoes.

(SK)

4. Remove rocks from the excavation and then place an old carpet or carpet liner in the bottom of the hole to prevent rocks from heaving upward through the rubber pond liner. A heavy plastic tub with a special spout will serve as a biological filter.

(SK)

5. Place a heavy-gauge rubber pond liner in the bottom of the pool. Be sure to use a nontoxic product especially designed for this purpose, such as EPDM, a synthetic rubber sheeting. Firestone Rubber Company produces an EPDM product called PondGuard that carries a 20-year warranty.

(SK)

6. Place native stone over the edges of the rubber to create a natural look.

7. Introduce insect-eating fish such as topminnows and fathead minnows. They will likely breed in the pool, eat mosquito larvae, and may attract an occasional heron. Purchase minnows at a local bait shop.

8. To prepare the associated bird-bathing pool:

- Use the soil from the excavated pool to build an adjacent mound about 1 foot tall.

- Use a rubber pond liner to create a channel leading from the mound to the pool and cover this with a few large rock slabs.

- Use native rock and chisel a natural-looking pathway for water to trickle toward the pool. Use fine concrete to fill any holes where water might escape.

- Place a birdbath rock (a flat rock with a shallow depression) so that it collects water before it trickles into the pool. If you cannot find such a rock at garden shops or local quarries, create it by chiseling a depression in a rock. Alternatively, create a depression by using *thermaling*, a technique where a propane torch carves out the depression.

(SK)

9. This water garden pool is 12 × 5 feet and the birdbath rock is 5 × 3 feet with a bathing depression 2 × 1½ feet, but less than 2 inches deep in the center.

Maintenance:

- Water gardens are dynamic, living systems. Expect the water to change color according to season and water temperature. Fish excrement contributes greatly to the quantity of nitrates in the water and this is the single greatest factor favoring algae growth. In most healthy pools, the water is not always crystal clear. The health of the pool is best maintained by circulating water from the pool through a biological filter and by encouraging submerged beds of aquatic plants such as anacharis and hornwort.

- Floating plants such as water lilies and pondweeds help to reduce algae growth as they prevent sunlight from reaching the water. Ideally, cover about two-thirds of the pond surface with floating leaf plants that are rooted in pots on the bottom of the pool. Also, encourage emergent plants such as arrowhead and pickerelweed by growing them in pots along the edge of the pool. Place a submersible water pump in the deepest part of the pool and connect this to tubing that leads underground to a biological filter, positioned at the head of your tiny waterway. Avoid powerful pumps—a trickle is better than a gusher!

- To make the biological filter, fill a tub with gravel or plastic "bioballs" (from a water garden supplier) on which nitrogen-consuming bacteria grow. Then introduce native plants such as water iris in the tub. The circulating water will reach the tub, pass through the roots of the established plants before overflowing on its path back to the pool. Use native, perennial plants and the effects will be long lasting and increasingly successful as the plants develop dense root masses.

- To reduce algae growth and the possibility of mosquitoes breeding in the bathing pool, scrub it about once each week with a stiff bristle brush.

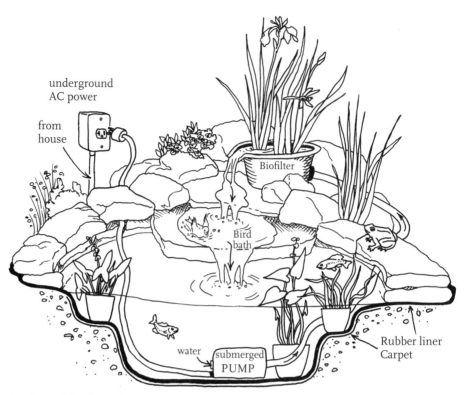

underground
AC power

from
house

Biofilter

Bird
bath

Rubber liner
Carpet

water

submerged
PUMP

A submersible lilypond pump moves about 275 gallons of bottom water to the "biofilter." The water then overflows the filter and meanders into a shallow-rock birdbath before tumbling into the pool. Slow water movement is more attractive than a gushing waterfall. (CD)

"Guzzlers" for Desert Birds

In semiarid habitats, collect and store rain from occasional downpours for wildlife by using a variety of catchment schemes, collectively known as *guzzlers*. Guzzlers are very successful for increasing populations of desert quail and songbirds that are limited by scarce water supplies.

Although the forms vary considerably, the basic idea is similar to a cistern in which water coming off a roof is caught and tunneled into a secure tank for later use. Corrugated sheet metal forms an "apron" that catches rain and guides it into a steel, fiberglass, or concrete tank, which may hold up to 1000 or more gallons. To reduce evaporation, locate guzzlers on a north-facing slope in areas secure from floods. For this reason, avoid placing guzzlers in a wash or gully. Cover the holding tank with a removable lid to reduce evaporation and the growth of algae and to facilitate annual cleaning. Protect guzzlers from wandering cattle by installing a sturdy, barbed-wire fence around the entire water-collection area.

Regardless of the size of the water-collecting tank, it is essential that the approach to the water does not become a deathtrap for birds. Larger tanks should have sloping ramps so that birds can walk to the water. To improve traction, tack small wooden slats or a piece of hardware-cloth wire to the ramp.

To construct a smaller-scale water catcher, slant two pieces of corrugated metal to feed water into an eave gutter that delivers it into a small pool or pan. Theodore Nelson of Crockett, California, suggests a simple, safe water-collection device for such small-scale guzzlers. He has found that a galvanized oil-collection pan equipped with a hardware-cloth cone will keep quail chicks from drowning in the pan. For a 16½-inch-diameter oil pan, he suggests using a 22-inch-diameter circle of hardware cloth. The circle of mesh is cut on a radius from the edge to the center and the interior is cut into an open circle before overlapping and forming a rim over the pan.

Sizes of Rain-collecting Aprons

Minimum Annual Rainfall (in.)	Square Feet of Collecting Surface Required		
	600 g.	700 g.	900 g.
1	965	1127	1453
2	482	563	726
3	322	376	485
4	242	282	365
5	192	225	290
6	162	189	243
7	138	161	208
8	121	141	182
9	107	125	161
10	97	113	146
11	87	102	132
12	80	94	121

Adapted from Stanford D. Schemnitz, ed. 1980. *Wildlife Management Techniques Manual.* 4th edition. Washington, DC: Wildlife Society.

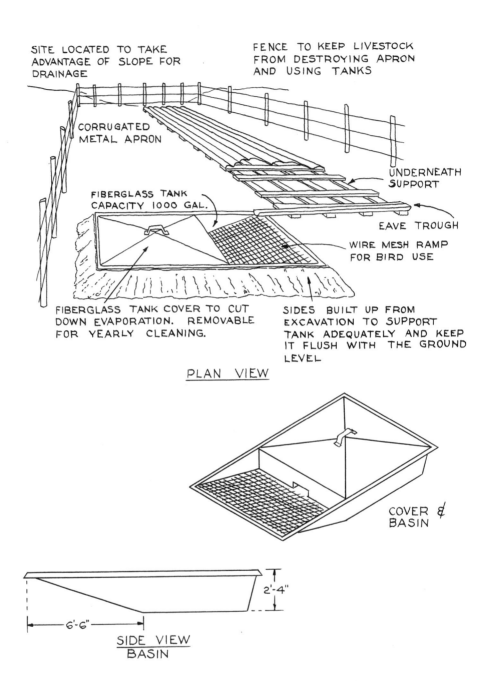

SITE LOCATED TO TAKE
ADVANTAGE OF SLOPE FOR
DRAINAGE

FENCE TO KEEP LIVESTOCK
FROM DESTROYING APRON
AND USING TANKS

CORRUGATED
METAL APRON

UNDERNEATH
SUPPORT

FIBERGLASS TANK
CAPACITY 1000 GAL.

EAVE TROUGH

WIRE MESH RAMP
FOR BIRD USE

FIBERGLASS TANK COVER TO CUT
DOWN EVAPORATION. REMOVABLE
FOR YEARLY CLEANING.

SIDES BUILT UP FROM
EXCAVATION TO SUPPORT
TANK ADEQUATELY AND KEEP
IT FLUSH WITH THE GROUND
LEVEL

PLAN VIEW

COVER &
BASIN

2'-4"

6'-6"

SIDE VIEW
BASIN

Large-scale "apron" guzzler with detail of water-holding tank. (AF)

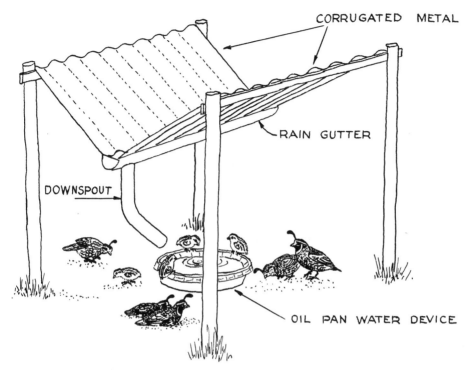

CORRUGATED METAL

RAIN GUTTER

DOWNSPOUT

OIL PAN WATER DEVICE

Water pan design for small guzzler.

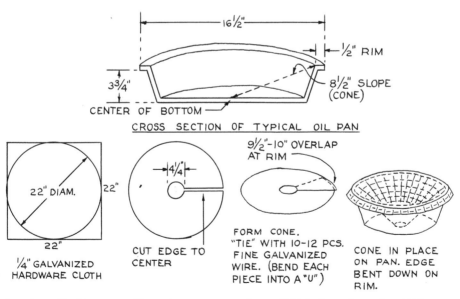

16½"

½" RIM

3¾"

8½" SLOPE (CONE)

CENTER OF BOTTOM

CROSS SECTION OF TYPICAL OIL PAN

22" DIAM.   22"

22"

¼" GALVANIZED HARDWARE CLOTH

4¼"

CUT EDGE TO CENTER

9½"-10" OVERLAP AT RIM

FORM CONE.
"TIE" WITH 10-12 PCS.
FINE GALVANIZED
WIRE. (BEND EACH
PIECE INTO A "U")

CONE IN PLACE
ON PAN. EDGE
BENT DOWN ON
RIM.

A water-collection pan with a wire cone prevents small birds from drowning. (AF)

Designing Ponds and Marshes for Birds

Ponds and marshes can be constructed at almost any site with suitable soil and a freshwater source such as a natural spring or a flowing stream or an adequately sized watershed that will permit enough water to fill the impoundment. Most farm ponds are designed for fishing and swimming, but this usually means they are not especially good for birds.

Ideally, bird ponds should be shallow, with gently sloping shorelines and a scattering of small islands. Half-submerged boulders and logs make ideal resting places for waterfowl and turtles. To attract more herons and fewer nuisance Canada geese, avoid mowing to the edge of the water. Impoundments should also be equipped with a drawdown gate that will permit various levels of drainage for shorebird management. Such structures also make it easier for future dredging operations if it becomes necessary to control aquatic vegetation such as cattails.

Prevent cattle from grazing and wallowing at the pond edge as they will trample vegetation and muddy the water. If there are cattle near your pond, fence it to keep the cattle out. Provide water for cattle with a special valve-controlled pipe that brings water through a dike to a nearby watering tank.

When designing a new wetland project that favors waterbirds, strive to increase the amount of shoreline. The edge of the wetland is an extremely rich habitat for a great variety of aquatic animals, such as insects, frogs, turtles, and crayfish, and it is the place where young fish and amphibian larvae find the best shelter. Shallow water is essential for encouraging submerged plants, tadpoles, small fish, and such aquatic insects as dragonflies and mayfly nymphs. These are important foods for ducks and marsh birds.

To increase the proportion of shoreline to surface area of a pond, construct the pond with an irregular shore, striving to create points and coves. This pattern also increases visual isolation and permits birds of the same species to nest in more secluded areas out of site of each other. For example, in this way more than one pair of territorial mallards can occupy the same pond; there may also be feeding space for two or more great blue herons rather than just one.

Small islands not only add valuable shoreline but also serve as favorite roosting and nesting places for waterfowl. Loons and grebes most frequently build their nests in the emergent vegetation around small islands.

Because of their isolation on water, islands are usually safer nesting places than adjacent shorelines, where predators such as fox and raccoon can sneak up on incubating birds with little warning. Similarly, artificial loafing and nesting rafts are attractive to Canada geese, common terns, and common loons. Large islands can accommodate more nesting birds, but even small islands of only 30 square feet are big enough to shelter at least one waterfowl nest.

For attracting birds, there also should be at least 5 hours of direct sunlight each day to favor growth of aquatic plants and suitable adjacent vegetation for food and cover.

Dense brush adjacent to the pond on at least one side is attractive to many songbirds, and standing dead trees in the water or along the shoreline are frequently used as nest sites by woodpeckers and tree swallows and often double as perches for kingfishers, flycatchers, and herons. Where trees are not available, consider "planting" dead trees. This will require a backhoe to dig a hole about 5 feet deep and other heavy equipment to move the trees into proper position. Black locust is the ideal species for creating such perches.

Mud flats are also an important feature of a bird pond, as they are choice feeding areas for shorebirds and popular loafing areas for waterfowl. Ponds and marshes constructed with a variable-level drawdown are ideal for creating mud flats. For ponds without a drawdown gate, you can create a small mud flat by spreading a piece of heavy plastic along a section of the shore. Secure the plastic by burying the edges in soil and cover it with several inches of sand or soil. Occasional raking will help keep plants from colonizing this small mud flat.

Ponds can provide habitat for both birds and fish, but it is necessary to pay careful attention to water depth. Large fish require at least 8 feet of water to survive northern winters. By creating the pond with both deep and shallow waters (with a minimum gradient of 6 : 1), the fish will have room, and the shallows will benefit birds and fish. Wetlands without predatory fish such as bass are highly attractive to waterbirds, as the big fish compete for small fish, invertebrates, and amphibians and will even eat small ducklings.

Gently sloping shorelines provide slightly different microhabitats in the various vegetation belts that soon circle the pond. Variety in shoreline vegetation leads to a greater diversity of birds. When emergent vegetation completely dominates the water area, by definition the pond becomes a marsh. Marshes make excellent bird habitat for certain species such as bitterns, rails, and marsh wrens, but it is best to strive for both open water and marsh habitats to benefit the greatest variety of species.

To improve the quality of marshes for waterbirds, try to prevent a single plant species from dominating the habitat. This is especially important for invasive species such as purple loosestrife and phragmites that have little wildlife value. Manual cutting, dredging, burning, and artificial changes in water level are all useful tools to maintain some open water and a high diversity of aquatic plants.

To protect waterbirds and other aquatic life in your pond or marsh, avoid using herbicides whenever possible. Before resorting to herbicides, it is best to manually pull small patches of invasive plants or otherwise kill them by cooking them under black plastic or burning with a propane torch. Some biological controls are also useful, but these typically require larger infestations before they are appropriate. Where herbicides are deemed necessary for controlling woody shrubs, trained workers should cut them and paint the herbicide onto the cut stems. Eye protection and gloves should be used. For details on the best techniques for your vicinity, contact your local office of the Natural Resources Conservation Service or Cooperative Extension Service.

A 3:1 shoreline gradient (1 foot deep at 3 feet from shore) creates the preferred fish habitat; wading birds will gravitate toward the shallower shoreline gradient of 6:1 (1 foot deep at 6 feet from shore). (AF)

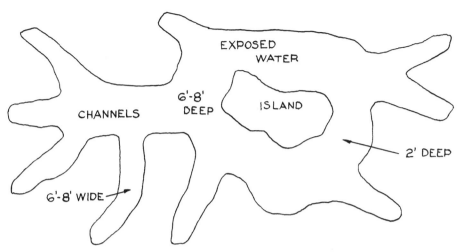

EXPOSED
WATER

CHANNELS

6'-8'
DEEP

ISLAND

2' DEEP

6'-8' WIDE

When creating new wetlands, strive to create an amoeba-shaped habitat with peninsulas that form numerous points and coves, maximizing the proportion of shoreline. Small islands provide nesting and loafing areas for waterfowl. (AF)

Constructing Wetlands

Soil type is the most important characteristic of any potential pond site. Soils with heavy clay content will hold water and are necessary for building ponds. Ponds constructed over sandy or gravel soils will surely leak.

The first step is to dig a test pit with a backhoe. Usually, digging several pits is best to sample the soil column throughout the proposed site. Even if your neighbor has a pond or marsh, it is necessary to thoroughly check the soil on your property so that no surprises, such as layers of gravel or sand, turn up after construction begins. Even a thin layer of sand (known as a *lens*) can drain water out of a pond basin. Coordinate the digging of test pits with a visit from your local representative of the Natural Resources Conservation Service (formerly Soil Conservation Service) or U.S. Fish and Wildlife Service. The representative can tell by examining the soil from the test pits if your site is likely to hold water.

If the soil is too sandy, you have a couple of choices aside from abandoning the project. The pond can be lined with a heavy clay known as *bentonite*, which is best installed within bats that consist of the clay sandwiched between plastic fiber. If bats are not used, then layer bentonite 3 inches deep over the entire basin or area suspected of leaking. Alternatively, an artificial rubber liner (EPDM) can be laid down over the entire basin of small projects. After bentonite or the rubber liner is in place, cover these surfaces with 3 inches of topsoil.

The natural resources agent will survey your wetland site, mark the boundaries of the new wetland, and design the location and size of the dike and water-control structures. If these are appropriate, the agent can also find local contractors experienced at pond construction. The size of the wetland will likely be determined by property boundaries and the size of the surrounding watershed that will drain into the site.

If bentonite or a pond liner is not necessary, a $^{1}/_{2}$-acre pond can be built for under $1500. The only major costs will be the fees for the bulldozer operator and the construction of a water-control device. With one bulldozer, run by a capable operator, the entire construction can be complete in 2 days.

Before construction begins, draw up a detailed map to scale, showing the size, shape, and slope of the project. Then review the details of your plan with the bulldozer operator. This is the time to insist on shallow slopes for most of the shoreline, irregular contour, locations for islands, and other design details. This may be contrary to the experience of your bulldozer operator, who is probably more familiar with steep-sided, round ponds built for fishing and swimming. Here are the steps to follow:

- Clear all trees, shrubs, and sod from the pond site. Some of these plantings should be saved for creating brush piles (see Chapter 1). Then all topsoil is stripped and piled aside.
- The bulldozer operator excavates the basin of the pond, using the heavy clay to build a dike on the downhill side. A core trench may be excavated inside of the dike and filled with clay to prevent water from leaking below the dike.
- This is also the time to build up islands within the basin and for the bulldozer to compact the soil in the bottom of the excavation.
- The final step is for the bulldozer to spread the topsoil over the dike, islands, and basin of the excavation. Without replacement of topsoil, it would be nearly impossible to establish vegetation.
- The dike and islands should be fertilized and grass planted as soon as possible after construction to reduce erosion. Plant wildlife shrubs and trees on at least one side of the pond, but avoid planting on the dike as roots may damage its structure.

Controlling Water Levels

The ability to control the water level is an important feature of a bird-attracting wetland. In general, waterfowl impoundments should be drained every 5 years because the fertility of the soil and water in artificial waterfowl pools sharply declines after the first 4 years. At the same time, useful waterfowl vegetation is replaced by less abundant and less attractive foods.

To improve aging wetlands for waterfowl, drain the site in late winter or early spring and disk the bottom to mix decomposed organic matter with mineral soils. Burning will also help to release nutrients. These techniques provide a suitable soil for favorite duck foods such as smartweeds (*Polygonum* spp.). If smartweeds or other suitable plants do not appear, plant the pond bottom with buckwheat (*Fagopyrum* spp.) and Japanese millet (*Echinochloa crusgalli frumentacea*) at 25 pounds of seed per acre. Let these mature over the summer and then flood the pond again in the fall. In the provinces and northern U.S. states, waterfowl impoundments should remain filled during spring and summer for the next 4 years as duck-breeding habitat. Reduce the water levels in the fall to create shorebird habitat and to promote growth of duck foods.

Green-tree Reservoirs

Green-tree reservoirs are bottomland forests flooded for waterfowl. Hardwood forests with oak, beech, sweetgum, and tupelos are ideal for this purpose. Suitable forests for this technique are located in valleys with a small stream. Here a low dam creates a temporary backwater, flooding the forest floor with 1 or 2 feet of water. The technique is useful in southern states where there is open water throughout the winter.

By flooding woodlands in late fall or early winter, acorn and other mast crops become available to wintering waterfowl that would not otherwise visit dry woodland habitats. If there is ample sunlight over the wetland, then increase food production for waterfowl by planting Japanese millet, corn, or grain sorghum during late spring. Late-fall flooding apparently benefits trees, and as long as the water is drained from the woodland when leaf buds swell in the spring, there will be no damage to the trees.

STOP PLANK GATE

USE CEDAR
FOR PLANKS.
4' LONG

SLIDING GATE VALVE

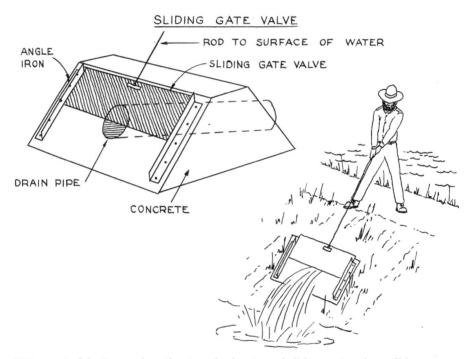

ROD TO SURFACE OF WATER

SLIDING GATE VALVE

ANGLE
IRON

DRAIN PIPE

CONCRETE

Water-control devices such as the stop plank gate and sliding gate valve will lower water levels when pond soil and water quality need rejuvenation. (AF)

WINTER:
KEEP WATER UP.

SPRING:
DRAW DOWN BEFORE
BUDS OPEN.

SUMMER:
WOODS ARE DRY. ACORNS
GROW. WEEDS THRIVE
IN CLEARINGS.

FALL:
FLOOD AFTER LEAF FALL.
TREE SEEDS PROVIDE
DUCK FOOD.

Green-tree reservoirs serve as a food supply, attracting waterfowl to areas, especially in the southern states, that might otherwise be too dry. (AF)

Shorebird Management

Most migratory shorebirds such as sandpipers and plovers rely mainly on exposed mud habitat during their annual migrations between Arctic nesting grounds and tropical winter homes. The conservation of both coastal and inland populations is a matter of great urgency, as serious declines have occurred in the numbers of many species.

In coastal habitats, most shorebirds habitually concentrate at a few key stopover areas. Here, they face loss of habitat due to development, disturbance, pollution, and overfishing of food sources such as horseshoe crabs. Fortunately, many coastal natural shorebird stopover habitats are now protected, and some tidal impoundments are managed for shorebirds by agencies such as the National Wildlife Refuge System. Managers communicate about the conservation of shorebird populations through an interagency conservation group known as the Western Hemisphere Shorebird Reserve Network. One of the greatest concerns in these areas is human disturbance. To benefit shorebirds using coastal beaches, managers should work to:

- Discourage people from letting dogs run free where shorebirds roost and feed.
- Establish no-disturbance zones where shorebirds can roost and feed without disturbance from joggers, dog walkers, and vehicles. Where suitable habitat exists, managers can establish such areas at isolated points of land.
- Create shorebird-viewing areas with interpretive signs.

Shorebirds that migrate through interior North America once used an extensive system of smaller wetlands between the Gulf of Mexico and their Arctic nesting habitat, but this region is now largely dominated by agriculture and developments that have replaced most natural wetlands. Vast shorebird populations that once migrated through this region were decimated in the late nineteenth century by hunting, and these populations have not rebounded, even though they are now protected. Today, effective management of artificial wetlands on private and agency-owned lands offers promise for helping shorebirds find suitable refueling habitat during migration.

Shorebirds that stop over at freshwater impoundments eat mostly invertebrates such as midge larvae that they probe from mud and rotting vegetation along the shoreline. Managers of wetlands with water-control structures can lower water levels at key times and thus provide necessary food. The following management regimes are appropriate for managers of large and small freshwater wetlands where there is not a significant invasion of perennial woody plants or invasive weeds such as purple loosestrife and where there is no history of disease such as botulism.

Spring migration[1]

Wetland impoundments suitable for spring shorebird management require flooding in the fall approximately 1 month before the first heavy freeze and the continued maintenance of flooded conditions to enable chironomids (midges) and other invertebrates to lay eggs and to ensure survival of larvae over the winter. During the spring migratory season, units should have extensive areas of open water or areas only partially covered with emergent vegetation (less than 50 percent). The water should be drawn down slowly (about 1 inch per week) to make invertebrates continuously available to the shorebirds that forage in open, shallow water and mud flats. If more than one unit is drawn down for shorebirds, the drawdowns should be staggered to extend the availability of habitat.

Summer and fall migration

Impoundments suitable for summer and fall shorebird management require two different strategies:

- Impoundments that remained flooded through spring and early summer should be drawn down slowly if natural evaporation does not expose the bottom.
- Impoundments that remained dry over the summer should be flooded to a shallow depth 2–3 weeks before migration begins. This allows time for invertebrates to repopulate the newly created habitat. To ensure a food supply for shorebirds, it is best to disk the vegetation that is growing in the basin of the impoundment. The type of disking is critical. Shallow disking converts plant biomass to detritus, which is an excellent substrate for invertebrates. In contrast, deep disking completely buries the vegetation, resulting in fewer invertebrates for shorebirds.

Establishing Food in New Wetlands for Waterbirds

New ponds and water impoundments will naturally attract a surprising variety of aquatic plants and animals. The first animals to appear in new ponds are small

---

[1]Adapted from D. L. Helmers. 1992. *Shorebird Management Manual*. Wetlands for the Americas Publication No. 3. Manomet, MA: Western Hemisphere Shorebird Reserve Network.

but vitally important to waterbirds. A close examination of pond water will show it alive with tiny crustaceans and insects. These aquatic invertebrates provide important food for waterfowl. Invertebrates are high in protein and they are essential in the diets of laying females and molting adults. They are especially important foods for rapidly growing young.

Tiny aquatic crustaceans find their way into impoundments from adjacent wetlands and on the feathers and feet of waterfowl. Some may also be blown in by the wind, while others can live for years as eggs in dry soil. Most aquatic insects, such as midges, mayflies, and dragonflies, have flying adult forms and these are quick to colonize new bodies of water. The number and variety of invertebrates are at their greatest within the first 2 years and are constant by 4 or 5 years. When impoundments back water up over upland vegetation, there is a dramatic peak in the abundance of crustaceans and insects, as the flooding releases abundant nutrients through the decay of vegetation.

Aquatic plants usually find their way to new ponds by either wind or waterfowl. A rapid succession begins with submerged and floating leaf plants and proceeds toward increasing amounts of emergents, such as cattails and bulrushes. The advanced stages of succession are less productive for most waterfowl, but they favor marsh birds such as rails and bitterns.

Frogs, toads, salamanders, and crayfish can hop, slide, and crawl miles to the nearest pond or marsh to reach a new habitat. Such travels are usually made on mild, rainy nights. Once a few frogs or toads colonize a new pond, their calls will attract others until they occupy all the available shoreline. Population growth is very rapid for amphibians. For example, a female bullfrog (*Rana catesbeiana*) may lay 20,000 eggs each year. The abundance of tadpoles becomes a prime attractant for herons, kingfishers, and other predatory birds. Fish may naturally colonize new ponds from such connecting water sources as streams, or they may arrive as eggs clinging to the feathers of birds.

Natural colonization by aquatic plants and animals may proceed at a slower than desired rate where new ponds are isolated from well-established ponds or marshes. To speed up colonization of preferred species of fish, amphibians, crayfish, and vegetation, transplant amphibian eggs, small fish, or young plant specimens from nearby waters. Many of these species are also available from plant and animal dealers and restoration specialists.

Minnows are the preferred fish for attracting herons, kingfishers, rails, mergansers, and many other freshwater birds. The best species for stocking will vary from one region to the next, so it is best to check with your local Cooperative

Extension Service office. Minnows are usually readily available at local fishing bait shops.

IMPORTANT WETLAND AND AQUATIC PLANTS

Waterfowl and marsh birds, such as coots, rails, and gallinules, are intimately tied to various amounts of emergent, floating, and submerged vegetation. Most of the plants in this group are prolific seed producers, an adaptation that increases a given plant's chances for its seed to find an ideal place for germination. Waterbirds benefit by eating the seed, and sometimes spread it to new locations. They also feed on rootstocks, underground tubers, plant stems, and even leaves of certain marsh and aquatic plants.

Because most wetland and aquatic plants distribute their prolific seeds effectively, plant succession usually occurs rapidly without assistance from humans. However, obtaining a desirable mix of the proper aquatic plants for attracting birds is often a difficult task because succession quickly changes ponds into marshes and marshes into brushy fields. Wetland managers must frequently manipulate water levels by using dikes and levees, and sometimes must burn woody and dry grass off marshes to expose root systems for waterfowl. In other areas, dredging may be necessary to deepen water or remove such unproductive, competitive plants as purple loosestrife.

Some aquatic plants—among them arrowheads, chufa sedge, paspalum, smartweeds, wild rice, naiads, pondweeds, and water lilies—are available through commercial suppliers for stocking small ponds and marshes.

Arrowheads (*Sagittaria* spp.)

Arrowheads occur along pond and lake edges throughout North America, but they are most abundant and important for wildlife in the eastern half of the continent. Waterfowl consume both the seeds and tuberous roots, but the tubers are by far the most important and have even given the arrowheads another common name—duck potato. Arrowhead tubers are most readily available when the plants are growing partially submerged or in soft mud. The two most abundant and useful species are *Sagittaria latifolia* and *S. cuneata*, although the former species often has tubers that are too large or buried too deep for ducks. Arrowheads are especially important to the canvasback, black duck, gadwall, wood duck, ring-necked duck, trumpeter and whistling swans, sandhill crane, and king rail. They are also occasionally eaten by at least another 10 kinds of dabbling and diving waterfowl.

Sagittaria latifolia

ARROWHEADS (*Sagittaria* spp.) (AF)

Bulrushes (*Scirpus* spp.)

Bulrushes are among the most important wetland plants for water and marsh birds. These tall, perennial native sedges often form dense stands or fringes along the shores of ponds and lakes. Of the more than 40 species found in North America, common three-square (*Scirpus americanus*) and hard-stem bulrush (*S. acutus*) are two of the most widespread and important kinds. Not only do bulrushes produce abundant seed crops, but the stems and root-stocks are important food for geese, swans, cranes, godwits, and rails. Bulrushes also provide important nesting cover for marsh wrens, blackbirds, waterfowl, bitterns, coots, and grebes. Bulrush seeds are important foods for at least 24 kinds of waterfowl.

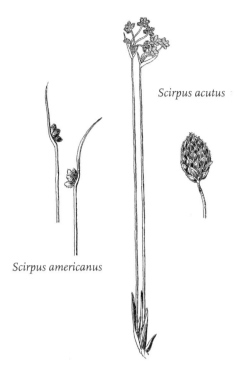

Scirpus acutus

Scirpus americanus

BULRUSHES (*Scirpus* spp.) (AF)

Chufa Sedge (*Cyperus esculentus*)
Chufa, sometimes known as *nut grass*, is by far the most important member of the *Cyperus* sedges as a wildlife food. Introduced from Africa, chufa now grows in damp, sandy soils and mud flats throughout most of the United States and southern Canada. Waterfowl and songbirds readily eat both the edible tubers and the seeds. Sometimes it occurs as an unwelcome weed in cultivated fields and gardens, but here too birds have discovered its food value. At least 12 species of waterbirds, including the

CHUFA SEDGE (*Cyperus esculentus*) (AF)

American coot, sandhill crane, mallard, and green-winged teal, readily eat chufa tubers.

Cordgrasses (*Spartina* spp.)

Two species of cordgrass dominate the salt marshes of the eastern and Gulf coasts. In brackish coastal waters from Newfoundland to Texas, marsh cordgrass (*Spartina alterniflora*) grows at the edge of the water, while the shorter, mat-forming salt hay (*S. patens*) grows at slightly higher levels. The seeds of

CORDGRASSES (*Spartina* spp.) (AF)

these perennial grasses provide important food for the black duck, clapper rail, Virginia rail, seaside sparrow, and sharp-tailed sparrow. The tender sprouts are a favorite food of brant, whooping crane, and Canada and snow geese.

Paspalum (*Paspalum* spp.)

The paspalum grasses are most abundant in the southeastern United States, where 42 species are known. At least 6 kinds occur west to the Pacific coast. Most paspalum grasses are perennial natives, growing in a wide variety of habitats, from dry, upland sites to marshland. Field paspalum (*Paspalum laeve*) and fringeleaf paspalum (*P. ciliatifolium*) are especially common in the eastern United States, occurring in fields and other dry habitats. Bull paspalum (*P. boscianum*) grows in moist meadows, marshes, and roadside ditches. At least 16 bird species are known to eat paspulum seed. Purple gallinule, sora, ground dove, wild turkey, mottled duck, and snow geese especially prefer it.

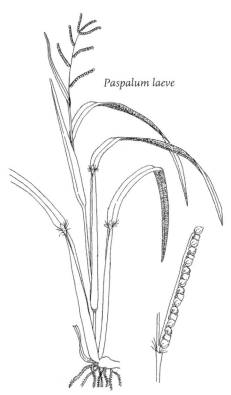

Paspalum laeve

PASPALUM (*Paspalum* spp.) (AF)

Rice Cutgrass (*Leersia oryzoides*)

Rice cutgrass is a native perennial grass that often grows in the shallow water around ponds and lakes. It is common throughout the eastern United States and southern Canada and also occurs on the Pacific coast in freshwater wetlands. Named for the serrate edges to its leaves, it should not be confused with saw grass, the dominant sedge of southern swamps and marshes. At least 12 species of waterfowl readily eat the seeds and many also dig up and consume the roots. The black duck, common goldeneye, mallard, shoveler, and blue-winged teal especially favor it.

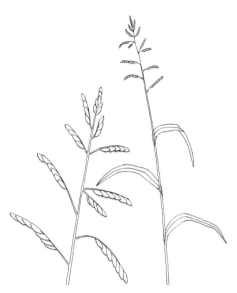

RICE CUTGRASS (*Leersia oryzoides*) (AF)

Wild Rice (*Zizania aquatica*)

Wild rice is a prolific seeding, annual grass. It grows in shallow water where there is deep, soft mud with enough circulation to prevent stagnation. Wild rice often fringes lakes and slow-moving rivers in the northern United States and southern Canadian provinces. It occurs along the Atlantic coast to Florida, but it is most abundant and has its greatest value to birds in the northern part of its range. The large seeds of this plumelike grass are favorite foods for many waterbirds. In Minnesota, wild rice comprises between 25 and 50 percent of the food of mallards during late summer. It is also an important food for the red-winged blackbird, bobolink, Virginia rail, sora,

WILD RICE (*Zizania aquatica*) (AF)

black duck, blue-winged teal, wood duck, redhead, ring-necked duck, and lesser scaup.

Sedges (*Carex* spp.)

There are at least 500 species of *Carex* sedges in North America. Although they represent a nightmare for most plant taxonomists, they are a delight to at least 53 species of waterfowl, shorebirds, upland game birds, and songbirds that feed on their abundant seeds. *Carex* sedges occur most commonly in wet meadows and marshy habitats, but some kinds grow in dry fields. Many kinds grow in dense clumps, a growth habitat that provides excellent nesting cover for waterfowl

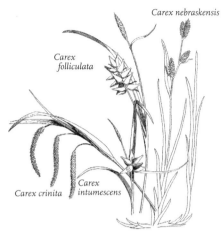

SEDGES (*Carex* spp.) (AF)

and many other types of ground-nesting birds. *Carex* seeds are especially favored by green-winged and cinnamon teal, sora, yellow rail, young ruffed grouse, snow bunting, Lapland longspur, and swamp sparrow.

Chara (*Chara* spp.)

Chara, sometimes known as *muskgrass* or *stonewort*, is a group of about 50 species of branching, lime-encrusted algae. The chara algae occur throughout most of North America in fresh, alkaline, or brackish water habitats, ranging from large lakes to farm ponds, roadside ditches, and coastal estuaries. Chara sometimes forms large, floating mats that are especially attractive to waterfowl when it is in its reproductive stage, bearing multitudes of microscopic oogonia. Chara algae

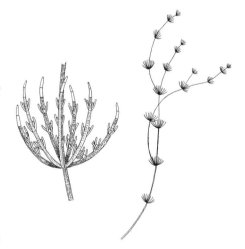

CHARA (*Chara* spp.) (AF)

are available to both dabbling and diving waterfowl, as the various species live in water ranging from a few inches to over 30 feet deep. Chara is an important food for the American coot, pintail, redhead, ring-necked duck, greater scaup, green-winged teal, American widgeon, and ruddy duck. It is also commonly eaten by at least 15 other species of diving and dabbling waterfowl.

Naiads (*Najas* spp.)

Naiads are annual freshwater herbs found mainly in eastern North America. Opposite or whorled leaves that have fine teeth on both edges identify them. Naiads can tolerate less light than many other freshwater plants and sometimes occur in deep water, though they most commonly grow where water is only 1–4 feet deep. Of the 8 species that occur in eastern North America, northern naiad (*Najas flexilis*) and southern naiad (*N. guadulupensis*) are the most abundant and important for wild birds. Southern naiad is somewhat tolerant of brackish water, but it and the northern species occur mainly in freshwater ponds and lakes. Waterfowl readily consume the abundant naiad seeds (nutlets) found in leaf axils as well as plant leaves and stem. Naiads are important foods for the coot, American widgeon, lesser scaup, bufflehead, teal (both blue- and green-winged), canvasback, and Canada goose.

SOUTHERN NAIAD

NAIADS (*Najas* spp.) (AF)

Smartweeds (*Polygonum* spp.)

Several wetland species in the *Polygonum* genus are especially important to waterfowl and land birds. Collectively grouped under the common name *knotweeds* (also known as *smartweeds*), two of the most important are lady's thumb (*P. persicaria*), named for the purple "thumbprint" on the center of each leaf, and pink knotweed (*P. pennsylvanicum*). These and several other members of this group grow on

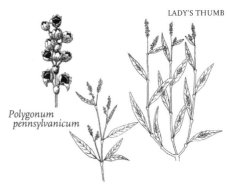

LADY'S THUMB

Polygonum pennsylvanicum

SMARTWEEDS (*Polygonum* spp.) (AF)

mud flats, on pond and marsh edges, and sometimes in moist, cultivated fields.

A useful management practice for attracting waterfowl is to drain ponds or lakes down a couple of feet during early spring, plant a crop of knotweed on the exposed mud, and then flood the mature plants in time for the fall waterfowl migration. At least 24 waterfowl species eat knotweed seed, but the black duck, mallard, pintail, and blue-winged teal especially enjoy it. The seed is also readily eaten by 37 other bird species, including the northern bobwhite, cardinal, and common redpoll, as well as the fox, song, swamp, and white-throated sparrows.

Spike Rushes (*Eleocharis* spp.)

Spike rushes are leafless sedges that grow in shallow water and the muddy shorelines of freshwater ponds and marshes throughout North America. There are approximately 45 species, and these range from only a few inches to several feet in height. Some kinds are annual and others are perennial, but almost without exception, spike rushes are a favorite food readily consumed by at least 27 species of waterfowl and marsh bird, such as coots, rails, and snipe. The American widgeon, black duck, mallard, shoveler, green-winged teal, and Canada and snow geese especially prefer the compact seed heads that give spike rushes their name.

**SPIKE RUSHES
(*Eleocharis* spp.)
(AF)**

Wild Celery (*Vallisneria americana*)

Wild celery, sometimes known as *freshwater eelgrass*, is an aquatic, submerged perennial of shallow ponds and lakes. It does not tolerate strong brackish waters. Wild celery spreads by creeping rootstocks, but also produces flowering stems that float on the surface. Both diving and dabbling ducks readily consume the leaves, rootstocks, and seeds. As its Latin name suggests, the canvasback (*Aythya valisineria*) has a special preference for wild celery. Where this plant is abundant, it may comprise between 25 and 50 percent of the canvasback's food. Wild celery is also an important food for the American coot, black duck, ring-necked duck, ruddy duck, common goldeneye, redhead, lesser and greater scaup, and tundra swan.

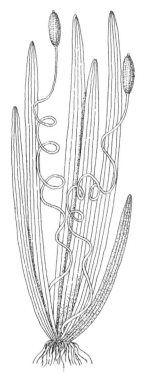

WILD CELERY (*Vallisneria americana*) **(AF)**

Widgeon Grass (*Ruppia maritima*)

Widgeon grass is one of the most important waterfowl foods in North America because of its preference for alkaline or saline waters. It thrives in brackish water along the Atlantic, Gulf, and Pacific coasts and is the dominant aquatic plant in many alkaline lakes and marshes from the prairies to the West Coast. This preference for saline and alkaline waters excludes it from most freshwater ponds and lakes of the eastern United States and Canada. Another merit of widgeon grass as a waterfowl food is that its roots, stems, leaves, and seeds are edible. Within its range, it is a staple food for the gadwall, shoveler, blue-

WIDGEON GRASS (*Ruppia maritima*) **(AF)**

and green-winged teal, redhead, greater and lesser scaup, oldsquaw, brant, and
Canada goose. It is also eaten by the mallard, pintail, mottled duck, canvasback, king eider, and purple gallinule.

Duckweeds (*Lemna* spp.)

Duckweeds and the closely
allied genera *Spirodela*, *Wolffia*,
and *Wolffiella* are tiny green
plants capable of totally covering
small ponds, swamps, and
marshes with their leaves. By far
the most abundant and most
important is common duckweed
DUCKWEEDS (*Lemna* spp.) (AF)

(*Lemna minor*). These tiny green plants are a staple in the diet of the common
coot and American widgeon. They are also eaten by at least 14 kinds of ducks,
purple gallinule, and sora.

Pondweeds (*Potamogeton* spp.)

Pondweeds are the dominant aquatic
vegetation in many ponds and lakes
throughout North America. Their abundance in terms of both quantity and
variety of species is greatest in the
northeastern United States, but
throughout their wide range,
pondweeds rank at the top of the list
for submerged and floating plants as
wild bird foods. Pondweeds are important not only for seed production but
also for the tender stems and leaves

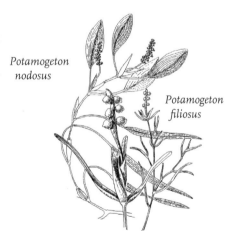

*Potamogeton
nodosus*

*Potamogeton
filiosus*

PONDWEEDS (*Potamogeton* spp.) (AF)

and edible tubers of certain varieties, all
of which contribute to their attractiveness to wetland birds. Sago pondweed
(*Potamogeton pectinatus*), a narrow-leafed, submerged species, is especially
important to waterfowl because of its edible tubers and seeds. In addition to
coots, avocets, dowitchers, and godwits, 25 species of waterfowl rely on
pondweeds for food.

Water Lilies (*Nymphaea* spp.)

The familiar water lilies of ponds, lakeshores, and other shallow freshwaters are both an attractive addition to quiet waters and a useful wild bird food. Water lilies occur almost exclusively in eastern North America, and although there are at least 8 species found in this region, the seeds, stems, and rootstocks of the white-flowered American water lily (*Nymphaea odorata*) and the yellow-flowered banana water lily (*N. flava*) of Gulf coast waters are the most frequently used members of this genus. Canvasbacks are known to feed extensively on the roots of the banana water lily. Ten other kinds of ducks are known to eat water-lily seeds and rootstocks. Water-lily stems, roots, and seeds are also a favorite food of sandhill cranes and gallinules. Few waterfowl eat the familiar yellow-flowered cow lilies, also known as yellow pond lilies (*Nuphar* spp.).

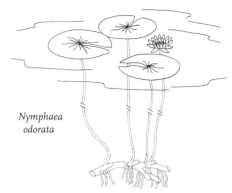

Nymphaea odorata

WATER LILIES (*Nymphaea* spp.) (AF)

USEFUL SOURCES

For mail-order sources for aquatic plants and animals, see Appendix B.

For contacts on agency help for construction of wetlands, see Appendix C.

The Aquatic Ecosystems Restoration Foundation:
　http://www.aquatics.org/

Aquatic Plant Management Society:
　http://www.apms.org/

The Western Aquatic Plant Management Society:
　http://www.wapms.org/

7

Nesting and Roosting Structures

Scarcity of nest sites often prevents birds from occupying otherwise suitable habitat. When a lack of nest sites limits population growth, artificial nesting structures have led to dramatic increases in bird numbers. For example, artificial nest boxes have helped to boost the populations of bluebirds, wood ducks, tree swallows, and many of the other 86 species of North American cavity-nesting birds.

Other types of artificial structures can provide nesting opportunities for many species other than cavity-nesters. Imaginative projects have recently demonstrated that many types of birds that usually use treetop nests, such as the osprey, eagles, double-crested cormorant, great horned owl, great gray owl, and long-eared owl, will accept artificial nesting platforms. Likewise, certain aquatic birds, such as terns, loons, ducks, and geese, which face a scarcity of predator-safe islands, will nest on artificial floating platforms. Even the endangered Everglade kite will nest in specially constructed metal baskets in preference to building its flimsy nest in swaying marsh vegetation.

Songbirds, such as sparrows, finches, and warblers, may be excluded from otherwise good habitat because they are unable to find adequate support for their nests. Pruning shrubs and low trees to create such sites can provide a useful way to increase populations of such songbirds.

Sometimes artificial nest structures provide more secure nesting places than natural sites, because artificial structures can be constructed to resist predators, parasites, and destruction from the elements. Bluebird boxes, for example, may be made with entrance holes small enough to exclude starlings, and they can be equipped with a special predator guard on the mounting pole. Likewise, artificial nest platforms for osprey built on top of rigid poles may be more secure than ageing treetop nests that could topple in strong winds.

Just as the number of suitable sites may limit population size, the availability of adequate roosting sites may also limit populations. This is especially true in windswept habitats where artificial roosting trees can serve a vital function for open-country birds such as quail. Likewise, roosting boxes for forest birds such as chickadees and titmice may provide essential cover from extreme winter weather.

Poorly designed or constructed artificial nesting sites could prove to be a detriment. For example, wrens and tree swallows will nest in milk cartons and tar-paper birdhouses, but the heat of long summer days on such thin-walled homes can overheat and kill the young. Aesthetics are also important. Artificial nests and roosts should be constructed from economic building supplies and designed with an eye to letting the structure become part of the habitat. This could minimize disturbance from curious neighbors.

NEST BOXES

Artificial nest boxes may entice birds to occupy a new habitat. Sometimes birds that normally nest only in large trees (i.e., barred owl, screech owl, and flicker) can be lured to younger forests or to forests where snags have been previously cleared. Artificial nest boxes simulate large tree trunks with significant-sized cavities.

Recent interest in the conservation of North American bluebird populations through the use of nest boxes has resulted in many effective nest box designs for small cavity-nesting birds. This interest has contributed to a wide range of management options for other cavity-nesting birds and useful information about common problems, such as parasite control and exclusion of nest predators and competitors.

Construction Materials

The best materials for building nest boxes are 1 × 8 inch pine, spruce, or poplar boards for bluebird-size boxes and 1 × 12 inch boards for screech owl–sized boxes.

Cedar is more weather tolerant, but much more expensive. Rough-grade lumber is ideal for nest boxes as the rugged cuts give a natural look and aid the birds in climbing out of the boxes. Rough slabs covered with bark from sawmill waste are excellent for building birdhouses, as they too have a natural appearance. Avoid using unseasoned woods or plywood, as these will warp or separate as they weather. Also avoid pressure-treated woods because they are impregnated with toxic chemicals such as arsenic.

Birds will nest in boxes constructed from almost anything—milk cartons, coffee cans, plastic jugs, sheet metal, tar paper, PVC sewer pipe—but these materials usually offer more problems from overheating, chilling, leaking, and condensation than they are worth. Exceptions are metal martin and wood-duck houses, which may have higher occupancy and nesting success rates than wooden boxes because they are safer from raccoon predators. Also, milk-carton nest boxes are helpful for providing abundant housing opportunities for pro-thonotary warblers, which nest in forested southern swamps.

When you are assembling wooden houses, it is not necessary to use glue to hold the parts together. Unsealed joints provide additional ventilation and drainage. Use galvanized sheet rock screws—these will long outlast steel nails. For top-opening boxes, use brass or stainless-steel hinges. Thick rawhide is a useful substitute for metal hinges.

Finishes

After a single field season, most woods will weather to a pleasing light gray that approximates the color of tree bark. Cedar lasts much longer than pine, but pine nest boxes will last for 20 years when painted with a generous coat of linseed oil. Avoid using lead-based alkyd paints, wood preservatives, or creosote. Although bright colors are unnecessary, the exterior of purple martin houses and gourds should be painted white to reduce temperatures in these comparatively thin-walled and exposed structures.

The interior of boxes should not be painted or treated with preservatives.

Drainage

Natural tree cavities, such as woodpecker holes, usually have excellent drainage, as wood chips rest on absorbent, dry heartwood, creating a snug cavity with thick, insulating walls. Also, woodpecker holes are generally located on the underside of leaning trunks, a feature that further improves drainage. With the water-safe characteristics of natural cavities in mind, nest boxes should be constructed to keep adults, eggs, and young as dry as possible while they are in the nest. Bluebirds and American kestrels are exceptions to this rule, as they can nest successfully in deep, open-topped boxes that simulate broken-off snags. Such boxes help to discourage house sparrows and tree swallows, which prefer dark cavities.

To keep rain from running into the boxes, the roof should be extended at least 3 inches beyond the front of the box. Flat-roofed houses should have a $\frac{1}{8}$-inch-deep drip line cut parallel to the face of the box; this keeps water from draining back toward the front of the box. To provide drainage, cut the corners off the floor of the box or drill $\frac{3}{8}$-inch drainage holes in each corner of the bottom. Also, be sure not to mount houses on leaning trees that would angle the boxes toward the sky.

Ventilation

Boxes constructed from 1-inch-thick wood generally have ample insulation to protect birds from excessive summer heat and unseasonably cold weather during the nesting season. Ventilation in well-sealed boxes can be improved by drilling several vent holes near the top of the sides or by dropping the front of the box down from the roof by $\frac{1}{4}$ inch. In addition to ventilation, these spaces provide a light source that may be useful to encourage birds to enter nest boxes early in the season when they are exploring for new cavities. Long ago, John Burroughs noted that when prospecting cavity-nesters poke their heads into a tight-fitting entrance hole, they totally block all light from the cavity, as their body fills the entrance hole. The total blackness may spook inexperienced birds unaccustomed to the suddenly dark interior.

Wood Chips

Since most small cavity-nesting birds depend on woodpecker excavations for nest sites, it helps to study a woodpecker cavity to determine preferred dimensions, height above the ground, and thickness of the walls for nest boxes. Since most woodpecker holes have a soft layer of wood chips in their bottom, many birds accustomed to this—wood duck, American kestrel, screech owl, barred owl, and flicker, among others—will reject artificial nest boxes without 3–4 inches of wood shavings or small wood chips in the bottom. Avoid using sawdust in nest boxes, as this soaks up and retains water.

Since chickadees are capable excavators, they prefer to make their own nesting cavities, so pack a nest box completely full of wood shavings and let the chickadees excavate a cavity of their preference. This technique may also prove useful for attracting flickers, downy, and other small woodpeckers that normally shun artificial nest boxes.

Feathers

Many species incorporate feathers into their nests, but barn, tree, and violet-green swallows are notable for lining their nests with feathers. Recent research conducted at the Cornell Laboratory of Ornithology demonstrates that these feathers provide important insulation for swallow eggs and that nests without the feathers are associated with lower hatching success. These swallows are so keen to obtain feathers that they will pluck them from the air. A simple way to provide feathers is to take a handful from an old pillow and toss them into the air soon after swallows return in the spring. Alternatively, place them in a wire basket and hang from a tree near a window so you can watch the swallows snatch them in their beaks and then fly to their nests.

Mounting Nest Boxes

Nest boxes for small cavity-nesting birds should usually be placed on special mounting poles or fence posts to reduce the chances of predation and to facilitate cleaning. Steel pipes (used for natural gas) with a $^3/_4$-inch internal diameter make excellent mounting poles. To set the poles easily and safely, use a post pounder rather than wielding a heavy sledge from the top of a ladder. Post pounders can often be rented or they can be built at home. A post pounder is a heavy pipe with a cap that fits over the mounting pole. The pounder is lifted a couple of feet above the post and then dropped onto it, driving the post into the ground. A homemade pounder can be constructed from a $2^1/_2$-foot length of $1^1/_2$-inch-internal-diameter steel pipe with one threaded end onto which a heavy steel cap is tightened.

Mount nest boxes for forest species directly to trees at the recommended height as outlined later under Nest Site and Nest Box Characteristics.

Positioning Boxes

Recent research from the Birdhouse Network Program of the Cornell Laboratory of Ornithology has found that in northern states and Canadian provinces, it is best to face nest box entrances to the east. This warms the box by exposing its broad face to the morning sunlight. In southern states, the east-facing position is not as important.

Cleaning Nest Boxes

Boxes that are packed with old bird nests and mouse nests are seldom occupied by birds, so cleaning is important. Cleaning can also help to control parasitic insects, mites, and lice, although studies conducted as part of Cornell's Birdhouse Network Program were inconclusive as to the benefits of cleaning boxes to reduce risk from parasitic blowflies. Researchers found similar numbers of blowflies in boxes where old nests were removed in comparison to boxes where old nests remained.

Nest boxes with a swing-out side are easiest to clean. In this design, a single wood screw holds the bottom of the wall secure to the base of the box. Side- or front-opening boxes are much easier to clean than top-opening boxes, which must first be taken off their mounts.

Although top-opening boxes are more difficult to clean, they are the best choice for researchers. They have the advantage of permitting researchers to band young and check adults, for young birds are less likely to prematurely fledge and adults can be easily trapped on their nests. Young birds that do leave the nest early probably will not stay in the nest box even if they are returned, although they are not likely to survive outside.

When cleaning boxes, use a spatula or ice scraper and remove the old nest from the immediate vicinity. Boxes that are under close inspection should be cleaned between broods to remove infertile eggs, dead nestlings, and nest parasites. Removing the first nest keeps the adults from building a new nest on top of it, a behavior that raises the nest contents dangerously near the entrance hole, where they are more vulnerable to predation by starlings and raccoons.

NEST BOX MOUNTING TECHNIQUES

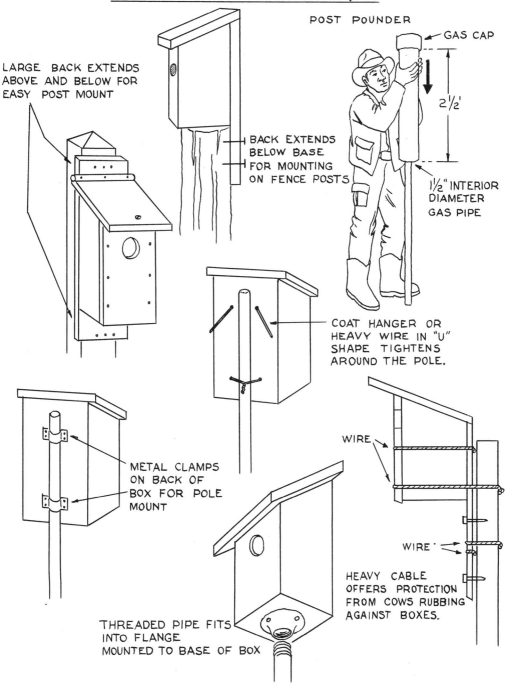

POST POUNDER

GAS CAP

2½'

1½" INTERIOR DIAMETER GAS PIPE

LARGE BACK EXTENDS ABOVE AND BELOW FOR EASY POST MOUNT

BACK EXTENDS BELOW BASE FOR MOUNTING ON FENCE POSTS

COAT HANGER OR HEAVY WIRE IN "U" SHAPE TIGHTENS AROUND THE POLE.

METAL CLAMPS ON BACK OF BOX FOR POLE MOUNT

WIRE

WIRE

HEAVY CABLE OFFERS PROTECTION FROM COWS RUBBING AGAINST BOXES.

THREADED PIPE FITS INTO FLANGE MOUNTED TO BASE OF BOX

Various techniques for mounting nest boxes on fence posts and metal poles. (AF)

PARASITES

An active bird nest contains a community of living creatures that find food from the nest in various ways. Some mites are harmless, scavenging on food scraps and feathers, but most invertebrates found in nests feed directly on nestling birds and their parents. In small numbers, the mites, lice, flies, and wasps that naturally occur in bird nests are not dangerous; large numbers, however, may cause fatalities and necessitate limited control.

An important reason for the annual spring cleaning is to remove nesting material that may harbor the pupae of blowflies. Species of the genus *Protocalliphora* (formerly *Apaulina*) have larvae that specialize in drinking blood from nestling birds. Several studies have found that over 80 percent of bluebird nest boxes contain blowfly larvae. This cycle starts when adult blowflies lay their eggs on newly hatched nestlings. The eggs hatch and the larval flies attach themselves to the young birds. The larvae feed on nestlings at night, a behavior that may permit them to avoid predation by adult birds tending the young during the day. At night the larvae emerge from the nesting material, feed on the nestlings, and then disappear back into the nest bottom during daylight hours.

Normally, small numbers of blowfly larvae are not a problem for healthy young birds, but if the numbers grow too high (over 150 larvae in a nest), they can kill the young. However, even small numbers can weaken young birds, making them more vulnerable to predators, extreme weather, or poor food supplies. Blowflies are known to parasitize bluebirds, tree swallows, American robins, house wrens, barn swallows, cliff swallows, and many other small landbirds.

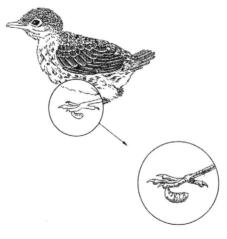

Parasitic blowfly larvae usually attach themselves to the soft parts of nestling birds, especially feet and facial areas. (AF)

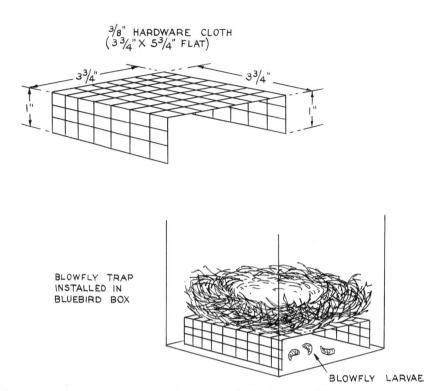

³/₈" HARDWARE CLOTH
(3³/₄" X 5³/₄" FLAT)

3³/₄"   3³/₄"

1"   1"

BLOWFLY TRAP
INSTALLED IN
BLUEBIRD BOX

BLOWFLY LARVAE

This simple blowfly trap, designed by Ira Campbell of Timberville, Virginia, is made of hardware cloth. The mesh covers the bottom of the bluebird nest box and traps the blowfly larvae below as they fall through. (AF)

An innovative trap for blowfly larvae was designed and tested by Ira Campbell of Timberville, Virginia. His clever design is based on the habits of the legless blowfly larvae. Noting that the larvae hide at the bottom of the nest box during the day and then wiggle their way back through the nest material at night to feed on the nestlings, he designed an easy-to-build trap that consists of a piece of ³/₈-inch-square hardware cloth cut and bent so that it sits 1 inch off the bottom of the box and covers the entire floor of the nest box. In boxes equipped with these traps, blowfly larvae move to the bottom of the nest, but fall through the mesh and are trapped in the bottom. In controlled field tests, Campbell found that bluebirds accepted boxes fitted with the wire traps just as frequently as boxes without the traps. He had no losses to blowfly parasitism in 53 boxes with the false bottoms, but 12 nestling bluebirds died in 47 control boxes without traps.

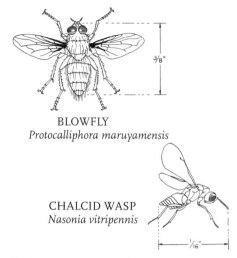

BLOWFLY
Protocalliphora maruyamensis

CHALCID WASP
Nasonia vitripennis

Adult blowfly (*Protocalliphora maruyamensis*) and its much smaller predator, the chalcid wasp (*Nasonia vitripennis*). (AF)

One of the natural population checks on blowflies is a small chalcid wasp (*Nasonia vitripennis*). This tiny wasp is only about $\frac{1}{16}$ inch long, but it does an effective job reducing blowfly populations. Chalcid wasps seek out the blowfly pupal cases in the nesting material and lay their eggs on the fly pupae within. When the eggs hatch, the wasp larvae consume the blowfly pupae.

Knowledge of the life cycles of the blowfly and the predatory chalcid wasp is essential, because while it is important to remove old bird nests with their overwintering blowfly pupae, the old nesting material is also the overwintering habitat for chalcid wasp larvae. If nesting material is cleaned from boxes in the fall and scattered on the ground or burned, the larvae of the useful chalcid wasps will be lost along with the blowflies. For this reason, John Terres, in *Songbirds in Your Garden*, recommends a mid-March cleaning of nest boxes. At this season the nest contents are collected and scattered on the ground away from the nest boxes. This spring cleaning is also a good time to remove mouse nests, open drainage holes, and repair broken boxes for the coming nesting season.

When checking nest boxes, you may discover lice and mites on nestlings and nesting material. Bird lice of the order Mallophaga are brown, wingless insects about the size of a pinhead. They are among the most common bird ectoparasites. Most birds have at least a few of these tiny, wingless insects. A few lice will cause little harm to healthy birds, as they eat mainly feather fragments, with occasional blood meals from newly emerging feathers. Young birds, however, sometimes have large infestations of lice and these may seriously weaken nestlings, reducing their chances for survival. Bird lice will not bite or infest humans.

Mites are also common external parasites on wild birds. As with lice, small numbers of mites are usual on most wild birds, but large populations of some kinds can prove fatal. The most easily seen mites look like tiny red spiders. These hide in bird nests and come out at night to suck blood from nestlings and adults. *Dermanyssus hirundinis* is often common in bluebird, tree swallow, house wren, and purple martin nests, and it can be a serious health hazard to nestlings. These mites not only weaken nestlings by drinking blood, but also can carry virus infections. A favorite hiding place for *Dermanyssus* mites is in the cracks and crevices in the bottoms of nest boxes. Most birds also carry feather mites of the family Analgesidae. These are the tiniest bird ectoparasites, most not exceeding $\frac{1}{32}$ inch. Feather mites do not drink blood but nibble on feathers and surface skin, doing little harm.

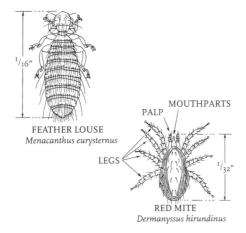

FEATHER LOUSE
Menacanthus eurysternus

PALP
MOUTHPARTS
LEGS
$\frac{1}{16}''$
$\frac{1}{32}''$

RED MITE
Dermanyssus hirundinus

Feather lice, such as *Menacanthus eurysternus*, and red mites, such as *Dermanyssus hirundinus*, feed mainly on feather fragments. Small numbers of these insects do little harm, but large populations require burning old nests and scrubbing box interiors with a 10 percent bleach solution. (AF)

Small populations of lice and mites are normal and should not cause concern. When large populations (hundreds) occur, all nesting material should be burned and the boxes thoroughly cleaned and scalded with boiling water or washed with a 10 percent bleach solution, paying special attention to all cracks and crevices.

NEST PREDATORS

Raccoons

Raccoons are probably the most common nest box predator. Their keen sense of smell and capable climbing skills permit them to raid bird nests in even the highest treetops. To these talents, add a quick mind and long, finger-like paws and it is easy to see why raccoons can be a serious threat to cavity-nesting birds. Look for claw marks on nest boxes or nest contents that have been pulled out of box entrances as evidence of a raccoon raid.

The simplest protection from raccoons is to deepen the entrance hole by mounting a block of wood, 1¼ inches thick, over the entrance to the nest box. This helps to prevent raccoons from reaching deep into the box (adult raccoons have front legs that are about 10–11 inches long).

To keep raccoons from climbing nest box and feeder poles, mount a 2-foot length of 4-inch-diameter galvanized stovepipe, aluminum downspout, flower-pot, or PVC pipe under the nest box (see Chapter 8). To help deter climbing snakes and mice, plug the top of the guard with a wooden plug. Nest boxes that are attached to isolated trees may be protected from climbing cats and raccoons by strapping a 3-foot collar of aluminum flashing around the tree. This technique usually only works where nest boxes sit away from trees.

For wood-duck boxes mounted on poles in standing water, the best protection from pole-climbing raccoons is a 2-foot length of 4-inch stovepipe hanging under the nest box or a cone baffle with a 36-inch diameter. A flat-type raccoon guard is a simplified version of the cone baffle. This can be constructed from a 40 × 40 inch piece of sheet metal and mounted on either metal or wood posts. Baffles constructed from garbage can lids, such as those described for defending feeders from squirrels, can also be effective if the diameter of the lid is at least 36 inches.

Another approach to protecting cavity-nesters from raccoons is to attach a 5-inch collar constructed of ½-inch mesh hardware cloth around the entrance hole. For details of the Noel Predator Guard and other techniques for excluding predators, visit the Web site http://birds.cornell.edu/birdhouse/bhbasics/bhbasics_index.html.

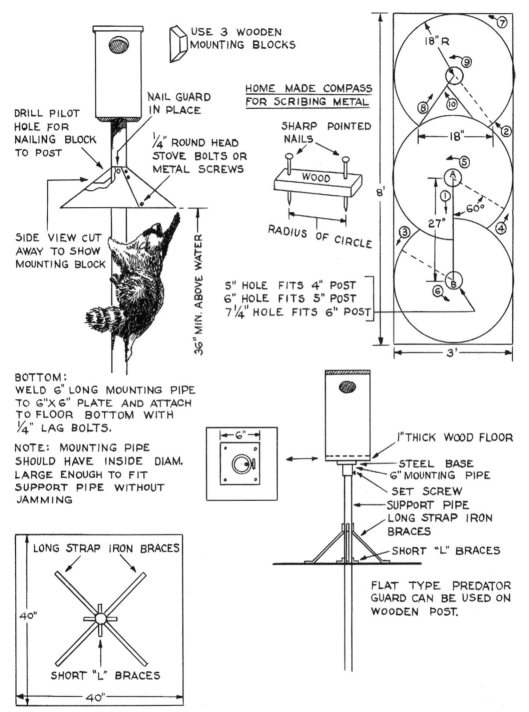

USE 3 WOODEN MOUNTING BLOCKS

DRILL PILOT HOLE FOR NAILING BLOCK TO POST

NAIL GUARD IN PLACE

¼" ROUND HEAD STOVE BOLTS OR METAL SCREWS

SIDE VIEW CUT AWAY TO SHOW MOUNTING BLOCK

36" MIN. ABOVE WATER

HOME MADE COMPASS FOR SCRIBING METAL

SHARP POINTED NAILS

WOOD

RADIUS OF CIRCLE

18"R

18"

27"

60°

8'

3'

5" HOLE FITS 4" POST
6" HOLE FITS 5" POST
7¼" HOLE FITS 6" POST

BOTTOM:
WELD 6" LONG MOUNTING PIPE TO 6"X 6" PLATE AND ATTACH TO FLOOR BOTTOM WITH ¼" LAG BOLTS.

NOTE: MOUNTING PIPE SHOULD HAVE INSIDE DIAM. LARGE ENOUGH TO FIT SUPPORT PIPE WITHOUT JAMMING

6"

1" THICK WOOD FLOOR
STEEL BASE
6" MOUNTING PIPE
SET SCREW
SUPPORT PIPE
LONG STRAP IRON BRACES
SHORT "L" BRACES

FLAT TYPE PREDATOR GUARD CAN BE USED ON WOODEN POST.

LONG STRAP IRON BRACES

40"

40"

SHORT "L" BRACES

Raccoons are frequent predators of nesting wood ducks. Raccoons can swim, climb, and pry open even secure nest boxes, and therefore all wood-duck boxes should be protected with carefully constructed raccoon guards. Redrawn from U.S. Department of Interior. 1976. "Nest Boxes for Wood Ducks." Wildlife Leaflet WL 510. Washington, DC: U.S. Department of Interior. (AF)

Snakes

Snakes are rarely a threat to adult birds, but tree-climbing snakes such as rat snakes (*Elaphe* spp.) can eat the eggs and nestlings of cavity-nesting birds. This happens mostly in southern states where black rat and corn snakes are locally common. The best way to deter tree-climbing snakes is to secure smooth 2-foot-long guards (described for deterring raccoons under nest boxes), taking care to leave no passage where the pole passes through the guard. Four-inch-diameter guards should be adequate, but larger guards or large inverted flowerpots may be necessary depending on the species of snake.

Ants and Wasps

Paper wasps of the genus *Polistes* often establish their hanging colonies from the roof of nest boxes in early spring before birds begin to nest. Although wasps rarely kill birds in nest boxes, it is not surprising that few birds will attempt to nest in a box already claimed by a well-established paper wasp colony.

If you discover ant or wasp colonies when checking nest boxes in early spring before birds begin looking for nest sites, spray the interior of the box with a liberal dose of pyrethrum spray at night when most of the insects will be in the box. After spraying through the entrance hole, plug it with a rag. The spray will kill most of the insects by morning.

Fire ants (*Solenopsis invicta*) are a serious threat to cavity-nesting birds in the southeastern United States. This tenacious, predatory ant is native to South America, but for the past 65 years it has spread through much of the Southeast. According to R. B. Layton of Jackson, Mississippi, the ants will not invade nest boxes equipped with his homemade ant barriers. Layton's technique for discouraging fire ants is to place a barrier such as an empty thread spool covered with STP™ oil treatment between the nest box and the mounting pole. Ants that climb the pole cannot make it past this sticky barrier. He recommends readily available, dried seed balls of sweetgum (*Liquidambar styraciflua*) treated with STP™ as an ideal barrier. Hide the barrier well behind the box to reduce risk to birds. A band of sticky duct tape tacked to the base of nest box poles will also keep ants from invading boxes. Do not place tape or grease on mounting poles as birds may become accidentally entangled or oiled.

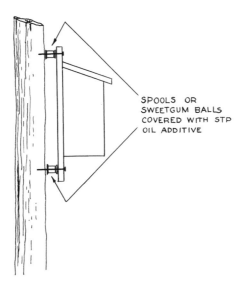

SPOOLS OR
SWEETGUM BALLS
COVERED WITH STP
OIL ADDITIVE

Spools or sweetgum seed balls covered with STP oil treatment prevent fire ants from invading nest boxes. (AF)

Livestock

Cattle and horse pastures are excellent habitats for bluebirds and tree swallows, as there is usually abundant insect food and little competition from house wrens, which frequent brushy fencerows. Unfortunately, nest boxes attached to fence posts or positioned atop isolated poles within pastures are often used by cattle as rubbing posts, and one such encounter is enough to destroy a nest box and its contents.

A simple livestock guard designed by Richard Tuttle of Delaware, Ohio, consists of two 24-inch sections of angle iron secured perpendicular to each other 3 feet from the ground and attached to a metal pole with a U-bolt. The guard is completed by addition of a ring of barbed wire. Although horses and cattle will rub against unyielding barbed-wire fences, the livestock guard is different. When livestock lean against the guard, the pole will slightly bend, and then snap back at the animal, striking it with the barbed wire—a second experience is seldom necessary.

Livestock guards should be painted a light color to reduce the chances of an animal stumbling over it at night. Guards mounted in horse pastures should also be marked to avoid collisions by frolicking horses. Two 3-inch-wide rings of white 4-inch-diameter PVC pipe dangling below the birdhouse will warn most horses during the day and night. The poles that support the livestock guard and nest box should be protected by 4-inch-diameter metal or PVC sheathing. Be sure to have the enthusiastic approval of livestock owners before mounting nest boxes in pastures.

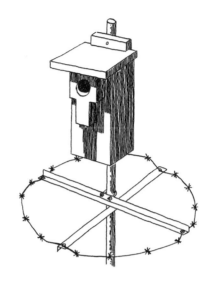

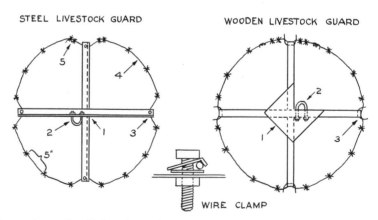

Paint livestock guards a light color and position them under nest boxes located in pastures. One brush with the barbed wire is usually enough to deter livestock from rubbing against the post. Redrawn from Richard M. Tuttle. 1982. "Livestock Guards Make Bossie, Black Beauty, and Bluebirds Compatible." *Sialia* 4(2):65–69. (AF)

House sparrow, Orville Rice (OR), © Cornell Laboratory of Ornithology

Competition for quality nesting cavities is often very intense for native birds because of the introduction of two European species, the house sparrow and European starling. Since both species are resident in breeding habitats throughout the year, they usually have first pick of the best nest sites. Migratory birds, such as the tree swallow, great-crested flycatcher, and bluebirds, often find themselves competing with these aggressive aliens when they return from winter migrations.

Both house sparrows and starlings not only are competitive when it comes to housing but also will destroy eggs and nestlings when they evict less aggressive species from nesting cavities. House sparrows are even known to kill adult male bluebirds as they fight for occupancy rights of a choice nest site. If the adult bluebird or large young are killed in a nest box, the house sparrows will build their nests on top of the carcasses. Starlings can be even more aggressive in fights over suitable nesting sites. Not infrequently they attack and kill downy woodpeckers, and will even take on the much larger flickers and American kestrels as they fight over nesting sites.

House sparrows and starlings are most abundant in open habitat near human housing. House sparrows are rarely found far from human habitation, but starlings sometimes live in mature forest, where they occupy vacant woodpecker cavities.

Entrance holes of 1½ inches exclude starlings from nest boxes intended for wrens, chickadees, titmice, bluebirds, and tree swallows (mountain bluebirds require a 1⁹⁄₁₆-inch hole). Although starlings can't squeeze into a 1½-inch hole, they can sometimes reach in and peck eggs or nestlings. To further protect cavity-nesters, place a 1½-inch-thick block of wood over the entrance hole. This extra thickness is usually enough of a barrier to keep starlings and raccoons from reaching into the boxes. There is no way to exclude starlings from larger nest boxes such as those intended for flickers, screech owls, and kestrels.

Although house sparrows can be excluded from boxes that have up to a 1⅛-inch entrance hole, other species requiring boxes with larger holes are very vulnerable to nest competition and predation by house sparrows, and to date no completely successful exclusion technique has been devised to keep them out of most nest boxes.

House sparrows and starlings are intelligent, adaptable, successful birds and that is why they are so abundant. Destruction of some individuals may be necessary through trapping, as they cannot be excluded from most nest boxes, but it should always be done as expediently and humanely as possible.

Several features of the house sparrows' behavior can reduce competition with other cavity-nesting birds. Placement of the nest box is probably the most important. Because house sparrows seldom occur far from human habitation, they will less frequently use boxes located far from houses and barns. Likewise, they do not like to nest below 3 feet from the ground, while bluebirds and chickadees will nest closer to the ground. Low placement is not recommended, however, if feral cats are in the neighborhood.

Timing is also important. Since house sparrows are resident in their territories all winter, they may occupy boxes before the arrival of migratory birds. By keeping nest entrances plugged or removing boxes from their mounting posts until preferred species arrive, house sparrows will be unable to stake early claims. This technique is especially useful for purple martin houses.

If a house sparrow is discovered using a nest box, its nest should be removed and the entrance covered for a few days. This may encourage the sparrow to go elsewhere, but if there is a high population of sparrows and a low number of suitable nest sites, the sparrow will likely attempt renesting in the same or a nearby nest box. Persistent removal of nests can succeed in discouraging house sparrows, but nests may have to be removed every few days for a week or more.

Where sparrow populations are high and they dominate most nest boxes, the only realistic way to lower populations will be trapping and removal. Many effective live traps for capturing large numbers of sparrows are available from the Web site http://www.nwtrappers.com/catalog/traps/sparrow.asp. Trapping offers some temporary relief for nest competition. Once sparrows are trapped, they should be humanely destroyed.

Trapping efforts have demonstrated that if a territorial male house sparrow is removed from a nest box, his mate will soon abandon the site. In contrast, however, if the female is removed, the male will quickly remate and stay on territory, actively defending the nest box from other prospecting birds.

Sparrow traps need to be checked hourly for species other than house sparrows. Trap operators should be well versed in sparrow identification to be sure that only house sparrows are detained. Because they are introduced species, house sparrows, starlings, and pigeons are not protected by wildlife laws, but all other birds (including their nests, eggs, and parts) are protected by federal and state/provincial laws and cannot legally be captured or held without special permits.

NEST SITE AND NEST BOX CHARACTERISTICS

The location of a nest box is one of the most important considerations in not only attracting birds, but also in optimizing their chances for successful nesting. Most birds select nest sites based on a mixture of innate ability and learned experience. Wood ducks, for example, prefer to nest in tree cavities near quiet, shallow water, a preference that has obvious benefit for newly fledged broods. When offered a variety of artificial homes, they usually prefer wooden homes to metal ones, but after some experience with metal houses, they will nest just as readily and may actually prefer them in areas where raccoon predation is a serious problem. Wood ducks, therefore, have a genetic preference for nesting near wooded, quiet water, but within the habitat they learn which nest sites are most likely to prove successful.

Preferences for specific nest-site characteristics, such as height above the ground, distance to water, or proximity to food, usually have adaptive value. Birds that deviate too far from normal nesting situations are likely to fail rearing their young. With this in mind, it becomes all the more important to place nest boxes not only within the right habitat, but to pay attention to microhabitat needs, such as height above the ground, distance to dense cover, and spacing between boxes. Such specific requirements vary from one species to the next and are unfortunately largely unknown for most birds. The following discussion of nest site characteristics describes some of the habitat needs of selected cavity-nesting birds.

A standard wooden box for cavity-nesting birds will serve many species if the size of the floor, depth of the box, and size and shape of the entrance hole are changed. The following table summarizes recommended box sizes for 32 species, with suggestions for positioning the box at various heights for different birds. The table also recommends preferred habitats for locating boxes.

Nest Box Dimensions for Common Cavity-nesting Birds

Species	Floor (in.)	Chips*	Depth (in.)	Entrance above Floor (in.)	Diameter of Entrance (in.)	Height (ft.) above Ground or Water (W)	Preferred Habitat Code†
Wood duck	12 × 12	+	22	17	4	20–10, 6W	3, 5
Common goldeneye	12 × 12	+	24	20–22	4–5	4–20	3, 5
Barrow's goldeneye	6–9 × 6–9	+	9–52	7–48	3–4	4–20	3, 5
Bufflehead	7 × 7	+	16	13–14	$2\frac{7}{8}$	10–20	3, 5
Hooded merganser	10 × 10	+	15–18	10–13	5	4–6	3, 5
Common merganser	9–11 × 9–11	+	33–40	28–35	5	8–20	3, 5
American kestrel	8 × 8	+	12–15	9–12	3	10–30	1, 4
Barn owl	10 × 18	+	15–18	0–4	6	12–18	4
Barred owl	12 × 12	+	20–24	14	6 × 6	15–20	5
Screech owl	8 × 8	+	12–15	9–12	3	10–30	2
Boreal owl	6–7 × 6–7	+	9–18	7–15	$2\frac{1}{2} \times 4\frac{1}{2}$–5	10–25	9
Saw-whet owl	6 × 6	+	10–12	8–10	$2\frac{1}{2}$	12–20	2
Red-headed woodpecker	6 × 6	+	12	9	2	10–20	2
Golden-fronted woodpecker	6 × 6	+	12	9	2	10–20	2
Downy woodpecker	4 × 4	+	9	7	$1\frac{1}{4}$	5–15	2
Hairy woodpecker	6 × 6	+	12–15	9–12	$1\frac{5}{8}$	12–20	2
Northern flicker	7 × 7	+	16–18	14–16	$2\frac{1}{2}$	6–30	1, 2
Great crested flycatcher	6 × 6	+	8–10	6–8	$1\frac{9}{16}$‡	8–20	1, 2
Ash-throated flycatcher	6 × 6	+	8–10	6–8	$1\frac{1}{2}$‡	8–20	1, 6
Purple martin	6 × 6		6	1	$2\frac{1}{4}$	10–20	1
Tree swallow	5 × 5		6–8	4–6	$1\frac{1}{2}$‡	4–15	1
Violet-green swallow	5 × 5		6–8	4–6	$1\frac{1}{2}$‡	4–15	1
Chickadees	4 × 4	+	9	7	$1\frac{1}{8}$	4–15	2
Titmouse	4 × 4	+	9	7	$1\frac{1}{4}$	5–15	2

315

Nest Box Dimensions for Common Cavity-nesting Birds—cont.

Species	Floor (in.)	Chips*	Depth (in.)	Entrance above Floor (in.)	Diameter of Entrance (in.)	Height (ft.) above Ground or Water (W)	Preferred Habitat Code[†]
Nuthatches[§]	4 × 4	+	9	7	$1\frac{3}{8}$	5–15	2
Carolina wren	4 × 4		6–8	4–6	$1\frac{1}{2}$[‡]	5–10	2, 7
Bewick's wren	4 × 4		6–8	4–6	$1\frac{1}{4}$	5–10	2, 7
House wren	4 × 4		6–8	4–6	$1–1\frac{1}{4}$	4–10	2, 7
Bluebirds (eastern and western)	4 × 4		8–12	6–10	$1\frac{1}{2}$[‡]	3–6	1
Mountain bluebird	4 × 4		8–12	6–10	$1\frac{9}{16}$[‡]	3–6	1
Prothonotary warbler	4 × 4		6	4	$1\frac{3}{8}$	4–12, 3W	3, 5

*Plus sign means add 2–3 inches of wood chips.

[†]Preferred habitat codes:

1. Open areas in the sun (not shaded permanently by trees), pastures, fields, or golf courses.
2. Woodland clearings or the edge of woods.
3. Above water, or if on land, the entrance should face water.
4. On trunks of large trees, or high in little-frequented parts of barns, silos, water towers, or church steeples.
5. Moist forest bottomlands, flooded river valleys, swamps.
6. Semiarid country, deserts, dry open woods, and wood edge.
7. Backyards, near buildings.
8. Near water; under bridges, barns.
9. Mixed conifer-hardwood forests.

[‡]Precise measurement required; if diameter is larger, starlings may usurp cavity.

[§]Brown-headed and pygmy nuthatches ($1\frac{1}{4}$), red-breasted nuthatch ($1\frac{1}{4}$), and white-breasted nuthatch ($1\frac{3}{8}$) will all use the same box. However, the smaller opening sizes where appropriate may discourage use by house sparrows.

Adapted from Daniel D. Boone. 1979. *Homes for Birds*. U.S. Fish and Wildlife Service Conservation Bulletin 14. Washington, DC; also Susan E. Quinlan. 1982. *Bird Houses for Alaska*, vol. 1, no. 3. Alaska Wildlife Watcher's Report. Juneau: Alaska Department of Fish and Game.

Bluebirds

Bluebirds once nested mostly in natural tree cavities. Today the majority use nest boxes.
William Dilger (WD), © Cornell Laboratory of Ornithology

People have provided housing for bluebirds for at least 150 years, but only in the past 40 years have declines in bluebird populations sparked interest in using nest boxes to help increase their numbers.

Bluebird populations declined due to the regrowth of abandoned farmlands into forest, widespread use of persistent pesticides, and the introduction of house sparrows and European starlings. Loss of nest cavities in old apple orchards and wooden fence posts, and removal of dead snags from forests also contributed to the decrease.

Nest boxes have helped to reverse this decline. To facilitate monitoring, nest boxes are usually mounted along "trails" where nest contents are easily checked and the boxes can receive regular cleaning and maintenance. Some bluebird trails span impressive areas, crossing hundreds of miles in Canada and the United States. One of the longest trail stretches for over 2000 miles from the vicinity of Winnipeg, Manitoba, westward beyond Saskatoon, Saskatchewan. On this trail, bluebird boxes are mounted on fence posts about every 100 yards. Several thousand bluebirds fledge from these boxes each year.

Proper location of bluebird nest boxes is more important than subtleties of box design. Bluebirds rarely nest in urban or forested areas. They prefer open countryside with a scattering of trees and low undergrowth. Large lawns, pastures, golf courses, parks, and other open areas are their preferred habitats. Bluebird nest boxes should be mounted 3–6 feet above the ground. Although bluebirds will nest lower, the chances of predation increase and it becomes too difficult to clean boxes mounted higher than about 5 feet. Because bluebirds are highly territorial, it is usually unproductive to mount adjacent nest boxes closer than 100 yards.

Although not always necessary, when possible locate bluebird boxes within 50 feet of a tree, fence, or other structure on which fledglings can perch after their first flight. This reduces the chances of the young birds landing on the ground, where they are more vulnerable to cats and other predators, and provides parents a convenient perch from which they pounce on insect prey.

Proper location of nest boxes can also help to minimize nest competition with other birds, such as house wrens and house sparrows. To reduce competition from house wrens, locate bluebird boxes away from brushy fencerows. House sparrows are much more difficult to discourage, but competition can sometimes be reduced by locating bluebird boxes far from human habitation.

Nest boxes provide secure places from predators and nest competitors when mounted in appropriate habitat. John Schmitt (JS), © Cornell Laboratory of Ornithology

While careful location of boxes may help to discourage wrens and house sparrows, the preferred habitat for bluebirds is also the favorite habitat for tree and violet-green swallows. Both swallows are aggressive nest competitors with bluebirds, and in areas where swallow populations are large and nest sites are scarce, the swallows may usurp nest boxes from bluebirds and sometimes even build their own nests on top of bluebird nests containing eggs and nestlings.

If paired nest boxes are placed a few feet apart, a territorial pair of swallows will chase other swallows from the vicinity of their nest, and in so doing they keep the other box available for bluebirds. In areas where both tree and violet-green swallows nest, boxes should be set out in threes, so that each species of swallow can use a box and there will still be one remaining for bluebirds.

Dick Peterson of Brooklyn Center, Minnesota, has designed a unique nest box that is now widely used throughout the United States. The special feature of this box is the steep sloping roof and front of the box, which results in a very small floor space. According to Peterson, the advantage of this box is that parent bluebirds expend less time carrying nesting material to build a suit-able-sized nest and there is less space for blowfly larvae to hide. This box also has an elongated entrance hole, $1\frac{3}{8}$ inches wide and $2\frac{1}{4}$ inches long. The hole keeps starlings out without a nest guard and permits the bluebirds to slip in with ease.

During winter nights, bluebirds conserve body heat by roosting together, with as many as a dozen birds in the same tree cavity. Bluebirds use natural cavities more frequently than nest boxes for roosting, probably because such sites have fewer cold-air leaks. Recently, Richard Tuttle "winterized" some of his bluebird houses by plugging drainage holes with $\frac{1}{4}$-inch wooden dowels and securing felt weather-stripping to all ventilation slots, thus restricting drafts and improving the boxes for roosting purposes. He found that bluebirds roosted more often in his winterized houses than those not sealed for winter. He also noted that early-spring clutches are more likely to succeed in winterized boxes than those with usual drainage and ventilation holes. Winterizing materials are removed after spring weather stabilizes.

There are several bluebird recovery groups around the United States and Canada, the largest of which is the North American Bluebird Society. This group publishes *Sialia*, a very useful journal that reports on various techniques for improving the status of bluebirds and other cavity-nesting birds.

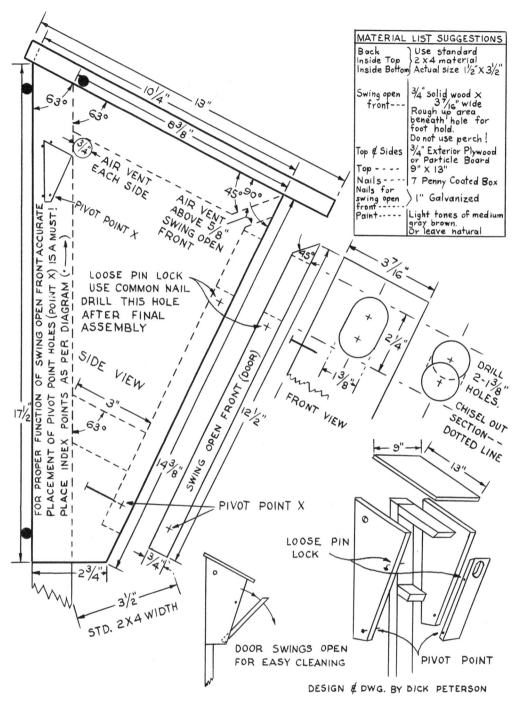

63°
63°
10¼"
13"
8⅜"
¾
AIR VENT EACH SIDE
AIR VENT ABOVE ⅝" SWING OPEN FRONT
45°90°
PIVOT POINT X

FOR PROPER FUNCTION OF SWING OPEN FRONT ACCURATE PLACEMENT OF PIVOT POINT HOLES (POINT X) IS A MUST! PLACE INDEX POINTS AS PER DIAGRAM (⟶)

LOOSE PIN LOCK USE COMMON NAIL DRILL THIS HOLE AFTER FINAL ASSEMBLY

SIDE VIEW

17½"

3"
63°

14⅜"

12½"

SWING OPEN FRONT (Door)

45°

3⁷⁄₁₆"

2¼"

1⅜"

FRONT VIEW

DRILL 2-1⅜" HOLES.

CHISEL OUT SECTION - DOTTED LINE

9"
13"

PIVOT POINT X

LOOSE PIN LOCK

2¾"
¾"
3½"
STD. 2X4 WIDTH

DOOR SWINGS OPEN FOR EASY CLEANING

PIVOT POINT

DESIGN & DWG. BY DICK PETERSON

Dick Peterson of Brooklyn Center, Minnesota, designed this small-bottomed box. The small floor space may be advantageous as it reduces the amount of time adults spend on nest building. The smaller nest bottom may also attract fewer blowfly larvae. Redrawn from original plan by Dick Peterson. (AF)

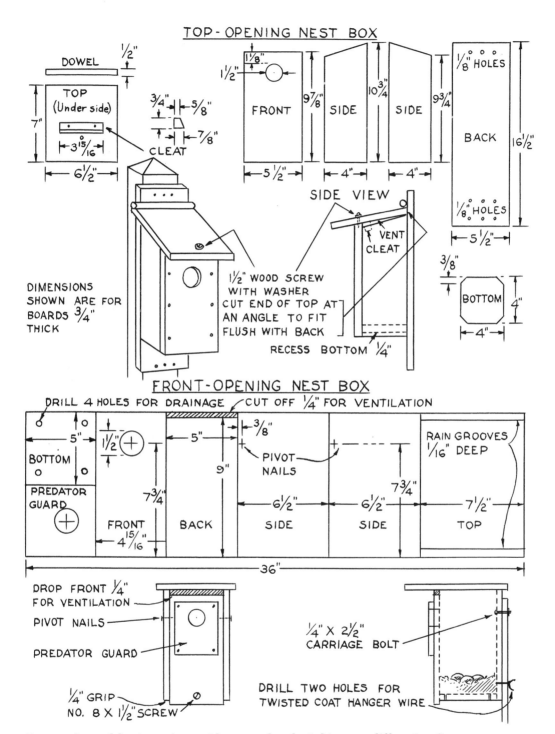

TOP-OPENING NEST BOX

DOWEL

½"

TOP (Under side)

7"

3 15/16"

6½"

CLEAT

¾" | 5/8"

7/8"

1 1/8"

FRONT

1½"

9 7/8"

5½"

SIDE

10 ¾"

SIDE

9 ¾"

4"   4"

1/8" HOLES

BACK

16½"

5½"

1/8" HOLES

3/8"

BOTTOM

4"

4"

SIDE VIEW

VENT CLEAT

1½" WOOD SCREW WITH WASHER

CUT END OF TOP AT AN ANGLE TO FIT FLUSH WITH BACK

RECESS BOTTOM ¼"

DIMENSIONS SHOWN ARE FOR BOARDS ¾" THICK

FRONT-OPENING NEST BOX

DRILL 4 HOLES FOR DRAINAGE

CUT OFF ¼" FOR VENTILATION

BOTTOM

5"

PREDATOR GUARD

FRONT

4 15/16"

1/2"

7¾"

5"

BACK

9"

3/8"

PIVOT NAILS

SIDE

6½"

SIDE

6½"

7¾"

RAIN GROOVES 1/16" DEEP

TOP

7½"

36"

DROP FRONT ¼" FOR VENTILATION

PIVOT NAILS

PREDATOR GUARD

¼" GRIP

NO. 8 X 1½" SCREW

¼" X 2½" CARRIAGE BOLT

DRILL TWO HOLES FOR TWISTED COAT HANGER WIRE

Top-opening and front-opening nest boxes can be adapted to many different cavity-nesting birds (see page 315). This top-opening box is redrawn from Lawrence Zeleny. 1976. *The Bluebird* Bloomington: Indiana University Press. The front-opening box is redrawn from *Blueprint for a Bluebird*. Anon. Publication No. 339. Ohio Division of Wildlife, Columbus. (AF)

Purple Martins

Today almost all purple martins nest in artificial nesting structures, but it was not always that way. Before Europeans colonized North America, purple martins nested in woodpecker-riddled snags and crevices in cliffs (some West Coast martins still use this habitat). They probably were rare in the vast eastern forests and were most abundant in open, grassy valleys along rivers, lakes, and seacoast marshes. The greatest populations in precolonial times were probably in partly forested central regions of North America, an area that remains the heart of the purple martin's current distribution.

Native Americans were the first to attract martins to artificial nesting structures. Their technique was to hang dried gourds from trees near villages so that martins would consume nuisance insects. Today, gourds have become a popular way to house martins throughout North America. When given a choice of purple martin houses or gourds, martins often choose the gourds, while European starlings and house sparrows often prefer houses.

To make a gourd into a birdhouse, first thoroughly dry 8–14-inch bottle gourds before cutting a $2\frac{1}{8}$-inch entrance hole through the middle of the side. Then scrape out the gourd seeds and save them for a new crop. Drill $\frac{5}{8}$-inch holes in the bottom of the gourds for drainage and drill a $\frac{1}{4}$-inch hole through the top of the neck to attach a line. Then paint the outside with an exterior white latex paint to reflect heat. Cut a hole just below the neck to create an access door for cleaning. Seal this with the opaque lid of a kitchen storage container using silicon caulk to hold the lid in place for the season. Plastic gourds are also available from sources listed by the Purple Martin Society and the Purple Martin Conservation Association.

As with all martin houses, mount gourds atop a pole approximately 14 feet tall. Position the mounting pole in an open area *at least* 40 feet from overhanging limbs or buildings, as the martins like to circle their colony and appear to shun homes that are vulnerable to climbing predators. A location near open water such as a pond, river, or lake is especially attractive.

Because martins are highly social, they prefer multiple housing units. Adults often return to the same colony year after year and huge houses can accommodate as many as 200 pairs. More typically, colonies contain 10–20 pairs. Some of the young produced in a colony also return to the same house, but most join nearby colonies or start new colonies in the vicinity of their original home.

For those hoping to start a new colony, the Purple Martin Conservation Association offers a tape and CD titled the *Purple Martin Dawnsong*. Adult males sing this song in predawn hours for 6 weeks after their arrival at the colony site. Apparently, established males use the song to lure newly arrived subadult males to join their colony.

Aluminum martin houses have the advantage of lighter weight than wooden houses and this reduces the chances of the house falling in strong winds and makes it easier to raise and lower. However, properly designed wooden houses offer better insulation and these are preferred as long as they can be easily lowered for winter maintenance (models T14 and PMC 2000 are recommended by the Purple Martin Conservation Association).

Recently, martin enthusiasts have discovered that the number of pairs occupying a multiple house will increase with the use of porch dividers. These partitions create visual blocks on the porches, preventing squabbles between residents and new arrivals. This permits new breeders to more readily prospect for future nest sites. Porch dividers can increase occupancy from 50–65 percent to 75–100 percent. Most new houses do not come with the dividers, but it is possible to install aluminum partitions made from aluminum flashing. These should extend from the wall of the house to the railing and from the porch floor to the ceiling. The porch dividers are fastened to the railing and should have all cut edges finely sanded to prevent injuries.

Purple martins spend 7 months each year either going to, residing in, or returning from their South American wintering habitat. Prior to their return from migration, resident house sparrows and starlings often usurp nesting boxes. Since purple martins prefer a $2\frac{1}{8}$-inch hole, both starlings and house sparrows can easily gain access to martin nest boxes.

To reduce competition with starlings, the Purple Martin Conservation Association (PMCA) recommends crescent-shaped entrance hole covers that are exactly 3 inches wide and $1\frac{3}{16}$ inches tall. (Patterns are available from the PMCA.)

House sparrows are much more difficult to discourage, as they thrive in a wide variety of nest sites and find martin houses ideal. The best way to discourage house sparrows is to lower the houses in the fall, clean them over the winter, and put them up again when the first martins return. Martin houses located far from human dwellings and barns are less appealing to house sparrows. Unless martin houses are closed off in the winter, they are likely to become sparrow colonies. Because of the necessity of lowering and raising martin houses, the mounting pole design is an especially important part of the house.

A cluster of dried gourds is an inexpensive and time-proven nesting structure for purple martins. Martins are generally more successful in gourds than in either aluminum or wooden houses. (AF)

PLANS FOR A MARTIN HOUSE

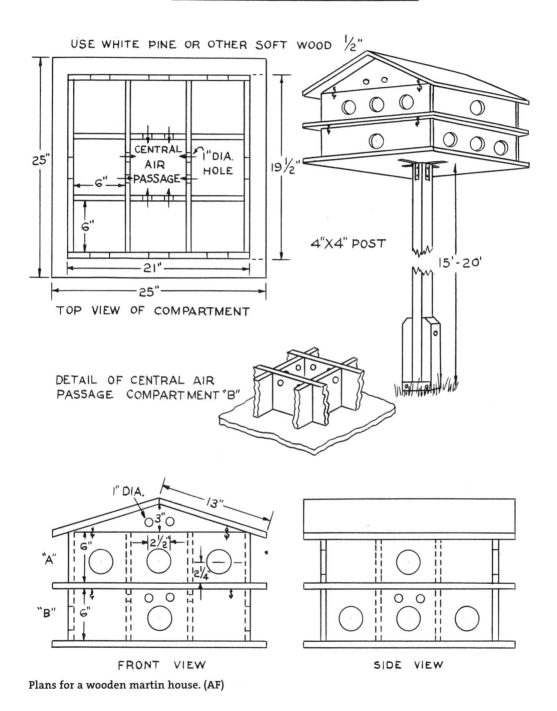

USE WHITE PINE OR OTHER SOFT WOOD ½"

25"

19½"

CENTRAL AIR PASSAGE

1" DIA. HOLE

6"

6"

21"

25"

TOP VIEW OF COMPARTMENT

4"X4" POST

15'-20'

DETAIL OF CENTRAL AIR PASSAGE COMPARTMENT "B"

1" DIA.

13"

3"

"A"

6"

2½"

2¼

"B"

6"

FRONT VIEW

SIDE VIEW

Plans for a wooden martin house. (AF)

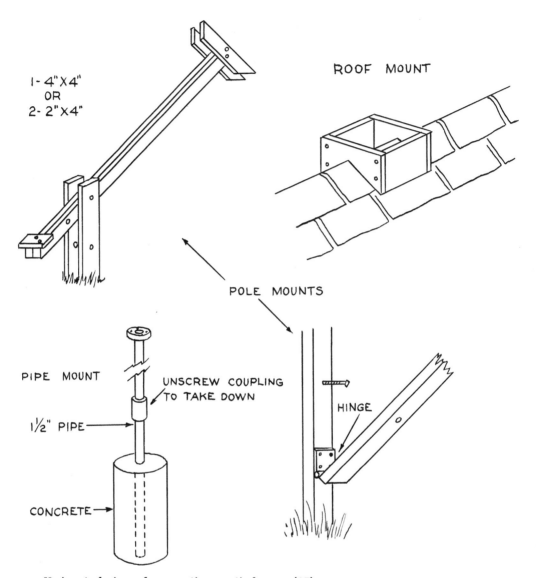

1- 4"X4"
OR
2- 2"X4"

ROOF MOUNT

POLE MOUNTS

PIPE MOUNT

UNSCREW COUPLING
TO TAKE DOWN

1½" PIPE

HINGE

CONCRETE

Various techniques for mounting martin houses. (AF)

Wrens

House wren. (OR)

For bluebird enthusiasts, the ambitious nest-building habits of house, Bewick's, and Carolina wrens are often unappreciated, as they frequently fill several nest boxes full of sticks and only rear their young in one box. Bluebird boxes are best placed far from brushy thickets to avoid wren competition, but where this is not possible, several boxes built especially for wrens may help to discourage them from using boxes intended for bluebirds.

Although wrens will nest in larger boxes, the sizes recommended in the table on page 315 are large enough to meet their needs, as they must do more work gathering sticks if they nest in a larger box. An oval entrance is best because it is much easier for wrens to pull nesting sticks through such an opening. For house wrens, openings should be $\frac{7}{8}$ inch high by $2\frac{1}{2}$ inches long. Bewick's wrens require a somewhat larger, 1-inch-tall opening, and Carolina wrens must have a $1\frac{1}{2}$-inch-tall opening. House sparrows will not be able to squeeze through 1-inch-diameter holes. Wrens readily use thin twigs cut 3–4 inches long and placed near nesting boxes.

Wood Ducks

The wood duck's magnificent plumage and its cavity-nesting habits contributed to a serious decline in numbers during the twentieth century. Other factors were the conversion of eastern forests to cropland, draining of swamplands, introduction of cavity-competing starlings, and market hunting.

Since the early 1930s, the U.S. Fish and Wildlife Service and many state wildlife agencies have launched impressive wood duck restoration efforts through the use of artificial nest boxes. While it is impossible to separate the effects of nest boxes from those of the regrowth of woodlands and protection of wetlands since the 1940s, it is clear that at least locally, nest boxes have substantially increased wood duck populations.

Several features of their behavior make wood ducks especially responsive to nest box programs. As with most ducks, female wood ducks usually return to the vicinity of their hatching place when they reach breeding age. Here they select a nest site similar to the one they remembered from their duckling days. Once a nest site is selected, they often reuse it year after year. Also, wood ducks are surprisingly colonial in their nesting habits. It is not uncommon for females to occupy nest boxes positioned only inches apart or even several boxes nailed together, apartment fashion.

Although wood ducks are sometimes desperate for nest sites (even trapping themselves in chimneys), a good nest box positioned in poor habitat can be a hazard rather than a help. Quality wood duck habitat consists of shallow water with abundant nearby shrubs and trees. Although it is important to protect nesting birds from excessive human disturbance, sizable wood duck "colonies" sometimes occur in even tiny urban wetlands. The water should have ample aquatic vegetation and food for ducklings, such as insect larvae and tiny crustaceans. Staff from local state or provincial wildlife departments can help to determine habitat quality.

Without protection, poorly placed boxes may lure birds to nest in predator-vulnerable locations. For this reason, the best location for a wood-duck box is on a separate pole, positioned about 6 feet above the water. One way to sink wood-duck poles into a pond or marsh bottom is to cut a hole through the ice in the winter and then pound the sharpened post well into the bottom muck. Because wood ducks will nest in cluster housing and it is often more difficult to erect boxes than it is to build them, it makes sense to position more than one box on a good nest box support.

Boxes mounted on trees at the edges of ponds are more vulnerable to predators, as it is easier for raccoons and snakes to climb into nesting trees from adjacent vegetation. If boxes must be located on land, they should be mounted at least 10–20 feet high on trees at or near water. Although wood ducks will nest considerable distances from water, the young are very vulnerable to predators if they must perform a long overland trek to the nearest swamp or marsh.

Since wood ducks naturally nest in tree cavities with soft heartwood or on chips from a woodpecker excavation, they will not use artificial nest boxes unless there are several inches of wood shavings or wood chips to cushion their eggs. To meet this need, add about 4 inches of fresh wood chips each year to the bottom of wood-duck houses. A strip of hardware cloth tacked on the inside front panel below the entrance hole gives the ducklings a rough surface to grip as they leave the box.

An entrance hole 3 inches tall and 4 inches wide will discourage some raccoons from reaching into nest boxes. A more successful entrance for eliminating raccoon predation is a 6-inch-square sleeve constructed from $^3/_4$-inch wood that fits over a 4-inch entrance hole (see illustration A). While this guard prevents raccoon predation, it may attract starlings, and is therefore not recommended where starlings are a problem. Starlings can totally fill wood-duck nest boxes with sticks and other vegetation, even building their nests over complete wood duck clutches. Where competition with starlings is a problem, slowly replace standard boxes with horizontal nesting structures that permit more light to reach the nesting cavity (see illustration B). Similarly, some experimental boxes with clear Plexiglas roofs also discourage starlings.

Wood ducks usually prefer to nest in wooden boxes. They will also use metal "boxes," and will even nest in specially modified plastic buckets. Illustration C shows plans for a standard wooden wood-duck house constructed from one piece of 10-foot-long, 1 × 12 inch rough-cut lumber. An alternative is a rocket-shaped metal house especially useful for discouraging raccoons, squirrels, and snakes (see illustration D).

Within their breeding ranges, the hooded merganser, common merganser, bufflehead, and common goldeneye may also use artificial nest boxes. See page 315 for nest box dimensions.

RACCOON- AND STARLING-PROOF
WOOD DUCK BOXES

3"   6"   9"

6"

10"

4"

NAIL BRACES ON SIDES OF
TUNNEL BEFORE TOP &
BOTTOM

A. RACCOON-PROOF BOX

B. STARLING-PROOF BOX

12 GAUGE WIRE

12"

HOLES FOR SUPPORT WIRE
STOVEPIPE

24"

½" DRAIN

FRONT

¼ X 2" ANCHOR BOLT

13"

8"

13"

WASHER

NUT

4"

4"

2 HEAVY GAUGE
ALUMINUM PLATES
ONE INSIDE, ONE
OUTSIDE "STOVEPIPE"

13"

BACK (VIEWED
FROM FRONT)

(A) The raccoon-proof wood-duck box prevents raccoon predation by lengthening the
box opening, thereby placing duck eggs out of their reach. (B) The interior of the
starling-proof wood-duck box is too brightly lit for most starlings. (AF)

C. STANDARD WOODEN WOOD DUCK BOX

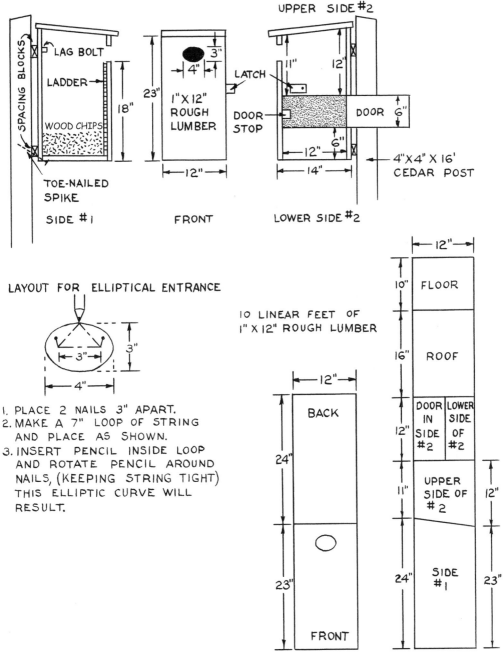

SPACING BLOCKS
LAG BOLT
LADDER
WOOD CHIPS
TOE-NAILED SPIKE
18"
SIDE #1

23"
1"X12" ROUGH LUMBER
3"
4"
12"
FRONT
LATCH
DOOR STOP

UPPER SIDE #2
11"
12'
DOOR 6"
6"
12"
14"
LOWER SIDE #2
4"X4" X 16' CEDAR POST

LAYOUT FOR ELLIPTICAL ENTRANCE
3"
3"
4"

1. PLACE 2 NAILS 3" APART.
2. MAKE A 7" LOOP OF STRING AND PLACE AS SHOWN.
3. INSERT PENCIL INSIDE LOOP AND ROTATE PENCIL AROUND NAILS, (KEEPING STRING TIGHT) THIS ELLIPTIC CURVE WILL RESULT.

10 LINEAR FEET OF 1"X12" ROUGH LUMBER

12"
BACK
24"
23"
FRONT

12"
10" FLOOR
16" ROOF
12" DOOR IN SIDE #2 | LOWER SIDE OF #2
11" UPPER SIDE OF #2 | 12"
24" SIDE #1 | 23"

(C) Standard design for a wooden wood-duck box. (AF)

D. ROCKET WOOD DUCK BOX

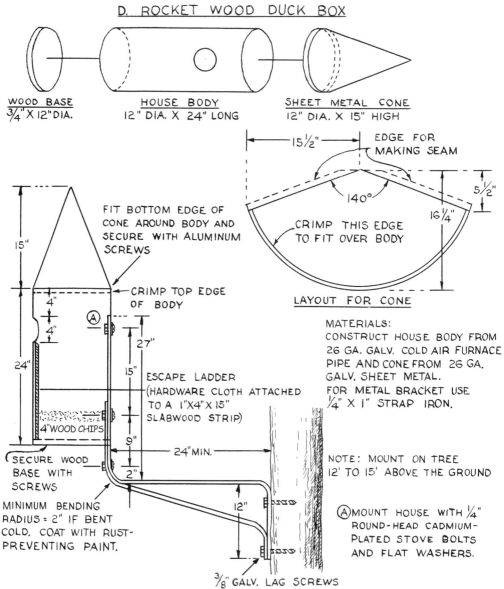

WOOD BASE
3/4" X 12"DIA.

HOUSE BODY
12" DIA. X 24" LONG

SHEET METAL CONE
12" DIA. X 15" HIGH

FIT BOTTOM EDGE OF CONE AROUND BODY AND SECURE WITH ALUMINUM SCREWS

CRIMP TOP EDGE OF BODY

15"

4"
4"
Ⓐ

24"

27"

15"

ESCAPE LADDER (HARDWARE CLOTH ATTACHED TO A 1"X4" X 15" SLABWOOD STRIP)

4" WOOD CHIPS

9"

2"

24" MIN.

SECURE WOOD BASE WITH SCREWS

MINIMUM BENDING RADIUS = 2" IF BENT COLD. COAT WITH RUST-PREVENTING PAINT.

12"

3/8" GALV. LAG SCREWS

15½"

EDGE FOR MAKING SEAM

140°

5½"

16¼"

CRIMP THIS EDGE TO FIT OVER BODY

LAYOUT FOR CONE

MATERIALS:
CONSTRUCT HOUSE BODY FROM 26 GA. GALV. COLD AIR FURNACE PIPE AND CONE FROM 26 GA. GALV. SHEET METAL.
FOR METAL BRACKET USE ¼" X 1" STRAP IRON.

NOTE: MOUNT ON TREE 12' TO 15' ABOVE THE GROUND

Ⓐ MOUNT HOUSE WITH ¼" ROUND-HEAD CADMIUM-PLATED STOVE BOLTS AND FLAT WASHERS.

(D) The rocket wood-duck box is useful on trees or unshielded wood posts. The metal design protects nesting ducks from raccoons, squirrels, and snakes. B, C are redrawn from U.S. Department of Interior. 1976. "Nest Boxes for Wood Ducks." Wildlife Leaflet WL 510. Washington, DC: U.S. Department of Interior. D is redrawn from U.S. Department of Agriculture. 1975. "Wood Duck Nest Boxes." Soil Conservation Service JS 234. Washington, DC: U.S. Department of Agriculture. (AF)

Barn Owls

Where nesting sites limit barn owl populations, nest boxes or shelves can have dramatic effects. One of the best examples of this is the project of Carl Marti and Kathryn Denn of Weber State College, Ogden, Utah, and Phillip Wagner of the Utah Division of Wildlife Resources. They noted that barn owls regularly roosted in abandoned silos, but only 1 in 50 silos had a suitable surface on which the owls could nest. In 1977 and 1978 they placed a total of 30 boxes in silos and of these, 24 were used by barn owls. During this period, 154 young owls fledged from their nesting boxes.

The actual dimensions of barn owl nest boxes are probably not nearly as important as placement of nesting structures in suitable habitat near good feeding areas. In northwestern Connecticut, Arthur Gingert of the National Audubon Society's Miles Wildlife Sanctuary lured barn owls to breed on an open shelf placed high in abandoned silos. His nesting shelf has a 12-inch-tall rim to keep young owls from falling out of the nest prematurely and an 8-inch-high divider across the middle of the shelf to help separate young and reduce competition for food.

Where good feeding habitat exists but abandoned silos and barns are not available, an exterior barn-owl box may prove suitable. The box illustrated here was designed by Larry McKeever of the Owl Rehabilitation Research Foundation, Vineland Station, Ontario. It has an extended roof that provides protection over a large landing platform in front of the box. Another unique feature of the box is the detachable base, which facilitates cleaning. This is useful because barn owl nests require a thorough scrubbing at the end of breeding season. Barn owl boxes and shelves should be filled with several inches of coarse wood shavings and pine needles, and nesting structures should be installed by late winter and positioned at least 10 feet off the ground.

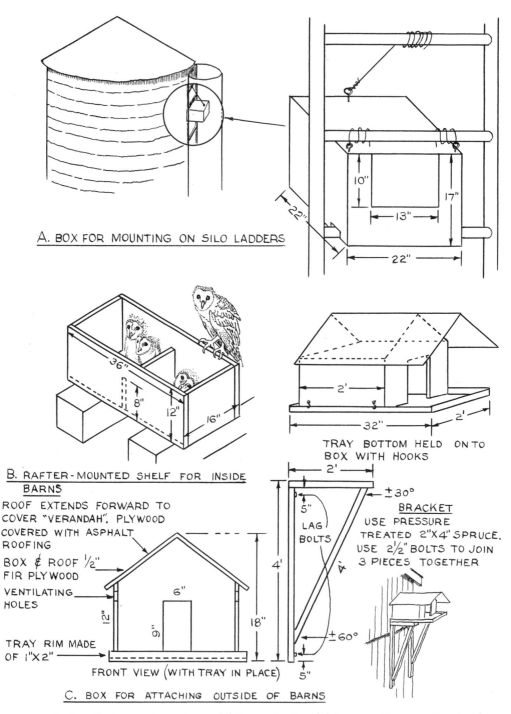

A. BOX FOR MOUNTING ON SILO LADDERS

10"

17"

13"

22"

22"

36"

8"

12"

16"

B. RAFTER-MOUNTED SHELF FOR INSIDE BARNS

2'

2'

32"

2'

TRAY BOTTOM HELD ON TO BOX WITH HOOKS

ROOF EXTENDS FORWARD TO COVER "VERANDAH". PLYWOOD COVERED WITH ASPHALT ROOFING

BOX & ROOF ½" FIR PLYWOOD

VENTILATING HOLES

TRAY RIM MADE OF 1"X2"

12"

6"

9"

18"

FRONT VIEW (WITH TRAY IN PLACE)

C. BOX FOR ATTACHING OUTSIDE OF BARNS

2'

± 30°

5"

LAG BOLTS

4'

4'

± 60°

5"

BRACKET
USE PRESSURE TREATED 2"X4" SPRUCE. USE 2½" BOLTS TO JOIN 3 PIECES TOGETHER

Designs for barn owl nest boxes: (A) for use in silos, (B) for mounting on rafters inside barns, and (C) for the exterior of barns and other large outbuildings. (AF)

Barred Owls

David Johnson of Park Rapids, Minnesota, demonstrated that barred owls would use nest boxes of the proper dimension when placed in suitable habitat. Johnson field-tested 35 specially constructed barred owl boxes in various forest habitats in north central Minnesota. In this study, he had 8 pairs of barred owls nest in 35 boxes. These produced a total of 28 young. Bernard Forsythe of Wolfville, Nova Scotia, has had a similar success in luring barred owls to nest boxes in Nova Scotia.

The boxes should be 20–24 inches tall and 12 inches square. Entrance holes should have 6 inches in diameter or an opening 6 inches square. Several inches of wood chips, dried leaves, or moss should be added to the bottom of the nest box. Barred owl boxes should be mounted at least 17 feet up in a tree with a substantial trunk in wet forests near a pond, stream, or swamp. The use of barred owl boxes in young forests, without suitable large nesting trees, demonstrates that as long as there is an ample food base, nest boxes can substitute for old-age natural cavities and permit barred owls to inhabit younger forests.

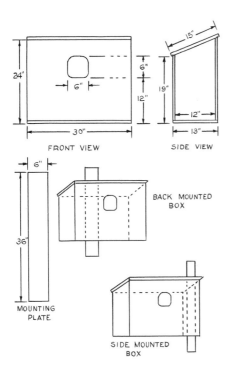

The barred owl nest box, designed by David Johnson, attracts owls because of its 6-inch entrance hole and suitable dimensions. A wet forest environment is the proper habitat. (AF)

American Kestrels

American kestrel. (OR), © Cornell Laboratory of Ornithology

American kestrels occur throughout North and South America, but they are declining throughout most of their North American range. Kestrels typically nest in tree cavities of solitary trees located in open fields. Often such natural sites are scarce or starlings may occupy them. The American kestrel is an adaptable species that can survive in suburban areas, given proper nesting sites.

Kestrels will nest in wood duck–size boxes or in custom boxes with an 8 × 8 inch floor. The boxes should be mounted 10–30 feet above the ground on solitary trees or utility poles. These boxes may increase the number of wintering kestrels by acting as shelters and roost sites.

Frances Hammerstroms's American kestrel nest box program demonstrates such an increase. In a 20-year period before her nest box effort began in central Wisconsin, she found only three pairs of nesting kestrels using 8330 acres of open countryside. In the 5 years following placement of 50 kestrel nest boxes, she found 8–12 broods per year raised in her boxes.

In 1983 Ron Andrews of the Iowa Department of Natural Resources originated the interstate nest box program for American kestrels. Working in cooperation with the Iowa Department of Transportation, nest boxes were attached to the backs of information signs along the interstate rights-of-way. Twenty nest boxes were placed on signs along I-35 in northern Iowa that first year as an Eagle Scout project, and eight were used by kestrels. Nearly every mile of I-35 from Missouri to Minnesota now has nest boxes, representing the nation's first statewide kestrel trail along an interstate system. These efforts have been coordinated by the Iowa Department of Natural Resources Nongame Wildlife Program and implemented at the local level by state nongame personnel, county conservation personnel, and a host of volunteers. Hundreds of nest boxes have been attached to highway signs elsewhere in Iowa. The study has demonstrated that collisions with automobiles are uncommon. Many other states, including Rhode Island, Nebraska, and Idaho, have adopted the kestrel box program.

NEST PLATFORMS AND SUPPORTS

A diverse assemblage of birds, including eagles, American robins, barn swallows, mourning doves, double-crested cormorants, ospreys, and great horned owls, will nest on suitable platforms when faced with a scarcity of natural sites. Most species will not attempt breeding unless there is ample food, but where this exists, the presentation of a secure nesting platform in the right habitat may be all that is necessary to encourage nesting.

American Robins, Phoebes, and Barn Swallows

Robins build their mud-lined nests in a variety of places, including deciduous and evergreen trees and shrubs. One of their favorite places is under building eaves where they find a secure supporting structure. Before human dwellings became an option for nesting, phoebes usually built their nests under bridges near moving water or in a natural rock crevice near a stream. As with robins, they also construct nests under protected building eaves if they can find a secure base for support, even if it is over a frequently used doorway.

Christmas wreaths are an excellent support for nesting robins, house finches, juncos, and other birds that typically nest in trees and shrubs. After using the wreath on your door, move it to a more secluded wall so that it will be ready for use by birds in the spring.

To encourage robins and phoebes to nest on your home or outbuildings (and away from doorways), construct a nesting shelf and attach it under a protected eave. For somewhat exposed areas, follow design A, and for areas with protection, use B. A few sprigs of evergreen needles, such as arborvitae, stapled to the face of robin nest shelves may increase acceptance of the platform.

As their name suggests, barn swallows usually nest in barns, but they often attempt to nest in abandoned buildings and under porches. A simple L-shaped platform (design C) provides an ideal base for swallow nests. Cliff swallows or cave swallows (southwestern Texas only) will also use this platform when it is mounted under building eaves.

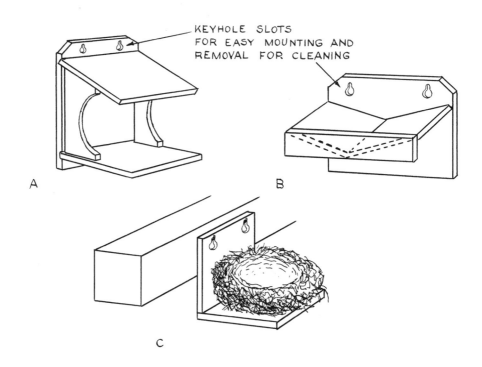

	FLOOR DIMENSIONS INCHES	HEIGHT OFF GROUND FEET
PHOEBE	6X6	8 – 12
ROBIN	6X8 (DEEP)	6 – 15
BARN SWALLOW	6X6	8 – 12

Nest platforms for phoebes, robins, and barn swallows. Design A is for somewhat exposed locations. Design B is for attachment under eaves and other protected sites. Phoebes and robins will use designs A and B. The L-shaped platform (design C) is an appropriate nest structure for barn swallows. (AF)

Creating Supports for Land Bird Nests

Land birds such as vireos, warblers, and sparrows that nest in shrubs and trees select branch arrangements that will support a nest. Two basic types of nest sites occur in trees and shrubs. One is on horizontal branches where three or more branches arise from one location. The second type is a crown site where branches arise in a whorl and where terminal growth is stunted. By examining trees and shrubs with this in mind, it is possible to find potential locations for nests and to prune branches to create a structure favorable for nest building.

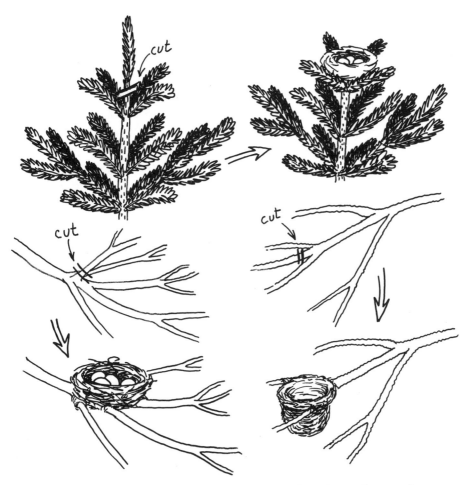

Pruning can help to create nest sites on both horizontal branches and crowns for warblers, vireos, thrushes, finches, sparrows, and other shrub- and tree-nesting birds. (CD)

Mourning Doves

**Mourning doves build loose stick nests and readily accept nest platforms. (OR), ©
Cornell Laboratory of Ornithology**

Mourning doves usually build a flimsy stick nest in a tree or shrub crotch, but these are often destroyed by strong winds and rain. Survival can be improved by building cone-shaped mourning dove nests from $\frac{1}{4}$- or $\frac{3}{8}$-inch hardware cloth. The cones are then positioned in forked branches 6–16 feet high in trees with moderate shade (either conifers or deciduous trees). Good nest sites should have an excellent view of the ground and a clear flight path to and from the nest. Since mourning doves sometimes nest in loose colonies, several nesting cones can be placed near each other in the same tree.

The nesting cones should be secured to the tree using two nails, one on each side of the cone, or wire. After installation, carefully bend down the lip of the cone to give a smooth landing place. Best results in the Central Valley of California were obtained by installing nest cones in late February, March, and April before most doves established their nesting territories. Old nests should be cleared from the wire cones each spring.

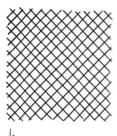
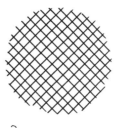
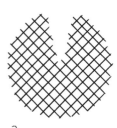

I.
2.
3.

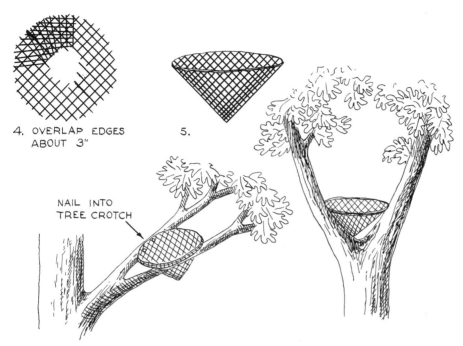

4. OVERLAP EDGES ABOUT 3"

5.

NAIL INTO TREE CROTCH

Nest cones for mourning doves. Cones are constructed from a 12-inch square of ¼- or ⅜-inch galvanized hardware cloth. The squares (1) are cut into a circle (2), notched (3), and overlapped in a cone (4, 5). These are then secured to tree crotches with nails or wire. (AF)

Great Horned, Long-eared, and Great Gray Owls

Tree-nesting owls that rely on the vacant nests of crows and hawks frequently face a shortage of secure nesting sites. Great horned owls begin nesting in January or February throughout much of North America, long before other birds begin to nest. They sometimes take over the favorite nesting sites of the osprey and bald eagle, but more frequently they nest in weathered crow or hawk nests that often crumble before their young can fledge.

Bernard Forsythe of Wolfville, Nova Scotia, has successfully lured both great horned and long-eared owls to artificial nesting platforms constructed high in living coniferous trees. Climbing up a suitable tree, he nails a board or stout pole across two branches, forming a triangular support for a chicken-wire basket. He attaches the chicken wire to the trunk and branches using tacks or staples and creates a shallow basket with a depth of 1 or 2 inches. Inside the basket, he builds a stick nest, tying a few branches to the mesh with string. The nest is lined with coniferous branches that are woven into the chicken wire. The nest is completed by a soft layer of twigs, leaves, and moss with several inches of sphagnum moss laid on top.

The space around owl nests should be fairly open so that the adults can easily fly into the nest, yet the site should not be so exposed that it is easily discovered by crows. For great horned owls, position the nest about 20 feet off the ground and cut away all branches within 24 inches over the nest (see illustration A). Position long-eared owl nests 15 feet off the ground with a 15-inch clearance above the nest (see illustration B).

In the woods between Lac du Bonnet, Manitoba, and the boglands of north Minnesota, Robert Nero, Ray Tuokko, and Herb Copland have built more than 140 artificial or reconstructed great gray owl nests. Like great horned and long-eared owls, great gray owls depend primarily on old crow and hawk nests, many of which deteriorate before their young fledge. Of 45 recent nesting attempts between 1974 and 1981, 26 nestings in their study area occurred in artificial nests.

Robert Nero and his associates build their nests 15–25 feet up in a crown of upright limbs in deformed tamarack (American larch). They attach the cradle of chicken wire and then build up a 2-foot-high nest using crushed tamarack twigs, bark, and moss for the dense lining. The whole structure is about 18–24 inches across. Usually they build three or more nests in nearby trees to provide a choice of nest sites.

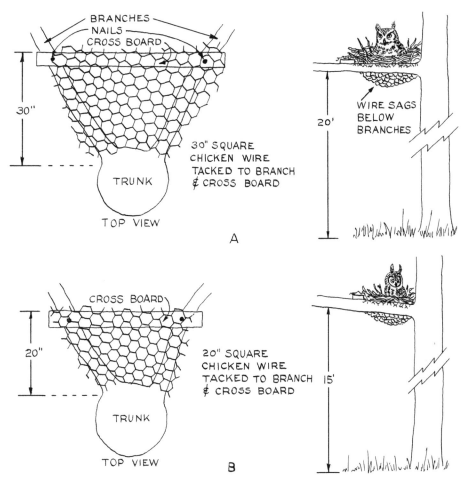

Artificial nest structures built in mature conifers for the great horned owl (A) and the long-eared owl (B). The basket is constructed from chicken wire attached to a board or pole that rests on adjacent branches. Designed by Bernard Forsythe of Wolfville, Nova Scotia. (AF)

Eagles, Ospreys, and Hawks

Nest sites for eagles, ospreys, and hawks are often scarce in western range-lands and coastal marshes. When natural sites are unavailable, these birds often resort to nesting on manmade structures such as windmills, utility poles, and navigational markers. Unfortunately, their nests are often removed from such locations. To lure them away from such hazards, an increasing number of wildlife agencies, conservation groups, and concerned individuals are creating artificial nest sites.

Where possible, the best technique is to cut the top off a large, solitary tree and build a nest platform on top of the trunk. Where suitable trees are not available, artificial nesting poles and structures are often accepted.

Ospreys are especially quick to use artificial nest platforms in both inland and coastal areas. Peter Ames and Paul Spitzer of Old Lyme, Connecticut, have designed osprey nesting platforms and mounting poles that have withstood the rigors of salt marsh habitats in Connecticut and Massachusetts for over 20 years. Their mounting posts and support structures are constructed from 16-foot, 4 × 4 inch seasoned oak or white cedar. The mounting poles are buried at least 3 feet into a salt marsh and braced by four 6-foot strut braces built of seasoned oak. The braces are predrilled and are held together with galvanized nails.

The platform is constructed around a pine sheath that slips over the top of the mounting pole. Four 2 × 4 inch, 30-inch-long fir struts form a foundation for eight 1 × 2 inch fir strips that support a 3 × 3 foot piece of turkey wire tacked to the struts.

Ospreys, bald and golden eagles, red-tailed and ferruginous hawks, great horned owls, and ravens have successfully used artificial nesting platforms similar to the one described here. Nesting platforms constructed in sunny, arid habitats should have a wooden protective canopy the size of the nest platform to provide partial shade.

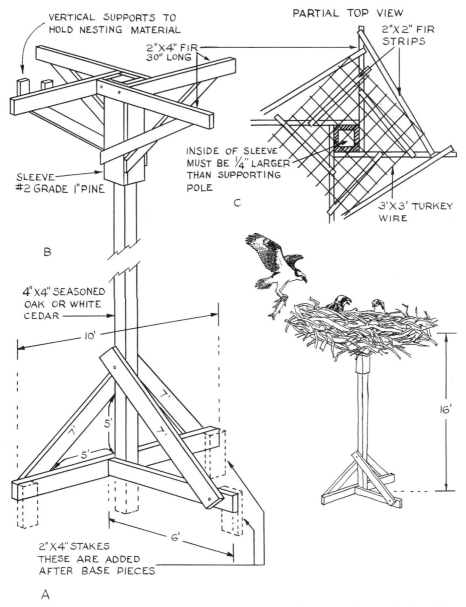

VERTICAL SUPPORTS TO
HOLD NESTING MATERIAL

2"X4" FIR
30" LONG

PARTIAL TOP VIEW

2"X2" FIR
STRIPS

INSIDE OF SLEEVE
MUST BE ¼" LARGER
THAN SUPPORTING
POLE

SLEEVE
#2 GRADE I"PINE

C

3'X3' TURKEY
WIRE

B

4"X4" SEASONED
OAK OR WHITE
CEDAR

10'

7'

5'

7'

5'

7'

16'

6'

2"X4" STAKES
THESE ARE ADDED
AFTER BASE PIECES

A

Nesting platform for ospreys and other treetop raptors. The post and supports should be constructed out of seasoned oak or white cedar. Designed by Peter Ames and Paul Spitzer of Old Lyme, Connecticut. (AF)

Ducks and Geese

Canada geese, mallards, black ducks, and other waterfowl prefer to nest on small islands where they can watch for predators. Even beaver and muskrat houses often serve as nesting sites. Where natural islands are not available, waterfowl will use floating 6 × 6 foot wooden rafts built over a Styrofoam core. Such rafts should be anchored to the bottom using bleach bottles filled with sand or concrete mix. Fill the raft with straw and paint the Styrofoam a dark brown color to help it blend with the environment. To help young birds find food and shelter, position the raft near emergent vegetation at the edge of a pond or lake.

Geese and ducks will use special nesting platforms constructed on 7-foot-long steel post legs set into the marsh soil. The platform consists of a 2 × 4 inch frame that supports 1 × 8 inch planks. A truck tire wired to the platform and filled with straw makes an excellent goose nest site.

A

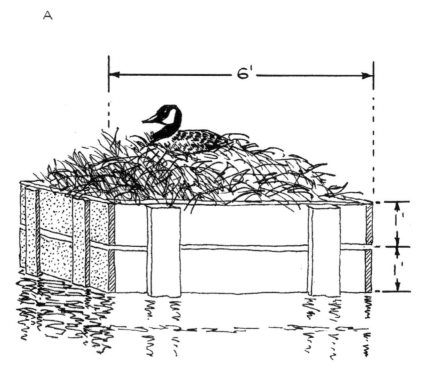

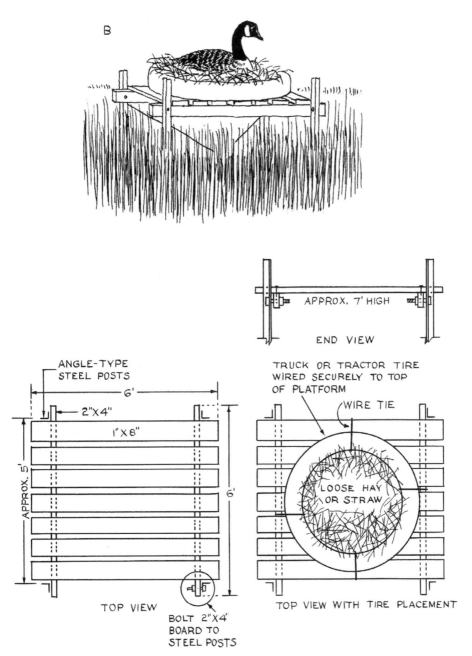

B

ANGLE-TYPE
STEEL POSTS

6'

2"X4"

I"X 8"

APPROX. 5'

6'

TOP VIEW

BOLT 2"X4'
BOARD TO
STEEL POSTS

APPROX. 7' HIGH

END VIEW

TRUCK OR TRACTOR TIRE
WIRED SECURELY TO TOP
OF PLATFORM

WIRE TIE

LOOSE HAY
OR STRAW

TOP VIEW WITH TIRE PLACEMENT

Designs for waterfowl nesting platforms: floating raft (A) and raised platform for marshes (B). (AF)

Loons

Loon populations in the northern United States and southern Canada are vulnerable, owing to loss of wetlands, disturbance by careless boaters, loss of fish from acid precipitation, and predation by increasing numbers of raccoons. The use of artificial nesting rafts has helped increase the numbers of loons by providing safe nesting places.

Loon conservation groups in Maine, New Hampshire, and Wisconsin have experienced success with such artificial platforms. For example, in 1982 the New Hampshire Loon Preservation Committee placed 50 nesting rafts and found loons nesting on 15 of these floating structures. These accounted for one-fifth of the loon chicks produced in New Hampshire in 1982.

The successful loon nesting structures used in New Hampshire are constructed from four 8-inch-diameter, 6-foot-long barkless cedar logs. These are notched to create a low profile and are held together with 8-inch-long galvanized spikes. A 5 × 5 foot piece of turkey wire (2 × 4 inch mesh) is then attached to the raft with 1½-inch galvanized fence staples to create a slightly sagging basket that holds a thick mat of sod, soil, and rotting wood. Marsh plants such as cattail, bulrush, and other emergent vegetation are then planted on the "island." The completed nesting surface of the raft measures 4 feet on a side. It is secured 30–50 yards from shore in 4–6 feet of water by two wire-cable anchor lines, each attached to an 8 × 8 × 16 inch cinder block.

Quiet ponds and lakes where loons are observed during the summer are the best sites for locating loon nesting-rafts. To learn more about loons and to find the nearest loon conservation group, contact the North American Loon Fund (see page 355).

CONSTRUCTION

A

25 SQ.FT.
1"X2" MESH
GALVANIZED

8"-10' DIAM.
GALVANIZED
WIRE

"U" CLAMP

2 CEMENT BLOCKS
FOR ANCHORS

72" CEDAR LOG
(UNTREATED)

8" GALVANIZED
SPIKES. 2
PER CORNER

HEAVY GALVANIZED
STAPLES. USED TO
ATTACH WIRE MESH
½ WAY UP SIDE OF LOG.*

B

48"

48"

"U" CLAMPS

"U" CLAMP - 2 ON
EACH ANCHOR LINE
TO SECURE WIRE.

*BE SURE SHARP ENDS OF WIRE ARE HAMMERED INTO THE LOG.

PLACEMENT

PROTECTED COVE
BEST AREA
FOR ISLAND
50'-100' FROM
SHORE

NOT A GOOD AREA
OPEN TO WIND AND
WAVE ACTION

45°

45°

LEAVE 2' SLACK

4'-6' WATER DEPTH

PREVAILING WINDS

FLOATING SIGN

LOON
NESTING
SANCTUARY
PLEASE STAY
AWAY

OVERALL DIMENSIONS
3'X 3'

ALL WOOD

FLOATLINE

LOON
NESTING
SANCTUARY

Construction and placement of loon nesting platforms. Redrawn from "An Artificial Island for Loons." Meredith, NH: North American Loon Fund. (AF)

Common and Forster's Terns

Terns may experience a shortage of nesting sites where vegetation has grown up too high or where nest site competitors, such as herring and great black-backed gulls, crowd terns onto marginal habitats.

Artificial nesting platforms may prove useful where vegetation management is not a solution to habitat needs. In such circumstances, the Royal Society for Protection of Birds and the Wisconsin Department of Natural Resources have used artificial nesting platforms to assist, respectively, common and Forster's terns.

In Wisconsin, Forster's terns usually nest on floating phragmites mats in well-protected areas. The chances of storm damage to nests on such ephemeral sites are so great that few nests produce chicks. When given a choice early in their nesting season of using emergent vegetation or 19 artificial platforms, a colony of about 200 terns on Lake Poygan abandoned natural sites in favor of the more secure platforms. All 19 platforms were used, producing at least 56 chicks.

The platforms used in Wisconsin consisted of a frame built of $^3/_4 \times 1^3/_4$ inch lumber over 1-inch-thick sheets of rugged blue waterproof Styrofoam. Bundles of phragmites wired every 6 inches to the frame formed a rim 4 inches high around the platform. The platform interiors were then filled with a layer of loose phragmites and cattail for a nesting substrate. The platforms were positioned near each other in shallow water. One-quarter-inch polypropylene cord attached each raft to an anchor made from concrete poured into used paint pails. Drag hooks protruding from the base of the anchor helped to keep the rafts from drifting.

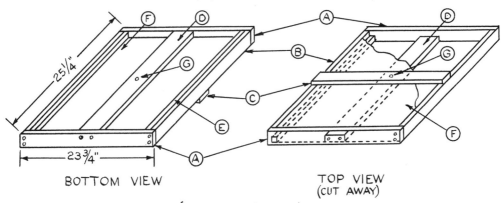

BOTTOM VIEW

TOP VIEW
(CUT AWAY)

FRAMES CUT FROM 1"X4"X8' NO. 3 PINE

(A) ENDS (2) ¾" x 1¾" X 23¾"
(B) SIDES (2) ¾" x 1¾" X 23¾"
(C) CENTER BRACE, TOP (1) 1¾" X ¾" X 23¾"
(D) CENTER BRACE, BOTTOM (1) ¾" X 1¾" X 23¾"
(E) STYROFOAM SUPPORT, BOTTOM (2) ¾" X ⅞" X 23¾"
(F) STYROFOAM FLOTATION PANEL (1) 1" X 22" X 23¾"
(G) ANCHOR ROPE HOLE ½" I.D.

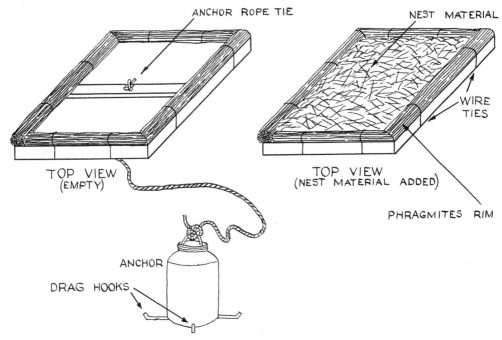

Nesting platforms anchored in shallow water provide suitable nesting habitat for Forster's tern. Redrawn from Arlen F. Linde and Carl Cierke. 1980. "Forster's Tern Nesting Platform Study." Bureau of Research, Wisconsin Department of Natural Resources. Madison. (AF)

SOCIAL ATTRACTANTS

For colonial birds, such as terns, and many other species that nest in groups, new colonies are often slow to start, even when nest sites and food supplies are abundant. My research with terns, puffins, razorbills, and Leach's storm-petrels on offshore Maine islands demonstrates the importance of encouraging the first pioneering colonial birds to nest.

Social attraction relies on the use of decoys and recordings of breeding birds to encourage nesting at former colony sites. These techniques have lured common, arctic, and roseate terns to breed on many islands along the Maine coast. Broadcasting the underground mating calls of "established breeders" from artificial burrows has helped to establish colonies of Leach's storm-petrels (robin-sized relatives of albatross) on former breeding sites on offshore Maine islands. Petrels will not visit these burrow sites without recordings, but they are readily attracted when they hear the call of established breeders. Likewise, social attraction may help rare land birds to establish new populations. For example, playback recordings are now a commonly used technique to encourage nesting by purple martins.

Research with black-capped vireos along the Rio Grande demonstrates that songbirds may also respond to social attraction. Researchers have broadcast the song of these rare birds from suitable habitat and have encouraged some of them to colonize, thus helping to redistribute the birds into additional nesting groups where they are safer from predators.

These studies suggest that other types of colonial birds, such as barn swallows, herons, and burrowing owls, may start new colonies more readily if they are socially stimulated. Decoys and recorded vocalizations help to advertise available nest sites and attract enough birds to start new colonies.

An arctic tern offers a small shrimp to a decoy in a courtship attempt. Decoys and tape recordings have helped to restore many tern colonies in New England. (SK)

ROOSTING SITES

At night and in extreme weather, birds must find suitable protective cover. Cavity-nesting birds such as woodpeckers, chickadees, and titmice usually sleep in tree cavities. Some such as chickadees and bluebirds often huddle together with other members of their winter flock. Cavity-nesting birds will use nest boxes, especially if they have a minimum of cracks and other drafty openings. There is some evidence that nest boxes that are sealed by plugging drain holes and closing ventilation slots are more readily accepted as winter roosts by bluebirds than boxes that are not "winterized."

Special weathertight roosting boxes designed with an entrance hole at the bottom so warm air is retained and alternating perches to keep birds from "decorating" their neighbors at night may also be helpful in providing protection during extreme cold weather. Roosting boxes should face toward the south to maximize direct sunlight during winter and be positioned away from the prevailing wind.

Birds of arid regions, such as songbirds and desert quail, are especially dependent on adequate roosts to moderate the extreme temperature changes from day to night. In such habitats, a scarcity of roost sites may severely limit bird populations. Here, artificial roosting trees provide much-needed protection.

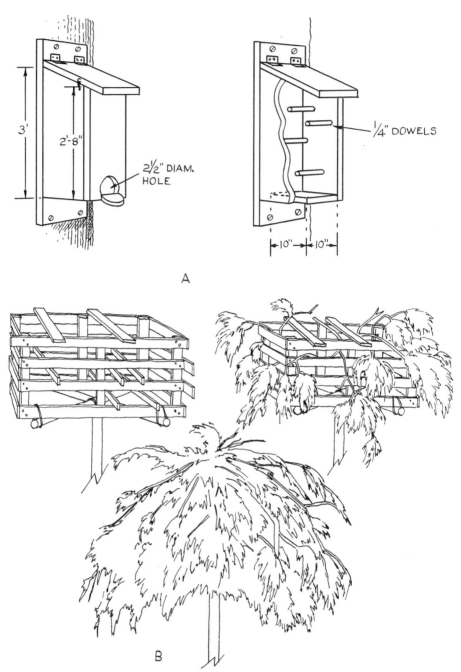

In harsh climates roosting shelters may provide essential cover for birds. Weather-tight roosting boxes provide shelter for small land birds in cold, northern climates (A); southern exposure should be maximized. Artificial tree roosts provide critical cover in arid regions (B). Redrawn from Yoakum et al. 1980. "Habitat Improvement Techniques," in S. D. Schemnitz, ed. *Wildlife Management Techniques Manual.* 4th edition. Washington, DC: Wildlife Society. (AF)

USEFUL SOURCES

The Cornell Laboratory of Ornithology's Birdhouse Network:
   http://birds.cornell.edu/birdhouse/
On nest box design and maintenance:
   http://birds.cornell.edu/birdhouse/bhbasics/bhbasics_index.html
On sparrow traps:
   http://www.nwtrappers.com/catalog/traps/sparrow.asp
On bluebirds:
North American Bluebird Society, Inc.:
   http://www.nabluebirdsociety.org/
On purple martins:
Purple Martin Conservation Association:
   http://www.purplemartin.org
Purple Martin Society NA:
   http://www.purplemartins.com
On American kestrels:
   http://www.npwrc.usgs.gov/resource/tools/kestrel/kestrel.htm
On loons:
   http://www.adkscience.org/loons/info.htm

8

Supplemental Feeding

About 54 million residents of the United States feed wild birds at backyard feeders.[1] This massive feeding effort would seem to improve the well-being of many birds, but the effects of supplemental feeding vary greatly between species and regions because many factors in bird environments are changing at the same time. For the past several decades we have not only fed birds but also altered the landscape as small farms have been replaced by expansive plantings of single-species croplands. Likewise, suburbs and pavement have spread over millions of acres of prime bird habitat, forests have regrown on abandoned farmland, and grasslands, shrublands, and wetlands have become increasingly scarce.

These changes are obvious, but less conspicuous ones are also occurring. For example, invasive plants are competing with natural foods, introduced birds such as starlings and house sparrows are competing for food and nesting places, while

[1]2001 National Survey of Fishing, Hunting and Wildlife-Associated Recreation, Washington, DC: U.S. Fish and Wildlife Service and U.S. Department of Commerce.

vast deer herds browse back undergrowth, exposing nests to thriving populations of small predatory mammals and predatory birds such as grackles, jays, and hawks. Within our dynamic, changing landscape, what can we say about the effects of feeding wild birds?

To put bird feeding into perspective, consider even the most regular visitors at feeders will not feed exclusively on human handouts. Most birds are quick to use whatever foods they can find in their environment, and when they are away from feeders they continue to forage on weed seeds, fruits, insects, and other foods. Feeders provide a supplement to natural food supplies and only rarely do they comprise the bulk of a wild bird's diet. Clearly, birds have survived and thrived in North America long before the present enthusiasm for feeding birds, which dates only to the early 1950s. If all feeding were to stop overnight, there would probably be no species extinctions or even major population declines.

Plants, birds, and mammals have coevolved over thousands of years to disperse seeds and find food. Many surprising and often intricate interactions exist. For example, the fruits of trees and shrubs, such as hawthorn and crabapple, attain their bright bird-attracting colors only when the fruits are ripe and ready for dispersal by birds. Likewise, the same gray squirrels that may drive backyard bird watchers to distraction by consuming grain may also help wild birds by tunneling through several feet of snow to reveal and crack open otherwise unavailable bird foods, such as osage orange, walnuts, and acorns, and certainly the squirrels plant many oak trees.

In general, wild birds depend on foods that they find away from bird feeders, and they find them with remarkable efficiency. Their senses are finely tuned to recognize and consume foods as they become available. Such availability has probably been a major factor affecting the timing and direction of migration. Considering the many generations of birds that have adapted to finding the proper mixes of food, cover, and water, it is unlikely that even the species that are most abundant at feeders are now seriously dependent on the charity of bird feeders. Yet the questions remain, where food is unusually concentrated in rich supplies, what effect does this have on migration, survival, and population growth? And does supplemental feeding enhance populations of predatory birds such as jays and grackles, which also consume the eggs and young of birds that don't use feeders such as warblers and thrushes?

In some cases, supplemental feeding has altered normal winter dispersals and detained birds from their usual migrations. Such was the case at the Horicon

National Wildlife Refuge in southeastern Wisconsin, where crops planted especially for Canada geese attracted increasingly large numbers until as many as 208,000 geese crowded onto the refuge rather than migrating down the Mississippi to their usual wintering grounds in Louisiana. Such numbers resulted in overcrowding and competition with other waterfowl for food and space. The crowding also created a setting for disastrous disease outbreak.

After several generations of supplemental feeding, there was concern that the migratory habits of the geese would change and that the ancestral migration to Louisiana would be forgotten. Recent changes in supplemental feeding and habitat management have reduced Canada goose numbers at Horicon and encouraged them to resume their traditional migration route. Such wintering shifts may occur to small land-bird populations in response to food availability, but they are very difficult to detect.

It is likely that some species or populations benefit from supplemental feeding far more than others. For example, small birds such as common redpolls have body temperatures that may be over 105 degrees Fahrenheit on frigid winter nights. Even with an insulating covering of feathers, heat loss is a potentially serious problem because of their comparatively high proportion of skin surface area to small body mass. Such birds benefit from dependable supplies of high-energy food like sunflower and nyjer seeds.

Although heat loss may be a danger, studies of black-capped chickadees show how behavioral, social, and physiological adaptations help them survive the rigors of winter weather. When temperatures drop, chickadees respond by fluffing their well-insulated plumage and huddling together at night with flock members in tree cavities or other sheltered places. Chickadees can also store food and remember places where they found a good meal at least 8 months later.

Chickadees also have remarkable physiological adaptations for conserving body heat during long, winter nights. As temperatures drop to freezing, they enter a torpid condition to which body temperatures may drop by 20 degrees.

Susan M. Budd, a Cornell University researcher, found that black-capped chickadees living off a normal diet of insects and wild plant seeds put on enough fat during daylight hours to increase their body weight by an average of 7.5 percent before each long winter night. Usually this fat was depleted by morning. In contrast, chickadees that ate a diet of sunflower seeds put on an average of 11.8 percent fat. Young birds, sick birds, or others that are not as efficient at finding food are especially vulnerable to starvation.

The more we know about winter birds, the better we can appreciate how well adapted most species are to their environments. Small birds such as chickadees have many adaptations for surviving the rigors of winter, but they have little in the way of reserve foods, and are usually quick to eat supplemental food supplies offered at feeders. For such species, supplemental feeding may make a life or death difference under prolonged, extremely cold weather conditions or during sudden ice storms.

Some nonmigratory birds are, in general, more likely to benefit from supplemental feeding than are highly mobile species. A study of nonmigratory mourning doves conducted by A. Starker Leopold and Mark F. Dedon of the University of California in Berkeley illustrates this point. While most North American mourning doves are migratory, apparently doves that live in Berkeley and several other areas in central and southern North America are not. The study reveals that in Berkeley, a developed community with no vacant lots for weed seeds and other natural foods, mourning doves are heavily dependent on bird feeders and probably could not exist in that community without supplemental feeding. In contrast to mourning doves, highly mobile, flocking species such as the evening grosbeak and American goldfinch will quickly move on when foods run low. They can simply fly to a neighbor's feeder or leave the area entirely.

Food availability throughout the year is certainly a limiting factor for many kinds of birds. When food limits are removed, it is interesting to see how some birds respond. The extraordinary population growth of red-winged blackbirds in North America illustrates the link between food availability and population growth. Red-winged blackbirds were originally restricted to marshlands where food was scarce and competition with other birds was intense. However, the recent trend toward large farms that specialize in vast fields of corn, wheat, and other grains is likely one of the principal factors contributing to the growth of red-winged blackbird populations.

Similarly, populations of herring and great black-backed gulls in New England were also limited by scarce food at the sea edge, especially in winter. Since early in the 1900s, these gull populations have increased greatly due to the abundance and availability of newly found foods from garbage dumps, fish-processing plants, and fishing boats. The response of these species to large supplemental food supplies suggests that the same effect could favor certain backyard-feeder birds.

Perhaps the tons of grain consumed each year from North American feeders may temper population fluctuations resulting from poor local food supplies or harsh winters. Supplemental feeding may also help to explain the explosive range expansion of the house finch, a native of the western United States that was introduced in western Long Island, New York, about 1940. In the past 60 years, house finches have spread across North America, frequently inhabiting back-yards with active feeding stations. Similarly, feeding could also help to explain the northward range extensions of southern seed-eating birds such as the cardinal, tufted titmouse, mourning dove, and red-bellied woodpecker. But the question remains, have these species leapfrogged their way north along a sunflower seed pipeline, or is their recent range expansion due to other factors such as global warming?

Range expansions following bird feeders would seem a clear-cut case, except that northern range extensions are not unique to seed-eating birds. Recently, the northern mockingbird, blue-winged warbler, Louisiana waterthrush, blue-gray gnatcatcher, and turkey vulture have also experienced northward range extensions. Climate change may explain these increases, but it is not as clear why some northern birds such as the evening grosbeak, American robin, and barn swallow have expanded their breeding ranges to the south.

Range expansions and contractions probably result from varied causes, including changes in climate, land-use patterns, and changes in the distribution of important cover or food plants. However, the recent growth of supplemental bird feeding warrants its inclusion as one of the several likely factors influencing population size and range expansion for certain, but probably not all, species that visit feeders.

While it is important to minimize the hazards associated with concentrating birds at feeders, we need not search too far for a rationale for feeding birds beyond introducing children and adults to the joys of watching them. Without feeders, the elusive and highly mobile nature of wild birds makes it difficult to close the distance and glimpse their beauty.

FEEDING BIRDS THROUGH THE SEASONS

Spring

Early spring is an important season for feeding birds because most preferred natural foods have been consumed during the winter. At this time of year, late snows and ice storms may bury any remaining food supplies. Ample food and water supplies are especially attractive to migrating birds because of the great energy cost of migration; for this reason, supplemental feeding may provide useful refueling stops for migrants. Resident birds such as chickadees that are already familiar with feeders may help attract migrants.

It is likely that where other requirements exist, the availability of a constant supply of food and water will increase nesting populations or entice birds to breed on properties they might otherwise avoid. Where food is scarce, birds may not breed because ample food is a prerequisite for attaining reproductive condition.

To increase your chances for attracting breeding birds, provide nesting materials, such as chicken feathers, hair, and short (3–4 inch) pieces of yarn and string. If mud is not readily available, wet a patch of soil to provide nesting material for robins, swallows, and phoebes. Crushed eggshells or finely crushed oyster shells are good supplements to feed at this season, as the calcium requirements for females are very high just prior to egg laying. Early spring is also the season to position new nest boxes, clean out old ones, and plant bird-attracting trees, shrubs, and vines.

Materials such as strips of grapevine bark, string, yarn, and chicken feathers are often used for nest building by northern orioles and other birds. String and yarn should be only 3–4 inches long to prevent the birds from becoming accidentally entangled. (AF)

Summer

Summer is the season of greatest natural food abundance. Insect populations are at their highest and many tree, shrub, and vine fruits are available. But it is also the period of greatest food needs, as parent birds must provide food for themselves and their young. The rapid growth rates of young birds necessitate high-protein diets. For this reason, most birds (even seed-eating specialists) feed their growing young a diet consisting mostly of insects.

In *Songbirds in Your Garden*, John K. Terres lists 33 species of insect- and seed-eating birds that readily consumed his mixture of peanut butter (one part), cornmeal (four parts), flour (one part), and vegetable shortening (one part). Using this mixture in the summer, he attracted a surprising variety of such birds as tanagers, thrushes, and warblers that usually eat insects. This is a better mixture to use in the summer than suet-based mixes or raw suet, as suet will turn rancid at summer temperatures and may mat facial and breast feathers, possibly resulting in infection of facial skin, poor insulation, and reduced waterproofing. Such alternative suet mixtures are readily eaten by parent birds, which sometimes feed them to their young and later bring young to the feeders. Place the mixture in hanging food logs, cupcake baking trays, or suet feeders.

Another way to attract insect-eating birds is to offer mealworm larvae. Mealworms are inch-long, hard-shelled larvae of darkling beetles. Cardinals, towhees, sparrows, and many kinds of insect-eating birds readily eat mealworm larvae. Place the mealworm larvae in either a shallow glass or smooth, metal-walled container on a feeding table or offer the mealworms by hand. When mealworms are tossed onto the ground, wild birds will soon overcome their fear of humans and approach for a handout.

Breed your own supply of mealworms in an aquarium, shoebox, or other smooth-walled container. For mass production, use a 55-gallon steel drum. Fill the container half full of bran mixed with breadcrumbs, cornmeal, farina, or crushed crackers. For moisture, place a few thin slices of apple on the surface and cover the grain and apple with several layers of newspapers. After several months, replenish the moisture by adding another layer of bran mixture, more apple slices, and newspaper. Be sure to cover the container with a tight-fitting but well-ventilated lid, such as window screening, to keep the flying adults and larvae in the container. Mealworms are available at most pet shops or through the mail.

Insect-eating birds such as this eastern towhee are attracted to mealworm larvae. To keep the larvae accessible and contained, place them in a shallow, smooth-walled tray. (AF)

Summer feeding can also attract fruit-eating birds in addition to seed- and insect-eating species. Fruit sometimes attracts tanagers, orioles, and certain woodpeckers. Overripe citrus fruits and bananas are favorites. Cut fruit open to display the interiors and place them on feeding tables or on spikes.

Grapefruit and orange halves are an excellent way to attract fruit-eating birds such as this red-crowned woodpecker. (AF)

Summer is also the season for feeding hummingbirds and other nectar-eating birds. The best way to attract hummingbirds to your yard is to provide abundant orange and red tubular flowers from late spring to early fall. Hummingbirds not only feed on flower nectar, but also eat insects and small spiders they find in the flowers. Supplemental feeding of hummingbirds may be useful to hold birds in your yard until flowers bloom or as a lure to entice hummers into better-viewing areas.

Take care to keep hummingbird feeders clean of fungus. To avoid this problem, clean feeders every 2 or 3 days under hot running tap water, scrubbing carefully with a bottlebrush. Although honey water is more nutritious than gran-ular-sugar water, it ferments faster in the sun than sugar water and cultures mold that can kill hummingbirds. For this reason, do not use honey-water mixtures as hummingbird food.

Mixtures of water and granular white or brown sugar are the best food for hummingbirds, as they offer less risk from fermentation and mold. However, there is some danger that mixtures with more than 1 part sugar to 4 parts water can harm hummingbirds by enlarging their livers. Although sugar-water mix-tures do not ferment as rapidly as honey-water mixes, it is important to clean feeders after several days. To prepare a sugar-water solution, mix sugar and water together in equal (1:1) proportion, then boil the mixture to retard fermentation and dissolve all sugar. Then dilute to 1 part sugar to 4 parts water by adding cold water. Store the unused quantity in a refrigerator.

Use 1 part sugar to 4 parts water when first attracting hummingbirds, but decrease the proportion to 1 part sugar to 6 parts water after hummers learn the location of your feeders. This reduces the danger to the liver and encourages the birds to feed more on natural foods. To help attract hummingbirds to new feeders, tie a cluster of plastic red flowers over the feeder entrance. Red food coloring is not necessary to attract hummingbirds.

Sometimes ants, bees, and wasps drink more sugar water than humming-birds. When this happens, discourage ants by hanging feeders on thin monofil-ament fishing line. Coating the feeding portals with salad oil will deter most bees and wasps.

Worldwide, about 1600 species of birds (20 percent of all living birds) eat nectar. Most of these live in the tropics where flowers bloom year-round. In North America, at least 53 bird species are known to visit sugar-water feeders. Orioles, mockingbirds, grosbeaks, tanagers, and several warblers readily eat the same sugar solution that attracts hummingbirds. Feeders of various sizes, separated in different locations, will help to minimize competition. Many commercial hummingbird feeders are available, but simple homemade feeders are easy to make. A mouse- or hamster-watering bottle (available at most pet stores) makes an excellent oriole feeder.

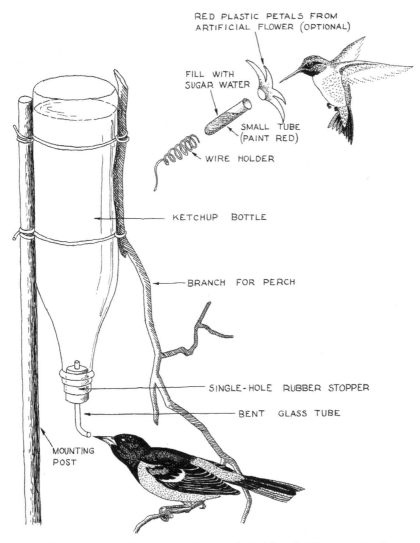

RED PLASTIC PETALS FROM
ARTIFICIAL FLOWER (OPTIONAL)

FILL WITH
SUGAR WATER

SMALL TUBE
(PAINT RED)

WIRE HOLDER

KETCHUP BOTTLE

BRANCH FOR PERCH

SINGLE-HOLE RUBBER STOPPER

BENT GLASS TUBE

MOUNTING
POST

A homemade sugar-water dispenser made out of a ketchup bottle may attract hummingbirds and larger perching birds such as orioles. Carefully measure the proportion of sugar to water, clean the feeder, and provide fresh sugar water every few days. (AF)

Fall

Early fall is the best time of year to plant trees and shrubs that have their roots wrapped in burlap or those that were grown in containers. It is also the best season for hanging roosting boxes for overwintering birds. Nest boxes that are set in place at this season can double as roosts. They will also have a chance to weather to more natural color and they will already be in place for returning migrants.

Although natural foods such as insects and fruit are especially abundant in the fall, this is also a season of great food demand, as bird populations are at their highest levels owing to the new crop of fledglings. During this season, insects are important as most birds replace all of their feathers prior to migration and this requires a protein-rich diet.

There is also great need for migrants to put on ample fat to power their long migrations. Oil-rich seeds, such as sunflower and nyjer seeds, are readily eaten at this time of year. Likewise, many native plants such as flowering dogwoods, spicebush, and magnolias have high-lipid-fat fruits. Some migrants such as the white-crowned sparrow increase their body weight by as much as 40 percent before starting their southern migration. While traveling to their winter habitat, birds can rebuild such fat deposits in only 3–5 days if they stop over in an area with a rich food supply.

Surviving the first year of life is a major accomplishment for most birds. In many species, it is normal for 80 percent of young birds to die in their first year. This heavy toll comes from a variety of causes, including predation, accidents, weather, and poor navigation, but certainly high on the list must be the bird's success in finding food. The transition from dependence to independence happens in only a few days for most songbirds. Supplemental feeding in the fall could make a difference for some young birds.

By feeding birds in early fall, you may have a greater chance of seeing fall migrants. Also, adults and young of many southern species scatter from their breeding areas in the fall and some are likely to visit feeders at this time. Often such early-fall dispersals result in movements that take southern seed-eating birds such as cardinals and tufted titmouse into new habitat in the north. Its likely that when such birds wander north of their original range and find abundant food supplies, they will stay for the winter, acting as pioneers to further expand the species' range.

Winter

Winter is the most difficult season for many northern-latitude birds. The relatively few birds that remain in northern habitats must contend with frigid temperatures, chilling winds, and long nights that reduce the amount of time available for foraging. Natural foods become scarce from the onset of the first killing frost until spring growth.

In addition, already sparse food supplies may be completely unavailable under deep layers of snow and ice. These are the circumstances when supplemental feeding is most useful to wild birds. Dawn and dusk are the best times to provide seed and suet as these are the greatest periods of bird foraging. This pattern is especially apparent after a long winter night of subfreezing temperatures.

Beef kidney suet provides a rich supply of fat and is readily eaten by at least 80 species of North American birds, including many insect-eating species, such as woodpeckers, chickadees, titmice, wrens, orioles, shrikes, thrushes, and warblers. It is difficult to explain exactly why suet has such broad appeal since it looks so unlike most foods eaten by these birds. Although chickadees and some other suet-eaters are known to pick fat from deer carcasses and thus may have experience with fat, its likely that the white, greasy, and stringy consistency resembles the fatty bodies of overwintering insect eggs and pupae. These are normally gleaned from tree bark and leaf litter. What a bonanza a chunk of suet must seem to a chickadee accustomed to tediously searching for tiny insect eggs.

Feed suet to birds whole, or melt and solidify it for a more workable form. Melt suet by first chopping it into small pieces and then cook the pieces slowly in a large pot or double boiler. The pieces can then be chopped to a fine mix in a food processor or blender, and then returned to the pot for melting. Melting suet does not change its nutritional value.

To increase the variety of birds that feed on suet, mix it with such ingredients as cornmeal, shortening, bacon grease, and peanut butter until the mixture is the consistency of bread dough. Suet mixtures are best offered in hanging food sticks, pressed into the crevices of large pine cones, or in cupcake baking tins. Hang raw suet in mesh onion bags or offer it in hardware cloth feeders.

Mixing suet and seed is counterproductive because it attracts both seed- and suet-eaters to the same feeder. Seed-eating birds will peck through the mixture for preferred seeds, wasting most other ingredients. To avoid competition, crowding, and waste, offer the food separately at nearby feeders. It is also likely that greasy seeds extracted from suet balls are harder to crack open than dry seed.

Winter is also a good time to put out food for fruit-eating songbirds such as the northern mockingbird and eastern bluebird. If you see these birds near your feeder, sprinkle a few raisins or currants on a conspicuous surface such as a flat rock or table feeder. Dried or frozen fruits such as grapes and cherries are very useful for attracting winter birds such as robins, mockingbirds, and waxwings.

If there is little shelter near bird feeders, you can plant balled and burlapped evergreens. Low-growing junipers and other evergreen shrubs with prickly branches provide excellent cover throughout the year, but quality cover during late fall and winter is especially important.

Another technique is to tie several discarded Christmas trees together and secure this bundle to a post positioned near the feeder. Empty birdhouses and special overnight roosting boxes provide additional shelter from extremely low temperatures and also afford protection from such nocturnal predators as cats and raccoons that sometimes prey on sleeping songbirds.

In northern latitudes, open water may be unavailable for several months. Most northern birds can survive by obtaining moisture from their food and from eating snow and ice, but even hardy northern species will drink and bathe in open water at birdbaths.

SETTING UP A FEEDING STATION

Variety is the most important consideration when setting up a new bird-feeding station. Since bird species have different preferences, the best way to attract many species is to offer a variety of feeders. Place several kinds of feeders at different heights above the ground and different distances from human activity and the nearest cover. Provide millet and cracked corn on the ground for sparrows, doves, and quail; sunflower seeds, mixed grain, and fruit at tabletop level for cardinals, grosbeak, and finches; and suet feeders on tree trunks or hanging from tree limbs for woodpeckers and chickadees.

Another value of multiple feeders is that you can provide selective feeding. Although chickadees and titmice are so fearless they will take seed from feeders mounted directly on windows (or even from your hand or teeth), house sparrows will not venture so close. In addition, feeders designed to exclude certain birds because of size, weight, or behavior can help to make more expensive grain available only to preferred species.

Separate feeders for different kinds of seed also reduce competition at feeders and avoid unnecessary waste. Seed mixtures containing sunflower seeds are often largely wasted, as the many birds with an appetite for sunflower seeds will pick and scratch through most other seeds, discarding them to the ground where they will be lost or left to rot. Another reason for avoiding mixes is that birds that eat sunflower seeds generally prefer to eat from hanging feeders, while the species that prefer millet and cracked corn prefer to feed at table and ground feeders.

Another good way to reduce congestion at feeders is to provide a convenience perch for birds that are waiting in line. The convenience perch may also provide a suitable surface for chickadees and titmice to perch while they extract seeds from sunflower hulls. Create a convenience perch by attaching a branch to a feeder. This gives birds a convenient spot to wait for an opportunity to drop into a busy feeding location.

When selecting feeder locations, consider visibility from your home, distance from shrubs, and proximity to good perches. When possible, choose southern exposures. This reduces spillage from strong northern winds and provides a somewhat warmer, more protected area for birds to congregate. Also try to locate feeders within about 20 feet of nearby shrubs or thicket cover. This gives birds a ready place to escape if hawks or cats attack, but avoid placing feeders over shrubs as this may give cats a hiding place for stalking birds that forage directly under the feeders.

CONVENIENCE PERCH ATTACHED TO SIDE OF FEEDER.

A convenience perch attached to a feeder reduces congestion and provides a ready place for chickadees and titmice to crack open seeds. (AF)

Expectations

The speed with which your feeding station is discovered and visited by birds depends not only on the location and visibility of the feeder but also on the kinds of birds in your vicinity and the sizes of the populations. In general, forested habitats have fewer birds than shrubby edge habitats; therefore, it may take longer for birds to discover feeders in wooded areas. Similarly, urban habitats may have fewer birds than suburban or rural habitats, but even feeders placed outside windows in tall apartment buildings have a chance of attracting sparrows, starlings, house finches, and the occasional migrant.

The numbers of birds and frequency with which they visit feeders are also related to the amount of bird feeding in your neighborhood. If you have the only feeders in the neighborhood, you are likely to have more birds at your feeders. For these reasons, it may take from a few minutes to several months before birds start visiting your feeders. To attract birds more quickly to new feeding stations, scatter grain on the ground or on the top of roofed feeders. A simple table feeder set in an open site is the most conspicuous manner to display foods and it is a good way to start a bird-feeding station. After birds become accustomed to visiting a table feeder, replace it with a hopper feeder or other weatherproof feeder to reduce exposure of the food to rain and snow.

The variety of birds that will visit feeders also depends on ranges. The farther north you live, the fewer species nest and winter in your area. However, many of the birds that winter in northern latitudes feed on seed or forage on invertebrates gleaned or chiseled from tree trunks and these are especially quick to visit feeders.

If you have chickadees in your neighborhood, they will probably be the first to discover new bird feeders, as these inquisitive, active birds are constantly searching for food. They are usually joined by a variety of other species, such as nuthatches, titmice, and woodpeckers, forming a mixed winter flock. Chickadees not only lead the way for other species, but also, as shown by banding studies, remember feeder locations many months and probably return to the same feeders for years. Research also shows that black-capped chickadees are quick to find new feeders in the fall, but they discover new feeders much more slowly by January, presumably because winter feeding territories are established during fall.

Feeding Continuity

One of the most commonly repeated beliefs for operating a feeding station is, "Once you start, keep the food coming." This idea rests on the thought that birds become dependent on a feeding area in the winter and are at risk if their food supply were to disappear in midwinter when their needs are greatest. This may apply at isolated locations where feeding stations are few and where feeders provide large amounts of food from early fall into the winter. These stations might detain migrants in the fall and concentrate them in unusually large numbers, making birds vulnerable to food shortages caused by heavy snows. In reality, however, this situation is probably rare.

More commonly, feeder birds do not depend on either single food supplies or solely on food that they find at feeders. Most birds feed in mixed-species flocks that forage over at least several acres in the winter. Within this area they have a pattern of feeding that may include many different backyards. Dan Gray, a Cornell University researcher, studied the movements of winter flocks of color-banded black-capped chickadees as they moved from feeder to feeder. He noted that the birds followed a "trapline," regularly searching in places where they previously found food. If a feeder was empty, the chickadees simply moved on to the next likely feeding site and could remember successful feeding locations at least 8 months later. Other winter feeder birds likely feed in similar ways, often moving in mixed-species flocks with chickadees.

Certainly, in nature there are never cornucopia plants that consistently provide food. Birds are so mobile and aware of the presence of others of their species that in most situations, they probably have little trouble finding food if the feeders at one residence (in a neighborhood of many feeding stations) suddenly dry up. Also, many species such as chickadees, titmice, nuthatches, and jays that winter in northern habitats store food when it is abundant. This caching helps to avoid starvation when they are faced with temporary shortages.

One good reason to keep your feeders full is that once you stop, it may be difficult to attract a variety and number of birds later in the winter if birds have learned to feed elsewhere. But if you live in a neighborhood where there are other feeders, a stop in feeding for a few days in midwinter is unlikely to cause death for backyard-feeder birds.

FEEDING SEED TO WILD BIRDS

A wide variety of birds consume seeds because they contain concentrated nourishment and are often available for extended periods when other foods may be difficult to find. Birds have strong preferences for certain types of seeds because of differences in nutritional quality, taste, availability, and ease of opening.

Opening Seeds

Small birds with seed-cracking beaks, varying from the tiny beak of the siskin to the massive beaks of the grosbeaks, use subtle movements of their mandibles to first crush and then open seeds.

Small birds such as finches open seeds by rolling the seed back and forth over a projection on the lower mandible while the seed balances in a ridge in the upper mandible. The sharp mandible edges, powered by strong jaw muscles, apply crushing pressure until the seed coat opens. Then lateral movements of the mandibles separate the seed from the coat, dropping the seed contents into the mouth and expelling the seed coat onto the ground. This all happens in a split second, and the great piles of sunflower hulls under feeders are testimony to the efficiency of the technique.

Seed-eating birds that do not have crushing beaks (i.e., chickadees, nuthatches, titmice) are usually also insect-eaters and must therefore use other techniques for cracking seeds. These birds usually place the seed in a bark crevice (nuthatches) or hold it in their feet (titmice and chickadees) and pound away until they break through the seed coat.

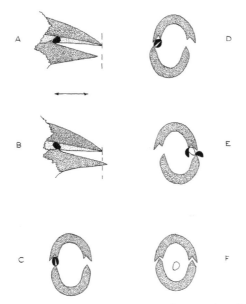

Techniques for cracking a seed in the beak. Redrawn from Joel Carl Welty, *The Life of Birds* (2nd ed.), W.B. Saunders Co., Philadelphia, 1975. Reprinted by permission of CBS College Publishing. (AF)

Grit

Once seed-eating birds break through outer protective shells, the seeds are broken into digestible form by the muscular gizzard. Wild turkey can crush whole hickory nuts and acorns in their gizzards. In a similar manner, small seed-eating birds also grind and crush seeds in their muscular, gravel-packed gizzards and require a supply of tiny gravel or grit throughout the year for this purpose.

Birds can usually find plenty of grit along gravel roadsides and other sandy places. Winter is probably the only season when grit is scarce, as snow may cover most supplies. During this season birds often feed along roadsides searching for seeds and gravel, and infrequently they become casualties to passing cars as a result.

You can reduce this hazard by mixing 5–10 pounds of grit to every 100 pounds of bird seed mixture. Beach sand or similar-sized quartz sand mixed with ground oyster shell is the ideal grit mixture. Hard quartz sand gives excellent abrasion for grinding seed.

Calcium

Calcium is important both as a grit for digestion and for developing sturdy eggshells. It is especially important during egg-laying season. Yet calcium may be scarce, especially in the north where acid rain leaches it from the soil. Crushed oyster shell (available from poultry feed suppliers) and crushed chicken eggshells are excellent sources.

The Birds and Calcium Project of the Cornell Laboratory of Ornithology found that at least 67 birds eat crushed chicken-egg shells provided at feeders. Such varied birds as ovenbirds, eastern phoebes, scarlet tanagers, and Baltimore orioles ate crushed eggshells placed on the ground or on platform feeders. Even swallows landed under feeders to pick up pieces of crushed eggshell. Jays are especially fond of eggshells, while thrushes, woodpeckers, and wrens rarely eat the shells. Some participants in the study observed cardinals, common grackles, purple martins, and several species of sparrows feeding eggshells to their young, which suggests its importance for building strong bones in developing nestlings.

To provide eggshells, rinse and be sure to bake them for 20 minutes at 250 degrees to kill *Salmonella* bacteria. Let the eggshells cool, then crush them into pieces smaller than a dime. Offer the eggshells in a dish or low platform feeder, separate from seed.

FOOD PREFERENCES

Birds show definite, predictable preferences for certain foods. Their choices are certainly influenced by both abundance and availability, but when given choices of equally abundant, available foods it is interesting to see what different species will select. Although most birds are generally thought to have a poorly developed sense of taste compared to mammals, birds usually select food by tasting various samples and later use visual cues and memory to return to favorite supplies.

The high fat and protein content of sunflower seeds probably explains why this favorite is in a class of its own as the preferred seed choice of most feeder birds. Sweet foods, such as sugar water are a ready source of fructose and sucrose, forms of sugar that provide quick energy. After consumption, these sugars break down into glucose, which readily supplies calories for maintaining high body temperatures and levels of activity. The high demand for sugar is apparent from the fact that the average concentration of glucose in bird blood is about twice that found in mammalian blood.

The need for fat and sugar helps to explain why some unlikely foods such as doughnuts are a special favorite of many birds. This sweetened, deep-fried bread dough provides a ready source of carbohydrate, fat, and sugar. In general, birds eat foods that will give them the greatest amount of energy for the least amount of effort.

Seed Preferences

While sunflower seed, millet, and fine-cracked corn are highly preferred seeds for attracting birds, there are at least a dozen other grains that find their way into the commercial bird seed trade. Some, such as milo, wheat, oats, and rice, are well known as human foods, but studies of bird stomach contents confirm that these grains are also readily eaten by a wide variety of wild birds. It would seem, therefore, that they would be logical additions to birdseed mixtures, especially since they are grown in enormous quantity and prices are often low because of surplus stocks.

Dr. Aelred D. Geis of the U.S. Fish and Wildlife Service conducted a detailed, comparative study of the food preferences of 19 common feeder birds of the northeastern United States for 23 different kinds and forms of birdseed.[2] These findings were later substantiated by follow-up studies conducted in Maine, Ohio, and California.[3] By offering food from identical feeders and rotating these in a random way, he compared various seeds to black-striped sunflower and white proso millet to determine preferences. This study confirmed what many have long noticed. Some common grains in birdseed mixtures are rarely eaten and are so unappealing that they are usually discarded. His studies have also shown that even sunflower seed will not attract all desirable species. Some, such as sparrows and towhees, will visit feeders primarily to take millet and cracked corn.

Among the least desirable seeds are the common cereal grains: milo, wheat, oats, and rice. Although many birds will glean these grains from cultivated fields where they have few other choices, these seeds are often rejected when offered at bird feeders.

Undesirable birdseed mixes are often easy to identify because of the distinctive reddish color of milo (grain sorghum). Even at a glance, the largely reddish background color of certain low-priced mixes is evidence of a large proportion of milo. Milo is generally less expensive because it is grown in large quantities for other agricultural markets. In contrast, blends with a light yellow color consist primarily of fine-cracked corn and white millet. Certain birdseed blends (especially low-priced grocery store mixes) become increasingly loaded with milo, wheat, oats, and other commercial grains that have less value as wild bird foods. These mixes are especially attractive to house sparrows, starlings, cowbirds, and feral pigeons. While this general rule holds throughout most of North America, milo is often eaten at feeders in the southwestern United States, especially where quail and doves are abundant. Some milo varieties are less palatable than others.

[2]Aelred D. Geis. 1980. "Relative Attractiveness of Different Foods at Wild Bird Feeders." Special Scientific Report—Wildlife No. 233. Washington, DC: U.S. Fish and Wildlife Service.
[3]Aelred D. Geis. 1983. "Results of Nation-Wide Tests of Wild Bird Feeding Preferences." Unpublished summary report. Washington, DC: U.S. Fish and Wildlife Service.

Preferred bird seeds: top row, left to right—oil sunflower, striped sunflower, hulled sunflower (kernels) and white proso millet; middle row, whole corn, cracked corn, safflower, milo; bottom row: canary seed, nyjer ("thistle"), and peanuts. (SK)

PREFERRED SEEDS

Sunflower Seed (*Helianthus annuus*)

Sunflower seeds are the favorite of chickadees, evening grosbeaks, tufted titmice, blue jays, house finches, purple finches, and cardinals. As long as sunflower seed is available, these birds will eat little else at feeders. Sunflower seed is also readily eaten by at least another 40 species, including wild turkeys, nuthatches, scrub jays, black-headed grosbeaks, and downy and hairy woodpeckers. Sunflower seeds may have such broad appeal because they have higher proportions of fat and protein than other common grains, such as Japanese millet, proso millet, milo, cracked corn, and oats.

Sunflower seed specialists are so eager to obtain these seeds that it is best to offer pure sunflower seed in separate feeders, to prevent sunflower seed–eating birds from spilling large quantities of blended grain while they search through less preferred seed.

For years the black-striped sunflower seed (confectioner's sunflower) was the only type sold for birdseed. Then, in about 1975, an especially large crop of the smaller, black oil sunflower seed found its way to the birdseed market. Previously, this high-oil-content seed was grown only for production of sunflower seed oil. Studies by Dr. Geis and the Cornell Laboratory of Ornithology have demonstrated that certain birds greatly prefer the smaller oilseed over the larger striped seed. For example, in Dr. Geis's study, chickadees found the oil sunflower seed 3.5 times as attractive as the larger striped sunflower seeds. In addition, evening grosbeaks, American goldfinches, house finches, and purple finches showed strong preference for the oilseeds. Only tufted titmice, common grackles, and blue jays selected the striped seed over oilseed. Birds may prefer the oilseed because it has a comparatively thinner hull that is easier to remove. It is also smaller and easier to manipulate, an advantage for small birds, and has more oil for its weight than the striped seed.

Sometimes seed companies stock the extra large gray-striped sunflower seeds. These imported African seeds have no advantage over black-striped sunflower seeds and are not nearly as attractive as the small, all-black oil sunflower seed.

Hulled sunflower seeds (broken and whole kernels) are by far the most attractive food for the American goldfinch—even more attractive than the expensive imported nyjer seed. The manageable size of the hulled kernels makes them more attractive to the white-throated sparrow, but most other birds do not favor them over the seed with its hull. As with shelled grains, hulled sunflower seed is more vulnerable to deterioration in the weather than is the unhulled seed, but since the seed is so attractive, birds generally do not give it a chance to spoil. Hulled sunflower seed is an excellent choice for those wishing to avoid an accumulation of sunflower hulls under their feeder.

Proso Millet (*Panicum miliaceum*)

There are two color types of proso millet—white and red. Although both types are readily eaten, most species preferred white proso millet in Dr. Geis's study. Ground-feeding birds such as sparrows and the mourning dove especially favor it. The following species are listed in order of their preference for this useful and inexpensive grain: tree sparrow, song sparrow, brown-headed cowbird, dark-eyed junco, house sparrow, mourning dove, and white-throated sparrow.

Red proso millet looks much like white millet except for color. As with white millet, it is readily eaten, but it is not as attractive to most birds. In addition to sparrows and doves, proso millet is also eagerly eaten by the northern bobwhite, painted bunting, dickcissel, eastern towhee, and several species of waterfowl, including the mallard, redhead, shoveler, American widgeon, and green-winged teal.

In addition to wild bird feed, millet is used for cattle and poultry feed and cereals for human consumption. A distinct advantage of proso millet as a bird food is that its hard seed coat resists swelling and rotting. This makes it an excellent choice for tube feeders and hopper feeders as it is less likely to clog feeders.

Corn (*Zea mays*)

Whole corn kernels, either on or off the cob, are favorite foods of several medium-sized feeder birds, such as the mourning dove, blue jay, common grackle, and red-bellied woodpecker. Whole grain is much more resistant to weather deterioration than cracked corn, but the large kernel size and tough seed coat discourage most smaller birds. Larger ground-feeding birds such as the pheasant and wild turkey can consume whole kernels, but most species that visit backyard feeders prefer cracked corn. Whole corn is a favorite food of at least 16 species of ducks, geese, crows, and sandhill cranes.

Whole-grain corn, with its large kernel and resilient seed coat, is a favorite food of red-bellied woodpeckers and other mediumsized to large birds. Display whole corn in conspicuous places by mounting it on sharp spikes. (SK)

Smaller birds prefer fine-cracked corn, but it deteriorates quickly in wet weather. White-throated sparrows, dark-eyed juncos, cardinals, mourning doves, tree sparrows, and other desirable feeder birds eat fine-cracked corn, but it is also a favorite food of squirrels, house sparrows, and blackbirds. Fine-cracked corn (also called chick corn) is eaten by more species than coarse-cracked corn. Cracked and whole corn make inexpensive feeds for luring squirrels, house sparrows, and blackbirds away from feeders offering more expensive, preferred foods, such as sunflower seed, white millet, and nyjer seed. Cracked corn is best offered on table feeders or the ground. Because it is soft and water absorbent, it is not a useful grain for dispensing from hanging hopper feeders, as it easily molds and cakes, resulting in clogged feeders.

Nyjer Seed (*Guizotia abyssinica*)

Sometimes known as *thistle*, this seed is imported from the tropical environments of India, Nigeria, and Ethiopia. It is not even closely related to the familiar prickly thistle of pastures and roadsides, and will not become a nuisance in gardens. Nyjer seed is an excellent though very expensive food for finches. American goldfinches consume nyjer seed almost as readily as they eat sunflower seed. The purple finch, house finch, redpoll, pine siskin, chickadees, mourning dove, song sparrow, white-throated sparrow, and dark-eyed junco also readily consume the tiny black seeds.

Special nyjer feeders with tiny holes help reduce spillage and competition from "nonfinches" whose beaks are too large to extract seeds from the tiny holes. House sparrows, however, will sometimes enlarge nyjer feeder holes by nibbling at plastic, and in this way they may gain access to the seed. Nyger feeders that have the perches above the feeding ports permit the more acrobatic finches to feed, and discourage house sparrows and house finches. Mesh bags sold for dispersing nyjer seed are not as selective as tube feeders and often substantial amounts of seed are spilled.

A nyjer ("thistle") feeder houses this imported tiny black seed, a favorite food of the common redpoll and other small-beaked winter finches. (SK)

OTHER SEEDS

Buckwheat (*Fagopyrum sagittatum*)

Buckwheat is an occasional additive to low-priced bird foods. As with wheat and oats, wild birds often glean it from cultivated cropland, and it is known from the stomachs of at least 21 different wild birds. Among these it is most readily eaten by game birds such as the ring-necked pheasant and greater prairie chicken. However, when it is placed on the feeding table with highly preferred foods, such as white proso millet and cracked corn, it is almost always ignored. In Dr. Geis's study, the brown-headed cowbird and mourning dove showed some interest in buckwheat, but even these were much more readily attracted to white millet.

Canary Seed (*Phalaris canariensis*)

Canary seed is an annual, introduced grass whose seeds are a common addition to birdseed mixtures. The seed is eaten by most of the species that eat white millet, such as the mourning dove, dark-eyed junco, eastern towhee, and most sparrows, but comparative studies show that most of these birds prefer proso millet over canary seed. Since canary seed is usually more expensive than millet, it does not pay to offer it at feeders.

Hulled Oats (*Avena sativa*)

Analysis of stomach contents reveals that oats are an important food for at least 72 kinds of wild birds. Most of these glean discarded oats from cultivated fields. In this way, oats are especially important to the greater prairie chicken, blackbirds (Brewer's, red-winged, yellow-headed, and bobolink), horned lark, western meadowlark, and many sparrows (especially grasshopper, white-crowned, and lark). Yet when compared to proso millet, the only birds that preferred hulled oats in Dr. Geis's study were starlings. In this study, whole oats were totally ignored. For this reason, it appears that oats are an undesirable addition to grain mixtures.

Japanese Millet (*Echinochla crusgalli* var. *frumentacea*)

Japanese millet, also known as *duck millet*, is an annual, cultivated strain of barnyard grass. Dr. Geis found it less attractive than white proso millet for the species in his studies, but it is known to be a choice food for the bobolink, bobwhite, indigo bunting, blue grosbeak, and several species of waterfowl, including the gadwall, mallard, pintail, and American widgeon.

Milo (*Sorghum vulgare*)

Milo, also known as *grain sorghum*, is an introduced grass from Africa. Each year, approximately 13 million acres are planted with sorghum in Kansas, Texas, and Nebraska, accounting for an annual production of about 45 billion pounds of grain. Most of the milo crop is used for livestock forage and cereals for human consumption, but such mass production makes milo available as an ingredient in low-priced birdseed mixtures. Milo is often substituted for corn and millet when the prices for these grains increase. It is a favorite food of many large game birds such as the ring-necked pheasant, northern bobwhite, wild turkey, and mallard. However, with the exception of starlings, the mourning dove, and brown-headed cowbird, most feeder birds seldom eat it. Perhaps the larger size, thick seed coat, and relatively low fat content all contribute to the low desirability of this seed. White sorghum may be eaten more often than the usual reddish seed, but milo of any color should generally be avoided unless it is to be used for feeding doves, quail, mallards, and pheasants.

Safflower (*Carthamus tinctorius*)

Safflower seed is most notable as a favorite food for cardinals and is sometimes even sold as "cardinal bait." It is, however, only about one-third as attractive as the cardinal's favorite food, sunflower seed. Safflower seed is also readily eaten by the white-winged dove, purple finch, and evening grosbeak. It is also eaten, but with less favor, by the mourning dove, blue jay, ring-necked pheasant, and tufted titmouse. An advantage of safflower seed is that gray squirrels do not readily eat it.

Wheat (*Triticum aestivum*)

Wheat, as with oats, is one of the most important wildlife foods because of the extent to which it is planted. No fewer than 76 different kinds of wild birds feed on wheat by gleaning it out of farmers' fields after cultivation. However, when wheat is offered as part of a mixed blend, few birds will eat it as long as white proso millet, cracked corn, and sunflower seed are available. Wheat is readily eaten by house sparrows.

Peanuts (*Arachis hypogaea*)

Whole peanut kernels are a favorite food of the tufted titmouse, blue jay, Carolina chickadee, and white-throated sparrow. The red-winged blackbird, indigo bunting, catbird, black-capped chickadee, crow, American goldfinch, dark-eyed junco, ruby-crowned kinglet, and warblers (yellow-rumped, orange-crowned, and pine) also readily eat them. Whole peanuts probably appeal to both insect- and seed-eating birds because of their high fat and protein content.

Peanut hearts are a common peanut product used in certain food mixtures. They are the embryos removed from the seed in the manufacture of peanut butter. Although peanut hearts are a relatively inexpensive food, Dr. Geis's study showed that they are the preferred food for starlings, which consumed peanut hearts in preference to all other choices. Where starlings are aggressive competitors at feeders, it is best to eliminate peanut hearts from your feeder menu.

An entertaining way to offer whole peanuts is to thread them onto a section of fishing line or skewer them onto a length of galvanized wire. Bend the bottom end of the wire to hold the peanuts and shape a hook at the other end to hang it in a squirrel-safe place. Jays and woodpeckers will hang on the peanut skewer, skillfully balancing as they shred the shells to retrieve the nuts. Although titmice and blue jays enjoy whole peanuts, they ignore peanut hearts.

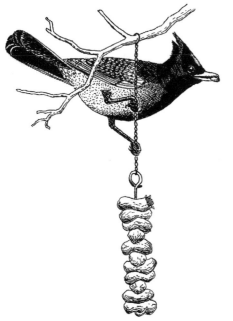

Stellar's jay (illustrated) and blue jays readily eat whole peanuts threaded on galvanized wire. (AF)

OTHER FOODS

Wild birds will eat a remarkable variety of foods at backyard bird feeders. The greater the variety of choices offered through the seasons, the more kinds of birds will visit your feeders. Here are a few possibilities:

Fruit

To attract a greater variety of birds to your feeders in the summer, try offering apples, oranges, grapefruits, and bananas. These are favorite foods for many tropical migrants such as tanagers, orioles, and warblers. Red-bellied and hairy woodpeckers especially favor sliced apple, and jays, bluebirds, the American robin, and Swainson's and hermit thrushes also readily eat it. Sectioned grapefruit and oranges are one of the best ways to lure orioles, mockingbirds, catbirds, and thrashers.

Currants and Raisins

Currants and raisins are most useful for attracting wild birds in late winter when preferred natural foods are scarce. Blue jays, bluebirds, the American robin, varied thrush, and Bohemian and cedar waxwings may eat raisins and currants. The best way to display the fruit is to scatter it on table feeders or other open, conspicuous places.

Bread and Doughnuts

At least 83 different kinds of North American birds are known to eat bread scraps. Certainly the high number of such species reflects the availability of bread as a bird food, but it may seem surprising that it is sometimes consumed by such diverse species as the red-headed woodpecker, brown creeper, cactus wren, eastern bluebird, and cedar waxwing. Even kestrels and shrikes are known to eat bread. This wide popularity most likely results because bread consists of both finely ground grains and shortening (fats). Doughnuts are also highly attractive to a wide variety of birds that apparently enjoy the high fat and sugar content. Bread scraps and day-old doughnuts are readily eaten by house sparrows, grackles, starlings, and many other birds that seem to be just as satisfied with these scraps as with expensive foods such as sunflower seeds.

Melon Seeds

The seeds of pumpkin, cantaloupe, watermelon, and squash are readily consumed by at least 20 different kinds of seed-eating birds, including the mourning dove, blue jay, white and red-breasted nuthatches, northern cardinal, and rose-breasted grosbeak. Smaller birds such as chickadees and yellow-rumped warblers can more readily obtain the nutritious seed hearts if melon seeds are first passed through a meat grinder before they are offered at feeders.

Nutmeats

Nutmeats exposed from the thick hulls of acorns, walnuts, hickory nuts, coconuts, and pecans provide high-energy foods for wild birds. They may be eaten by red-headed and pileated woodpeckers, blue jays, chickadees, nuthatches, and wrens. Even ruby-crowned kinglets and eastern bluebirds sometimes eat nutmeats.

Peanut Butter

Pure peanut butter is readily eaten by at least 50 kinds of birds. The combination of peanut butter oil and sugar make this an especially attractive food to chickadees, titmice, Carolina wrens, and many other feeder birds. To stretch the rather expensive peanut butter supplies, mix peanut butter with cornmeal at proportions of 1 cup of peanut butter to 5 cups of cornmeal. Place peanut butter and mixtures in one-inch-diameter holes drilled into hanging logs.

PRECAUTIONS FOR OPERATING FEEDING STATIONS

Because feeders usually create unnaturally large concentrations of birds, responsible operators should take care to avoid the associated dangers.

Window Collisions

Sheet glass is effectively invisible to birds. Collisions occur at windows as small as garage doors to entire glass walls such as in multistory office buildings. Glass kills indiscriminately, taking both fit and unfit birds during every season and throughout the day and night. At least 25 percent of all North American species are known to collide with glass. Researchers with Project Feederwatch of the Cornell Laboratory of Ornithology found window collisions killed more birds than either disease or predators, and that on average between 1 and 10 birds might be killed per building, resulting in the annual death of as many as a billion birds in the United States alone. Window collisions often stun birds, which makes them vulnerable to house cats and other predators and reduces their success of completing migration.

Birds usually crash into windows for one of the following reasons:

- Glass is in the path of flight and birds don't see it.
- Birds are using feeders near a window and are startled by a hawk or other danger.
- The angle of the window reflects an expansive scene such as a large lawn, woodland, or other open space.
- Windows may be aligned so that birds see an apparent open passage through your home.
- During nesting season, birds may see their reflections in the window and take chase.

The simplest solution to window collisions near feeders is to relocate the feeder. Surprisingly, feeders that are very close (or attached) to windows are not as great a risk as those set back more than 3 feet. The risk of collisions near feeders increases with distance from windows up to about 30 feet. Birds flushed near windows are usually not injured because they do not gather enough momentum before striking the glass.

To make glass more visible, attach objects such as stained glass, decals or other decoration outside the window or suspend mobiles, wind chimes, or other objects to show birds that the window is not a clear passage. Objects attached on the inside of windows (or hanging inside windows such as potted plants) do little to save birds from collisions.

Silhouettes of diving falcons attached to the outside of the window may reduce window collisions, but any opaque shapes would probably be just as effective at breaking up the expanse of open glass. For the greatest success, place these 2–4 inches apart.

Fruit tree netting stretched over the outside of the window is the best solution. This fine black plastic netting is nearly invisible during most hours of the day. Use molding to attach the netting to the edges of the window or secure the netting in custom-built frames like window screens. Fruit tree netting is available at most garden shops.

If a bird hits a window and is only stunned, place it inside a cardboard box with a secure lid and then take it indoors to a warm, quiet place. If the bird is likely to survive, you'll hear it walking around in the box within a few hours. This simple "box treatment" gives the bird a chance to recover without the added dangers of prowling neighborhood cats and dogs. After recovery, release the bird near a dense thicket or hedge where it can find shelter.

If you find a freshly killed bird under your window, put the bird in a plastic bag along with the date, location, and apparent cause of death. Then freeze the bird and call a local museum, nature center, or university zoology department to see if it can be added to the institution's teaching or research collections. Some excellent collections have grown almost entirely from accidentally killed birds. With the exception of introduced birds, such as the starling, house sparrow, and domestic pigeon, it is illegal to keep birds (alive or dead), their feathers, parts, nests, or eggs without both state/provincial and federal permits.

Feeder Preservation

Bird feeders built from cedar or exterior-grade plywood will have the longest life expectancy. To protect pine and other soft woods, coat the wood with linseed oil. Do not build feeders from pressure-treated wood or wood soaked in creosote. Also, resist the temptation to paint feeders, as the paint will eventually peel and birds may consume the flakes with the seed. Lead-based paints are especially problematic, but paint of any variety is unnecessary.

Salt

Birds sometimes eat salty soils and not infrequently pick up salt along with grit at roadsides. Such northern birds as crossbills and other finches are especially eager salt eaters. Road salt sometimes causes fatalities among turkeys, crossbills, and other birds by paralyzing their central nervous systems, giving them a tame appearance. Generally, however, birds seem to tolerate the low-salt contents of peanut butter and bacon grease. Poultry growers find that approximately 1 percent salt in grain seems to meet the needs of chickens; they can tolerate up to 4 percent salt without obvious ill effects. This low level is usually available from soil, gravel, and natural food. To avoid possible salt poisoning, do not add salt to grain mixtures.

Freezing to Metal

A common concern at feeders is that birds will freeze to metal perches and other feeder parts. This idea probably arises from the fact that human skin will stick to subfreezing bare metal. The concern, however, has little relevance to birds because their feet, unlike our skin, do not have sweat glands. The horny scales that cover bird feet are perfectly dry, as evidenced by the fact that birds can safely perch on wire fences at the coldest winter temperatures. In *A Complete Guide to Bird Feeding*, John V. Dennis reports one incident of a purple finch that was found with its eye frozen to a metal feeder, but such observations are extremely uncommon. The reflex reactions of healthy birds are so fast that their moist eyes rarely touch anything. Freezing to metal feeders is not a serious hazard for healthy wild birds.

FEEDER DISEASES AND CHALLENGES

The unusually crowded conditions at feeding stations increase the probability of contagious diseases spreading, especially where uneaten food and bird droppings accumulate. Also, regular food supplies at feeders may permit diseased birds to survive longer than they would without supplemental food, and the longer they reside at feeders, the more likely they are to spread disease to healthy birds. The bird diseases discussed here are not contagious to humans, but they are deadly serious to birds and everything should be done to prevent their occurrence or spread at your feeders.

A common disease problem at bird feeders results from accumulating wet grain that serves as a medium for the growth of the mold *Aspergillus fumigatus.* The spores of this mold are widely distributed in nature and will readily grow on wet grain. Feeder birds such as juncos, cowbirds, grackles, and many others can contract aspergillosis by inhaling mold and spores while eating moldy grain. It can also be a very serious problem for ducks and other waterfowl.

Aspergillosis usually attacks the lungs, air sacs, and occasionally the windpipe. To recognize this disease, watch for birds at your feeders that gasp and wheeze or sit quietly for long periods with fluffed feathers. Birds that are about to die from the disease are easy to approach. In the final days of the sickness, they may develop diarrhea and become increasingly lethargic.

Mourning doves and domestic pigeons are especially susceptible to trichomoniasis, a disease caused by the flagellated protozoan *Trichomonas gallinae.* This protozoan lives in the throat and causes ulcers and swelling that obstruct the esophagus, crop, or pharynx, eventually leading to starvation.

Salmonellosis is the disease caused by infection with *Salmonella* spp. bacteria. Salmonellosis outbreaks are more common at bird feeders during late winter and early spring when birds are stressed and crowded near feeders. Late summer is also a vulnerable time when birds are crowded near water. Regular cleaning of feeders and bird baths reduces risk of this disease.

Avian pox is another disease that sometimes infects birds at feeding stations. As with the diseases mentioned above, avian pox will not spread to humans, but it is contagious and can easily contaminate other birds. This virus produces warty protuberances on the feet or head and/or damage to the lining of the throat and respiratory tract.

Avian conjunctivitis is caused by a unique strain of the bacterium *Mycoplasma gallisepticum*, which is a common pathogen in domestic turkeys and chickens. Although infected birds have swollen eyes, the disease is primarily a respiratory infection. The infection poses no known health threat to humans. Researchers at various institutions are currently trying to learn more about the transmission, genetics, and development of this disease.

The disease has spread through the eastern population of house finch and now occurs throughout the Midwest to the Pacific. Although the disease is most prominent in the house finch, it is also confirmed in the American goldfinch, purple finch, evening grosbeak, and pine grosbeak, all members of the family Fringillidae. This disease is recognized by the presence of oozy and crusted eyes. An ongoing study is underway at the Cornell Laboratory of Ornithology. To report occurrences of avian conjunctivitis, contact the House Finch Disease Survey, Cornell Laboratory of Ornithology, 159 Sapsucker Woods Road, Ithaca, NY 14850, or send an e-mail to housefinch@cornell.edu, or visit the Web site: http://birds.cornell.edu/hofi/

West Nile virus was first identified in Uganda in 1937 and it first appeared in the Western Hemisphere in August 1999 in the New York City vicinity. Since its first detection, it has spread rapidly across North America and by 2002 was known from all but four of the contiguous states. Unlike most avian diseases, West Nile virus can spread to humans. In 2002 it affected 4,161 people, with 277 fatalities. Most birds are vulnerable to this mosquito-borne disease. It is especially common among crows and jays, but to date 138 species ranging in size from bald eagles to chickadees have died from the disease in North America.

To reduce the risk to people and birds, it is important to prevent mosquitoes from breeding in birdbaths and garden pools. The best way to control mosquitoes in garden pools is to establish populations of mosquito-eating fish such as gambusia. These fish are appropriate throughout the Southeast. In cooler climates, fat-headed minnows will eat the larvae. Bait stores are a good place to obtain minnows for ponds and pools. It is also important to scrub birdbaths with a stiff bristle brush at least once a week, replacing standing water with fresh supplies.

Feeder Maintenance

The best way to reduce the danger of diseases at your feeding stations is to keep grain dry and to clean up spilled grain before it has a chance to rot. Feeding preferred seeds, such as sunflower, white proso millet, and fine-cracked corn, will lead to less waste at feeders and less opportunity for molds to grow in wet grain. In winter, it is best to feed birds from hopper feeders or other enclosed feeders rather than spreading grain on open feeding tables or the ground, where it is likely to be covered by snow. In the spring, rake the area under feeders to remove accumulated grain and hulls. Mix this into your compost pile. Cleaning under feeders also reduces the risk of attracting nuisance squirrels, rats, and raccoons.

If you find sick or dead birds at your feeders, it is best to stop feeding for at least a few days to let the birds disperse. Rake rotting grain and discarded seed hulls, then bury or compost this accumulation far from the feeding area.

Feeder should be cleaned several times each year, especially in early fall or spring. Use a powerful hose to blast accumulated grain from inside tube feeders and carefully scrub all feeders with stiff brushes, rinsing thoroughly with a 10 percent bleach solution (mix 1 part bleach to 10 parts water).

If you find an occasional dead bird under your feeders, bury it far from the feeders. If you find more than an occasional dead bird, call your state wildlife conservation office. Likewise, report injured or sick birds to your local wildlife conservation department. The staff may know of a nearby licensed rehabilitation program that has the specialized skills and treatments necessary for healing birds. Without appropriate state/provincial or federal permits, it is illegal to keep wild birds in captivity.

Hawks and Owls

Large concentrations of birds at backyard feeders are likely to attract bird-eating hawks. Cooper's hawk, sharp-shinned hawk, American kestrel, and goshawk are the most frequent predators that visit feeders. Screech and great horned owls may also take their share of feeder birds, but the activities of these nocturnal predators are rarely observed. The greatest danger of hawks visiting feeders is that each time a hawk appears, the smaller birds will scatter and some are likely to hit nearby windows in their panic to escape.

If hawks habitually capture birds at your backyard feeders, the best approach is to let the feeders go empty for a few days. This will temporarily lower feeder populations and decrease vulnerability to hawks. With their prey dispersed, hawks will soon move on to feed elsewhere.

Consider yourself fortunate to witness hawks in action. Their predatory skills are a thrill to observe, as they are masters of coordination and agility, but it is best to do your hawk watching away from feeders as hawks are also at risk from fatal window collisions. Healthy birds can usually evade predators at feeders if there is suitable escape cover within approximately 15–20 feet of feeders.

Cats[4]

The combined total of pet and free-ranging cats in the United States is likely more than 100 million. Nationwide, cats probably kill hundreds of millions of birds each year, and because of their close association with humans, much of this happens near our homes and farms. Cats are especially dangerous to birds during the nesting season because they can climb to nests or catch fledglings that have not yet learned to fly. In some areas, the number of cats exceeds the combined numbers of native predators such as raccoons, skunks, and fox. Here are some ways to take action:

- For the sake of your cat and local wildlife, keep your cat indoors. This will eliminate unwanted reproduction and predation on wild animals. Bells on cat collars are largely ineffective in preventing predation because by the time the bell rings, its usually too late for the prey. Declawing may reduce hunting success, but many declawed cats are still effective predators. Keeping your cat indoors helps protect the wildlife around your yard and prevents your cat from picking up diseases from strays or getting injured. If cats must be allowed outdoors, consider using a fenced enclosure or runway.
- Neuter or spay your cat or prevent it from breeding.
- Locate bird feeders in sites that do not provide cover to ambush birds. To prevent cats from climbing to bird nests, put animal guards (2-foot-wide band of aluminum flashing) around nesting trees.
- Do not release unwanted cats in rural areas. Cats suffer in an unfamiliar setting. Contact your local animal welfare group for help.
- Do not feed stray cats. Feeding strays maintains high densities of cats that kill and compete with native wildlife populations. Cat colonies will form

[4]Adapted from J. S. Coleman, S. A. Temple, and S. R. Craven. 1997. *Cats and Wildlife—A Conservation Dilemma*. Madison, WI: Wisconsin Cooperative Extension. 6 pp.

around sources of food and grow to the limits of the food supply. In such colonies, cats suffer from disease and injury, while native wildlife populations decline.

- On farms, keep only the minimum number of free-ranging cats needed for rodent control and neuter or spay these to limit populations. Well-fed, spayed females will stay closest to farm buildings and do most of their killing where rodent control is most needed. Traps and rodenticides, as well as rodent-proof storage for grains, are more successful approaches to rodent control than maintaining large numbers of cats.

Squirrels and Raccoons

(©MD)

Squirrels will challenge even the most ambitious bird-feeding enthusiasts by their remarkable gymnastic talents. Gray squirrels can leap 8 feet from a nearby tree or house onto a feeder or drop 11 feet down to a feeder from an overhanging tree. They may also have the expensive habit of gnawing through wood or plastic to obtain the last bit of grain in a feeder.

Gray squirrels cause the most problems, but in the midwestern and southern states, fox squirrels do their share of mischief. Red squirrels are the principal grain grabbers of the northern and mountain coniferous forests, and even the nocturnal flying squirrel can make a significant dent in sunflower seed supplies. Raccoons are not as agile as squirrels, but they make up for this on their night raids with abilities to use their paws to open feeders. In some areas, black bears are becoming increasing problems. If sturdy feeders are pulled to the ground, a black bear could be the culprit. Raccoons and bears are especially fond of suet.

Trapping and removing squirrels might seem like a logical solution, but new arrivals will soon fill the vacancies. Also, mammals that are trapped and released in new territory with the thought that they will lead a happy future actually may have a grim chance of surviving because most suitable habitat is usually already occupied. For these reasons, trapping and relocating is usually illegal in most states and provinces. Likewise, shooting is not a legal or wise option, especially in city limits. Squirrels and raccoons are game animals protected by hunting laws and may be taken legally only during short seasons in the fall. Some feeders are especially designed to discourage squirrels and heavier birds. These rely on the weight of the squirrel or large bird to drop a protective shield over the grain supply.

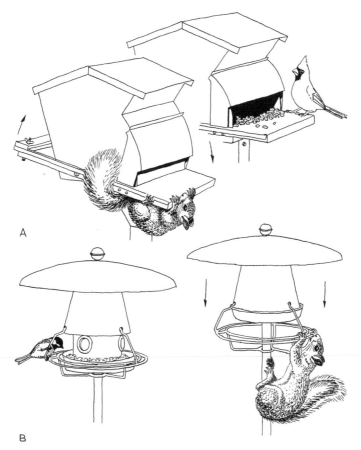

Weight-adjusted feeders exclude squirrels whose weight causes the door to shut. These feeders can also select against heavy birds such as jays and grackles. (AF)

Where possible, place bird feeders on 5- to 6-foot-tall poles away from trees or other perches from which squirrels can leap or drop onto feeders. Although homemade baffles above hanging feeders, such as a stack of wobbly 33⅓ rpm phonograph records separated by large thread spools, or commercial plastic baffle domes, will deter some of the squirrels part of the time, a truly determined squirrel will often keep trying until its efforts to reach the feeder succeed.

Merrill Wood of State College, Pennsylvania, experimented with horizontal wires of various weights to find the thinnest weight that a squirrel could walk. He found that gray squirrels could not walk upright on a No. 9 wire, but they could reach his feeders by clinging upside down, like a very fast sloth. Horizontal wires can be squirrel proofed with elaborate baffles and other devices to stumble even surefooted squirrels. Pat Ellis of Columbus, Ohio, has successfully deterred gray squirrels by lacing thread spools onto a wire and placing flat metal baffles (such as CDs) at either end of the spool lineup. She reports that squirrels climb upside down on the spools without the baffles, but the combination has kept her feeders squirrel-free. Such elaborate efforts emphasize that *it is much more difficult to deter squirrels from approaching feeders from above than it is to keep them from climbing up to feeders from the ground.* If the feeder is placed on a wire, protect it with baffles. Phonograph records, CDs, and wooden thread spools will help discourage squirrels and prevent most from reaching feeders.

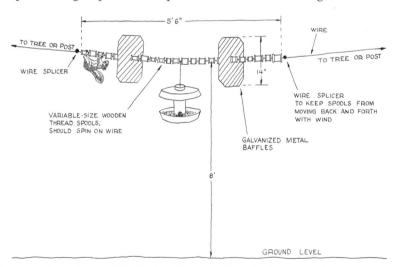

This homemade squirrel baffle, designed by Pat Ellis of Columbus, Ohio, combines the use of thread spools and flat metal baffles to provide an effective deterrent for gray squirrels. (AF)

Whenever possible, position feeders on poles in open sites to restrict squirrels to climbing rather than leaping and dropping from overhead perches. Several homemade baffles are easy to build. Dick Tuttle of Delaware, Ohio, designed one of the simplest homemade baffles. His squirrel baffle consists of a 12-inch length of 4-inch-diameter PVC sewer pipe positioned just under the feeder with hooks. Squirrels climbing the pole find themselves inside of the wobbly pipe, with no way to get around this slippery baffle. A similar idea is to cut the bottom off of a gallon milk jug or bleach bottle and then secure it just under the feeder. Likewise, an inverted plastic flowerpot makes an ideal squirrel baffle as squirrels can climb the feeder pole, but are unable to get around the walls of this easy-to-construct baffle.

In a similar manner, metallic cone-shaped baffles of various sizes will keep squirrels, raccoons, and cats from climbing feeder poles. Twenty inches appears to be the minimum size to baffle squirrels. Such baffles are readily available in most bird feed accessory shops.

To construct a cone with a 20-inch diameter at its base, use tin snips to cut a circle with a 15-inch radius from galvanized sheet metal. Then cut a wedge with a 31-inch arch from the circle, and snip a circular opening in the center of the piece. Form the cone by overlapping the metal by an inch and securing the joint with self-taping metal screws. To mount the cone on the feeder pole, first attach 1 × 6 inch strips of metal to the narrow end of the cone to create a collar; then nail the collar to the pole or use a tight-fitting radiator clamp.

Dana Buckelen of Bethany, West Virginia, has successfully baffled squirrels and even house cats from climbing the poles to his feeders by securing a garbage can lid to the feeder pole. He does this by using a tin snip to cut a circular hole in the center of the lid, leaving the cut-out flap attached at one end. The garbage-can handle is cut at one end and used along with the cutout to secure the lid onto a wooden pole.

David Cooper of Lewiston, New York, has devised an equally simple squirrel baffle. He suggests cutting out a 24-inch circular piece of sheet metal with a central hole large enough to slide over the feeder pole. This flat baffle is free to wobble, tilt, and rotate, as the only thing holding it in place is a ball of duct tape wound beneath it around the pole. Marjorie Edelen of Lambertville, Michigan, suggests a similar technique. She simply took a child's sliding saucer and inverted it between the feeder and the top of a wooden post, completely baffling her gray squirrels.

E. Stuart Mitchell of Portland, Connecticut, was having trouble with squirrels chewing on his feeders. In retaliation, he discovered an ingenious deterrent. To "cure" squirrels of their chewing mischief, he applies a thin coat of clear silicon bathtub caulk to trouble spots on his feeders and imbeds a thick coating of red pepper or chili powder into the caulking. He finds that several layers of the mixture are excellent protection to his feeders.

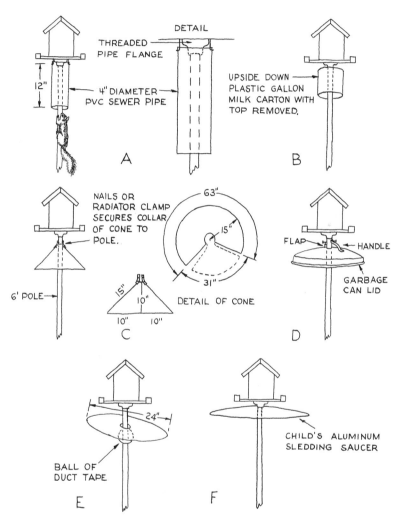

Squirrel baffles for pole feeders: (A) sewer pipe baffle, (B) milk jug baffle, (C) sheet metal cone, (D) garbage can lid, (E) wobbly sheet metal disk, and (F) sledding saucer baffle. (AF)

Rats and Mice

Rats and mice will find their way into grains stored in paper bags, and will even chew through plastic garbage cans. Only metal garbage cans with tight-fitting lids will keep rats and mice out of stored grain. Store these inside a shed or garage to discourage raccoons from lifting off lids and helping themselves.

Rats and mice may be quick to discover spilled grain under bird feeders, and will climb up feeder poles and into feeders that are not equipped with squirrel baffles. Burrows with 2–3-inch openings in the ground near feeders are likely to be rat dens. If you observe rats using such burrows, clean up spilled grain and baffle your feeders. To further minimize danger to birds, stop feeding at this location for several weeks.

FEEDER DESIGNS

Mounting Feeders on Living Trees

Whenever possible, avoid nailing bird feeders and houses onto living trees. Nails often cause sapwood to die and may create an avenue for either internal rot or external infection to spread through the tree's living tissues. Also, bark will eventually grow over exposed nails, hiding them from woodcutters' saws. One hidden nail can destroy a chain-saw blade and will greatly decrease the value of prime lumber trees.

Bob Burrell of Arlington, Illinois, recommends a technique commonly used for hanging feeders and birdhouses in Sweden. This method consists simply of a wooden strut attached to the back of the feeder or birdhouse. This supports the feeder in a tree crotch without using nails. The length of the strut is cut to fit specific trees.

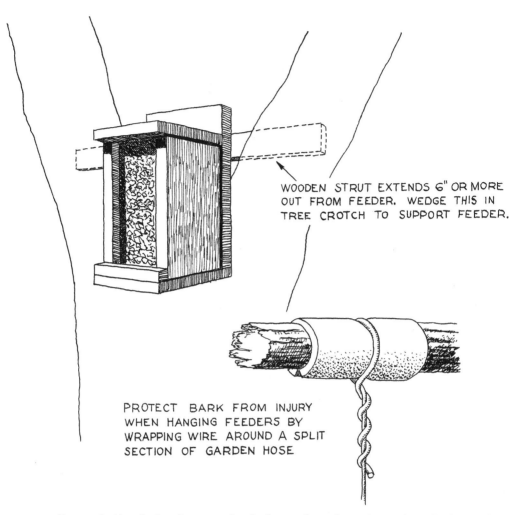

WOODEN STRUT EXTENDS 6" OR MORE
OUT FROM FEEDER. WEDGE THIS IN
TREE CROTCH TO SUPPORT FEEDER.

PROTECT BARK FROM INJURY
WHEN HANGING FEEDERS BY
WRAPPING WIRE AROUND A SPLIT
SECTION OF GARDEN HOSE

Tree-protecting devices for mounting feeders and nest boxes lower the risk of rot and infection. (AF)

Since squirrels can easily chew through cotton or nylon line, it is best to suspend hanging feeders with wire or small-link chains. This, however, can seriously damage living tree limbs, for the wire will eventually cut into growing tissue as the tree limb matures. To avoid this problem on narrow branches, thread the wire through a split section of garden hose.

Suet Feeders

Whole suet and suet mixtures are easy to provide for winter birds. Press suet into 1-inch holes drilled in hanging suet logs (food sticks) or pack it into holes drilled in dead snags. Other ways to provide suet are in hanging onion/citrus bags, soap dishes strapped to trees, and a variety of other simple and more elaborate dispensers. The selection of which design to use depends more on available materials and carpentry skills than on differences in attractiveness to birds.

Although squirrels do not usually have a taste for suet, it is a favorite of raccoons, dogs, and starlings, all of which can rob and destroy feeders in their eagerness to get at suet.

To protect suet feeders, hang them well above the reach of the largest neighborhood dog or serve suet only from raccoon-baffled feeders. Starlings are probably the most difficult suet eaters to discourage. One way to shield suet from starlings is to serve it only to small birds, such as chickadees and titmice, from a dispenser completely protected by a square chicken-wire cage through which only small birds can enter. Be sure to use 1½-inch chicken wire, as starlings can squeeze through the 2-inch openings of larger-mesh chicken wire. Although this technique excludes starlings, it also keeps woodpeckers out.

Since chickadees, titmice, nuthatches, and woodpeckers can feed upside down, it is possible to provide suet to these bark-clinging birds and avoid feeding the starlings. A suet feeder designed by Richard Tuttle of Delaware, Ohio, selectively excludes starlings while giving woodpeckers, chickadees, and nuthatches ready access. First attract suet-eating birds to a couple of display holes in the upright log section of the feeder. After birds have become familiar with the feeder, suet is then offered only from holes underneath the horizontal top section. Woodpeckers, nuthatches, titmice, and chickadees will cling upside down to obtain suet, but starlings cannot.

Frederick Sweet of Manchester, Connecticut, designed another innovative starling-proof feeder. This hanging feeder is based on the fact that starlings cannot climb vertical logs. To reach the suet basket in Sweet's feeders, birds must either cling to the suspended log and hike their way up to the feeder basket or be small enough (as are chickadees) to hop through the 1½-inch-mesh chicken-wire cage.

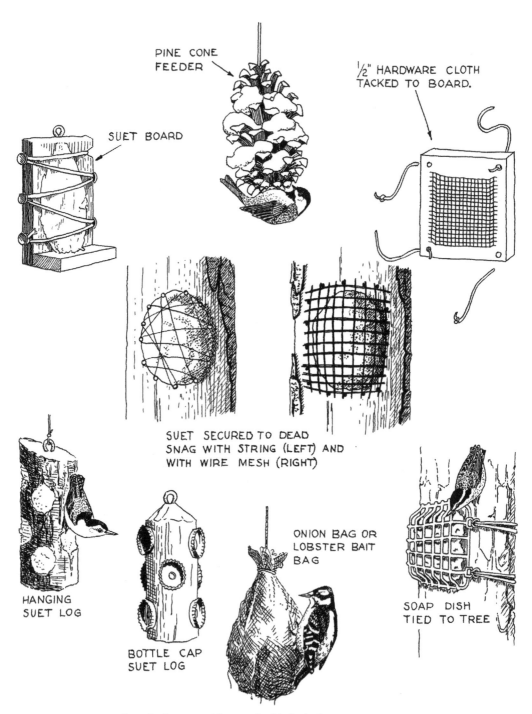

PINE CONE
FEEDER

SUET BOARD

½" HARDWARE CLOTH
TACKED TO BOARD.

SUET SECURED TO DEAD
SNAG WITH STRING (LEFT) AND
WITH WIRE MESH (RIGHT)

HANGING
SUET LOG

BOTTLE CAP
SUET LOG

ONION BAG OR
LOBSTER BAIT
BAG

SOAP DISH
TIED TO TREE

A variety of methods to provide suet for birds. (AF)

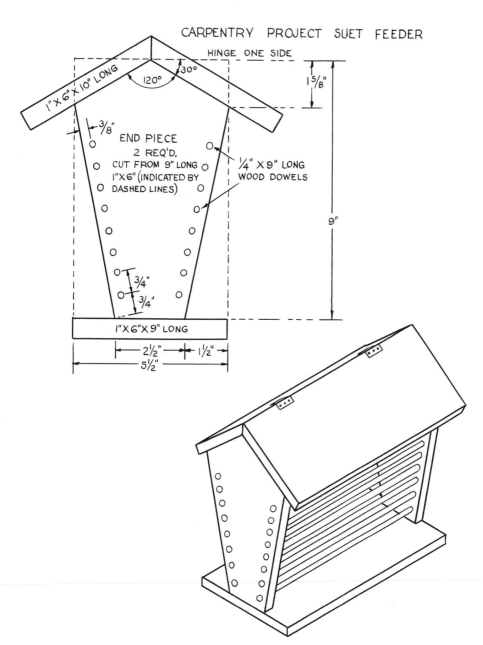

CARPENTRY PROJECT SUET FEEDER

HINGE ONE SIDE

1" X 6" X 10" LONG

120°

30°

1 5/8"

3/8"

END PIECE
2 REQ'D.
CUT FROM 9" LONG
1"X6" (INDICATED BY
DASHED LINES)

1/4" X 9" LONG
WOOD DOWELS

9"

3/4"
3/4"

1"X 6"X 9" LONG

2 1/2"   1 1/2"
5 1/2"

Plans for suet feeders. (AF)

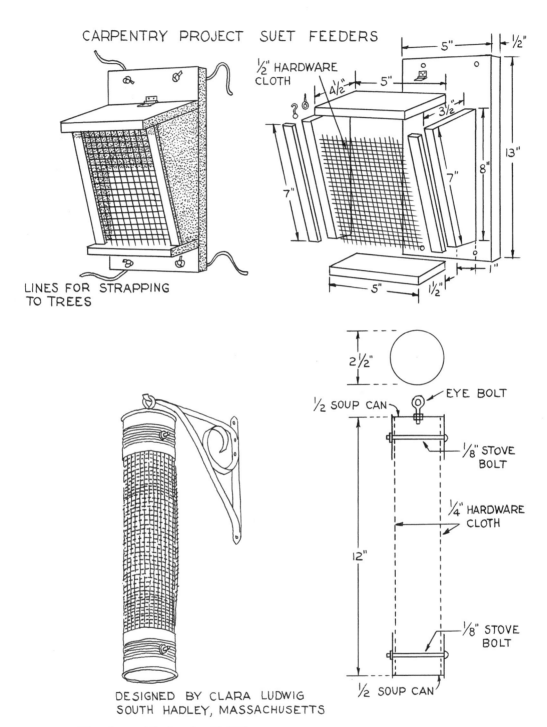

CARPENTRY PROJECT SUET FEEDERS

LINES FOR STRAPPING
TO TREES

½" HARDWARE
CLOTH

EYE BOLT

½ SOUP CAN

⅛" STOVE
BOLT

¼" HARDWARE
CLOTH

⅛" STOVE
BOLT

½ SOUP CAN

DESIGNED BY CLARA LUDWIG
SOUTH HADLEY, MASSACHUSETTS

Plans for suet feeders (cont.). (AF)

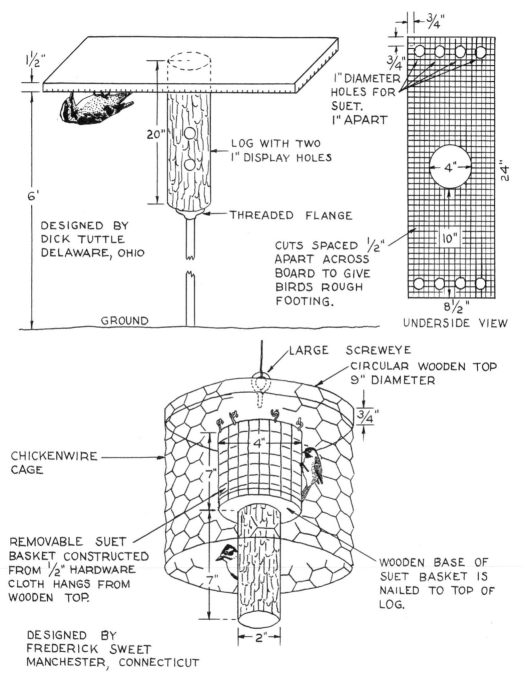

1½"

6'

20"

LOG WITH TWO
1" DISPLAY HOLES

THREADED FLANGE

DESIGNED BY
DICK TUTTLE
DELAWARE, OHIO

CUTS SPACED ½"
APART ACROSS
BOARD TO GIVE
BIRDS ROUGH
FOOTING.

GROUND

¾"

¾"

1" DIAMETER
HOLES FOR
SUET.
1" APART

4"

24"

10"

8½"

UNDERSIDE VIEW

LARGE SCREWEYE

CIRCULAR WOODEN TOP
9" DIAMETER

¾"

4"

7"

CHICKENWIRE
CAGE

REMOVABLE SUET
BASKET CONSTRUCTED
FROM ½" HARDWARE
CLOTH HANGS FROM
WOODEN TOP.

7"

2"

WOODEN BASE OF
SUET BASKET IS
NAILED TO TOP OF
LOG.

DESIGNED BY
FREDERICK SWEET
MANCHESTER, CONNECTICUT

Plans for suet feeders (cont.). (AF)

Grain Feeders

There is a special satisfaction in luring birds to homemade feeders. Perhaps it is the idea that one can build something that works as well as expensive commercial products, or perhaps it is just the pleasant notion of using "throwaway" items, such as milk cartons, soda bottles, and scrap wood, for a good purpose.

Of course, birds do not really care how much a feeder costs or what it looks like. Cost and aesthetics aside, the only thing that is really important is that food does not deteriorate before the birds have an opportunity to eat it. Moisture is the greatest problem in bird feeders, as it can turn grain to mush in a matter of hours, creating a medium for mold that can prove fatal to birds.

Feeders with roofs are especially important during winter, when snow readily covers and soaks grain. Even feeders with secure lids may take on excessive moisture through feeding portals, so some drainage is important in nearly all feeders. The weathervane feeder helps to keep birds and grain out of direct wind and precipitation.

Feeders that exclude larger birds, such as jays and grackles, permit smaller birds access to grain without waiting for leftovers from the larger, more aggressive species. Such selective feeders as the coffee can feeder or hanging soda bottle with 1-inch holes in its ends are excellent ways to provide choice food only for chickadees and titmice, which can duck into the tiny holes. Perch length can also help to attract one species over another. For example, American goldfinches will perch on feeders with $^3/_4$-inch-long perches, but this is usually too small for the competitive house finches.

The stacked bowl feeder with varying entrances can provide food for small and large birds at the same time by varying feeding levels and size of entrances to the grain. Likewise, the "harmony feeder" permits hundreds of flocking birds such as grosbeaks to feed at the same time by providing many feeding levels and expansive surfaces for displaying grain.

June Osborne of Waco, Texas, tried for years to attract goldfinches to her yard with sunflower and thistle seeds, but could not lure them to her feeders, even though her neighbor regularly hosted many. Apparently, one of the main differences between Osborne's yard and her neighbor's was the presence of mature sycamore trees near her neighbor's home. These were heavy with sycamore fruit, a favorite goldfinch food. Within 3 days of tying dozens of sycamore balls to a barren mimosa tree, Osborne finally lured goldfinch to her yard. First they visited the sycamore fruits, then discovered her feeders. Her experience emphasizes that feeders placed in unsuitable habitat will attract few birds, and the presence of certain bird species is usually explained by the presence of specific plants and plant communities.

Although bird feeders may attract birds to your property for brief visits, long-term improvements will occur only when feeding is part of general landscaping improvements that are made with birds in mind.

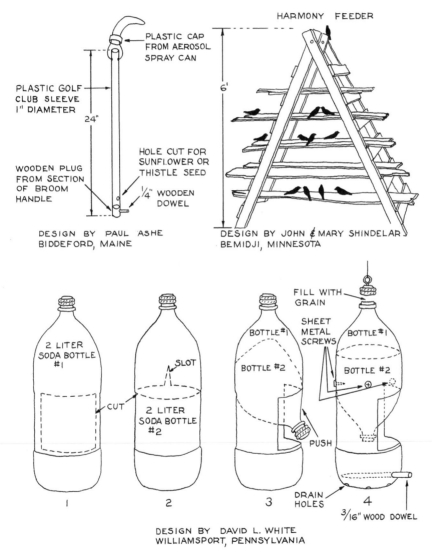

Simple seed feeders. (AF)

THISTLE SEED FEEDER

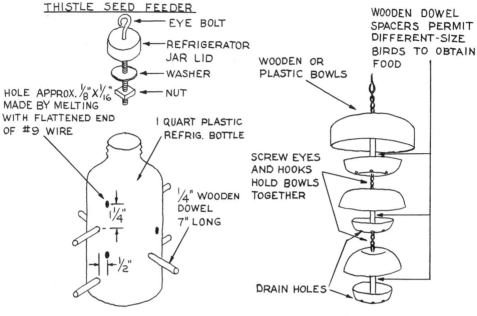

EYE BOLT

REFRIGERATOR JAR LID

WASHER

NUT

HOLE APPROX. $\frac{1}{8}"$ X $\frac{1}{16}"$ MADE BY MELTING WITH FLATTENED END OF #9 WIRE

1 QUART PLASTIC REFRIG. BOTTLE

$\frac{1}{4}"$

$\frac{1}{4}"$ WOODEN DOWEL 7" LONG

$\frac{1}{2}"$

WOODEN OR PLASTIC BOWLS

WOODEN DOWEL SPACERS PERMIT DIFFERENT-SIZE BIRDS TO OBTAIN FOOD

SCREW EYES AND HOOKS HOLD BOWLS TOGETHER

DRAIN HOLES

DESIGN BY RICHARD WASON
LISLE, ILLINOIS

DESIGN BY ALEXANDER HILLIARD
ORANGE PARK, FLORIDA

DONUT FEEDER

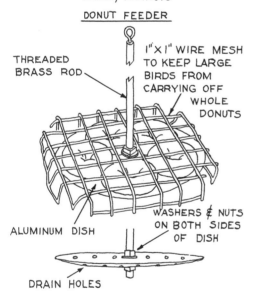

THREADED BRASS ROD

1" X 1" WIRE MESH TO KEEP LARGE BIRDS FROM CARRYING OFF WHOLE DONUTS

ALUMINUM DISH

WASHERS & NUTS ON BOTH SIDES OF DISH

DRAIN HOLES

DESIGN BY LISA VON BOROWSKY
BROOKSVILLE, FLORIDA

SUNFLOWER SEED FEEDER FOR CHICKADEES & TITMICE

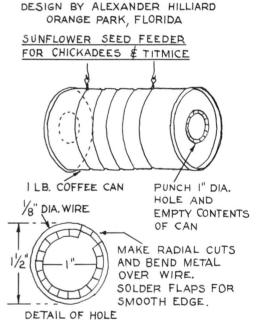

1 LB. COFFEE CAN

PUNCH 1" DIA. HOLE AND EMPTY CONTENTS OF CAN

$\frac{1}{8}"$ DIA. WIRE

$1\frac{1}{2}"$

1"

MAKE RADIAL CUTS AND BEND METAL OVER WIRE. SOLDER FLAPS FOR SMOOTH EDGE.

DETAIL OF HOLE

DESIGN BY CHRIS CHRISTIANSEN
MURRAY HILL, NEW JERSEY

Simple seed feeders (cont.). (AF)

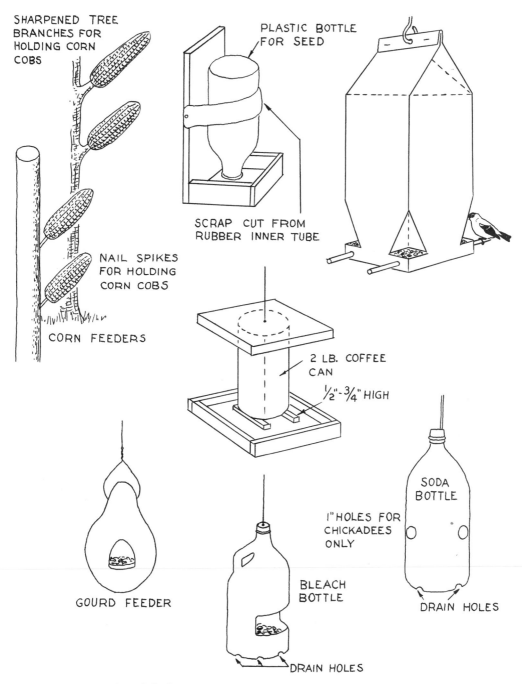

SHARPENED TREE
BRANCHES FOR
HOLDING CORN
COBS

PLASTIC BOTTLE
FOR SEED

SCRAP CUT FROM
RUBBER INNER TUBE

NAIL SPIKES
FOR HOLDING
CORN COBS

CORN FEEDERS

2 LB. COFFEE
CAN

$\frac{1}{2}$"-$\frac{3}{4}$" HIGH

SODA
BOTTLE

1" HOLES FOR
CHICKADEES
ONLY

GOURD FEEDER

BLEACH
BOTTLE

DRAIN HOLES

DRAIN HOLES

Simple seed feeders (cont.). (AF)

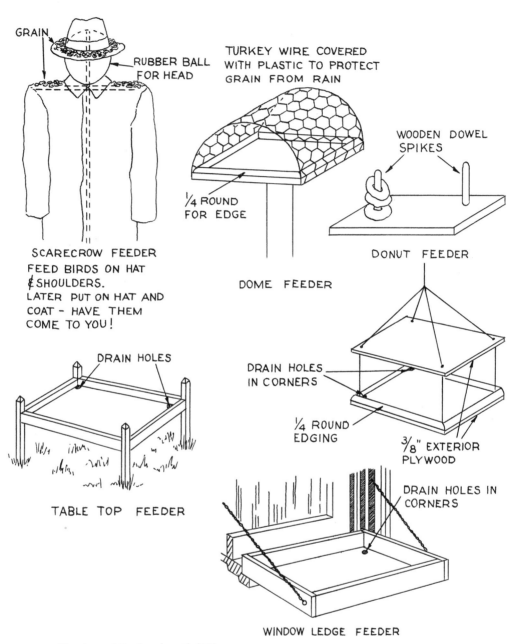

GRAIN

RUBBER BALL
FOR HEAD

SCARECROW FEEDER
FEED BIRDS ON HAT
& SHOULDERS.
LATER PUT ON HAT AND
COAT - HAVE THEM
COME TO YOU!

TURKEY WIRE COVERED
WITH PLASTIC TO PROTECT
GRAIN FROM RAIN

¼ ROUND
FOR EDGE

DOME FEEDER

WOODEN DOWEL
SPIKES

DONUT FEEDER

DRAIN HOLES

TABLE TOP FEEDER

DRAIN HOLES
IN CORNERS

¼ ROUND
EDGING

3/8" EXTERIOR
PLYWOOD

DRAIN HOLES IN
CORNERS

WINDOW LEDGE FEEDER

Simple seed feeders (cont.). (AF)

LEAN-TO GROUND FEEDER

← PREVAILING WIND

CONIFER BRANCHES FOR SHELTER

CORN ON SPIKES IN FEEDING TRAY

RIM ON FEEDING TRAY TO CONTAIN GRAIN

HOPPER FEEDER

DOUBLE HOPPER FEEDER

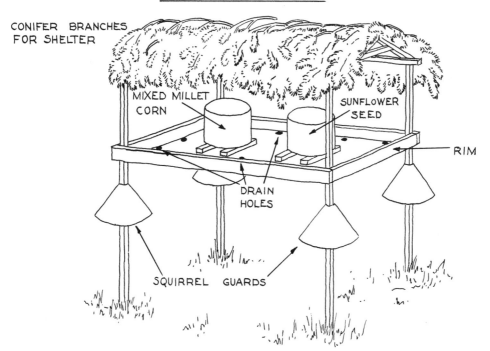

CONIFER BRANCHES FOR SHELTER

MIXED MILLET CORN

SUNFLOWER SEED

RIM

DRAIN HOLES

SQUIRREL GUARDS

Lean-to ground feeder and double-hopper feeder. (AF)

CARPENTRY PROJECT GRAIN FEEDERS
HOPPER FEEDER

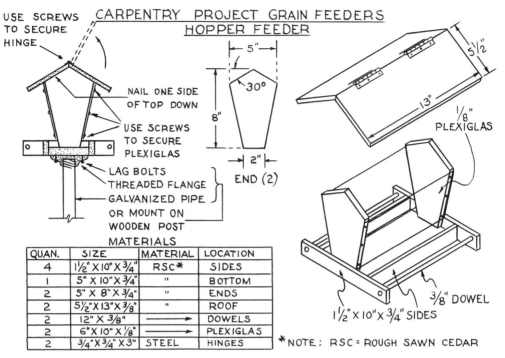

USE SCREWS TO SECURE HINGE

NAIL ONE SIDE OF TOP DOWN

USE SCREWS TO SECURE PLEXIGLAS

LAG BOLTS
THREADED FLANGE
GALVANIZED PIPE
OR MOUNT ON
WOODEN POST

5"

30°

8"

2"

END (2)

5½"

13"

⅛" PLEXIGLAS

MATERIALS

QUAN.	SIZE	MATERIAL	LOCATION
4	1½" X 10" X ¾"	RSC*	SIDES
1	5" X 10" X ¾"	"	BOTTOM
2	5" X 8" X ¾"	"	ENDS
2	5½" X 13" X ⅜"	"	ROOF
2	12" X ⅜"	⟶	DOWELS
2	6" X 10" X ⅛"	⟶	PLEXIGLAS
2	¾" X ¾" X 3"	STEEL	HINGES

⅜" DOWEL

1½" X 10" X ¾" SIDES

*NOTE: RSC = ROUGH SAWN CEDAR

WEATHER VANE BIRD FEEDER

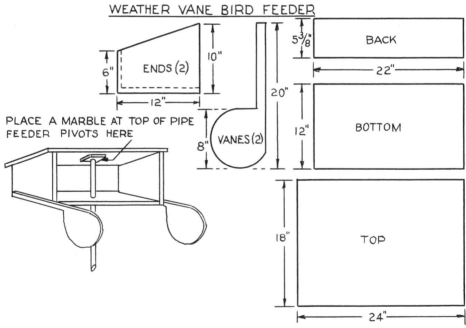

ENDS (2)

6"

10"

12"

5⅜"

BACK

22"

20"

12"

BOTTOM

PLACE A MARBLE AT TOP OF PIPE FEEDER PIVOTS HERE

8" VANES (2)

18"

TOP

24"

Carpentry project grain feeders—hopper feeder. (AF)

CARPENTRY PROJECT GRAIN FEEDERS
GROUND FEEDER

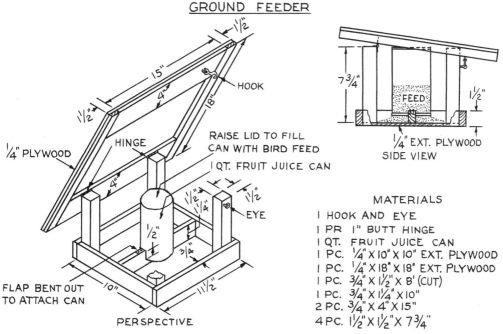

1/2"

15"

4"

18"

1 1/2"

HOOK

1/4" PLYWOOD

HINGE

4"

RAISE LID TO FILL
CAN WITH BIRD FEED

I QT. FRUIT JUICE CAN

1/2"
1/4"

1/2"

EYE

1/2"

3/4"

FLAP BENT OUT
TO ATTACH CAN

10"

11/2"

PERSPECTIVE

7 3/4"

FEED

1/2"

1/4" EXT. PLYWOOD
SIDE VIEW

MATERIALS

1 HOOK AND EYE
1 PR 1" BUTT HINGE
1 QT. FRUIT JUICE CAN
1 PC. 1/4" X 10" X 10" EXT. PLYWOOD
1 PC. 1/4" X 18" X 18" EXT. PLYWOOD
1 PC. 3/4" X 1/2" X 8' (CUT)
1 PC. 3/4" X 1 1/4" X 10"
2 PC. 3/4" X 4" X 15"
4 PC. 1 1/2" X 1 1/2" X 7 3/4"

ONCE-A-WEEK FEEDER

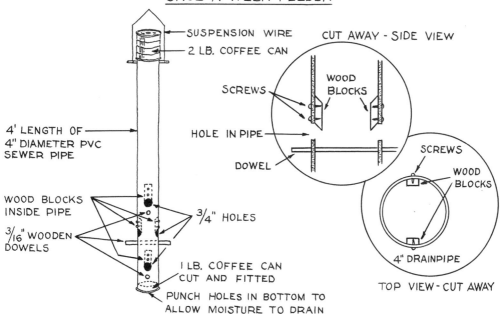

SUSPENSION WIRE
2 LB. COFFEE CAN

CUT AWAY - SIDE VIEW

SCREWS

WOOD
BLOCKS

HOLE IN PIPE

DOWEL

4' LENGTH OF
4" DIAMETER PVC
SEWER PIPE

WOOD BLOCKS
INSIDE PIPE

3/4" HOLES

3/16" WOODEN
DOWELS

1 LB. COFFEE CAN
CUT AND FITTED

PUNCH HOLES IN BOTTOM TO
ALLOW MOISTURE TO DRAIN

SCREWS

WOOD
BLOCKS

4" DRAINPIPE

TOP VIEW - CUT AWAY

Carpentry project grain feeders—ground feeder. (AF)

Bird feeding basics:

http://www.audubon.org/bird/at_home/bird_feeding/index.html

Backyard Citizen Science Projects such as Project Feederwatch, Christmas Bird
Count, Great Backyard Bird Count, visit Birdsource:

http://birdsource.org/

Mealworm supplier: Rainbow Mealworms, 126 E. Spruce Street, P.O. Box
4907, Compton, CA 90220. Email for information at
rainbowm@earthlink.net, or telephone 1-800-777-9676, or go to

http://www.rainbowmealworms.com

On avian conjunctivitis:

House Finch Disease Survey, Cornell Laboratory of Ornithology, 159 Sapsucker
Woods Road, Ithaca, NY 14850, or email housefinch@cornell.edu, or go to

http://birds.cornell.edu/hofi/

On West Nile virus:

http://www.cdc.gov/ncidod/dvbid/westnile/

On cats:

Cats Indoors! American Bird Conservancy, 1834 Jefferson Place, NW, Washington, D.C. 20036;

http://www.abcbirds.org/cats

Native Habitats, 17287 Skyline Blvd—PMB 102, Woodside, CA 94062-3780;

http://www.NativeHabitats.org

9 Healthy Habitats

More than 2 million acres of open land are annually converted to urban and suburban areas dominated by expansive lawns with a scattering of exotic trees and shrubs.[1] This bird-unfriendly habitat is further compromised, as approximately 50 percent of all U.S. households treat their yards with lawn and garden pesticides that may be lethal to birds.[2]

Not only do our garden and landscape choices affect the health of wildlife, plants, and humans in our backyards but also the effects can reach far from home, since pesticides and fertilizers often drift into the air and run into sewers, waterways, and ultimately to lakes, estuaries, and oceans. The following

[1]Natural Resources Conservation Service. 1996. *Framework for the Future of Wildlife* [electronic version]. Washington, DC: U.S. Department of Agriculture. Retrieved January 21, 2003, from http://www.ms.nrcs.usda.gov/whmi/pdf/framework.pdf.

[2]S. R. Templeton, D. Zilberman, and S. J. Yoo. 1998. "An Economic Perspective on Outdoor Residential Pesticide Use." *Environmental Science and Technology* 2:416A–423A.

guidelines provide specific ways to create healthy habitats for backyards and beyond.

REDUCE LAWN AND SAVE WATER[3]

Homes surrounded only by lawn provide no habitat for wildlife and require intensive watering, pesticides, and fertilizer. (SK)

Home lawns cover at least 21 million acres—an area larger than Maryland, Massachusetts, and New Hampshire combined. This is a vast commitment to

[3]This and the next section are adapted from National Audubon Society. 2002. *Audubon Guide for a Healthy Yard and Beyond.* 3rd edition. New York: National Audubon Society; National Audubon Society and Seattle Audubon Society. 2003. *Audubon at Home in Seattle: Gardening for Life.* New York: National Audubon Society; and National Audubon Society. 2003. *Healthier Choices: The Audubon at Home Guide to Healthier Pest Control.* New York: National Audubon Society.

lawns, especially considering that they require 2½–4 times more water than land planted with shrubs and trees.[4] On average, typical American lawns consume 10,000 gallons of water each year above and beyond rainwater.[5] Water that runs off lawns carries fertilizer and lawn chemicals into streams and rivers that eventually lead to lakes and oceans; runoff is greatest in the cities because of the amount of paved surface. For this reason, a typical city block generates about 9 times more runoff than a wooded area the same size.[6]

In contrast to thirsty lawns decorated with ornamental shrubs and trees, native plants are well adapted to local climates, and once established, they generally need little supplementary watering. Likewise, native plants do not usually require pampering with insecticides and herbicides. Unlike dense turf grass, the roots of native grasses, shrubs, and trees go deep into the soil, where they create pathways that lead rain and irrigation water down into the nearest aquifer. Here are some simple steps you can take to responsibly manage the lawn on your property:

1. Develop a plan to reduce your lawn by 25 percent this year. Replace some lawn with native trees and shrubs, and let other areas transition to meadow by not mowing.
2. When mowing the lawn, use sharp blades and mow high, leaving the grass 3–4 inches tall. Don't let the grass get too tall between cuttings; short clippings decompose faster and create less thatch.
3. Aerate lawns to promote dense, deep roots that require less water. Aerated lawns permit more rain to reach underlying aquifers.
4. Tolerate lawns that are less than uniform, knowing that lawns free of pesticides are safer for wildlife, children, and pets. Even brown late-summer lawns will become green again the following spring.

---

[4]American Water Works Association. 2001. "Water Use outside the Home: Basic Landscape Types and Corresponding 'S' Factor." Retrieved January 21, 2003, from Water-Wiser Web site: http://www.waterwiser.org/template.cfm?page1=wtruse/outdoor&page2=books_menu2.

[5]Amy Vickus. 2001. *Handbook of Water Use and Conservation.* Amherst, MA: Waterplow Press.

[6]U.S. Environmental Protection Agency. 1996. *Managing Urban Runoff.* Pointer No. 7, EPA841-F-96–004G, Polluted Runoff (Nonpoint Source Pollution) Factsheet. Retrieved January 21, 2003, from http://www.epa.gov/OWOW/NPS/facts/point7.htm.

5. Replace water-thirsty grasses such as bluegrass with drought-resistant species like buffalo grass or other warm-season grasses. Ask your local Cooperative Extension Service to recommend drought-tolerant grasses for your region.

PESTICIDES AND FERTILIZERS

Homeowners in the United States apply about 78 million pounds of insecticides, herbicides, and fungicides per year to their homes, lawns, and gardens, not including applications made by pest control or lawn care professionals.[7] On a per-acre basis, this is 3 times more pesticides than the amount used on agricultural crops! David Pimentel, professor of entomology at Cornell University, estimates that about 72 million birds die each year as a result of direct exposure to pesticides on agricultural lands, and an estimated additional 7 million die each year from lawn chemicals.

In a recent University of Washington study of pesticide exposure among children living in Seattle, traces of garden chemicals were found in 99 percent of tested children. Significantly higher concentrations were found in children whose parents reported using pesticides in their gardens.[8] Pesticides can wash into rivers and streams, blow into neighboring areas, and seep into the ground where they are routinely found in groundwater. Many pesticides persist in soil and garden litter and are readily tracked into our homes. Lawn and garden fertilizers are also problematic, as runoff contributes to algae blooms in streams, lakes, and ponds, which compromise the value of these critical habitats for wildlife.

Integrated Pest Management (IPM) is an approach to pest control that utilizes regular monitoring to determine if and when treatments are needed. The approach employs physical, mechanical, cultural, biological, and educational tactics to keep pest numbers low enough to prevent damage or annoyance. The

[7]D. Donaldson, T. Kiely, and A. Grube. 2002. *Pesticides Industry Sales and Usage: 1998 and 1999 Market Estimates.* Washington, DC: U.S. Environmental Protection Agency, Office of Prevention, Pesticides, and Toxic Substances.

[8]C. Lu, D. E. Knutson, J. Fisker-Andersen, and R. A. Fenske. 2001. "Biological Monitoring Survey of Organophosphorus Pesticide Exposure among Pre-school Children in the Seattle Metropolitan Area." *Environmental Health Perspectives* 109:299–303.

least-toxic chemical controls should be used only as a last resort.[9] Here are some simple steps you can take to reduce the use of pesticides and fertilizers.

1. Compost your household's organic waste, and use it in place of artificial fertilizers. This reduces the amount of organic waste sent to landfills, while creating "black gold"—the perfect fertilizer and soil conditioner for nurturing gardens and other plantings.

2. Mulch around plantings to block weed growth. Use wood chips, leaves, landscape fabric, or newspapers covered with straw as mulch.

3. Weed gardens and beds by hand early in the season to prevent weeds from becoming established and before they produce copious amounts of seed. Instead of herbicides, apply corn gluten meal to turf grass in early spring and fall to prevent the germination of dandelions, crabgrass, and other weeds; where weed control is desired on sidewalks and driveways, use boiling water, a propane torch, or white vinegar. Stay vigilant to watch for and remove the first incursions of invasive plants. To remove small patches of lawn or invasives, spread heavy-gauge black plastic sheets over the invasives during spring/summer to thermally kill the plants.

4. Tolerate blemishes on fruit and vegetables, finding satisfaction that fruit grown without pesticides is healthier for people, wildlife, and the planet. Likewise, appreciate the variety of plants in your lawn, knowing that plant diversity means greater wildlife diversity and a safer place for children and pets.

5. Use alternatives to pesticides. Identify backyard pests using an insect field guide to learn which pests you are attempting to control. Whenever possible, use nontoxic techniques rather than pesticides. For example, install mesh "row covers" to keep insects off garden plants, and use copper flashing to deter snails and slugs from garden beds, and protective oils against mites, aphids, thrips, and whiteflies. Pick off Japanese beetles and large garden pests. Dispose of them in alcohol and utilize techniques such as sticky tapes, pheromone traps, and plant vacuums. Prune to eliminate infestations, or rinse insects from plants with a garden hose.

6. Choose biological controls such as predatory lacewings, ladybird beetles, and dragonflies. Milky spore disease controls Japanese beetle grubs.

[9]William Olkowski. 1991. *Common-Sense Pest Control.* Newtown, CT: Taunton Press.

Some strains of the bacteria *Bacillus thuringiensis* (Bt) kill caterpillars and others kill mosquito larvae. Galerucella beetles (natural predators on purple loosestrife in Europe) are now destroying purple loosestrife without affecting native plants in North America.

7. Read labels before buying pesticides; study directions and precautions carefully. Avoid broad-spectrum pesticides that kill many species, especially those labeled "Danger" by the Environmental Protection Agency.

8. When limited herbicides are deemed necessary (e.g., to kill invasive shrubs and vines), apply to individual plants using a brush or focused spray. Use eye protection and gloves, applying neither more nor less than the recommended amount. Avoid application during windy conditions.

9. Inform your neighbors when you are using pesticides that can drift across property borders. Be sure to post notices around your yard if you treat your lawn with pesticide. These chemicals are usually dangerous to children, wildlife, and pets.

USEFUL SOURCES

National Audubon Society's Audubon at Home program provides recommendations for creating healthy habitats:
http://www.audubon.org/bird/at_home/index.html

National Wildlife Federation's Backyard Wildlife Habitat program certifies wildlife-friendly backyards:
http://www.nwf.org/backyardwildlifehabitat/

The Rachel Carson Council, Inc. provides information about the effects of pesticides:
http://members.aol.com/rccouncil/ourpage/index.htm

Cornell University's site concerns Integrated Pest Management and biological control:
http://www.nysaes.cornell.edu/ent/biocontrol/

Cornell University's Ecology and Management of Invasive Plants Program:
http://www.invasiveplants.net/

Suppliers of biological controls:
http://www.cdpr.ca.gov/docs/ipminov/ben_supp/contents.htm

Appendix A. References—Books, Magazines, Web sites

BOOKS

Landscaping Basics

Adams, George. 1998. *Birdscaping Your Garden*. Emmaus, PA: Rodale Press, 208 pages.

Barnes, Thomas G. 1999. *Gardening for the Birds*. Lexington: University Press of Kentucky, 280 pages.

Bormann, Herman, Diana Balmori, and Gordon T. Begalle. 2001. *Redesigning the American Lawn—A Search for Environmental Harmony*. New Haven, CT: Yale University Press, 192 pages.

Dieckelmann, John, and Robert Schuster. 1982. *Natural Landscaping—Designing with Native Plant Communities*. New York: McGraw-Hill, 277 pages.

Ernst, Ruth Shaw. 1996. *The Naturalist's Garden*. 3rd edition. Old Saybrook, CT: Globe Pequot Press, 224 pages.

Henderson, Carrol L. 1987. *Landscaping for Wildlife*. St. Paul: Minnesota Department of Natural Resources, 144 pages.

Kenfield, Warren G., and Happy K. Hamilton. 1991. *The Wild Gardener in the Wild Landcape*. New London: Connecticut Arboretum, 232 pages.

Kress, Stephen W. 1995. *The Audubon Society Bird Garden*. New York: Dorling Kindersley, 176 pages.

Leopold, Aldo. 1966. *A Sand County Almanac—With Other Essays on Conservation from Round River*. New York: Oxford University Press, 269 pages.

Mowery, Marci. 1997. *Native Plants in the Creation of Backyard, Schoolyard and Park Habitat Areas*. Camp Hill: Audubon Council of Pennsylvania, 38 pages.

Newfield, Nancy L., and Barbara Nielsen. 1996. *Hummingbird Gardens*. Shelburne, VT: Chapters Publishing, 144 pages.

Niering, William A., and Richard H. Goodwin. 1996. *Energy Conservation on the Home Grounds: The Role of Naturalistic Landscaping*. New London: Connecticut Arboretum, 28 pages.

Roth, Sally. 1998. *Attracting Birds to Your Backyard*. Emmaus, PA: Rodale Press, 308 pages.

Smyser, Carol A. 1982. *Nature's Design: A Practical Guide to Natural Landscaping*. Emmaus, PA: Rodale Press, 390 pages.

Stein, Sara Bonnett. 1995. *Noah's Garden: Restoring the Ecology of Our Own Backyards*. Boston, MA: Houghton Mifflin, 304 pages.

———. 1997. *Planting Noah's Garden*. Boston, MA: Houghton Mifflin, 464 pages.

Stokes, Donald. 1998. *Stokes Bird Gardening Book*. New York: Little, Brown, 96 pages.

Forest Management

Brett, Richard M. 1983. *Woodlot Primer— The Right Way to Manage Your Woodlot*. Brattleboro, VT: Country Journal Printing, 134 pages.

Decker, Daniel J., and John W. Kelley. Undated. *Enhancement of Wildlife Habitat on Private Lands*. Information Bulletin No. 181. Ithaca, NY: Cornell Cooperative Extension Service, 40 pages.

Hunter, Malcolm L., Jr., ed. 1999. *Maintaining Biodiversity in Forest Ecosystems*. New York: Cambridge University Press, 698 pages.

Martin, Thomas E., and Deborah M. Finch. 1995. *Ecology and Management of Neotropical Birds*. New York: Oxford University Press, 489 pages.

Grasslands and Shrublands

Askins, Robert A. 2002. *Restoring North America's Birds*. 2nd edition. New Haven, CT: Yale University Press, 332 pages.

Brown, Lauren. 1979. *Grasses: An Identification Guide*. Boston, MA: Houghton Mifflin, 240 pages.

——. 1976. *Weeds in Winter*. Boston, MA: Houghton Mifflin, 252 pages.

Mooberry, F. M., and Jane H. Scott. 1980. *Grow Native Shrubs in Your Garden*. Chadds Ford, PA: Brandywine Conservancy, 68 pages.

Packard, Stephen, and Cornelia F. Mutel, eds. 1997. *The Tallgrass Restoration Handbook*. Washington, DC/Covelo, CA: Island Press, 463 pages.

Shirley, Shirley. 1994. *Restoring the Tallgrass Prairie*. Iowa City: University of Iowa Press, 330 pages.

Smith, J. Robert. 1980. *The Prairie Garden*. Madison: University of Wisconsin Press, 220 pages.

Spurr, Joy. 1978. *Wild Shrubs—Finding and Growing Your Own*. Seattle, WA: Pacific Search Press, 95 pages.

Stein, Sara Bonnett. 2000. *My Weeds: A Gardener's Botany*. Gainesville: University Press of Florida, 229 pages.

Stokes, Donald W. 1981. *The Natural History of Wild Shrubs and Vines— Eastern and Central North America*. New York: Harper and Row, 256 pages.

Selecting and Growing Plants

Brenzel, Kathleen Norris, ed. 2001. *Western Garden Book*. Menlo Park, CA: Sunset Publishing, 768 pages.

Brooklyn Botanic Garden Handbooks (available from Brooklyn Botanic Gardens, 1000 Washington Avenue, Brooklyn, N.Y. 11225, and some local nurseries)
    Handbook No. 97, *Planting and Transplanting*.
    Handbook No. 99, *Nursery Source Manual* (for 1300 selected trees and shrubs).

Bruce, Hal. 1976. *How to Grow Wildflowers and Wild Shrubs and Trees in Your Own Garden*. New York: Alfred A. Knopf, 294 pages.

Cullina, William. 2002. *Native Trees, Shrubs, and Vines—A Guide to Using,*

*Growing, and Propagating North
American Woody Plants.* Boston, MA:
Houghton Mifflin, 354 pages.

DeGraaf, Richard M., and Gretchin M.
Witman. 1979. *Trees, Shrubs and Vines
for Attracting Birds—A Manual for the
Northeast.* Amherst: University of
Massachusetts Press, 194 pages.

Dirr, Michael. 1983. *Manual of Woody
Landscape Plants.* Champaign, IL: Stipes
Publishing, 826 pages.

Haehle, Robert G., and Joan
Brokwell. 1999. *Native Florida Plants.*
Houston, TX: Gulf Publishing, 360
pages.

Hightshoe, Gary L. 1987. *Native Trees,
Shrubs, and Vines for Urban and Rural
America.* New York: John Wiley and
Sons, 832 pages.

Johnson, Lorraine, and Andrew Leyerle.
2003. *Grow Wild: Low-Maintenance,
Sure-Success, Distinctive Gardening with
Native Plants.* Golden, CO: Fulcrum
Publishing, 160 pages.

Knopf, Jim, Sally Wasowski, John Kadel
Boring, Glenn Keator, Jane Scott, and
Erica Glasener. 1995. *Natural Gardening.*
San Francisco, CA: Time-Life Books,
288 pages.

Kress, Stephen W., ed. 1999. *Bird Gardens.*
New York: Brooklyn Botanic Gardens,
111 pages.

———, ed. 2000. *Hummingbird Gardens.*
Handbook No. 123. New York:
Brooklyn Botanic Gardens, 111
pages.

Kruckeburg, Arthur R. 1982. *Gardening
with Native Plants of the Pacific
Northwest.* Seattle: University of
Washington Press, 264 pages.

Lowry, Judith Larner. 1999. *Gardening with
a Wild Heart: Restoring California's
Native Landscapes at Home.* Berkeley:
University of California Press, 280
pages.

Martin, Alexander C., Herbert S. Zim, and
Arnold L. Nelson. 1951. *American
Wildlife and Plants—A Guide to
Wildlife Food Habits.* New York:
Dover Publications, 500
pages.

McKenny, Margaret. 1939. *Birds in the
Garden and How to Attract Them.*
Minneapolis: University of Minnesota
Press, 349 pages.

National Vegetation Committee, Arizona
Chapter, Soil Conservation Society of
America. 1973. *Landscaping with Native
Arizona Plants.* Tucson: University of
Arizona Press, 194 pages.

Nehrling, Arno, and Irene Nehrling.
1975. *Easy Gardening with Drought-
Resistant Plants.* New York: Dover, 320
pages.

Perry, Bob. 1981. *Trees and Shrubs for Dry
California Landscapes: Plants for Water
Conservation.* Los Angeles: Ecology
Center of Southern California, 184
pages.

Phillips, Harry R. 1985. *Growing and
Propagating Wild Flowers.* Chapel Hill:
University of North Carolina Press, 331
pages.

Phillips, Judith. 1995. *Plants for Natural
Gardens: Southwestern Native and
Adapted Trees, Shrubs, Wildflowers and
Grasses.* Sante Fe: Museum of New
Mexico Press, 160 pages.

Pope, Thomas, Neil Odenwald, and Charles
Fryling Jr. 1993. *Attracting Birds to*

Southern Gardens. Dallas, TX: Taylor Publishing, 164 pages.

Springer, Lauren, and Rob Proctor. 2003. *Passionate Gardening: Good Advice for Challenging Climates.* Golden, CO: Fulcrum Publishing, 336 pages.

Wasowski, Sally, and Andy Wasowski. 1997. *Native Texas Plants—Landscaping by Region.* 2nd edition. Houston, TX: Gulf Publishing, 407 pages.

Workman, Richard W. 1980. *Growing Native Plants for Landscape Use in Coastal South Florida.* Sanibel, FL: Sanibel-Captiva Conservation Foundation, 137 pages.

Nesting Structures/Supplemental Feeding

Barker, Margaret, and Jack Griggs. 2000. *The Feeder Watcher's Guide to Bird Feeding.* New York: HarperCollins, 135 pages.

Berger, Cynthia, Keith Kridler, and Jack Griggs. 2001. *The Bluebird Monitor's Guide.* New York: HarperCollins, 127 pages.

Burton, Robert. 1992. *National Audubon Society North American Birdfeeder Handbook.* New York: Dorling Kindersley, 223 pages.

Day, Susan, Ron Rovansek, and Jack Griggs. 2003. *The Wildlife Gardener's Guide to Hummingbirds and Songbirds of the Tropics.* New York: HarperCollins, 128 pages.

Dennis, John V. 1976. *A Complete Guide to Bird Feeding.* New York: Alfred A. Knopf, 296 pages.

Dunn, Erica H., and Diane L. Tessaglia-Hymes. 1999. *Birds at Your Feeder.* New York: W. W. Norton, 418 pages.

Harrison, Hal H. 1975. *A Field Guide to Birds' Nests.* Boston, MA: Houghton Mifflin, 257 pages.

Henderson, Carrol L. 1992. *Woodworking for Wildlife.* St. Paul: Minnesota Department of Natural Resources, 111 pages.

Kalmbach, E. R., and W. C. McAtee. 1979. *Homes for Birds.* U.S. Department of Interior, Fish and Wildlife Service, Conservation Bulletin No. 14. Washington, DC: U.S. Government Printing Office, #0-301-753, 22 pages.

Laubach, Rene, and Christyna M. 1998. *The Backyard Birdhouse Book.* Pownal, VT: Storey Books, 203 pages.

McKinley, Michael. 2001. *Ortho's All about Attracting Birds.* Des Moines, IA: Meredith Books, 96 pages.

Roth, Sally. 2000. *The Backyard Bird Feeder's Bible.* Emmaus, PA: Rodale Press, 368 pages.

Stokes, Donald and Lillian. 1987. *The Bird Feeder Book.* New York: Little, Brown, 86 pages.

——. 1989. *The Hummingbird Book.* New York: Little, Brown, 89 pages.

——. 1990. *The Complete Birdhouse Book.* New York: Little, Brown, 95 pages.

——. 1991. *The Bluebird Book.* New York: Little, Brown, 94 pages.

——. 1997. *The Purple Martin Book.* New York: Little, Brown, 96 pages.

Terres, John K. 1977. *Songbirds in Your Garden*. New York: Hawthorne Books, 299 pages.

Toops, Connie. 1994. *Bluebirds Forever*. Stillwater, MN: Voyageur Press, 128 pages.

U.S. Department of Agriculture, Forest Service. 1977. *Cavity Nesting Birds of North American Forests*. Washington, DC: U.S. Government Printing Office, #001-000-03726-9, 112 pages.

Zeleny, Lawrence. 1976. *The Bluebird*. Bloomington: Indiana University Press, 170 pages.

Ponds/Pools/Wetlands

Burrell, Charles Colston, ed. 1997. *The Natural Water Garden*. New York: Brooklyn Botanic Garden, 112 pages.

Helmers, Douglas L. 1992. *Shorebird Management Manual*. Manomet, MA: Wetlands for the Americas, 58 pages.

Ledbetter, Gordon T. 1989. *Water Gardens*. New York: Alphabooks, W. W. Norton, 160 pages.

Matson, Tim. 1983. *Earth Ponds: The Country Pond Maker's Guide*. Woodstock, VT: Countryman Press, 104 pages.

Nash, Helen. 1996. *The Complete Pond Builder*. New York: Sterling Publishing, 144 pages.

Healthy Habitats

Bean, George A. 1971. *Healthy Lawns without Toxic Chemicals*. Silver Springs, MD: Rachel Carson Council, 12 pages.

Clark, C. H. D. 1963. *Pesticides and the Naturalist*. Silver Springs, MD: Rachel Carson Council, 6 pages.

French, C. T. 1981. *A Look at Pesticides in Contract Lawn Maintenance*. Silver Springs, MD: Rachel Carson Council, 3 pages.

Lopez, Andrea Dawn, and Lynn Marie Cuny. 2002. *When Raccoons Fall through Your Ceiling: The Handbook for Coexisting with Wildlife*. Denton: University of North Texas Press, 192 pages.

Plant Sources

Andersen Horticultural Library's Source List of Plants and Seeds. Minnesota Landscape Arboretum, Andersen Horticultural Library, 3675 Arboretum Boulevard, Chanhassen, MN 55318.

Florida Native Nurseries, P.O. Box 436, Melrose, FL 32666.

Garden Catalog Profiles. Norell Software, Inc., 36940 Fremont Road, Caliente, CA 93518.

Hortus Northwest, P.O. Box 955, Canby, OR 97013.

Lady Bird Johnson Wildflower Center, 4801 La Crosse Avenue, Austin, TX 78739, (512) 292–4100.

Native Plant Sources, P.O. Box 515, Windsor, CA 95492.

New England Wild Flower Society at Garden in the Woods, 180 Hemenway Road, Framingham, MA 01701.

Nursery Sources for California Native Plants. California Department of Conservation Division of Mines Geology, 801 K Street, Sacramento, CA 95814, (916) 445-1825.

Stevens, Barbara, and Nancy Connor. 1999. *Where on Earth: A Guide to Specialty*

Nurseries and Other Resources for California Gardeners. Heyday Books, P.O. Box 9145, Berkeley, CA 94709.

PERIODICALS

Audubon. National Audubon Society, 700 Broadway, New York, NY 10003.

Bird Watcher's Digest. P.O. Box 110, Marietta, OH 45750.

Birder's World. Kalmbach Publishing Company, P.O. Box 1612, Waukesha, WI 53187-1612.

Living Bird. Cornell Laboratory of Ornithology, 159 Sapsucker Woods Road, Ithaca, NY 14850.

Native Plants Journal. Indiana University Press, 601 North Morton Street, Bloomington, Indiana 47404-3797.

Restoration and Management Notes. University of Wisconsin-Madison Arboretum, 1207 Seminole Highway, Madison, WI 53711.

Sialia. North American Bluebird Society, P.O. Box 244, Wilmot, OH 44689-0244.

Wildbird. P.O. Box 52898, Boulder, CO 80322.

INTERNET LINKS

Links about Bird Attracting and Gardening for Wildlife

American Bird Conservancy's Cats Indoors program Web site: http://www.abcbirds.org/cats/

American kestrel nest box programs: http://www.npwrc.usgs.gov/resource/tools/kestrel/kestrel.htm

Aquatic Ecosystems Restoration Foundation: http://www.aquatics.org

Automated feeders are available from: http://www.SweeneyFeeders.com

Cats Indoors! American Bird Conservancy: http://www.abcbirds.org/cats

Cornell Laboratory of Ornithology, Web site, All About Birds: http://www.birds.cornell.edu/programs/AllAboutBirds/

Cornell Laboratory of Ornithology's Birdhouse Network, find further details on construction and maintenance of nest boxes and view the nest box camera: http://birds.cornell.edu/birdhouse/

Cornell Laboratory of Ornithology, House Finch Disease Survey: http://birds.cornell.edu/hofi/

Cornell Laboratory of Ornithology's Web site for the program Birds in Forested Landscape: http://birds.cornell.edu/bfl/

Cornell Laboratory of Ornithology's Web site on excluding predators: http://birds.cornell.edu/birdhouse/bhbasic_index.html

Cornell University's Web site for gardens and much more: http://www.gardening.cornell.edu

Cornell University's Web site for integrated pest management and biological control: http://www.nysaes.cornell.edu/ent/biocontrol/

Deer fencing: http://www.deerfence.com/

Deer repellents: http://www.woodstreamcorp.com/msds.asp

http://www.treehelp.com/index.asp

Driftwood Wildlife Association (chimney swift houses): http://www.concentric.net/~dwa

Forest landowners guides and state forestry offices: http://www.na.fs.fed.us/pubs/misc/ir/index.htm

Migratory birds: http://www.PartnersInFlight.org http://www.audubon.org

National Audubon Society's Audubon at Home program presents ideas on how to improve your land by creating a healthy habitat for people and wildlife: http://www.audubon.org/bird/at_home/index.html

National Wildlife Federation's Backyard Wildlife Habitat program has certified thousands of properties as wildlife habitat that meet qualifying criteria: http://www.nwf.org/backyardwildlifehabitat/

North American Bluebird Society: http://www.nabluebirdsociety.org/

North American plants, descriptions and photographs: http://plants.usda.gov/links.html

Population trends at USGS Bird site: http://www.mbr-pwrc.usgs.gov

Prescribed fire: http://www.Firewise.org

Purple Martin Conservation Association: http://www.purplemartin.org

Purple Martin Society: http://www.purplemartins.com

Quail chicks and supplies: http://www.mcmurrayhatchery.com http://www.quailrestoration.com

Quail Unlimited, 868 Road 290, Americus, KS 66835: http://www.quailunlimited.org

Rachel Carson Council provides information about the effects of pesticides: http://members.aol.com/rccouncil/ourpage/index.htm

Sparrow traps: http://www.nwtrappers.com/catalog/traps/sparrow.asp

U.S. Department of Agriculture Zone Map with more detail: http://www.usna.usda.gov/Hardzone/ushzmap.html

Warm-season grass and wildflower seed: Ernst Conservation Seed: http://www.ernstseed.com/ Prairie Nursery: http://www.prairienursery.com Prairie Moon Nursery: http://www.prairiemoonnursery.com

West Nile virus: http://www.cdc.gov/ncidod/dvbid/westnile/

Links about Native Plants and Invasives

Biological controls: http://www.cdpr.ca.gov/docs/ipminov/ben_supp/contents.htm

Cooperative Extension Service offices in the United States: http://www.CSREES.usda.gov/extension/

Cornell University's Ecology and Management of Invasive Plants Program: http://www/invasiveplants.net

Invasive plants information including biological controls: http://www.invasive.org

http://www.lastgreatplaces.org

National Directory of Native Plant
Sources:
http://www.nps.gov/plants/restore/
directory/dsoupromo.htm

http://www.NativeHabitats.org

Native plant sources for the middle Atlantic
region:
http://www.mdflora.org/publications/
nurseries.html

Native plant sources for the Northwest:
http://tardigrade.org/natives/nurseries.
html

Native plant sources for Saskatchewan:
http://www.npss.sk.ca/listing_service/

Native Plants Journal and associated
database:
http://www.nativeplantnetwork.org

Native plants societies and sources for
native plants:
http://www.nanps.org/associations/
frame.shtml

North American Native Plant Society:
http://www.nanps.org/index.shtml

Stop Invasives, a National Audubon Society
Web site about invasive plants and
animals:
http://www.stopinvasives.org/

U.S. Department of Agriculture, Natural
Resources Conservation Service's
database of native plants featuring
descriptions and photographs:
http://plants.usda.gov/gallery.html

U.S. Department of Agriculture, Natural
Resources Conservation Service's native
plants and gardening links:
http://plants.usda.gov/cgi_bin/link_
categories.cgi?category=linknative

U.S. Fish and Wildlife Service's Species
Information on Threatened and
Endangered Animals and Plants:
http://endangered.fws.gov/wildlife.html

Weeds Gone Wild: Alien Plant Invaders
of Natural Areas:
http://www.nps.gov/plants/alien/

Wild Ones, promotes native and natural
gardens:
http://www.for-wild.org/

Appendix B. Plant Sources

Pacific Coast

ABBEY GARDEN CACTUS
P.O. Box 2249
Long Beach, CA 90632-2249
Telephone (direct): 562-905-3520
Specialties: cacti, succulents

ABUNDANT LIFE SEED FOUNDATION
P.O. Box 772
930 Lawrence Street
Port Townsend, WA 98368
Telephone (direct): 360-385-5660
Fax: 360-385-7455
Email: abundant@olypen.org
Web site: http://www.abundantlifeseed.org
Specialties: seeds for flowers, grains, herbs,
    native plants, vegetables

CLYDE ROBIN SEED COMPANY
P.O. Box 2366
4233 Heyer Avenue
Castro Valley, CA 94546-0366
Telephone (toll-free): 800-647-6475
Telephone (direct): 510-785-0425
Fax: 510-785-6463
Email: sales@clyderobin.com
Web site: http://www.clyderobin.com
Specialties: flowers, seeds, shrubs, trees

FOURTH CORNER NURSERIES (FOREST FLOOR
    RECOVERY)
P.O. Box 89
Lummi Island, WA 98262
Telephone (direct): 360-734-0079
Specialties: native plants

FRESHWATER FARMS, INC. (NORTH COAST
    NATIVE SEED BANK)
5851 Myrtle Avenue
Eureka, CA 95503-9510
Telephone (toll-free): 800-200-
    8969
Telephone (direct): 707-444-8261
Fax: 707-442-2490
Email: info@freshwaterfarms.com
Web site: http://freshwaterfarms.com
Specialties: flowers, fungi, herbs, seeds,
    water plants

LAS PILITAS NURSERY—NORTH/CENTRAL
3232 Las Pilitas Road
Santa Margarita, CA 93453
Telephone (direct): 805-438-5992
Fax: 805-438-5993
Email: bawilson@laspilitas.com
Web site:
    http://www.laspilitas.com/nurseries/
    laspilitas.htm
Specialties: native plants

LAS PILITAS NURSERY—SOUTH
8331 Nelson Way
Escondido, CA 92026
Telephone (direct): 760-749-
    5930
Email: bawilson@laspilitas.com
Web site:
    http://www.laspilitas.com/nurseries/
    escondido.htm
Specialties: native plants

MONROVIA
18331 East Foothill Boulevard
Azusa, CA 91702
Telephone (toll-free): 888-752-
6848
Telephone (direct): 626-334-9321
Web site: http://www.monrovia.com
Specialties: bulbs, ferns, flowers, grasses,
shrubs, trees, vines

SISKIYOU RARE PLANT NURSERY
2825 Cummings Road
Medford, OR 97501
Telephone (direct): 541-772-6846
Fax: 541-772-4917
Email: customerservice@srpn.net
Web site: http://www.srpn.net
Specialties: dwarf conifers, rare plants,
trough plants

YERBA BUENA NURSERY
19500 Skyline Boulevard
Woodside, CA 94062
Telephone (direct): 650-851-1668
Fax: 650-851-5565
Web site:
http://www.yerbabuenanursery.com
Specialties: ground covers, shrubs, trees
(for arid climates)

Mountains and Deserts

GRANITE SEED
1697 West 2100 North
Lehi, UT 84043
Telephone (direct): 801-768-4422
Fax: 801-768-3967
Email: info@graniteseed.com
Web site: http://www.graniteseed.com
Specialties: flowers, native plants, shrubs,
trees

GREAT BASIN NATIVES
P.O. Box 114
310 South Main Street
Holden, UT 84636
Telephone (direct): 801-768-4422
Fax: 801-768-3967
Email: gbn@greatbasinnatives.com
Web site:
http://www.greatbasinnatives.com
Specialties: flowers, grasses, native plants,
shrubs, trees

PLANTS OF THE SOUTHWEST—ALBUQUERQUE
6680 4th Street, NW
Albuquerque, NM 87107
Telephone (direct): 505-344-8830
Email: contact@plantsofthesouthwest.com
Web site:
http://www.plantsofthesouthwest.com
Specialties: grasses, southwestern plants,
trees and shrubs, wildflowers

PLANTS OF THE SOUTHWEST—SANTA FE
3095 Agua Fria Road
Santa Fe, NM 87507
Telephone (direct): 505-438-8888
Email: contact@plantsofthesouthwest.com
Web site:
http://www.plantsofthesouthwest.com
Specialties: grasses, southwestern plants,
trees and shrubs, wildflowers

SPRING CREEK NURSERY
3226 West Montgomery Road
Deer Park, WA 99006
Telephone (direct): 509-276-8278
Fax: 509-838-1957
Email: springcreekdpark@aol.com
Web site:
http://www.springcreekdeerpark.com
Specialties: conifers, fruit trees, shrubs

WILDLAND NURSERY
550 North Highway 89
Joseph, UT 84739
Telephone (direct): 435-527-1234
Email: janett@wildlandnursery.com
Web site: http://www.wildlandnursery.com
Specialties: flowers, native plants, shrubs, trees

Prairies and Plains

LINCOLN OAKES NURSERIES
P.O. Box 1601
3310 University Drive
Bismarck, ND 58502-1601
Telephone (direct): 701-223-8575
Fax: 701-223-1291
Email: lincolnoakes@tic.bisman.com
Web site: http://www.lincolnoakes.com
Specialties: shrubs, trees, vines

NATIONAL ARBOR DAY FOUNDATION
211 North 12th Street
Lincoln, NE 68508
Telephone (toll-free): 888-448-7337
Telephone (direct): 402-474-5655
Fax: 402-474-0820
Email: info@arborday.org
Web site: http://www.arborday.org
Specialties: trees

NATIVE AMERICAN SEED
127 North 16th Street
Junction, TX 76849
Telephone (toll-free): 800-728-4043
Telephone (direct): 325-446-3600
Email: info@seedsource.com
Web site: http://www.seedsource.com
Specialties: grasses, wildflowers

NATIVE TEXAS NURSERIES
1004 Mopac Circle Suite 101

Austin, TX 78746
Telephone (toll-free): 877-962-8483
Telephone (direct): 512-280-2824
Fax: 512-280-7725
Email: sales@nativetexasnursery.com
Web site:
   http://www.nativetexasnursery.com
Specialties: grasses, perennials, shrubs, trees

RENEWABLE RESOURCES, LLC
20471 436th Avenue
DeSmet, SD 57231
Contact: Roger C. Petersen
Telephone (direct): 605-854-3971
Fax: 605-854-3301
Email: rcp1@dtgnet.com
Web site:
   http://www.renewableresourcesllc.
   com

SHARP BROS. SEED COMPANY
202 South Sycamore
Healy, KS 67850
Telephone (toll-free): 800-462-8483
Telephone (direct): 620-398-2231
Fax: 620-398-2220
Email: buffalo@sharpseed.com
Web site: http://www.sharpseed.com
Specialties: grasses, wildflowers

Southeast

GARDENS OF THE BLUE RIDGE
P.O. Box 10
Pineola, NC 28662
Telephone (direct): 828-733-2417
Fax: 828-733-8894
Email: robyn@gardensoftheblueridge.com
Web site:
   http://www.gardensoftheblueridge.com

Specialties: wildflowers native to the Blue Ridge Mountains

LADYSLIPPER RARE PLANT NURSERY
7418 Hickory Flat Highway 140
Woodstock, GA 30188
Telephone (direct): 770-345-2998
Specialties: annuals, aquatic plants, bulbs, herbs, native plants, perennials

LEWIS STRAWBERRY NURSERY, INC.
3500 NC Highway 133
Rocky Point, NC 28457
Telephone (direct): 910-675-9409
Specialties: strawberry plants

LILYPONS WATER GARDENS—TX
839 Farm 1489 Road
Brookshire, TX 77423
Telephone (toll-free): 800-999-5459
Telephone (direct): 281-391-0076
Fax: 281-934-2000
Email: Info@lilypons.com
Web site:
    http://www.lilyponswatergardens.com
Specialties: aquatic plants

LOUISIANA NURSERY (DURIO NURSERY)
5853 Highway 182
Opelousas, LA 70570
Telephone (direct): 337-948-3696
Fax: 337-942-6404
Email: dedurio@yahoo.com
Web site:
    http://www.durionursery.com
Specialties: bulbs, flowers, shrubs, trees, vines

NATIVE GARDENS
5737 Fisher Lane
Greenback, TN 37742-2749
Telephone (direct): 423-856-0220

Specialties: ferns, grasses, perennials, seeds, shrubs, trees

NORTH CAROLINA BOTANICAL GARDEN
University of North Carolina at Chapel Hill
CB 3375, Totten Center
Chapel Hill, NC 27599-3375
Telephone (direct): 919-962-0522
Fax: 919-962-3531
Email: sandra_flora@unc.edu
Web site: http://www.ncbg.unc.edu
Specialties: southeastern plant seeds and spores

PARK SEED COMPANY
1 Parkton Avenue
Greenwood, SC 29647
Telephone (toll-free): 800-213-0076
Telephone (direct): 864-227-0717
Fax: 800-275-9941
Email: info@parkseed.com
Web site: http://www.parkseed.com
Specialties: bulbs, ground covers, seeds, shrubs, trees

SAVAGE NURSERY CENTER
6255 Beersheba Highway
McMinnville, TN 37110
Telephone (direct): 931-668-8902
Specialties: fruit trees, ornamentals, small plants

VERNON BARNES AND SONS NURSERY
273 Kesey Ford Road
P.O. Box 250S2
McMinnville, TN 37111
Telephone (direct): 931-668-8576
Specialties: bulbs, fruit and berries, perennials, shrubs, trees, tropical plants

WATER GARDEN
5212 Austin Road

Chattanooga, TN 37343
Telephone (direct): 423-870-2838
Fax: 423-870-3382
Email: info@thewatergarden.com
Web site: http://www.thewatergarden.
    com
Specialties: plants and pond supplies

WAYSIDE GARDENS
1 Garden Lane
Hodges, SC 29695
Telephone (toll-free): 800-213-0379
Telephone (direct): 864-585-8227
Email: info@waysidegardens.com
Web site: http://www.waysidegardens.com
Specialties: bulbs, perennials, rare plants,
    roses, shrubs, trees

WOODLANDERS, INC.
1128 Colleton Avenue, SE
Aiken, SC 29801
Telephone (direct): 803-648-7522
Specialties: exotics, native plants of
    southern piedmont and coastal plain,
    perennials, shrubs, trees, wildflowers

Northeast

AMERICAN MEADOWS (VERMONT
    WILDFLOWER FARM)
223 Avenue D, Suite 30
Williston, VT 05495
Telephone (toll-free): 877-309-7333
Telephone (direct): 802-951-5812
Fax: 802-951-9089
Email: donna@americanmeadows.com
Web site:
    http://www.americanmeadows.com
Specialties: flowers, seeds

BLUE MEADOW FARM
184 Meadow Road

Montague Center, MA 01351
Telephone (direct): 413-367-2394
Specialties: annuals, perennials, tropicals

BRECKS BULBS
P.O. Box 65
Guilford, IN 47022-4180
Telephone (direct): 513-354-1511
Fax: 513-354-1505
Web site: http://www.brecks.com
Specialties: bulbs

BURGESS SEED & PLANT CO.
905 Four Seasons Road
Bloomington, IL 61701
Telephone (direct): 309-662-7761
Email: CustomerService@eburgess.com
Web site: http://www.eburgess.com
Specialties: bulbs, perennials, ornamentals,
    seeds

BURPEE
300 Park Avenue
Warminster, PA 18974
Telephone (toll-free): 800-888-1447
Telephone (direct): 215-674-4915
Fax: 800-487-5530
Email: custserv@burpee.com
Web site: http://www.burpee.com
Specialties: garden gear, herbs, perennials,
    seeds

BUSSE GARDENS
17160 245th Avenue, Northwest
Big Lake, MN 55309
Telephone (toll-free): 800-544-3192
Telephone (direct): 763-263-3403
Fax: 763-263-1473
Email: customer.service@bussegardens.
    com
Web site: http://www.bussegardens.com
Specialties: perennials

CARROLL GARDENS
P.O. Box 310
444 East Main Street
Westminster, MD 21157
Telephone (toll-free): 800-638-6334
Telephone (direct): 301-848-5422
Fax: 410-857-4112
Email: info@CarrollGardens.com
Web site: http://www.carrollgardens.
   com
Specialties: bulbs, herbs, perennials, roses,
   vines, woody plants

CONLEY'S GARDEN CENTER
Route 27
Boothbay Harbor, ME 04538-1845
Telephone (direct): 207-633-5020
Fax: 207-633-5961
Specialties: bulbs

DUTCH GARDENS
144 Intervale Road
Burlington, VT 05401
Telephone (toll-free): 800-944-2250, 888-
   821-0448
Telephone (direct): 802-660-3500
Fax: 800-551-6712
Email: info-dg@dutchgardens.com
Web site: http://www.dutchgardens.com
Specialties: bulbs

EARL MAY SEED & NURSERY, L.C.
208 North Elm Street
Shenandoah, IA 51603
Telephone (toll-free): 800-831-4193
Telephone (direct): 712-246-1020
Fax: 712-246-1760
Email: cbranson@earlmay.com
Web site: http://www.earlmay.com
Specialties: aquatic plants, bulbs, seeds,
   shrubs, trees

FAR NORTH GARDENS
59400 Pontiac Trail
New Hudson, MI 48165
Telephone (direct): 248-486-4203
Specialties: perennials

FARMER SEED AND NURSERY
Division of Plantron, Inc.
818 NW 4th Street
Faribault, MI 55021
Telephone (direct): 309-663-9551
Email: CustomerService@farmerseed.
   com
Web site: http://www.farmerseed.
   com
Specialties: bulbs, perennials, seeds,
   shrubs, trees

FERRIS NURSERY & SHADE TREE MOVERS
8907 160th Street
Davenport, IA 52804
Telephone (direct): 563-381-2034
Specialties: shrubs, trees

GARDEN IN THE WOODS
New England Wild Flower Society
180 Hemenway Road
Framingham, MA 01701
Telephone (direct): 508-877-7630
Fax: 508-877-6553
Email: garden@newfs.org
Web site: http://www.newfs.org
Specialties: wildflowers

GURNEY'S SEED & NURSERY CO.
P.O. Box 4178
Greendale, IN 47025-4178
Telephone (direct): 513-354-1491
Fax: 513-354-1493
Email: service@gurneys.com
Web site: http://www.gurneys.com
Specialties: seeds

HENRY FIELD'S SEED & NURSERY
P.O. Box 397
Aurora, IN 47001-0397
Telephone (direct): 513-354-1494
Fax: 513-354-1496
Email: service@henryfields.com
Web site: http://www.henryfields.com
Specialties: seeds

HENRY LEUTHARDT NURSERIES, INC.
607 Montauk Highway
P.O. Box 666
East Moriches, NY 11940
Telephone (direct): 631-878-1387
Fax: 631-874-0707
Email: leuthardtnursery@aol.com
Web site:
    http://www.henryleuthardtnurseries.
    com
Specialties: berries, fruit trees, vines

HOUSE OF WESLEY
1704 Morrisey Drive
Bloomington, IL 61704
Telephone (direct): 309-664-7334
Email: CustomerService@houseofwesley.
    com
Web site: http://www.houseofwesley.
    com
Specialties: bulbs, perennials, roses, seeds,
    shrubs, trees

J.W. JUNG SEED COMPANY
335 South High Street
Randolph, WI 53957-0001
Telephone (toll-free): 800-247-5864
Telephone (direct): 920-326-3121
Fax: 800-692-5864
Email: info@jungseed.com
Web site: http://www.jungseed.com
Specialties: bulbs, perennials, seeds

LILYPONS WATER GARDENS—MD
6800 Lilypons Road
P.O. Box 10
Buckeystown, MD 21717-0010
Telephone (toll-free): 800-999-5456
Telephone (direct): 301-874-5133
Email: Info@lilypons.com
Web site: http://www.lilypons.com
Specialties: aquatic plants

MELLINGER'S, INC.
2310 West South Range Road
P.O. Box 157
North Lima, OH 44452
Telephone (toll-free): 800-321-7444
Telephone (direct): 330-549-9861
Fax: 330-549-3716
Email: mellgarden@mellingers.com
Web site: http://www.mellingers.com
Specialties: bulbs, perennials, seeds,
    shrubs, trees

MUSSER FORESTS, INC.
1880 Route 119 Highway North
Indiana, PA 15701
Telephone (toll-free): 800-643-8319
Telephone (direct): 724-465-5685
Fax: 724-465-9893
Email: info@musserforests.com
Web site: http://www.musserforests.com
Specialties: conifer and hardwood
    seedlings, ground covers, landscaping
    shrubs, ornamental grasses, perennials

OLDS SEED SOLUTIONS
2901 Packers Avenue
Madison, WI 53707-7790
Telephone (toll-free): 800-356-7333
Telephone (direct): 608-249-9291
Fax: 608-249-0695
Email: dbastian@seedsolutions.com

Web site: http://www.seedsolutions.
com
Specialties: seeds

MORNING SKY GREENERY
24774 450th Avenue
Hancock, MN 56244
Telephone (direct): 320-392-5282
Fax: 320-392-5286
Email: mornsky@fedtel.net
Web site: http://www.morningskygreenery.
com
Specialties: flowers, grasses, seeds

PRAIRIE MOON NURSERY
Route 3, Box 1633
Winona, MN 55987-9515
Telephone (toll-free): 866-417-8156
Telephone (direct): 507-452-1362
Fax: 507-454-5238
Email: info@prairiemoonnursery.com
Web site: http://www.prairiemoon.com
Specialties: cacti, ferns, grasses, seeds,
shrubs, trees, vines

PRAIRIE RESTORATIONS
P.O. Box 327
Princeton, MN 55371
Telephone (direct): 763-389-4342
Fax: 763-389-4346
Email: info@prairieresto.com
Web site: http://www.prairieresto.com
Specialties: grasses, plants, seeds,
wildflowers

REEDS "N" WEEDS
215 Normandy Court
Nicholasville, KY 40356
Telephone (direct): 859-887-5721
Fax: 859-887-5775
Email: info@reedsnweeds.com

Web site: http://www.waterponds.
com
Specialties: plants and pond supplies

SPRING HILL GARDEN CENTER
110 West Elm Street
Tipp City, OH 45371-1699
Telephone (direct): 513-354-1509
Fax: 513-354-1504
Web site:
http://www.springhillnursery.com
Specialties: bulbs, ground covers, shrubs,
trees, vines

STARK BRO'S NURSERIES & ORCHARDS CO.
Bus. Highway 54 West
Louisiana, MO 63353
Telephone (toll-free): 800-478-2759
Telephone (direct): 573-754-3113
Email: info@starkbros.com
Web site: http://www.starkbros.com
Specialties: fruit trees, roses

SUNNYBROOK FARMS NURSERY
9448 Mayfield Road
P.O. Box 6
Chesterland, OH 44026
Telephone (direct): 440-729-7232
Fax: 440-729-2486
Specialties: geraniums, herbs, perennials,
vines

VAN BOURGONDIEN BROTHERS
245 Farmingdale Road
P.O. Box 31000
Babylon, NY 11702
Telephone (toll-free): 800-622-9997
Telephone (direct): 631-669-3500
Specialties: bulbs

VERMONT BEAN SEED COMPANY
334 West Stroud Street

Randolph, WI 53956-1274
Telephone (toll-free): 800-349-1071
Telephone (direct): 802-273-3400
Fax: 888-500-7333
Email: info@vermontbean.com
Web site: http://www.vermontbean.com
Specialties: beans, herbs, perennials, seeds,
    small fruit

WAYNESBORO NURSERIES, INC.
2597 Lyndhurst Road
P.O. Box 987
Waynesboro, VA 22980
Telephone (toll-free): 800-868-8676
Telephone (direct): 540-946-3800
Fax: 540-946-3814
Email: tim@waynesboronurseries.com
Web site:
    http://www.waynesboronurseries.com
Specialties: wholesale orders only—ground
    covers, ornamental grasses, perennials,
    supplies, woody ornamentals

WILD EARTH NATIVE PLANT NURSERY
22 Conover Street
Freehold, NJ 07728-2308
Telephone (direct): 732-308-9777
Fax: 732-308-9777
Specialties: ferns, grasses, wildflowers

WILDLIFE NURSERIES, INC.
904 Bauman Street
Oshkosh, WI 54902-3427
Telephone (direct): 920-231-3780
Specialties: wildlife and game food
    consultants, wildlife and game plants

WINTERTHUR GARDENS
Route 52
Winterthur, DE 19735
Telephone (toll-free): 800-448-3883
Telephone (direct): 302-888-4600
Email: tourinfo@winterthur.org
Web site: http://www.winterthur.org
Specialties: cultivated plants and shrubs

Appendix C. Agencies That Can Help

Restoration and management of large-scale bird habitat is an expensive process that requires experience and technical support. Fortunately, several government-sponsored programs provide financial assistance and technical advice for private landowners who want to improve agricultural land and other large, privately owned fields.

The Agricultural Preservation Restriction Program

The Agricultural Preservation Restriction Program (APR) can help to protect agricultural land from development. In this voluntary program, farmers apply to the state to sell development rights to their land. Farmers are compensated by up to 90 percent of the value of the land. In return, the state acquires the deed restrictions on the land, stating that the land must remain in some form of agriculture. This allows other farmers to buy farmland at affordable prices but restricts purchases of the land for development. Contact your state Department of Agriculture office for information on this program:

http://www.statelocalgov.net/50states-agriculture.cfm

The Conservation Reserve Program

Since 1985, the U.S. Department of Agriculture (USDA) has offered the Conservation Reserve Program (CRP). This very successful program has resulted in the protection and restoration of more than 34 million acres. The purpose of the program is to reduce crop surplus, protect soil from erosion, and increase wildlife habitat. As a result, habitat (especially in the prairie states) has been created and enhanced for waterfowl and many grassland birds. Under this plan, landowners are paid to plant perennial vegetation (grasses, legumes, or trees) on eroding fields. This land cannot be grazed or harvested for a 10-year period. For more about the CRP, visit or call your local USDA office or visit the Web site:

http://www.fsa.usda.gov/dafp/cepd/crp.htm

The following projects will help to meet the needs of wild birds for food, water, cover, and nest sites by fulfilling their requirements with as much variety as possible.

The Conservation Reserve Enhancement Program

In 1997, the USDA's Farm Service Agency implemented a program under CRP called the Conservation Reserve Enhancement Program (CREP). CREP combines state and federal dollars with funding from non-government sources to work on agriculture-related environmental issues. CREP are initiated at local levels when a state, Indian tribe, local government, or nongovernment group identifies an issue such as river buffers, wetland management, and wildlife habitat. Incentives include cost sharing and one-time payments. For further information, contact the Farm Service Agency, U.S. Department of Agriculture, STOP 0506, 1400 Independence Avenue SW, Washington, DC 20250-0506, or visit the Web site: http://www.fsa.usda.gov/dafp/cepd/crep.htm

The Partners for Fish and Wildlife Program

This U.S. Fish and Wildlife Service (USFWS) program, Partners for Fish and Wildlife (PFW), exists to encourage fish and wildlife enhancement projects on private lands. The program offers financial and technical support to private landowners, including farmers, corporations, and private organizations to conduct habitat restoration projects such as reseeding fields into native vegetation and restoring wetlands. For more general information about the program, contact the U.S. Fish and Wildlife Service, Branch of Habitat Restoration, 4401 N. Fairfax Drive, Room 400, Arlington, VA 22203. Telephone: (703) 358-2201. Web site: http://partners.fws.gov/

The Wildife Habitat Improvement Program

This new program is administered by the Natural Resources Conservation Service (NRCS) of the USDA in each state through the 1996 Farm Bill. The purpose of the Wildlife Habitat Improvement Program (WHIP) is to help landowners develop habitat for upland wildlife, wetland wildlife, threatened and endangered species, and fish. Grassland restoration is a priority

under this program. Funds are available to improve grasslands through practices such as brush control, mowing, burning, native vegetation planting, and fencing. The NRCS can provide money through a 75 percent cost share with the private landowner. For local information on the WHIP program, call your county office of the NRCS (listed under USDA) or write to: Natural Resources Conservation Service, Conservation Communications Staff, P.O. Box 2890, Washington, DC 20013, or visit the Web site: http://www.nrcs.usda.gov/programs/whip/

The American Farmland Trust

This national nonprofit organization works to protect productive farmland while encouraging farmers to improve the stewardship of their land through practical conservation options. The American Farmland Trust (AFT) helps to create policies at the local, state, and national levels that protect farmland through voluntary land stewardship incentives. For example, landowners can place conservation easements on their property. This is a legally binding voluntary action that can restrict development while permitting farming that conserves natural resources such as topsoil, water quality, and wildlife habitat. Under this easement, a landowner may be eligible for tax benefits. For more information about agricultural conservation easements or other programs, contact the regional office of the AFT. The national office American Farmland Trust, is 1200 18th Street NW, Washington, DC 20036. Telephone: (202) 331-7300. Fax:

(202) 659-8339. Email: info@farmland.org. Web site:

http://www.farmland.org/regions/#

Private Stewardships Grants Program

This USFWS program provides grants directly to private landowners to implement conservation actions on behalf of rare species, both federally listed endangered and threatened species and state-listed species. The USFWS grants are used to protect and restore imperiled species and their habitats. Excluding land acquisition, the Private Stewardships Grants Program (PSGP) is open to a wide variety of projects. Typical ones may include managing nonnative, competing species; implementing measures to minimize risk from disease; restoring streams that support imperiled species; or planting native vegetation to restore a rare plant community. In addition to grants, the USFWS's land managers can provide technical assistance to private landowners. For additional information on how the service may be able to assist you, call or write the program's contact person in the USFWS regional office. Information is also available from the service's Internet site at:

http://www.fws.gov.

Additional information is also available at:

http://endangered.fws.gov/grants/privat e_stewardship.html

Or write to Washington, D.C. Office, U.S. Fish and Wildlife Service, Endangered Species Program, 4401 N. Fairfax Drive, Room 420, Arlington, VA 22203.

Landowner Incentive Grant Program

The Landowner Incentive Grant Program (LIP) was established in 2002 to provide financial grants and technical assistance to private landowners. The program is designed to protect and restore habitats on private lands to benefit federally listed, pro- posed, or candidate species or other species determined to be at risk (e.g., state-listed). Under this program, states apply for matching grants from the USFWS, and the states then partner with private landowners to carry out the conservation work. Grants are also available to tribal organizations. For further information, contact your state wildlife department, or the U.S. Fish and Wildlife Service, Division of Federal Aid, Arlington Square, Room 140, 4401 N. Fairfax Drive, Arlington, VA 22203. Tele- phone: (703) 358-2156. Web site:

http://federalaid.fws.gov/lip/lip.html

Author Biography

STEPHEN KRESS is Vice President for Bird Conservation for the National Audubon Society and manager of the society's Maine Coast Seabird Sanctuaries. As director of the Audubon's Seabird Restoration Program, he develops techniques for managing colonial nesting seabirds. In this capacity, he restored puffins and other rare and endangered seabirds to islands on the Maine coast and many other locations worldwide. Taking his interest in bird restoration to backyards and larger habitats, he recognized the parallels between restoring seabirds to islands and creating bird-friendly habitats. He lives with his wife, Elissa, and two sons on a thirty-three-acre rural property at the edge of Ithaca, New York, where he tests techniques for improving gardens and landscapes for birds.

He received his undergraduate and master's degrees in wildlife management from Ohio State University and his doctorate in environmental education from Cornell. He is currently a laboratory associate at the Laboratory of Ornithology, where for the past twenty-nine years he has developed and taught his well-known Spring Field Ornithology course. He teaches Ornithology sessions at the Audubon Camp in Maine on Hog Island. He is a member of the Cornell Plantations advisory board. Among his many books on birding and backyard wildlife management, he is author of *The Audubon Society Bird Garden*, *The Audubon Society Birder's Handbook*, *Project Puffin*, *Saving Birds*, and the Golden Guide *Birdlife* as well as many scientific papers on seabird biology and conservation.

Index

Aspen: bigtooth, 144; quaking, 145, 197, 206–7, 244

Aspergillosis, 389

Aspergillus fumigatus, 389

Aster, 28; China aster, 28

Aster spp., 28

Atriplex: brewerii, 252; *canescens*, 238–39; *hymenelytra*, 226, 245; *lentiformis*, 226, 245; *polycarpa*, 252

Audubon at Home, 4

Audubon Society, 333; Appleton-Whittell Research Ranch, 81–82

Audubon Watchlist, 2, 47

Avena sativa, 383

Avian conjunctivitis, 390

Avian pox, 389–90

Avocet, 293

A-Z Encyclopedia of Garden Plants (Brickell and Zuk), 121

Baccharis pilularis, 251

Bachelor's button, 28

Bacillus thuringiensis, 420

Bailey, Ethel Zoe, 119

Bailey, Liberty Hyde, 119

Banding, 372

Basket flower, 28

Bayberry, northern, 155, 179

Bearberry, 165, 180, 198, 245

Bears, 394

Beautyberry, American, 176

Beavers, 68

Bee balm, 30, 31

Beech, American, 145

Bentonite, 275

Berchemia scandens, 189

Berries, 33, 119–20, 124. *See also individual species*

Betula: alleghaniensis, 146; *lenta*, 145; *occidentalis*, 221; *papyrifera*, 145, 197;

papyrifera var. *humilis*, 199; *populifolia*, 145

Bilberry, bog, 165, 245

Bioballs, 267

Biofilters, 266, 267

Biological controls, 419–20

Birch: Alaskan paper, 199; gray, 145; paper, 145, 197; sweet, 145; water, 221; yellow, 146

Birdbaths, 258–63

Birdhouse Network Program, 300, 355

Birds and Calcium Project, 374

Birds-of-paradise, 32

Bison, 67, 68

Bittern, 273, 282, 284

Bittersweet, American, 168, 198

Blackberry, 135, 180; Allegheny, 160; California, 253; highbush, 203

Blackbird, 254; Brewer's, 383; feeding, 383; food sources, 19, 21, 26; nesting sites, 284; red-winged, 19, 21, 26, 155, 288, 359, 383; yellow-headed, 383

Black-eyed Susan, 28

Blackhaw, rusty, 184

Bladderbush, 251

Blessed thistle, 28

Blowflies, 300, 302–4, 319, 320

Bluebells, 28

Blueberry, 252; dwarf, 233; ground, 186; highbush, 134, 180; lowbush, 160; western bog, 227

Bluebird, 56; eastern, 73, 134, 138, 150, 151, 152, 158, 164, 172, 174, 182, 186, 195, 316, 386; feeding, 368, 386; food sources, 73, 106, 134, 138, 140, 150, 151, 152, 158, 172, 174, 182, 184, 186, 187, 195, 203, 221, 228, 254; mountain, 312, 316; nesting sites, 60, 151; nesting structures, 295, 296, 298, 316, 317–21; parasites, 302, 305; western, 214, 239, 316

Cavity-nesting birds, 56–61, 106, 130, 207;
dimensions for nest boxes, 315–16. *See
also* nesting and roosting structures
Ceanothus spp., 243–44; *fendleri*, 227, 243;
gloriossus, 243; *prostrates*, 243; *thrysiflorus*,
243–44
Cedar waxwings, 25, 128, 132
Celastrus scandens, 168, 198
Celery, wild, 291–92
Celosia: cristata, 28; *plumosa*, 28
Celtis: douglasii, 229; *laevigata*, 172–73, 197;
occidentalis, 147, 179, 191; *pallida*, 224;
reticulata, 199
Centaurea: americana, 28; *cineraria*, 28;
cyanus, 28; *hirta*, 28; *imperialis*, 28
Cephalanthus occidentalis, 155, 180, 198
Chalcid wasp, 304
Chara, 289–90
Chara spp., 289–90
Chat, yellow-breasted, 94
*Checklist of North American Plants for
Wildlife Biologists* (Scott and Wasser), 119
Chenopodium album, 23
Cherry: bessey, 203; bitter, 221, 227; black,
130, 197, 215; Catalina, 246; dwarf sand,
203; holly-leaved (Islay), 238; pin, 151,
197
Cherry laurel, Carolina, 187
Chickadee: black-capped, 207, 241, 358–59,
372, 385; Carolina, 171, 173, 385; chestnut-
backed, 241; diseases, 390; feeding, 361,
367, 368, 371, 373, 377, 378, 381, 385, 387,
401; food sources, 27, 106, 142, 145, 146,
171, 173, 246; nesting sites, 60, 130;
nesting structures, 299, 312, 315;
roosting structures, 296, 353
Chicken, 389, 390
Chilopsis linearis, 208
China aster, 28
Chionanthus virginicus, 185

Chironomids, 280, 281
Chokeberry: black, 155; red, 156
Chokecherry: common, 152, 189, 190–91,
215; Western, 253
Christmas berry (toyon), 177, 251
Christmas wreaths, 337
Chrysanthemum, 28
Chrysanthemum spp., 28
Chrysobalanus icaco, 187
Chufa sedge, 285–86
Circular planting, 104; shrublands, 104
Citris spp., 32
Citrus tree, 32
City birds, 32
Clear-cutting, 56–57
Clover, 113
Coccoloba: diversifolia, 181; *uvifera*, 188
Cocculus carolinus, 189
Cocoplum, 187
Colonies, 352–53. *See also* martin, purple;
swallow
Columbine, 30, 31
Commelina spp., 28
Complete Guide to Bird Feeding, A (Dennis),
389–90
Compost, 419
Condalia: knife-leaf, 227; lotebush, 227;
lotewood, 227
Condalia: lycioides, 227; *obtusifolia*, 227;
spathulata, 227
Coneflower, 28
Conifer plantations, 32–33
Conifers, 10
Conifer shelters, 34
Conservation easements, 65
Conservation plans, 4
Conservation Reserve Enhancement
Program (CREP), 441–42
Conservation Reserve Program (CRP),
441

Construction materials, for nest boxes, 296–97
Cooperative Extension Service, 41
Coot, 283, 284, 291, 293; American, 286, 290, 291; common, 293
Copland, Herb, 342
Coral bean, 32
Coralberry, 30, 161, 198
Cordgrasses, 286–87; marsh, 286; salt hay, 286
Coreopsis, 28
Coreopsis spp., 28
Cormorant, double-crested, 295
Corn, 112, 113, 379
Cornell Laboratory of Ornithology, 48, 374, 378, 387, 390; Birdhouse Network Program, 300, 355
Cornflower, 28
Cornstalk fields, 73–74
Cornus: alternifolia, 152, 179; *amomum*, 180, 194; *canadensis*, 166, 180, 198; *drummondii*, 194, 203; *florida*, 131–32, 179; *glabrata*, 228, 245; *nuttallii*, 221, 236–37; *occidentalis*, 244; *racemosa*, 194; *sessilis*, 228, 245; *stolonifera*, 135–36, 180, 194, 198, 215, 245
Corylus americana, 157
Cosmos, 28
Cosmos spp., 28
Cottonwood: black, 221; eastern, 197; Fremont, 221; narrowleaf, 221; plains, 199
Cowberry, 166
Cowbird, 376; brown-headed, 19, 21, 48, 51, 64, 103, 379; diseases, 389; feeding, 379; food sources, 19, 21
Coyote brush (dwarf chaparral broom), 251
Crabapple, 106, 120; flowering, 130–31, 179, 197; Oregon, 248; sargent, 131, 156;

sweet flowering, 130; toringo, 156. *See also* apple
Crabgrass, 112; hairy, 20, 21; smooth, 20, 21
Crane, 284; feeding, 379; sandhill, 283, 286, 294, 379; whooping, 287
Crataegus spp., 132, 197, 222; *brachyacantha*, 183; *chrysocarpa*, 200; *crus-galli*, 132, 152, 192, 244; *douglasii*, 209–10, 244; *marshalii*, 185; *mollis*, 200, 244; *nitida*, 200; *phaenopyrum*, 132, 244; *succulenta*, 200; *uniflora*, 157
Creeper, brown, 386
Creepers: common, 170, 198; Point Reyes, 243; trumpet, 178; Virginia, 141, 180, 198, 215
Crossbill, 32, 389; food sources, 143, 147; red, 129
Crotons (doveweed), 22
Croton spp.: *capitatus*, 22; *punctatus*, 22
Crow, 48, 379, 385, 390
Crowberry, black, 166, 180
Cuckoo, 168; yellow-billed, 95
Cultivated food plots, 27
Currant: American black, 161, 198; golden, 207–8; red-flowering, 240; sticky, 227; wax, 203, 215, 228
Cyperus esculentus, 285–86

Dahlias, 30
Dahlia spp., 30
Dahoon, 185
Dangleberry, 161, 180
Dawn census, 7
Dayflower, 28
Decoys, 352, 353
Dedon, Mark F., 359
Deer, 42–45, 47, 112
Deer Away/Big Game Repellent, 42
Deerberry, common, 188

Meadowlark, 68, 84; eastern, 84; western, 84

Meadowsweet, narrowleaf, 163

Mealworm larvae, 362, 363

Menispermum canadense, 170, 198

Merganser: common, 315, 329; hooded, 60, 315, 329

Mesquite, 211–12; screwbean, 223

Metal, freezing to, 389–90

Mice, 42–43, 74, 399

Migratory birds, 47; effect of feeding on, 357–58, 372; feeding, 366; nesting structures for, 312; purple martins, 323; shorebirds, 280–81

Miles Wildlife Sanctuary, 333

Milkweed, 30

Millet: Japanese (duck), 383–84; proso, 113, 378, 383

Milo, 112, 113, 376, 384

Mimosa tree, 32

Minnows, 266, 282–83, 390

Mirabilis jalapa, 30

Mitchella repens, 167

Mockingbird, 25, 128, 130, 137, 172, 176, 177, 214, 239, 360; feeding, 364, 368, 386; food sources, 149, 157, 161, 169, 181, 185, 187, 188, 189, 191, 237, 252, 255; nesting sites, 140, 187, 231

Mondarda didyma, 30

Monotonous landscapes, 1–4, 10–11

Moonseed, common, 170, 198

Morning glory, 31

Morus: microphylla, 201; *rubra*, 139, 179

Mosquitoes, 259, 264, 390

Moss rose, 28

Mountain-ash: alpine, 230, 245; American, 138, 179, 198, 244; European, 138, 153, 179, 198, 244; green, 210, 230, 245; Northern, 198; sitka, 231

Mountains and deserts, 13, 119, 353; additional recommended plantings, 214–15; ground covers, 233–34; other good choices, 216–234; pines, 215; plant sources, 432–33; recommended plantings, 206–14; shrubs, deciduous, 226–33; shrubs, evergreen, 224–26; trees, deciduous, 215, 220–23; trees, evergreen, 214, 216–20; vines, 234

Mowing, 70, 72, 80, 112

Mud flats, 273, 281

Mud habitat, 280

Mulberry: red, 139, 179, 244; Texas, 201; white, 139

Mulch, 419

Muskgrass, 289

Mycoplasma gallisepticum, 390

Myrica: californica, 241–42; *cerifera*, 186; *pensylvanica*, 155, 179

Naiads, 290

Najas spp., 290; *flexilis*, 290; *guadalupensis*, 290

Nannyberry, 196

Nasonia vitripennis, 304

Nasturtiums, 31

National Bird Conservation Initiative, 4

National Wildlife Refuge System, 280

Native Americans, 68, 322

Native plantings, 4

Natural Resources Conservation Service (NRCS), 4, 275, 442

Nero, Robert, 342

Nest boxes: cleaning, 300, 304; construction materials, 296–97; drainage, 297–98; mounting, 299, 301; positioning, 300; ventilation, 298; wood chips, 298–99

Nesting and roosting structures, 295–96; barn owls, 333–35; barred owls, 335;

247; *strobes*, 129–30; *taeda*, 171; *torreyana*, 248; *virginiana*, 182
Pinus ponderosa, 190
Plant/animal regions, 119, 121, 122
Plant names, 119
Plant predators, 4
Plants: aquatic, 282; evergreen or deciduous, 121; fruit period and type, 123; light requirements, 123; native vs. alien, 119–20; soils, 122; wetlands, 283–94; for wetlands, 283–94
Plants, for backyard pools, 267
Plant selection, 118–19
Plant sources, 431–39
Platanus: racemosa, 250; *wrightii*, 223
Platforms and supports, 337–51; for land bird nests, 339–41
Plover, 280
Plowing, 73–74
Plum: American, 186; sandhill, 204
Poinciana gillesii, 32
Pokeweed, 25
Polistes, 308
Pollution, 1–2, 48
Polygonum spp., 290–91; *aviculare*, 22, 23; *convolvulus*, 22, 23; *erectum*, 22, 23; *pennsylvanicum*, 290; *persicaria*, 290
Pome, 127
PondGuard, 265
Ponds and marshes, 272–74
Pondweeds, 293; sago, 293
Pools, backyard, 263–68
Poplar, balsam, 150, 215, 244
Populus: angustifolia, 221; *balsamifera*, 150, 215, 244; *deltoides*, 146, 197; *fremontii*, 221; *grandidentata*, 144; *sargentii*, 199; *tremuloides*, 145, 197, 206–7, 244; *trichocarpa*, 221
Portulaca, 28
Portulaca spp., 28; *grandiflora*, 28

Possum, haw, 186, 194–95
Potamogeton spp., 293; *pectinatus*, 293
Power lines, 96
Prairie chicken, 22, 204; greater, 191–92, 196, 221, 383
Prairies and plains, 74–75, 119; additional recommended plantings, 197–98; bobwhite in, 109; ground covers, 198; other good choices, 199–205; plant sources, 433; recommended plantings for, 190–205; shrubs, deciduous, 198, 203–5; shrubs, evergreen, 201–2; trees, deciduous, 199–201; vines, 198, 205
Predators, 357, 368; cats, 103, 114, 259, 313, 393–94; in forests, 48, 50–53; nesting structures and, 297, 300; of plants, 4; raccoons, 306–7, 314, 329, 394–98; in shrublands, 103; snakes, 308, 329; sparrows as, 51, 311–13
Prickly pear cactus, 212, 245
Prince's feather, 28
Prince's plumes, 28
Private Stewardship Grants Program, 443
Project Feederwatch, 387
Prosopis juliflora, 211–12
Protocalliphora maruyamensis, 300, 302–4
Prunus: americana, 186; *angustifolia*, 204; *besseyi*, 203; *caroliniana*, 187; *emarginata*, 221, 227; *ilicifolia*, 238; *lyonii*, 246; *pensylvanica*, 151, 197; *pumila*, 203; *serotina*, 130, 197, 215; *virginiana*, 152, 190–91, 215; *virginiana* var. *demissa*, 253
Pseudotsuga menziesii, 216, 244
Puffins, 352
Purple Martin Conservation Association (PMCA), 322, 323
Purple Martin Dawnsong, 323
Purple Martin Society, 322
Pyrrhuloxia, 19, 21, 22, 224

180; nannyberry, 159; possum haw, 186;
rusty black haw, 196–97; witherod, 159
Viburnum: acerifolium, 159, 180; *alnifolium*,
159, 180; *cassinoides*, 159; *dentatum*, 159,
180; *lentago*, 159, 196; *nudium*, 186;
prunifolium, 159; *rufidulum*, 184, 196–97;
trilobum, 158, 198
Vines, 65, 168–70; mountains and deserts,
234; Pacific Coast, 245, 256; prairies and
plains, 198, 205
Vireo: black-capped, 352; food sources, 141,
181, 203; nesting sites, 148, 168;
Philadelphia, 166; predators, 51; red-eyed,
48, 134, 150, 151, 181; warbling, 166, 237;
water sources, 258; white-eyed, 96
Vitis, 137; *acerifolia*, 205; *aestivalis*, 138, 169,
180; *arizonica*, 214; *cinerea*, 189; *labrusca*,
138, 169, 180, 198; *mustangensis*, 205;
novae-angliae, 168; *riparia*, 138, 169, 198;
vulpina, 169, 180
Vulture, turkey, 360

Wagner, Phillip, 333
Walnut, black, 151, 197
Warbler, 118; black-throated green, 51; blue-
winged, 96, 360; cerulean, 48, 49, 53;
chestnut-sided, 94, 96, 99; feeding, 364,
367, 385; food sources, 141; golden-
winged, 95; habitat, shrublands, 95, 96;
hooded, 65; Kentucky, 51; mourning, 65,
96; nesting sites, 137, 168, 188; nesting
structures, 295, 339; orange-crowned,
385; pine, 173, 385; prairie, 95, 96;
predators, 51; prothonotary, 60, 316;
water sources, 258, 259; worm-eating,
49, 51; yellow-rumped, 209, 241, 385, 387
Warm-season grasslands: native grasses
for, 88–93; steps for converting, 77–80;
wildflowers for, 76
Wasps, 304, 308

Wasser, Clinton H., 119
Waterfowl, 155, 284; establishing food in
new wetlands, 281–83; nesting
structures, 346–49; ponds and marshes
for, 272–74
Water lilies, 294
Water projects: backyard pools, 263–68;
birdbaths, 258–63; constructing
wetlands, 275–76; controlling water
levels, 277, 278; green-tree reservoirs,
277, 279; guzzlers for desert birds,
268–71; heating devices, 261–63; motion
devices, 259–61; ponds and marshes,
272–74; rubber liners, 265, 266, 275–76
Waxmyrtle, 186; Pacific, 241–42
Waxwing: Bohemian, 386; cedar, 135, 137,
138, 149, 152, 155, 157, 158, 164, 172, 174,
184, 186, 187, 195, 196, 203, 210, 213,
229, 233, 237, 247, 254, 255, 386;
feeding, 368, 386; food sources, 135, 138,
149, 152, 155, 157, 158, 164, 172, 174, 184,
186, 187, 195, 196, 203, 210, 213, 237,
254
Weber State College (Utah), 333
Weed food patches, 17–19
Weed management, 419; warm-season
grasslands, 77–78, 80
Western Hemisphere Shorebird Reserve
Network, 280
Western wheatgrass, 76
West Nile virus, 259, 390
Wetlands, 69, 280; constructing, 275–76;
establishing food, 281–83; plants,
283–94
Wheat, 384
Whortelberry, grouse, 233
Widgeon, American, 290, 291, 293, 384
Widgeon grass, 292–93
Wiegala, 32
Wiegala spp., 32

Wildlife Habitat Improvement Program (WHIP), 4, 442

Wildlife laws, 313–14

Willow: black, 151, 197; desert, 208; peach-leaved, 201; pussy, 160; sandbar, 201; scouler, 250

Windbreaks, 100–101, 113, 147; ponderosa pines, 190

Window boxes, 32

Winterberry, 137; common, 160, 180

Wintergreen, 167, 180, 233, 245; bush, 234

Winterizing nesting structures, 319, 353

Wisconsin Department of Natural Resources, 350

Wolfberry, Anderson, 233, 245

Woodbine, 205, 215

Wood chips, for nest boxes, 298–99

Woodpecker, 56, 58–60; acorn, 218; black-backed three-toed, *63*; downy, 59, 61, *63*, 152, 207, 299, 312, 315, 377, 386; feeding, 287, 363, 368, 374, 377, 379, 380, 386, 401; food sources, 130, 133, 146, 156, 157, 175, 183, 184, 185, 186, 188, 195, 228, 237, 239; gila, 233; golden-fronted, 212, 315; hairy, *63*, 134, 157, 238, 315, 377, 386; Lewis', 190, 249; nesting sites, 58–62, 130, 146, 273; nesting structures, 297–98, 299, 315; northern three-toed, *63*; pileated, 59, *63*, 132, 150, 161, 181, 185, 188, 189, 207, 237, 387; red-bellied, *63*, 146, 147, 175, 186, 189, 195, 360, 379, 380, 386; red-crowned, 363; red-headed, *63*, 133, 183, 184, 186, 213, 315, 386, 387; roosting sites, 353; western, 210; yellow-bellied sapsucker, *63*. *See also* flicker

World Conservation Union, 2

Wren, 16; Bewick's, 316, 327; cactus, 212, 224, 386; Carolina, 146, 316, 327, 387; feeding, 367, 374, 386, 387; house, 302, 305, 316, 318, 327; marsh, 273, 284; nesting sites, 60, 284; nesting structures, 296, 312, 318, 327; parasites, 302, 305; shelter for, 113

Wrentit, 234, 241, 242, 252

Xerophytes, 13

Yellow-bellied sapsucker, *63*

Yellowthroat, common, 99

Yew: Canada, 154, 179; Pacific, 220, 244

Zea mays, 379

Zinnia, 29, 31

Zinnia elegans, 29, 31

Zizania aquatica, 288–89